Frommer's®
Bermuda

Our Bermuda

by Darwin Porter & Danforth Prince

MARINERS OF YORE CALLED BERMUDA THE "ISLE OF THE DEVILS" because of the reefs that wrecked their ships. These days, the only "devils" you'll encounter on Bermuda are the high rollers who descend during the spring break from East Coast colleges. These hell raisers—and we were among them during our college years—will no doubt fall in love with the island and return every year, as we have done.

Bermuda is not about museums and manmade attractions but about spending time outdoors. This island nation is a vast natural wonder sitting isolated in the Atlantic, a serendipitous medley of land, ocean, and brilliant sunshine. And those beaches of (often pink) sand—what's not to love?

To fully enjoy your time in the sun, do a few things straightaway: First, buy a pair of pink Bermuda shorts—you'll fit right in. Then take a horse and buggy along Front Street in Hamilton selecting the shops you'll descend on later. Find yourself a moped so you can set out to explore Crystal Caves, a holdover from the dawn of the Ice Age. And at some point on your trip, take time out to golf (we always do), snorkel, or scuba dive.

Some Bermudians strike us as too "veddy British"—stiff upper lip and all that—for such a laid-back island. But we have come to love the islanders, their hospitality, and the lifestyle nevertheless. In the photographs and pages ahead, we'd like to share some of our favorite experiences in Bermuda.

© James Schwabel/Alamy

FRONT STREET (left) is the main street of the City of Hamilton, capital of Bermuda. Travel this water-bordering avenue by moped (if you're a visitor) or car (if you're a bonafide Bermudian). But most tourists walk and window shop, ducking into the prestigious pastel-colored stores to buy imported British goods such as Scottish tartans, English woolens, and fine china and crystal (including Royal Doulton).

In this **AERIAL VIEW (above)**, the archi-pelago of Bermuda rests under a mild cloud cover. The murky depths of the Atlantic Ocean enclose "The Rock," as Bermudians call their island, which originally rose up out of the sea as the result of a seismic shift in the Atlantic. Seventeenth-century English Poet Andrew Marvell imagined emigrants rowing "through the watery maze" to "an isle so long unknown, and yet far kinder than our own" (though Marvell himself never visited).

Yesterday's ocean-going tragedy provides today's **SNORKELING ADVENTURE (left).** The rocky coastlines of storm-tossed Bermuda have ripped the hulls of hundreds of ships. These wrecks in shallow waters are transformed into marine habitats that are virtual reefs of their own, teeming with schools of rainbow-hued fish. Exposure to seawater, sunlight, and air has rotted the upper hull of this Atlantic-crossing wreck, leaving an underwater shelter for coral, plankton, and all manner of fauna.

It took thousands of years of wind and water erosion to break down the massive limestone deposits and create the **NATURAL ARCHES (below),** on which vegetation grows. The arches, visible on several Hamilton beaches, are some of the island's most photographed features. Another iconic Bermuda beach sight— that pink sand—is a result of the microscopic red sea life that grows on coral reefs and eventually washes ashore, giving many beaches a distinctive hue.

Sea-bordering layouts with holes situated over the surging spray are a hallmark of **BERMUDA'S GOLF COURSES (above).** Premier golf architects such as Robert Trent Jones (both Sr. and Jr.) have created undulating, challenging courses— laid out in the best Scottish tradition but with considerably more lush terrain. When he played this course at St. George's, Babe Ruth proved better at his own game than at golf; his shots ended up in the drink a total of four times in one 18-hole round.

Limestone formations create **SHELTERED COVES (right)** where these children in their candy-striped towels find refuge. Families frolic on the beach from spring to autumn, and some even take a dip on warm winter days—but not Bermudians. Islanders have a strict rule that they won't go near the water any time before Queen Victoria's birthday on May 24, their official end of winter.

A shade corny but also fun, the traditional way to see the capital city of Hamilton is by **HORSE AND BUGGY (above)**. A driver, invariably in sunglasses and often a Jungle Jim hat, will be waiting for you along Front Street (the main street), near the flagpole or at the cruise-ship docks.

Following a strict dress code, this **HAMILTON BUSINESS EXECUTIVE (right)** hurries to work in his fashionable red Bermuda shorts that stop just 4 inches above a hairy knee. If the shorts showed more male leg, "we'd be putting on a girlie show in a burlesque house," a bank manager told us.

In Bermuda, visitors aren't allowed to rent the dreaded, gas-spewing automobile, an attempt to preserve the island's fragile environment. But they can **RENT A MOTORBIKE** and helmets and set out to explore the island, from St. George's in the east to Somerset in the west. This couple zooms past pastel-colored buildings that characterize the City of Hamilton. You can also rent bikes with pillions (the extra riding seat).

The blasting rhythms of the **GOMBEY DANCERS (above)**, the island's premier folk artists, keep alive the roots of West African tribal music on Bermuda. Taking to the streets on Boxing Day (December 26) and New Year's, the dancers appear to be merely "jumpin' up" to loud music, but actually perform carefully choreographed sequences.

Attired like Britain's Royal Marines, the **BERMUDA REGIMENT BAND (right)** evokes England in the tropics. This 600-person infantry battalion, mostly men with a few volunteer women, is often seen in parades, marching with their beating drums.

These **BERMUDIAN BAGPIPERS,** performing a winter skirling ceremony, aren't in Scotland—note the palm trees in the background—but on island. In the middle of the Atlantic, they carry on the Gaelic tradition of the bagpipe, that musical instrument of the Highlands that has come to symbolize Scottish identity and culture around the world.

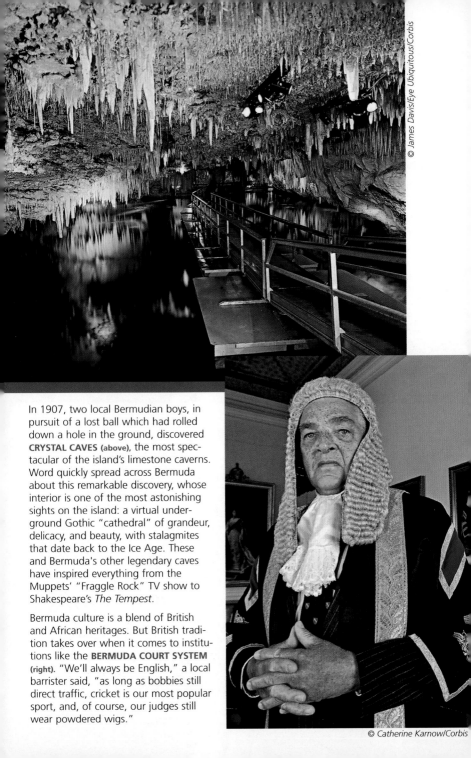

In 1907, two local Bermudian boys, in pursuit of a lost ball which had rolled down a hole in the ground, discovered **CRYSTAL CAVES (above)**, the most spectacular of the island's limestone caverns. Word quickly spread across Bermuda about this remarkable discovery, whose interior is one of the most astonishing sights on the island: a virtual underground Gothic "cathedral" of grandeur, delicacy, and beauty, with stalagmites that date back to the Ice Age. These and Bermuda's other legendary caves have inspired everything from the Muppets' "Fraggle Rock" TV show to Shakespeare's *The Tempest*.

Bermuda culture is a blend of British and African heritages. But British tradition takes over when it comes to institutions like the **BERMUDA COURT SYSTEM (right)**. "We'll always be English," a local barrister said, "as long as bobbies still direct traffic, cricket is our most popular sport, and, of course, our judges still wear powdered wigs."

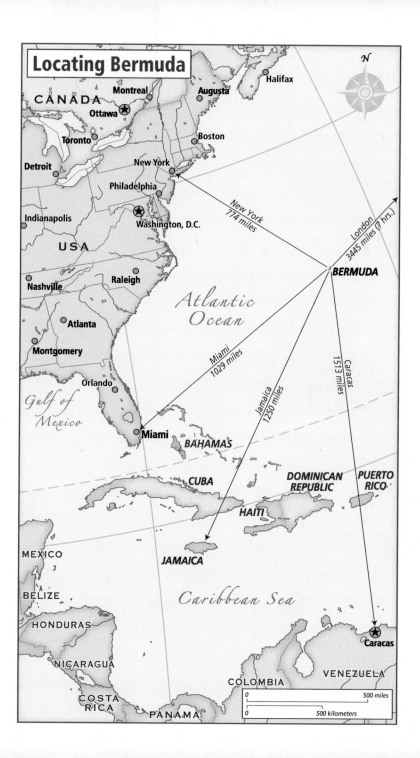

Locating Bermuda

CANADA

Montreal

Ottawa ★

Toronto

Detroit

Indianapolis

USA

Nashville

Atlanta

Montgomery

Orlando

Gulf of Mexico

MEXICO

BELIZE

HONDURAS

NICARAGUA

COSTA RICA

PANAMA

Halifax

Augusta

Boston

New York

Philadelphia

Washington, D.C. ★

Raleigh

Atlantic Ocean

Miami

BAHAMAS

CUBA

DOMINICAN REPUBLIC

HAITI

JAMAICA

Caribbean Sea

COLOMBIA

VENEZUELA

Caracas ★

PUERTO RICO

BERMUDA

New York 774 miles

London 3445 miles (7 hrs.)

Miami 1029 miles

Jamaica 1250 miles

Caracas 1513 miles

N

0   500 miles

0   500 kilometers

The Best of Outdoor Bermuda

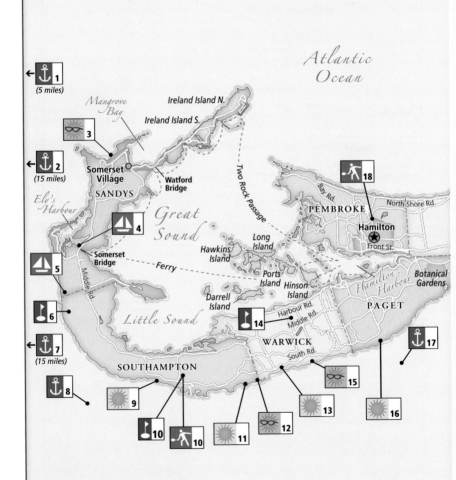

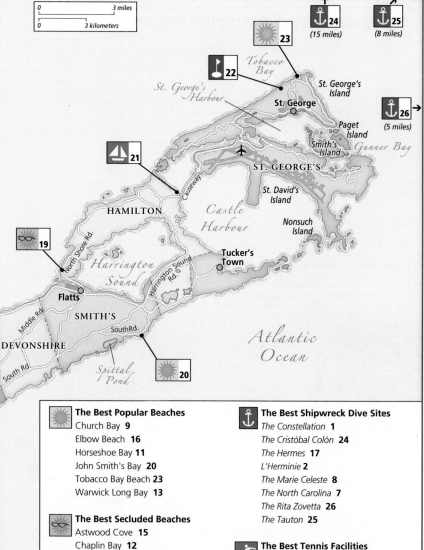

0		3 miles
0		3 kilometers

⚓ **24** ↑
(15 miles)

⚓ **25** ↗
(8 miles)

☀ **23**

Tobacco Bay

🚩 **22**

St. George's Harbour

St. George
St. George's Island

⚓ **26** →
(5 miles)

Paget Island

Smith's Island

Gunner Bay

⛵ **21**

HAMILTON

✈ **ST. GEORGE'S**

St. David's Island

Castle Harbour

Nonsuch Island

👓 **19**

North Shore Rd.

Harrington Sound

Tucker's Town

Harrington Sound Rd.

Flatts

SMITH'S

Middle Rd.

DEVONSHIRE

South Rd.

SouthRd.

Spittal Pond

☀ **20**

Atlantic Ocean

☀ **The Best Popular Beaches**
Church Bay **9**
Elbow Beach **16**
Horseshoe Bay **11**
John Smith's Bay **20**
Tobacco Bay Beach **23**
Warwick Long Bay **13**

👓 **The Best Secluded Beaches**
Astwood Cove **15**
Chaplin Bay **12**
Shelly Bay **19**
Somerset Long Bay **3**

⛵ **The Best Sailing Outfitters**
Blue Hole Water Sports **21**
Pompano Beach Club Watersports
   Centre **5**
Somerset Bridge Watersports **4**

⚓ **The Best Shipwreck Dive Sites**
The Constellation **1**
The Cristóbal Colón **24**
The Hermes **17**
L'Herminie **2**
The Marie Celeste **8**
The North Carolina **7**
The Rita Zovetta **26**
The Tauton **25**

🎾 **The Best Tennis Facilities**
The Fairmont Southampton **10**
Government Tennis Stadium **18**

🚩 **The Best Golf Courses**
Belmont Golf & Country Club **14**
Fairmont Southampton Golf Club **10**
Port Royal Golf Course **6**
St. George's Golf Club **22**

Bermuda's Best Accommodations

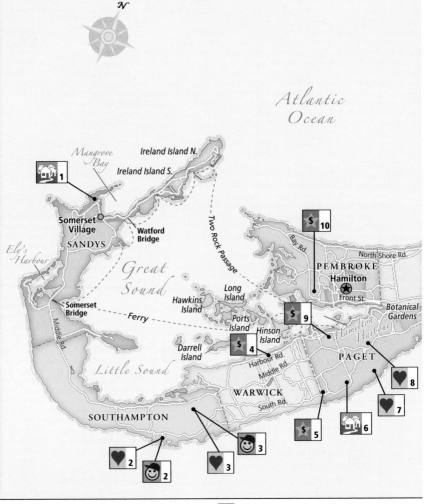

N

Atlantic Ocean

Mangrove Bay

Ireland Island N.
Ireland Island S.

1

Two Rock Passage

Bay Rd.

$ 10

North Shore Rd.

Somerset Village

Watford Bridge

SANDYS

PEMBROKE

Hamilton

Front St.

Ely's Harbour

Great Sound

Botanical Gardens

Hawkins Island

Long Island

Somerset Bridge

Ferry

Ports Island

$ 9

Hamilton Harbour

Hinson Island

$ 4

PAGET

Darrell Island

Harbour Rd.

Middle Rd.

Middle Rd.

Little Sound

WARWICK

♥ 8

♥ 7

South Rd.

SOUTHAMPTON

$ 5

6

♥ 2

😀 2

😀 3

♥ 3

The Best Resorts for Lovers & Honeymooners
Elbow Beach Hotel **7**
The Fairmont Southampton **3**
Grotto Bay Beach Resort **12**
Harmony Club **8**
Wyndham Bermuda Resort & Spa **2**

The Best Places to Stay with the Kids
Elbow Beach Hotel **7**
The Fairmont Southampton **3**
Grotto Bay Beach Resort **12**

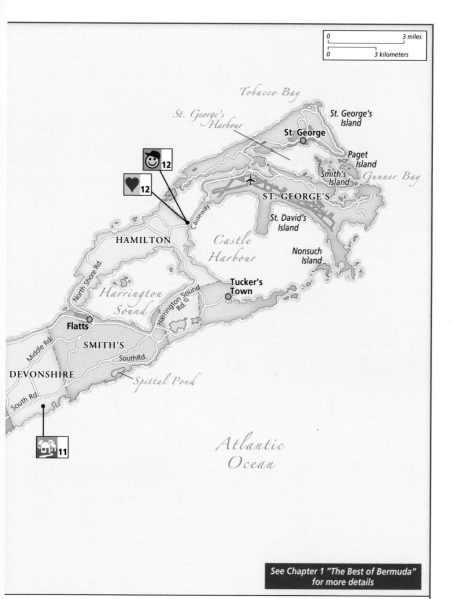

0   3 miles
0   3 kilometers

Tobacco Bay

*St. George's
Harbour*

*St. George's
Island*

St. George ○

*Paget
Island*

*Smith's
Island*   *Gunner Bay*

✈

ST. GEORGE'S

*St. David's
Island*

HAMILTON

*Castle
Harbour*

*Nonsuch
Island*

North Shore Rd.

*Harrington
Sound*

*Harrington
Sound
Rd.*

**Tucker's
Town**

Flatts ○

Middle Rd.

SMITH'S

South Rd.

DEVONSHIRE

Spittal Pond

South Rd.

 11

*Atlantic
Ocean*

See Chapter 1 "The Best of Bermuda"
for more details

 The Best Cottage Colonies
Ariel Sands Beach Club **11**
Cambridge Beaches **1**
Horizons and Cottages **6**

$ **The Best Hotel Bargains**
Astwood Cove **5**
Granaway Guest House & Cottage **4**
Rosemont **10**
Salt Kettle House **9**

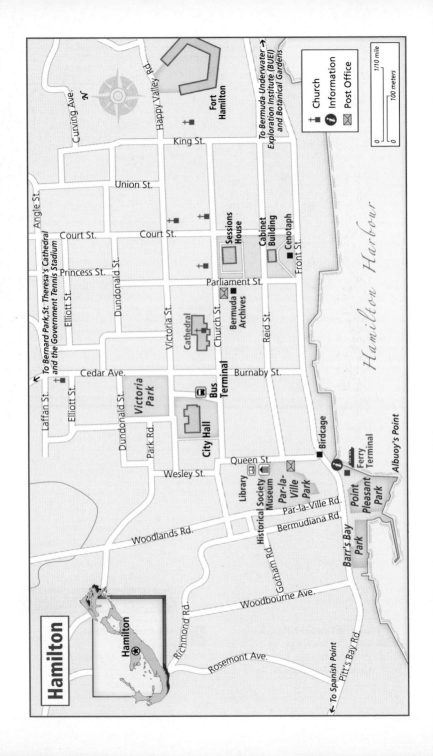

Frommer's®

Bermuda

2007

by Darwin Porter & Danforth Prince

Here's what the critics say about Frommer's:

"Amazingly easy to use. Very portable, very complete."

—*Booklist*

"Detailed, accurate, and easy-to-read information for all price ranges."
—*Glamour Magazine*

"Hotel information is close to encyclopedic."

—*Des Moines Sunday Register*

"Frommer's Guides have a way of giving you a real feel for a place."
—*Knight Ridder Newspapers*

Wiley Publishing, Inc.

About the Author

A team of veteran travel writers, **Darwin Porter** and **Danforth Prince** have written numerous titles for Frommer's, including bestselling guides to Italy, France, the Caribbean, England, and Germany. Porter is also a noted Hollywood biographer, his most recent releases being *Howard Hughes: Hell's Angels* (2005) and *Brando Unzipped* (2006). He is a radio commentator and newspaper columnist on popular culture, his broadcasts heard in all 50 states. Prince, formerly of the *New York Times* Paris bureau, is the president of Blood Moon Productions and other media-related firms.

Published by:

Wiley Publishing, Inc.

111 River St.
Hoboken, NJ 07030

ISBN 978-0-471-96224-3
ISSN 0-471-96224-4

Editor: Matthew Brown
Production Editor: M. Faunette Johnston
Cartographer: Anton Crane
Photo Editor: Richard Fox
Anniversary Logo Design: Richard Pacifico
Production by Wiley Indianapolis Composition Services

Front cover photo: Astwood Park Beach: couple walking, overhead view
Back cover photo: Warwick Long Bay: girl riding horse in the surf

For information on our other products and services or to obtain technical support, please contact our Customer Care Department within the U.S. at 800/762-2974, outside the U.S. at 317/572-3993 or fax 317/572-4002.

Wiley also publishes its books in a variety of electronic formats. Some content that appears in print may not be available in electronic formats.

Contents

8 Island Strolls 185

9 Shopping 197

10 Bermuda After Dark 210

Appendix: Bermuda in Depth 216

Index 232

List of Maps

Frommer's Star Ratings, Icons & Abbreviations

Every hotel, restaurant, and attraction listing in this guide has been ranked for quality, value, service, amenities, and special features using a **star-rating system.** In country, state, and regional guides, we also rate towns and regions to help you narrow down your choices and budget your time accordingly. Hotels and restaurants are rated on a scale of zero (recommended) to three stars (exceptional). Attractions, shopping, nightlife, towns, and regions are rated according to the following scale: zero stars (recommended), one star (highly recommended), two stars (very highly recommended), and three stars (must-see).

In addition to the star-rating system, we also use **seven feature icons** that point you to the great deals, in-the-know advice and unique experiences that separate travelers from tourists. Throughout the book, look for:

Finds	Special finds—those places only insiders know about
Fun Fact	Fun facts—details that make travelers more informed and their trips more fun
Kids	Best bets for kids and advice for the whole family
Moments	Special moments—those experiences that memories are made of
Overrated	Places or experiences not worth your time or money
Tips	Insider tips—great ways to save time and money
Value	Great values—where to get the best deals

The following **abbreviations** are used for credit cards:

AE	American Express	DISC	Discover	V	Visa
DC	Diners Club	MC	MasterCard		

Frommers.com

Now that you have the guidebook to a great trip, visit our website at **www.frommers.com** for travel information on more than 3,000 destinations. With features updated regularly, we give you instant access to the most current trip-planning information available. At Frommers.com, you'll also find the best prices on airfares, accommodations, and car rentals—and you can even book travel online through our travel booking partners. At Frommers.com, you'll also find the following:

- Online updates to our most popular guidebooks
- Vacation sweepstakes and contest giveaways
- Newsletter highlighting the hottest travel trends
- Online travel message boards with featured travel discussions

What's New in Bermuda

Even some diehard fans compare Bermuda to certain beauty queens—beautiful but dull. We prefer to think of it as "tranquil." If you're looking for exotic local color or sizzling rum- and reggae-filled nights, look farther south to the Caribbean. But if you need to escape the stress and strain of daily life, go to Bermuda.

This quiet island is one of the best places in the world for a honeymoon or a celebration of any romantic occasion. The joint may not be jumping, but it's the most relaxing—and safest—of the foreign islands off the American coast. Bermuda offers a relatively hassle-free environment where you can concentrate on your tan, minus the annoyance of aggressive vendors and worries about much crime. If you're into sunning and swimming, it doesn't get much better than Bermuda between May and September. Pink sand and turquoise seas—it sounds like a corny travel poster, but it's for real. As Mark Twain said, "Sometimes a dose of Bermuda is just what the doctor ordered."

Frankly, Bermuda is predictable, and its regular visitors wouldn't have it any other way. The tiny island chain has attracted vacationers for decades, and there aren't many secrets left to uncover. But those sandy pink beaches remain just as inviting as ever, no matter how many times you return.

Even to friends of Bermuda who make an annual pilgrimage to the island, the Bermudians can be a bit smug. They know their island is more attractive than Chicago, New York, Los Angeles, or Miami, and they're not above reminding you. Bit of an imperial attitude, isn't it? Exactly.

Some critics claim that Bermuda has become Americanized. That's true of islands much farther south, such as The Bahamas, but not of Bermuda. Indeed, the island and its population steadfastly adhere to British customs, even if, at times, that slavish devotion borders on caricature. (The afternoon tea ritual is pleasant enough, but the lawyers' and judges' powdered wigs are a bit much—those things must get hot in a semitropical climate!) Some visitors find all the British decorum rather silly on a remote island that's closer to Atlanta than to London. But many others find the stalwart commitment to British tradition colorful and quaint, enhancing the unique charm of the lovely, wonderful place that is Bermuda.

If you're looking for some of the best golf in the world, Bermuda is your mecca. It has the scenery, the state-of-the-art courses, and the British tradition of golfing excellence. Even the most demanding player is generally satisfied with the island's offerings.

If you're a sailor, you'll find the waters of Bermuda reason enough for a visit. The farther you go from shore, of course, the greater the visibility. Discovering a hidden cove, away from the cruise-ship crowds, can make your day.

If you hate driving on the left side of the road, that's fine with Bermudians. You *can't* drive here—they won't rent you a car. Bike around, or hop on a scooter and zip from one end of the island to the other.

We could go on and on with reasons for you to come to Bermuda, from exploring its natural wonderlands to playing on choice tennis courts with gentle sea breezes and warm sunshine. But we'll end here with a couple of warnings: Demanding foodies will find better dining on other islands, such as Martinique—although Bermuda has made much culinary progress of late. And if you want nightlife, glittering casinos, and all that jazz, head for San Juan. There is some nightlife in Bermuda, if you enjoy nursing a pint in a pub. It's always wise to bring along some good company (or a good book) to ensure a blissful night here.

Locals will always tell you, "If you want change, go to The Bahamas. We stay the same in Bermuda." Defying local wisdom, we've come up with some developments.

GETTING THERE Two daily nonstop flights between New York and Bermuda are now offered by **JetBlue Airways** (© 800/JET-BLUE), with one-way fares affordably priced at $129 per passenger. Two-hour flights depart from Kennedy International Airport. See p. 40.

ACCOMMODATIONS Owing to a lack of land, it's a big occasion when Bermuda gets a new hotel development. Such is the case with the **Newstead Belmont Hills Golf Resort & Spa,** 27 Harbour Rd., in Paget (© 441/236-5367), which is under construction. With its par-70 golf course, these digs will be among the most opulent on the island. Check out www.newsteadbelmonthills. com for the official opening date, which is currently set for early 2007. See p. 80.

A longtime favorite of ours, **Pink Beach Club & Cottages,** 116 South Shore Rd. at Tucker's Town in Smith's Parish (© 441/293-1666), is better than ever in the wake of grand improvements since being hit by Hurricane Fabian, in 2003. From its spacious, sparkling accommodations to its public rooms, the aura is one of glamour, attracting an affluent crowd. The cuisine has been greatly improved as well. See p. 88.

On a more modest level, **9 Beaches,** 4 Daniel's Head Lane in Sandys Parish (© 441/232-6655), is the newest hotel to open. It's also one of the most affordable, but far from luxurious. It's a well-maintained, comfortable choice in a compound spread across 7.3 waterfront hectares (18 acres). True to its name, the resort opens onto nine beaches, but only at high tide. See p. 91.

DINING Although it's been around awhile, **Silk,** 55 Front St. (© 441/295-0449), has only now begun to get the international acclaim it deserves. Many publications, including *Condé Nast Traveller,* have hailed this Thai restaurant with its authentic cuisine as the finest dining room in Bermuda. The delectable cuisine is based on long-cherished recipes from the ancient kingdom of Siam. See p. 127.

If an exotic restaurant opens on Bermuda, local foodies hail it as an event. **Café Cairo,** 95 Front St. (© 441/295-5155), in Hamilton, has brought an international cuisine to Bermuda, with a particular emphasis on the cuisine of Morocco, Lebanon, and Egypt. In an *Arabian Nights*–like setting, you can enjoy such delights as couscous or shish kebabs cooked on charcoal braziers at your table. See p. 121.

In the center of Hamilton, **Lemon Tree Cafe,** 7 Queen St. (© 441/292-0235), serves a Continental cuisine and also does a good breakfast or even sandwiches at lunchtime. Posted daily specials always include something good, such as fresh salmon with a garlic and blue cheese dressing. Stop in, too, for Hamilton's best chicken salad. See p. 130.

AFTER DARK Many locals vow that Bermuda will never become a Las Vegas in the Atlantic. But the "unthinkable" just might happen. The self-governing British colony is seriously considering legalizing gambling. If casinos open on the island, the face of Bermuda might be forever altered. Even though there is much resistance, gambling may be on the way, but not immediately.

Until the dice are tossed, you might head instead for the latest and hottest night club on Bermuda. It's **Splash,** Bermudiana Road (© **446/296-3848**), a split-level club with two full-service bars, evocative of New York. Expect the best DJs on island. To their sounds, you can dance until 3am. See p. 211.

1

The Best of Bermuda

If you've decided that Bermuda sounds like the perfect place to relax, feel free to start unwinding right now, because we've done all the legwork for you. Below you'll find our carefully compiled lists of the best that Bermuda has to offer, from beaches and dive sites to resorts, restaurants, and sightseeing—and nearly everything else you'll want to see and do. For the locations of many of these items, see the color maps "The Best of Outdoor Bermuda" and "Bermuda's Best Accommodations" at the front of this book.

1 The Best Beaches

Your first priority on your Bermuda vacation probably will be to kick back at the beach. But which beach? Hotels often have private stretches of sand, which we've described in each accommodations review (see chapter 4, "Where to Stay"). There are many fine public beaches as well. Here's our top-10 list, arranged clockwise around the island, beginning with the south-shore beaches closest to the City of Hamilton. For locations, see the color map "The Best of Outdoor Bermuda" at the front of this book. See chapter 6, "Fun in the Surf & Sun," for more details.

- **Elbow Beach** (Paget Parish): The pale pink sand stretches for almost a mile at Elbow Beach, one of the most popular beaches in Bermuda. At least three hotels sit on its perimeter. Because protective coral reefs surround it, Elbow Beach is one of the safest beaches on the island for swimming. Around Easter, it tends to be packed with college students who descend on Bermuda. See p. 139.

- **Astwood Cove** (Warwick Parish): At the bottom of the steep, winding

road that intersects with South Road, this beach is so remote that it's rarely overcrowded. Come here when you want to be alone. The trees and shrubbery of Astwood Park provide a verdant backdrop. See p. 140.

- **Warwick Long Bay** (Warwick Parish): This popular beach, on the south side of South Shore Park, features a half-mile stretch of sand against a backdrop of scrubland and low grasses. Despite frequent winds, an offshore reef keeps the waves surprisingly small. Less than 60m (200 ft.) offshore, a jagged coral island appears to be floating above the water. There is excellent snorkeling here—the waters are clear and marine life comes in close to shore. See p. 141.

- **Chaplin Bay** (Warwick and Southampton parishes): At the southern extremity of South Shore Park, straddling the boundary of two parishes, this small but secluded beach almost completely disappears during storms and particularly high tides. An open-air coral barrier rises from the water, partially separating one half of the beach from the other. See p. 142.

- **Horseshoe Bay** (Southampton Parish): This is Bermuda's most famous beach, and it's one of the best for families. Unlike most island beaches, Horseshoe Bay has a lifeguard on duty from May to September. The **Horseshoe Bay Beach Cafe** (© 441/238-2651) offers complete facilities, including watersports equipment rental. See p. 142.

- **Church Bay** (Southampton Parish): If you like to snorkel, this southwestern beach is for you. The relatively calm waters, sheltered by offshore reefs, harbor a variety of marine life. Sunbathers love the unusually deep, pink sands of this beach. See p. 143.

- **Somerset Long Bay** (Sandys Parish): The waters off this beach are often unsafe for swimming, but its isolation will appeal to anyone who wants to escape the crowds. With about a quarter-mile of sand, the crescent-shaped beach is ideal for strolling.

The undeveloped parkland of Sandys Parish shelters it from the rest of the island. See p. 143.

- **Shelly Bay** (Hamilton Parish): On the north shore, you'll discover calm waters and soft, pink sand—and you'll want for nothing else. This beach is well-known among beach buffs, but it's rarely overcrowded and there's always a spot in the sun just waiting for you. See p. 143.

- **Tobacco Bay** (St. George Parish): A popular stretch of pale pink sand, this is the most frequented beach on St. George's Island. It offers lots of facilities, including equipment rentals and a snack bar. See p. 143.

- **John Smith's Bay** (Smith's Parish): The only public beach in Smith's Parish is long and flat. It boasts the pale pink sand for which the south shore is famous. There's usually a lifeguard on duty from May to September—a plus for families. There are toilet and changing facilities on-site. See p. 144.

2 The Best Outdoor Pursuits

See chapter 6, "Fun in the Surf & Sun," for details on arranging any of these activities.

- **Golf:** Known for its outstanding courses, Bermuda attracts the world's leading golfers (and those who'd like to be). Over the years, such luminaries as President Eisenhower, President Truman, and the Duke of Windsor have hit the island's links. Rolling, hummocky fairways characterize the courses. Many avid golfers come to Bermuda to "collect courses," or play them all. Some holes, such as Port Royal's notorious 16th, are "from hell," as golfers say: Both the tee and the hole are high on cliff edges, with the rich, blue sea a dizzying 30m (98 ft.) below. See "The Best Golf Courses," below, for our top picks.

- **Boating & Sailing:** Yachters around the world agree: Bermuda is one of the world's top boating destinations. Many people forget that Bermuda isn't one island, but an archipelago, with all kinds of nooks and crannies waiting to be discovered. With the fresh wind of the Atlantic blowing in your hair, you can embark on your own voyage of discovery, exploring Great Sound and its islets, including Long Island and Hawkins Island. Tiny, secluded beaches beckon you to put down anchor and relax awhile. If you're a novice, try Mangrove Bay; it's protected and safer than some of the more turbulent seas. See "More Fun in the Water," in chapter 6.

- **Diving:** If you're happiest under the sea, Bermuda has what you're looking

Bermuda

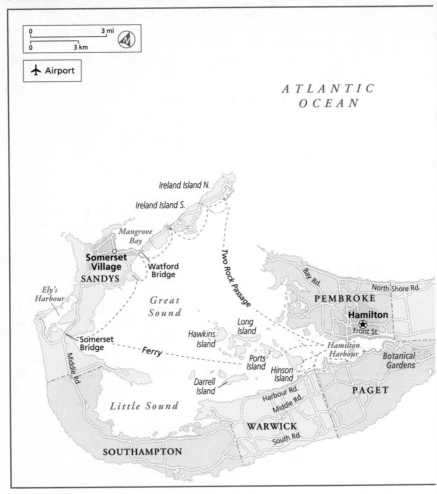

for. That includes the wrecks of countless ships, underwater caves, rich reefs, and, during most of the year, warm, gin-clear waters. All around the island you'll find a kaleidoscope of coral and marine life that's the most varied in this part of the world. Many scuba experts consider Bermuda one of the safest and best places to learn the sport. Seasoned divers will not be disappointed, either—Bermuda has terrific diving areas for experts. Depths begin at 7.5m (25 ft.) or less, but can exceed 24m (79 ft.). Some wrecks are in about 9m (30 ft.) of water, which puts them within the range of snorkelers. See "The Best Dive Sites," below, and "Scuba Diving," in chapter 6.

- **Biking:** You can't rent a car on Bermuda, so you might as well hit the

road on two wheels. Most of the island isn't great cycling terrain, because the roads are narrow and the traffic is heavy. So we suggest that you head for the Railway Trail, the island's premier bike path. The paved trail, which follows the former route of Bermuda's railway line, runs almost the entire length of the island. See "Other Outdoor Pursuits: Biking,

Horseback Riding & Tennis," in chapter 6.

- **Horseback Riding:** Steering a horse through the dune grass and oleander, especially at South Shore Park, is an experience you won't want to miss. Because this sport is restricted to supervised trails on Bermuda, it can be all the more memorable—you'll have the gorgeous seascapes all to yourself. Horseback-riding centers guide you on trails through the best of the countryside and to beautiful hidden spots along the north coast.

See "Other Outdoor Pursuits: Biking, Horseback Riding & Tennis," in chapter 6.

3 The Best Dive Sites

The following are some of the most exciting shipwreck and coral-reef dives. See "Scuba Diving," in chapter 6, for information about dive outfitters and for more about the sites described below. For locations, see the color map "The Best of Outdoor Bermuda," at the front of this book.

- **The *Constellation:*** This 60m (197-ft.), four-masted schooner, which wrecked en route to Venezuela with a cargo of glassware, drugs, and whiskey in 1943, lies in 9m (30 ft.) of water off the northwest side of the island, about 13km (8 miles) west of the Royal Naval Dockyard. The true story of this ship inspired Peter Benchley to write *The Deep.*

- **The *Cristóbal Colón:*** The largest known shipwreck in Bermuda's waters is this 144m (472-ft.) Spanish luxury liner; it ran aground in 1936 on a northern reef between North Rock and North Breaker. It lies in 9 to 17m (30–56 ft.) of water.

- **The *Hermes:*** This 50m (164-ft.) steamer ship rests in some 24m (79 ft.) of water about 1.6km (1 mile) off Warwick Long Bay on the south shore. It foundered in 1985. The *Hermes,* the *Rita Zovetta,* and the *Tauton* (see below) are Bermuda favorites because of the incredible multicolored variety of fish that populate the waters around the ships. You'll have a chance to see grouper, brittle starfish, spiny lobster, crabs, banded coral shrimp, queen angels, tube sponge, and more.

- ***L'Herminie:*** A first-class, 60-gun French frigate, *L'Herminie* was 17 days out of its Cuban port, en route to France, when it sank in 1838. The ship lies in 6 to 9m (20–30 ft.) of water off the west side of the island, with 25 cannons still visible.

- **The *Marie Celeste:*** This paddle-wheeler sank in 1864. Its 4.5m-diameter (15-ft.) paddle wheel, off the southern portion of the island, is overgrown with coral standing about 17m (56 ft.) off the ocean floor.

- **The *North Carolina:*** One of Bermuda's most colorful and well-preserved wrecks, this English sailing barkentine foundered in 1879 and now lies in about 12m (39 ft.) of water off the western portion of the island. The bow, stern, masts, and rigging are all preserved, and all sorts of vibrant marine life call the wreck home.

- **The *Rita Zovetta:*** A 180m (591-ft.) Italian cargo ship, lying in 6 to 21m (20–69 ft.) of water off the south side of the island, the *Rita Zovetta* ran aground off St. David's Island in 1924. It's a favorite with underwater photographers because of the kaleidoscope of fish that inhabit the area.

- **South West Breaker:** This coral-reef dive off the south shore, about 2.5km (1½ miles) off Church Bay, has hard and soft coral decorating sheer walls at depths of 6 to 9m (20–30 ft.).

- **Tarpon Hole:** Near Elbow Beach, off the south shore, this dive's proximity to the Elbow Beach Hotel makes it extremely popular. The honeycombed reef—one of the most beautiful off the coast of Bermuda—is known for its varieties of coral: yellow pencil, elkhorn, fire, and star.

- **The *Tauton:*** This popular dive site is a British Royal Mail steamer that sank in 1914. It lies in 4 to 12m (13–39 ft.) of water off the north end of the island and is home to numerous varieties of colorful marine life.

4 The Best Golf Courses

All four of these courses are 18 holes. For locations, see the color map "The Best of Outdoor Bermuda," at the front of this book.

- **Belmont Golf & Country Club** (Warwick Parish): Scotsman Emmett Devereux designed this par-70, 5,282m (5,776-yd.) course in 1923. It has been challenging golfers ever since, especially on its par-5 11th hole, a severe dogleg left with a blind tee shot. Trade winds play havoc with the listed lengths. Critics complain that the layout is "maddening," yet they continue to return for new challenges. The grass is dense thanks to a modern irrigation system. See p. 153.
- **Fairmont Southampton Golf Club** (Hamilton Parish): This is a par-54, 2,454m (2,684-yd.) course, with elevated tees, strategically placed bunkers, and an array of water hazards to challenge even the most experienced golfer. One golfer said of this course, "You not only need to be a great player, but have a certain mountaineering agility as well." See p. 154.
- **Port Royal Golf Course** (Southampton Parish): This public course ranks among the best on the island, public or private; in fact, it's one of the greatest public courses in the world. Jack Nicklaus apparently agrees—he's fond of playing here. Robert Trent Jones, Sr., designed the par-71, 6,003m (6,565-yd.) course along the ocean. The 16th hole is the most famous in Bermuda; photos of it have appeared in countless golf magazines. The hole is situated on a dramatic oceanside cliff with stunning views—one wrong hit from the club and your ball will go flying into the ocean below. Greens fees are relatively reasonable. See p. 154.
- **St. George's Golf Club** (St. George Parish): One of the island's newest courses—and one of its best—this par-62, 3,697m (4.043-yd.) course was designed by Robert Trent Jones, Sr. Within walking distance of the historic town of St. George, it lies on a windy headland at the northeastern tip of Bermuda. Although you'll enjoy panoramic vistas, your game is likely to be affected by Atlantic winds. The greens are the smallest on the island, at no larger than 7.2m (24 ft.) across. See p. 155.

5 The Best Tennis Facilities

For locations, see the color map "The Best of Outdoor Bermuda," at the front of this book.

- **The Fairmont Southampton** (Southampton Parish): This is Bermuda's premier destination for avid players. Its tennis court complex is the largest on the island, and is maintained in state-of-the-art condition. The deluxe hotel, one of the finest on Bermuda, offers 11 Plexipave (professional color surface) courts. The courts are somewhat protected from the north winds, but swirling breezes may affect your final score. See p. 157.
- **Government Tennis Stadium** (Pembroke Parish): Although Bermuda has been known as the tennis capital of the Atlantic since 1873, players often complain that the trade winds around the island affect their game, especially near the water. That's why

The Baffling Bermuda Triangle

The area known as the Bermuda Triangle encompasses 2,414,016 sq. km (932,057 sq. miles) of open sea between Bermuda, Puerto Rico, and the southeastern shoreline of the U.S. This bit of the Atlantic is the source of the most famous, and certainly the most baffling, legend associated with Bermuda.

Tales of the mysterious Bermuda Triangle persist, despite attempts by skeptics to dismiss them as fanciful. Below are three of the most popular. Can they be true? See what you think:

- In 1881, a British-registered ship, the *Ellen Austin*, encountered an unnamed vessel in good condition sailing aimlessly without a crew. The captain ordered a handful of his best seamen to board the mysterious vessel and sail it to Newfoundland. A few days later, the ships encountered each other again on the high seas. But to everyone's alarm, the crewmen who had transferred from the *Ellen Austin* were nowhere to be found—the ship was completely unmanned!
- Another tale concerns the disappearance of a merchant ship, the *Marine Sulphur Queen*, in February 1963. It vanished suddenly without warning, and no one could say why. The weather was calm when the ship set sail from Bermuda, and everything onboard was fine—the crew never sent a distress signal. In looking for explanations, some have theorized that the ship's weakened hull gave way, causing the vessel to descend quickly to the ocean floor. Others attribute the loss to more mysterious forces.
- The most famous of all the legends concerns an incident in 1945. On December 5, five U.S. Navy bombers departed from Fort Lauderdale,

many prefer inland courts, such as those at this government-owned stadium. It offers three clay and five shock-absorbing Plexicushion courts (three illuminated for night play). The facility, which is north of the City of Hamilton, requires players to wear proper tennis attire. On-site, you'll find a pro shop, a ball machine, and a pro offering private lessons. See p. 157.

6 The Best Day Hikes

- **The Bermuda Railway Trail** (Sandys Parish): Stretching for about 34km (21 miles), this unique trail was created along the course of the old Bermuda Railway. The railway served the island from 1931 to 1948 (automobiles weren't allowed on the island until the late 1940s). Armed with a copy of the *Bermuda Railway Trail Guide,* available at visitor centers, you can follow the route of the train known as "Rattle and Shake." Most of the trail still winds along a car-free route, and you can travel as much (or as little) of it as your stamina allows. See p. 156 and 192.
- **From the Royal Naval Dockyard to Somerset** (Sandys Parish): A 6.4km

Florida, on a routine mission. The weather was fine; no storm of any kind threatened. A short time into the flight, the leader of the squadron radioed that they were lost, and then the radio went silent. All efforts to establish further communication proved fruitless. A rescue plane was dispatched to search for the squadron—but it, too, disappeared. The navy ordered a search that lasted 5 days, but there was no evidence of any wreckage. To this day, the disappearance of the squadron and the rescue plane remains a mystery as deep as the waters of the region.

How do those who believe in the Bermuda Triangle legend account for these phenomena? Some contend that the area is a time warp to another universe; others think the waters off Bermuda are the site of the lost kingdom of Atlantis, whose power sources still function deep beneath the surface. Still others believe that laser rays from outer space are perpetually focused on the region, or that underwater signaling devices are guiding invaders from other planets, and that these aliens have chosen the site for the systematic collection of human beings for scientific observation and experimentation. (Smacks of *The X-Files*, doesn't it?) Some, drawing upon the Bible's Book of Revelation, are fully persuaded that the Bermuda Triangle is really one of the gates to Hell (in this version, the other gate lies midway between Japan and the Philippines, in the Devil's Sea).

No matter what your views on these mysteries, you're bound to provoke an excited response by asking residents what they think about it. On Bermuda, almost everyone has an opinion about the island's biggest and most fascinating legend.

(4-mile) walk leads from the dockyard, the former headquarters of the British navy on Bermuda, to Somerset Island. Along the way you'll cross a beautiful nature reserve; explore an old cemetery; view the Royal Naval Hospital, where thousands of yellow-fever victims died in the 19th century; and be rewarded with a sweeping panoramic view of Great Sound. Sandy beaches along the route are perfect for pausing from your hike to stretch out on the sand or take a dip in the ocean. See "Walking Tour 3: Sandys Parish," in chapter 8.

- **Spittal Pond Nature Reserve** (Smith's Parish): This 24-hectare (59-acre) sanctuary is the island's largest nature reserve, home to both resident and migratory waterfowl. You can spot some 25 species of waterfowl from November to May. Scenic trails and footpaths cut through the property. Explore on your own or take a guided hike offered by the Department of Agriculture. See p. 177.

7 The Best Sailing Outfitters

Bermuda is one of the Atlantic's major sailing capitals. Many sail-yourself boats are available for rent to qualified skippers, and kayaks, paddle boats, boards, and more are available for everyone. If you'd like to sail on a larger craft, the outfitters will provide you with a captain. Here are some of the best outfitters. For locations, see the color map "The Best of Outdoor Bermuda," at the front of this book.

- **Blue Hole Water Sports** (Grotto Bay Beach Hotel, Hamilton Parish; ℂ **441/293-2915;** www.bluehole water.bm): Here you'll find a large selection of watercraft, including Sunfish, sailboards, kayaks, Paddle Cats, and Sun Cats. Rentals are available for up to 8 hours. See p. 150.
- **Pompano Beach Club Watersports Centre** (Southampton Parish; ℂ **441/234-0222;** www.pompano.bm): This is the best outfitter in this tourist-laden parish. Open from May to late October, it offers a variety of equipment, including the O'Brien Wind-surfer, a popular sailboard suitable for

one person at the intermediate or advanced level. Its fleet also includes vessels that hold one or two people: Dolphin paddle boats, Buddy Boards, Aqua-Eye viewing boards, Aqua Finn sailboats, and kayaks. These can be rented for up to 4 hours. See p. 150.
- **Somerset Bridge Watersports** (Somerset Parish; ℂ **441/234-0914**): This is the best place to rent a Boston whaler, a small boat that can hold three or four passengers. It's an ideal craft for exploring the archipelago's uninhabited islands. This outfitter rents 4m (13-ft.) whalers and a 30-hp, 5m (16-ft.) Open Bowrider, a speed-craft often used to pull water-skiers, which accommodates four. See p. 150.

8 The Best Views

Bermuda is incredibly scenic, with lovely panoramas and vistas unfolding at nearly every turn. But not all views are created equal. Below are some of our personal favorites. See chapter 7, "Seeing the Sights," for additional suggestions.

- **Scaur Hill Fort Park:** From Somerset Bridge in Sandys Parish, head for this fort atop the parish's highest hill. Walk the fort's ramparts, enjoying the vistas across Great Sound to Spanish Point. You can also gaze north to the dockyard and take in the fine views of Somerset Island. On a clear day, a look through the telescope reveals St. David's Lighthouse, 23km (14 miles) away on the northeastern tip of the island. After enjoying the fantastic views from the fort, you can stroll through the fort's 9 hectares (22 acres) of beautiful gardens. See p. 167.
- **Gibbs Hill Lighthouse:** For an even better view than the one enjoyed by

Queen Elizabeth II when she visited the lighthouse in 1953, climb the 185 spiral steps of the lighthouse. Built in 1846, it's the oldest cast-iron lighthouse in the world. From the top, you can relish what islanders consider the single finest view in all of Bermuda—a panorama of the island and its shorelines. You can, that is, if the wind doesn't blow you away—be sure to hang on to the railing. In heavy winds, the tower actually sways. See p. 171.
- **Warwick Long Bay:** This stretch of pristine pink sand is a dream beach of the picture-postcard variety. It backs up to towering cliffs and hills studded with Spanish bayonet and oleander. A 6m-high (20-ft.) coral outcrop, rising some 60m (197 ft.) offshore and resembling a sculpted boulder, adds variety to the stunning beachscape. See p. 141.

9 The Best Historic Sights

See "The Best Places to Experience Old Bermuda," below, for a description of the Royal Naval Dockyard.

- **Fort St. Catherine** (St. George Parish): This fort—with its tunnels, cannons, and ramparts—towers over the beach where the shipwrecked crew of the *Sea Venture* first came ashore in 1609 (becoming Bermuda's first settlers). The fort was completed in 1614, and extensive rebuilding and remodeling continued until the 19th century. The audiovisual presentation on St. George's defense system helps you better understand what you're seeing. See p. 184.

- **Scaur Hill Fort Park** (Sandys Parish): Fort Scaur and Fort St. Catherine were part of a ring of fortifications that surrounded Bermuda. Built by the British navy, the fort was supposed to protect the Royal Naval Dockyard from an attack that never materialized. During World War II, U.S. Marines were billeted nearby. Overlooking Great Sound, the fort offers views of some of the island's most dramatic scenery. See p. 167.

- **St. Peter's Church** (St. George Parish): This is the oldest Anglican house of worship in the Western Hemisphere. At one time virtually everyone who died on Bermuda was buried here, from governors to criminals. To the west of the church lies the graveyard of slaves. The present church sits on the site of the original, which colonists built in 1612. A hurricane destroyed the first structure in 1712, but some parts of the interior survived. It was rebuilt on the same site in 1713. See p. 183.

- **Verdmont** (Smith's Parish): This 1770s mansion is on property once owned by William Sayle, founder and first governor of South Carolina. Filled with portraits, antiques, and china, the house offers a rare glimpse into a long-faded life of old-fashioned style and grace. Resembling a small English manor house, it's the finest historic home in Bermuda. See p. 177.

10 The Best Places to Experience Old Bermuda

Although much of Bermuda is modern, the first settlers arrived in 1609. The following places provide insights into the old, largely vanished Bermudian way of life. See chapter 7, "Seeing the Sights," for more details.

- **The Back Streets of St. George** (St. George Parish): Almost every visitor to the island has photographed the 17th-century stocks on King's Square in historic St. George. But it's in the narrow back alleys and cobblestone lanes, such as Shinbone Alley, that you'll really discover the town's old spirit. Arm yourself with a good map and wander at leisure through such places as Silk Alley (also called Petticoat Lane), Barber's Lane Alley (named for a former slave from South Carolina), Printer's Alley (where Bermuda's first newspaper was published), and Nea's Alley (former stamping ground of the Irish poet Tom Moore). Finally, walk through Somers Garden and head up the steps to Blockade Alley. On the hill is the aptly named Unfinished Cathedral. See "Walking Tour 2: Historic St. George Town," in chapter 8.

- **The Royal Naval Dockyard** (Sandys Parish): Nothing recaptures the maritime spirit of this little island colony more than this sprawling complex of attractions (with a multimillion-dollar cruise-ship dock) on Ireland Island. Britain began building this dockyard in 1809, perhaps fearing attacks on its fleet by Napoleon or greedy pirates. Convicts and slaves provided much of the construction labor, and the Royal Navy occupied the shipyard for almost 150 years. It closed in 1951, and the navy has little presence here today. The Maritime Museum—the most important museum on the island— and other exhibits on Bermuda's nautical heritage give you a good feel for a largely vanished era. See p. 170.

- **St. David's Island** (St. George Parish): Though most of Bermuda looks pristine and proper, you'll still find some vestiges of rustic maritime life on St. David's. Some St. David's Islanders never even bother to visit neighboring St. George, and to some locals, a trip to the West End of Bermuda would be like a trip to the moon. St. David's Lighthouse has been a local landmark since 1879. To see how people used to cook and eat, drop by Black Horse Tavern (p. 136).

11 Bermuda's Best-Kept Secrets

- **St. David's Island** (St. George Parish): Part of St. George Parish, this remote little island is often missed by many visitors, but it represents Bermuda at its most authentic (see listing above).
- **Remote, Natural Settings** (Sandys Parish; © 441/234-1831): Bermuda still has some oases that aren't overrun with visitors. One such place is the **Heydon Trust,** along Somerset Road, a sanctuary for migratory birds. It's a true walk through nature, with flowering bushes and citrus orchards. See p. 177.

- **Crystal Caves** (Hamilton Parish; © 441/293-0640): A spelunker's paradise, Bermuda has the highest concentration of limestone caves in the world. They form one of the island's major natural wonderlands. Their surreal formations took millions of years to come into being, and the great stalactites and stalagmites have a gothic grandeur. Crystal Caves, at Bailey's Bay, are the best. Discovered in 1907, these caves house crystal-clear Cahow Lake. See p. 178.

12 The Best Resorts for Lovers & Honeymooners

Bermuda has long been a favorite destination of newlyweds. Its hotels, from deluxe resorts to guesthouses, attract lovers of all kinds looking for a little peace, solitude, and seclusion.

Although some couples seek out small cottages and guesthouses, most prefer a package offered by one of the splashy resort hotels. The following resorts feature not only romance but also some of the best deals around.

Note: It's a good idea to consult a travel agent for help in getting the best bargain. Before you call any of these hotels directly, see "Packages for the Independent Traveler," in chapter 2. For full hotel reviews, see chapter 4, "Where to Stay." For locations, see the color map "The Best of Outdoor Bermuda," at the front of this book.

- **Elbow Beach Hotel** (Paget Parish; © 441/236-3535; www.mandarin oriental.com/bermuda): This hotel promises "marriages made in heaven." Its Romance Packages include a daily breakfast, plus a candlelit dinner for two in your room on the first night. Upon departure, newlyweds receive a copy of the *Elbow Beach Cookbook.* See p. 76.

- **The Fairmont Southampton** (Southampton Parish; © **800/441-1414** in the U.S., 800/268-7176 in Canada; or 441/238-8000; www.fairmont.com/southampton): The island's most luxurious hotel does everything it can to attract honeymooners seeking lots of activities, from watersports to nighttime diversions (other than those in the honeymoon suite). Its honeymoon packages, which start at 4 days and 3 nights, include breakfast and dinner on a MAP (modified American plan) "dine-around plan" (dinner and breakfast are included in the hotel rate, but you can dine in any of the two Princess resorts' restaurants), a bottle of champagne, a basket of fruit, admission to the exercise club, and even a special-occasion cake, plus a souvenir photo and a watercolor print by a local artist. See p. 72.

- **Grotto Bay Beach Resort** (Hamilton Parish; © **800/582-3190** in the U.S., 800/463-0851 in Canada, or 441/293-0188; www.grottobay.com): This resort, which actively caters to honeymooners, features everything from midnight swims at a private beach to cozy lovers' nests with private balconies overlooking the ocean. The honeymoon packages include romantic dinners and arrangements for cruises and walking tours, as well as optional champagne, fruit, and flowers. See p. 79.

- **Harmony Club** (Paget Parish; © **888/427-6664** in the U.S., or 441/236-3500; www.harmonyclub.com): If you shun the big splashy resorts that attract a lot of families with children, head to this small, couples-only all-inclusive resort. Guests are housed in romantic Queen Anne–style buildings in a setting of formal gardens and gazebos. Dinners are served by candlelight on fine china and crystal. Honeymoon packages are available. See p. 83.

- **Wyndham Bermuda Resort & Spa** (Southampton Parish; © **877/999-3223** in the U.S. or Canada, or 441/238-8122; www.wyndham.com): You'll find champagne chilling in your room when you arrive—and it just gets better from there. To set the mood, the staff will arrange an introductory horse-and-buggy ride in the old Bermuda tradition. The following day, they'll lend you a motor scooter for getting around. The sports director offers one free tennis or scuba lesson. The hotel is right on the beach, and also boasts a fully equipped, professionally staffed health spa. See p. 73.

13 The Best Places to Stay with the Kids

Bermuda is more kid-friendly than any place we know in the Caribbean or The Bahamas. It's a safe, clean environment in a politically stable country. Nearly all Bermuda hotels go the extra mile to welcome families with children, but the following are our top choices. Turn to chapter 4, "Where to Stay," for full reviews. For locations, see the color map "The Best of Outdoor Bermuda," at the front of this book.

- **The Fairmont Southampton** (Southampton Parish; © **800/441-1414** in the U.S., 800/268-7176 in Canada, or 441/238-8000; www.fairmont.com/southampton): From June through Labor Day, this hotel features the best children's program in Bermuda. Children under 17 stay free; and if the parents choose the MAP (breakfast and dinner included in the rates), kids also get free meals. With its many sports facilities, including two freshwater pools and 11 tennis courts, the Fairmont is definitely for families who enjoy the sporting life. The former Touch Club has been redesigned as Lenny's Loft, a social center for children's activities. From Lenny's Loft, kids are taken on excursions around the island. See p. 72.

• **Grotto Bay Beach Resort** (Hamilton Parish; ℭ **800/582-3190** in the U.S., 800/463-0851 in Canada, or 441/293-0188; www.grottobay.com): With its excellent summer children's program, this hotel attracts many families. It sits on 8.5 tropically landscaped hectares (21 acres), so guests usually don't mind its relative isolation across from the airport. The swimming pool has been blasted out of natural rock, and there are subterranean caves to explore. Beachside barbecues and other activities make this a lively place. See p. 79.

• **Elbow Beach Hotel** (Paget Parish; ℭ **441/236-3535;** www.mandarin oriental.com/bermuda): This longtime family favorite, on one of the best beaches in Bermuda, allows children under 13 to stay free when sharing a room with their parents. It also offers a year-round "Family Value Package," which grants very low rates for four people (usually two children and two parents) and includes buffet breakfast, 4 hours of babysitting, 1 hour of paddle boat rental, 2 hours of tennis, and free passes to the zoo and aquarium. Call the hotel or ask a travel agent for details. See p. 76.

14 The Best Hotel Bargains

For locations, see the color map "The Best of Outdoor Bermuda," at the front of this book.

• **Granaway Guest House & Cottage** (Warwick Parish; ℭ **441/236-3747;** www.granaway.com): This former private home from 1734 is a virtual picture-postcard cliché of Bermudian charm, with its pink walls and whitewashed roof. Opening onto views of Great Sound, it has been handsomely converted to receive guests—even the former slave quarters are now comfortable. See p. 99.

• **Astwood Cove** (Warwick Parish; ℭ **800/637-4116** in the U.S., or 441/236-0984; www.astwoodcove. com): This place is definitely a good buy in pricey Bermuda. For families seeking a self-contained studio or suite apartment with a fully equipped kitchenette and a private porch or patio, this is a great choice. You prepare your own meals and use the hotel's English bone china and wine glasses. Studio apartments have sofa beds that can accommodate a third person. See p. 93.

• **Salt Kettle House** (Paget Parish; ℭ **441/236-0407**). The name is not the only thing charming about this informal and secluded 2-centuries-old cottage. It's a real discovery, and bargain hunters eagerly seek it out, preferring it to the glitz of the megaresort hotels. You can swim in the nearby cove, retiring to your waterside cottage at night. See p. 99.

• **Rosemont** (City of Hamilton, Pembroke Parish; ℭ **800/367-0040** in the U.S., 800/267-0040 in Canada, or 441/292-1055; www.rosemont. bm): A collection of housekeeping cottages near the Hamilton Princess, Rosemont has long been a family favorite, offering a central location at a good price. The site offers panoramic views of Hamilton Harbour and the Great Sound. Guests often prepare their own meals. See p. 95.

15 The Best Restaurants

You don't come to Bermuda for grand cuisine. That said, there are quite a few places in which to enjoy a memorable meal.

- **Aqua** (Devonshire Parish; ⓒ **441/236-2332**): In the Ariel Sands Hotel, this restaurant, owned in part by actor Michael Douglas, has quickly become one of the island's best, with its savory blend of Bermudian and international recipes. Expect everything from Cajun cookery to Indian-style tandoori dishes. See p. 132.

- **Ascots** (City of Hamilton; Pembroke Parish; ⓒ **441/295-9644**): In the Royal Palms Hotel, this restaurant specializes in a Continental menu that is mostly inspired by France and Italy, and does it exceedingly well. Classic techniques and first-rate ingredients are combined to make this one of the most enduring restaurants on the island. See p. 120.

- **Black Horse Tavern** (St. George Parish; ⓒ **441/297-1991**): When you crave good, hearty food served in a casual atmosphere, this is the place to come. Islanders fill most of the tables at night, ordering shark hash or curried conch. See p. 136.

- **Lobster Pot & Boat House Bar** (City of Hamilton, Pembroke Parish; ⓒ **441/292-6898**): If you don't find the local foodies at the restaurants discussed above, they'll surely be at this local favorite, enjoying some of the island's best regional dishes. Black rum and sherry peppers are the secret ingredients in the fish chowder, and baked fish and lobster are sure to tempt you. See p. 125.

- **Mediterraneo Bar & Ristorante** (City of Hamilton, Pembroke Parish; ⓒ **441/296-5277**): The hottest new restaurant in Bermuda, as its name suggests, is the place to go to experience the savory cuisine of the Mediterranean, including an array of fresh fish and shellfish along with succulent pastas and piping-hot pizzas. The chefs also roam other parts of the world for culinary inspiration. See p. 122.

- **Newport Room** (Southampton Parish; ⓒ **441/238-8000**): Part of the Fairmont Southampton Princess, this nautically decorated restaurant attracts an upscale crowd, especially yachters. The glistening teak decor makes it the most expensively furnished restaurant in Bermuda, and the French cuisine is worthy of the decor. The rack of lamb with mixed-nut crust is the stuff of which memories are made. See p. 111.

- **Silk** (City of Hamilton; Pembroke Parish ⓒ **441/295-0449**): Some critics, including the discriminating readers of *Condé Nast Traveller,* are hailing Silk as the island's finest restaurant. We are inclined to agree after our most recent feast here. Recipes are inspired by the ancient Kingdom of Siam—read "Thai" to modern palates. See p 127.

- **Tamarisk Dining Room** (Sandys Parish; ⓒ **441/234-0331**): This is an elegant enclave at the western tip of Bermuda. Housed in one of the island's premier accommodations, Cambridge Beaches, it offers excellent service and a frequently changing menu of impeccably prepared international cuisine. For your main course, you can't do better than juicy tenderloin of beef with grain mustard and blanched garlic sauce. The wine cellar is up to the high standards of the menu. See p. 107.

- **Tom Moore's Tavern** (Hamilton Parish; ⓒ **441/293-8020**): The Irish poet Tom Moore reportedly was a frequent visitor to this restaurant, which dates from 1652 and overlooks Walsingham Bay. The menu, however, is no relic—it's quite innovative. Duck is a specialty, as is Bermuda lobster; but who can forget the quail in puff pastry stuffed with foie gras? See p. 134.

• **Waterlot Inn** (Southampton Parish; ℂ **441/238-8000**): In a historic inn and warehouse that's part of the Fairmont Southampton Princess, this restaurant serves the island's most famous Sunday brunch, but it's also an ideal choice for dinner. Everybody from Eleanor Roosevelt to Mark Twain has praised the Mediterranean cuisine. See p. 112.

2

Planning Your Trip to Bermuda

In this chapter, you'll find everything you need to plan your trip, from when to go to how to land the best package deals. Getting to Bermuda is easier than ever, thanks to more frequent flights from such gateway cities as New York, Boston, and Washington. We've also included information on several cruise lines that sail to the island from spring until late autumn.

1 Visitor Information

Some of your best sources of information may be relatives, friends, or colleagues who have been to Bermuda, so ask around. For information sources once you're in Bermuda, see "Orienting Yourself: The Lay of the Land," in chapter 3, "Getting to Know Bermuda."

THE BERMUDA DEPARTMENT OF TOURISM

IN THE UNITED STATES To receive a visitor information packet about Bermuda before you go, call ℂ **800/237-6832** (800/BERMUDA); www.bermuda tourism.com.

To speak to a travel representative, contact the **Bermuda Department of Tourism,** 205 E. 42nd St., New York, NY 10017 (ℂ **212/818-9800**); or 245 Peachtree Center Ave. NE, Suite 803, Atlanta, GA 30303 (ℂ **404/524-1541**).

IN CANADA Contact the **Bermuda Department of Tourism** at 1200 Bay St., Suite 1004, Toronto, ON, Canada M5R 2A5 (ℂ **416/923-9600**).

IN THE UNITED KINGDOM Contact the **Bermuda Department of Tourism** at 1 Battersea Church Rd., London, England SW11 3LY (ℂ **020/8410-8188**).

TRAVEL AGENTS

Travel agents can save you plenty of time and money by hunting down the best package deal or airfare. For the time being, most travel agents charge you nothing for their services—they're paid through commissions from the airlines and other agencies. However, most airlines have cut commissions, and increasingly, agents are finding they have to charge customers fees. Some unscrupulous agents may offer you only the travel options that bag them the juiciest commissions. Shop around and ask hard questions. The best way to use a travel agent is to make preliminary decisions using this guide, and go into your meeting as a smart and informed consumer.

If you decide to use a travel agent, make sure the agent is a member of the **American Society of Travel Agents (ASTA),** 1101 King St., Suite 200, Alexandria, VA 22314 (ℂ **703/739-2782;** fax 703/684-8319; www.astanet.com). To receive a copy of the free booklet *Avoiding Travel Problems,* send ASTA a self-addressed, stamped envelope.

Tips **Your Own Personal "Weblet"**

The Bermudian government remains committed to attracting more and more visitors. Its latest offering is to arrange a personalized Bermuda miniguidebook for potential visitors. Within minutes of hanging up the phone, Internet-connected **800/BERMUDA** callers receive a personalized "weblet" that gives specific, detailed information on hotels and activities based on information supplied by the caller. Your weblet's search engines allow you to supply personal criteria and receive a selection of hotels and restaurants designed to appeal to your taste and pocketbook. Special-interest buttons can be pressed for data on golf, honeymoon packages, nightlife, and sports facilities.

---

2 Entry Requirements & Customs

ENTRY REQUIREMENTS

As of January 1, 2008, under new Homeland Security regulations, Americans returning from Bermuda and the Caribbean must show passports when reentering the United States. Those returning to Canada will have to show passports starting December 31, 2006.

Bermuda Immigration authorities require **U.S. citizens** to have at least one of the following items in their possession: a birth certificate (or a certified copy of it accompanied by a photo ID), a U.S. naturalization certificate, a valid passport, a U.S. Alien Registration card, or a U.S. reentry permit. Go with the passport.

Canadian citizens must have either a birth certificate (or a certified copy), a Canadian certificate of citizenship, or a valid passport plus proof of Landed Immigrant status.

Bermuda Immigration authorities require visitors from the **United Kingdom** and **Europe** to show a valid passport. All visitors must have a return or onward ticket in addition to their valid passport or original birth certificate.

Any traveler staying in Bermuda longer than 3 weeks must apply to the **Chief Immigration Officer** in person, at the Government Administration Building, 30 Parliament St., Hamilton HM 12, Bermuda (© **441/295-5151**), for an extended stay. You will be asked to fill out an immigration application for an extended stay, which then will or will not be approved by authorities.

CUSTOMS
WHAT YOU CAN BRING INTO BERMUDA

Visitors may bring into Bermuda duty-free apparel and articles for their personal use, including sports equipment, cameras, 200 cigarettes, 1 liter of liquor, and 1 liter of wine. Certain foodstuffs may be subject to duties. All imports may be inspected on arrival. Visitors entering Bermuda may also claim a duty-free gift allowance.

Persons who are taking prescription medication must inform Bermuda customs officials at the point of entry. Medicines must be in labeled containers. Travelers should carry a copy of the written prescription and a letter from the physician or pharmacist confirming the reason the medicine is prescribed.

Bermuda customs authorities may enforce strict regulations concerning temporary importation into or export from Bermuda of items such as animals; arms, ammunition, or explosives; building sand, crushed rock, gravel, peat, soil, or synthetic potting media; foodstuffs (animal origin); fumigating substances; gaming machines; historic articles (relating to

Bermuda); lottery advertisements and material; motorcycles or motor vehicles; obscene publications; organotin anti-fouling paint; pesticides, plants, plant material, or fruits and vegetables (living or dead, including seeds); prescription drugs; prohibited or seditious publications; and VHF radios or radar and citizens band (CB) radios.

When you're leaving Bermuda (if you're flying back to the United States) a customs inspector will ask to see a copy of

Destination Bermuda: Pre-Departure Checklist

- Do you have the appropriate documents required by Bermuda's immigration department for your particular nationality? (It's recommended that U.S. citizens bring a valid passport, although Bermuda authorities will also accept an original birth certificate, a U.S. naturalization certificate, a U.S. Alien Registration card, or a U.S. reentry permit.) If you're flying, are you carrying a current, government-issued ID, such as a driver's license or passport?
- Have you checked with the United States **Centers for Disease Control and Prevention** (© 800/311-3435; www.cdc.gov) for up-to-date information on necessary vaccines, if any, and health hazards?
- Do any theater, restaurant, or travel reservations need to be booked in advance?
- Did you make sure your favorite attraction is open? Call ahead for opening and closing times.
- If you purchased traveler's checks, have you recorded the check numbers, and stored the documentation separately from the checks?
- Did you stop the newspaper and mail delivery, and leave a set of keys with someone reliable?
- Did you pack your camera and an extra set of camera batteries, and purchase enough film?
- Do you have a safe, accessible place to store money?
- Did you bring your ID cards that could entitle you to discounts, such as AAA and AARP cards, student IDs, and so on?
- Did you bring emergency drug prescriptions and extra glasses and/or contact lenses?
- Did you find out your daily ATM withdrawal limit?
- Do you have your credit card pin numbers? Is there a daily withdrawal limit on credit card cash advances? Five- or six-digit numbers generally work in Bermuda, but confirm this with your bank before leaving home.
- To check in at a kiosk with an e-ticket, do you have the credit card you bought your ticket with or a frequent-flier card?
- Did you leave a copy of your itinerary with someone at home?
- Do you have the measurements for those people you plan to buy clothes for on your trip?
- Did you check to see if any travel advisories have been issued by the U.S. State Department (http://travel.state.gov/travel) regarding your destination?

Traveling with Minors

It's always wise to have plenty of documentation when traveling in today's world with children. For changing details on entry requirements for children traveling abroad, keep up-to-date by going to the U.S. State Department website: http://travel.state.gov/foreignentryreqs.html.

To prevent international child abduction, governments have initiated procedures at entry and exit points. These often (but not always) include requiring documentary evidence of relationship and permission for the child's travel from the parent or legal guardian not present. Having such documentation on hand, even if not required, facilitates entries and exits. All children must have their own passport. To obtain a passport, the child *must* be present—that is, in person—at the center issuing the passport. Both parents must be present as well. If not, then a notarized statement from the parents is required.

All questions parents or guardians might have can be answered by calling the **National Passport Information Center** at ℂ **877/487-6868** Monday to Friday 8am to 8pm Eastern Standard Time.

---

the incoming Bermuda form that was stamped and given to you as you cleared Bermuda Customs. Make sure that you hold onto it and can produce it on short notice.

For additional information on temporary admission, export and customs regulations, and tariffs, contact **Bermuda Customs** at ℂ **441/278-7422** or customs_valuation@gov.bm, or visit the Bermuda Customs website at www.customs.gov.bm.

WHAT YOU CAN TAKE HOME FROM BERMUDA
U.S. Citizens

For specifics on what you can bring back and the corresponding fees, download the invaluable free pamphlet *Know Before You Go* online at **www.cbp.gov**. (Click on "Travel," and then click on "Know Before You Go!") Or contact the **U.S. Customs & Border Protection (CBP),** 1300 Pennsylvania Ave. NW, Washington, DC 20229 (ℂ **877/287-8667**), and request the pamphlet.

Canadian Citizens

For a clear summary of Canadian rules, write for the booklet *I Declare,* issued by the **Canada Border Services Agency** (ℂ **800/461-9999** in Canada, or 204/983-3500; **www.cbsa-asfc.gc.ca**).

U.K. Citizens

For information, contact **HM Customs & Excise** at ℂ **0845/010-9000** (from outside the U.K., 020/8929-0152), or consult their website at **www.hmce.gov.uk**.

Australian Citizens

A helpful brochure available from Australian consulates or Customs offices is *Know Before You Go.* For more information, call the **Australian Customs Service** at ℂ **1300/363-263,** or log on to **www.customs.gov.au**.

New Zealand Citizens

Most questions are answered in a free pamphlet available at New Zealand consulates and Customs offices: *New Zealand Customs Guide for Travellers, Notice no. 4.* For more information, contact **New Zealand Customs,** The Customhouse, 17–21 Whitmore St., Box 2218, Wellington (ℂ **04/473-6099** or 0800/428-786; **www.customs.govt.nz**.

3 Money

Time is money, and because Bermuda is less than 2 hours from most cities on the U.S. East Coast, the savings begin even before you land on the island. A 4-day, 3-night vacation in Bermuda can actually include 4 days of vacation for the price of 3 nights' accommodations. An 8:30am flight from New York gets you to Bermuda in time for lunch, with the whole afternoon to play.

The variety of accommodations—luxury resort hotels, small hotels, intimate guesthouses, and cottage colonies—allows visitors to indulge their preferences and tastes regardless of budget.

Hotel costs also depend on what time of year you travel. If you're seeking major discounts—sometimes as much as 60% off high-season rates—try visiting during the off season. (For more information, see "When to Go," below.) Off-season rates, which we've listed in this guide, are a bonanza for cost-conscious travelers—though you're not guaranteed that it'll be warm enough to truly enjoy the beach.

Travel agents sometimes offer special packages, which can represent a substantial savings over regular hotel rates for families, golfers, tennis players, honeymooners, and others; for more information, see "Packages for the Independent Traveler," later in this chapter.

Dining out is an expensive undertaking. In the top places, you can end up spending as much as $80 per person for a meal, excluding wine. Even moderate to expensive restaurants charge $25 to $50 per person. Any dinner under $25 per person is considered inexpensive. You might want to investigate the package plans that most of the large resorts offer, which include meals. For details on meal plans, see "Rates & Reservation Policies," in chapter 4, "Where to Stay." Other ways to reduce dining costs are to pack picnic lunches, or to have your main meal in the middle of the day, at a pub. To cut costs further, families and others planning to stay for a week or more might opt for a housekeeping unit (efficiencies and apartments are available), a cottage with a kitchenette, or even a condominium (some are rented like timeshare units).

In figuring your budget, be sure to consider transportation costs. Getting around the island isn't always easy, and because rental cars are not available, you'll have to rely on local transportation. With the exception of taxis, which are very expensive, public transportation is efficient and inexpensive. Options include the simple and comprehensive bus system, ferries, and bicycle or motorbike rentals; see the "Getting Around" section in chapter 3 for details. Once you reach a particular parish, many attractions are accessible on foot.

In general, athletic and cultural activities—such as tennis, riding, guided tours, museums, and attractions—are good values.

Tips Planning Pointer

Before leaving home, make copies of your most valuable documents, including the inside page of your passport that has your photograph. Also copy your driver's license, airline ticket, hotel vouchers, and any other pertinent documents. You should also make copies of the prescriptions for any medications you take. Leave one copy at home, place one copy in your luggage, and carry the original with you. The information on these documents is extremely valuable if your possessions are lost or stolen.

What Things Cost in Bermuda	US$/BD$	UK£
Average 15-minute taxi ride	$12–$15	£6.60–£8.25
Bus from the City of Hamilton to Ireland Island	$4.50	£2.50
Local telephone call	20¢	11p
Double room at Elbow Beach Hotel (expensive)	$395	£217
Double room at Rosemont (moderate)	$180	£99
Double room at Salt Kettle House (inexpensive)	$120	£66
Lunch for one at Tamarisk Inn's Dining Room (expensive)	$25	£14
Lunch for one at the Hickory Stick (inexpensive)	$9	£4.95
Dinner for one at Ascots (expensive)	$60	£33
Dinner for one at La Trattoria (moderate)	$32	£18
Dinner for one at The Beach (inexpensive)	$18	£9.90
Bottle of beer in a bar	$4.50	£2.50
Coca-Cola in a cafe	$3–$4	£1.65–£2.20
Cup of coffee in a cafe	$1.75–$4	95p–£2.20
Glass of planter's punch in a restaurant	$6.50–$7	£3.60–£3.85
Roll of ASA 100 color film, 36 exposures	$8.50	£4.70
Admission to Bermuda Maritime Museum	$10	£5.50

Golfers will find that greens fees are comparable to, or less than, fees at other destinations.

Costs are relative, of course. What is affordable for one visitor is a splurge for another. In general, prices in Bermuda are comparable to those in New York, but less expensive than those in London. If you live in rural Texas, the cost of even a so-called inexpensive restaurant in Bermuda will seem expensive to you because of the added import costs attached to most food items. There are no really cheap hotels in Bermuda.

CURRENCY

Legal tender is the Bermuda dollar (BD$), which is divided into 100 cents. It's pegged through gold to the U.S. dollar on an equal basis—BD$1 equals US$1.

U.S. currency is generally accepted in shops, restaurants, and hotels. Currency from the United Kingdom and other foreign countries is usually not accepted, but can be easily exchanged for Bermuda dollars at banks and hotels.

ATMs

The easiest and best way to get cash away from home is from an ATM. These machines are plentiful in Bermuda. The **Cirrus** (© **800/424-7787**; www.master card.com) and **PLUS** (© **800/843-7587**; www.visa.com) networks span the globe; look at the back of your bank card to see which network you're on, then call or check online for ATM locations at your destination. Be sure you know your personal identification number (PIN) and daily withdrawal limit before you depart. *Note:* Remember that many banks impose a fee every time you use a card at another bank's ATM, and that fee can be higher for international transactions (up to $5 or more) than for domestic ones (where they're rarely more than $2). In addition, the bank from which you withdraw cash may charge its own fee. For international withdrawal fees, ask your bank.

CREDIT CARDS

Credit cards are another safe way to carry money. They also provide a convenient record of all your expenses, and they generally offer relatively good exchange rates. You can withdraw cash advances from your credit cards at banks or ATMs, provided you know your PIN. Keep in mind that you'll pay interest from the moment of your withdrawal, even if you pay your monthly bills on time. Also, note that many banks now assess a 1–3% "transaction fee" on all charges you incur abroad (whether you're using the local currency or your native currency).

All major U.S. credit cards, including American Express, Diners Club, Discover, MasterCard, and Visa, are commonly accepted in Bermuda.

TRAVELER'S CHECKS

You can buy traveler's checks, which are widely accepted in Bermuda, at most banks. They are offered in denominations of $20, $50, $100, $500, and sometimes $1,000. Generally, you'll pay a service charge ranging from 1% to 4%.

The most popular traveler's checks are offered by **American Express** (© **800/ 807-6233** or © **800/221-7282** for card holders—this number accepts collect calls, offers service in several foreign languages, and exempts Amex gold and platinum cardholders from the 1% fee); **Visa** (© **800/732-1322**)—AAA members can obtain Visa checks for a $9.95 fee (for checks up to $1,500) at most AAA offices or by calling © **866/339-3378**; and **MasterCard** (© **800/223-9920**).

American Express, Thomas Cook, Visa, and **MasterCard** offer **foreign currency traveler's checks,** which are useful if you're traveling to one country, or to the Euro zone; they're accepted at locations where dollar checks may not be.

If you carry traveler's checks, keep a record of their serial numbers separate from your checks in the event that they are stolen or lost. You'll get a refund faster if you know the numbers.

4 When to Go

THE WEATHER

A semitropical island, Bermuda enjoys a mild climate; the term "Bermuda high" has come to mean sunny days and clear skies. The Gulf Stream, which flows between the island and North America, keeps the climate temperate. There's no rainy season, and no typical month of excess rain. Showers may be heavy at times, but the skies clear quickly.

Being farther north in the Atlantic than the Bahamas, Bermuda is much cooler in winter. Springlike temperatures prevail from mid-December to late March, with the average temperature ranging from the low 60s°F to 70°F (16°C–21°C). Unless it rains, winter is fine for golf and tennis but

---

Tips Easy Money

You'll avoid lines at airport ATMs by exchanging at least some money—just enough to cover airport incidentals and transportation to your hotel—before you leave home.

When you change money, ask for some small bills or loose change. Petty cash will come in handy for tipping and public transportation. Consider keeping the change separate from your larger bills so that it's readily accessible and so you'll be less of a target for theft.

not for swimming; it can be cool, and you may even need a sweater or a jacket. Water temperatures in winter are somewhat like the air temperature, ranging from about 66°F (19°C) in January to 75°F (24°C) through March. Scuba divers and snorkelers will find Caribbean waters appreciably warmer in winter. From mid-November to mid-December and from late March to April, be prepared for unseasonable spurts of spring or summer weather.

In summer, the temperature rarely rises above 85°F (29°C). There's nearly always a cool breeze in the evening, but some hotels have air-conditioning. And local water temperatures can be as high as 86°F (30°C)

during the summer—warmer than many inshore and offshore Caribbean waters.

As a result, Bermuda's off season is the exact opposite of that in the Caribbean. It begins in December and lasts until about March 1. In general, hotels offer off-season rates, with discounts ranging from 20% to 60%. This is the time to go if you're traveling on a tight budget. During autumn and winter, many hotels also offer discounted package deals. Some hotels close for a couple of weeks or months at this period.

A look at the official chart of temperature and rainfall will give you a general idea of what to expect during your visit.

Bermuda's Average Daytime Temperatures & Rainfall

	Jan	Feb	Mar	Apr	May	June	July	Aug	Sept	Oct	Nov	Dec
Temp. (°F)	65	64	64	65	70	75	79	80	79	75	69	65
Temp. (°C)	19	18	18	19	21	24	30	27	30	24	21	19
Rainfall (in.)	4	5	4.6	3	3.9	5.2	4	5.3	5.3	6	4.5	3

THE HURRICANE SEASON

This curse of the Caribbean, the Bahamas, and Bermuda lasts officially from June to November, but don't panic—fewer tropical storms pound Bermuda than the U.S. mainland. Bermuda is also less frequently hit than islands in the Caribbean. Satellite forecasts are generally able to give adequate warning of any really dangerous weather.

If you're concerned, you can call the nearest branch of the National Weather Service (it's listed under the U.S. Department of Commerce in the phone book). Radio and TV weather reports from the National Hurricane Center in Coral Gables, Florida, will also keep you posted.

To find the current weather conditions in Bermuda, and a 5-day forecast, go to Bermuda Weather at **www.weather.bm**.

HOLIDAYS

Bermuda observes the following public holidays: New Year's Day (Jan 1), Good Friday, Easter, Bermuda Day (May 24),

the Queen's Birthday (first or second Mon in June), Cup Match Days (cricket; Thurs and Fri preceding first Mon in Aug), Labour Day (first Mon in Sept), Christmas Day (Dec 25), and Boxing Day (Dec 26). Public holidays that fall on a Saturday or Sunday are usually celebrated the following Monday.

BERMUDA CALENDAR OF EVENTS

January & February

Bermuda Festival. Throughout January and February, island-wide events abound. They include golf and tennis invitationals, an international marathon, a dog show, open house and garden tours, and the Bermuda Festival, a 6-week international festival of the performing arts, held in the City of Hamilton. It features drama, dance, jazz, classical, and popular music, as well as other entertainment by the best international artists. Some tickets for the festival

> **Fun Fact** **Getting Sucked In: The Official Word on the Bermuda Triangle**
>
> In response to a flood of concern from travelers about the possibility of getting sucked into the so-called Bermuda Triangle and disappearing forever, the U.S. Board of Geographic Names has issued an official statement: "We do not recognize the Bermuda Triangle as an official name and do not maintain an official file on the area. The 'Bermuda or Devil's Triangle' is an imaginary area located off the southeastern Atlantic coast of the United States, which is noted for a high incidence of unexplained losses of ships, small boats, and aircraft. The apexes of the triangle are generally accepted to be Bermuda, Miami, and San Juan. In the past, extensive but futile Coast Guard searches prompted by search-and-rescue cases such as the disappearances of an entire squadron of TBM Avengers shortly after take-off from Fort Lauderdale, or the traceless sinking of *Marine Sulphur Queen* in the Florida Straits, have lent credence to the popular belief in the mystery and the supernatural qualities of the Bermuda Triangle."

are reserved until 48 hours before curtain time for visitors. For details and a schedule for the 2007 festival, contact **Bermuda Festival,** P.O. Box HM 297, Hamilton HM AX, Bermuda (© **441/ 295-1291;** www.bermudafestival.org).

The Bermuda International Race Weekend, with international and local runners, takes place the third weekend in January. For further information and entry forms, contact the **International Race Weekend Committee,** Bermuda Track and Field Association, P.O. Box DV 397, Devonshire DV BX, Bermuda (© **441/296-0951;** www.bermudatracknfield.com).

Bermuda Heart & Soul. Travelers 50 years of age or older can enjoy specially designed cultural activities throughout the month of February during this Golden Rendezvous month. Many hotels offer reduced rates to mature travelers, and discount coupons are also available at the Visitors Service Bureau in Hamilton. For more information, call the Department of Tourism at © **441/292-0023.**

March

Home and Garden Tours. Each spring, the Garden Club of Bermuda lays out the welcome mat at a number of private homes and gardens. A different set of houses, all conveniently located in the same parish, is open every Wednesday during this event. The program usually includes a total of 20 homes, many of them dating from the 17th and 18th centuries. The Bermuda Department of Tourism Office (see "Visitor Information," earlier in this chapter) provides a complete listing of homes and viewing schedules. The tours run from the end of March to mid-May.

April

Beating Retreat Ceremony. The Bermuda Regiment and massed pipes and drums (a military band and a drum corps) create an event that combines a marching band concert and a parade. The ceremony's roots are in the 17th century, when British soldiers were stationed on the island and a roll of the drums called them back to their garrisons at nightfall. It's presented once or twice per month, rotating among the City of Hamilton, St. George, and the Royal Naval Dockyard. The ceremony usually takes place from April to July, and in September and October. The Bermuda Department of Tourism Office (see "Visitor Information," earlier in this chapter) supplies exact times and schedules.

Bermuda International Film Festival. Film buffs and filmmakers (mainly independent ones) descend on Bermuda for the annual festival that combines screenings of independent works with movies from personal workshops. Participants get to meet and speak with industry leaders. After each film there is a Q & A session. During the festival, three daily screenings are held. For more information, log on to www.biff.bm or contact Duncan Hall at © **441/293-3456.** Mid-April.

Peppercorn Ceremony. His Excellency the governor collects the annual rent of one peppercorn for use of the island's Old State House in St. George. Mid- to late April. For information and the exact date, call © **441/297-1532** or 800/223-6106.

Agriculture Exhibit. Held over 3 days in late April at the Botanical Gardens in Paget, this event is a celebration of Bermuda's agrarian and horticultural bounty. In addition to prize-winning produce, the Agriculture Exhibit provides a showcase for local arts and crafts. For more information, contact the **Department of Environmental Protection,** P.O. Box HM 834, Hamilton HM CX, Bermuda (© **441/236-4201**), or the Bermuda Department of Tourism (see "Visitor Information," earlier in this chapter).

International Race Week. Every year, during late April and early May, this yachting event pits equivalent vessels from seven classes of sailing craft against one another. Yachting enthusiasts around the world follow the knockout elimination-style event with avid interest. The Marion-to-Bermuda Race (see below) takes place in June.

Other sailing contests are scheduled for alternate years. The world's most famous wind-driven contest, the Newport–Bermuda Race, falls next in June 2008. The record to date, which starts in Newport, Rhode Island, is a 56-hour transit.

Unfortunately for spectators, the finish lines for the island's sailing races usually lie several miles offshore. Afterward, boats are often moored in Hamilton Harbour; any vantage point on the harbor is good for watching the boats come in. Even better: Head for any of the City of Hamilton's harborfront pubs, where racing crowds celebrate their wins (or justify their losses) over pints of ale.

For information on all sailing events held off the coast of Bermuda, contact the **Sailing Secretary,** Royal Bermuda Yacht Club, P.O. Box HM 894, Hamilton HM DX, Bermuda (© **441/296-8598**), or (for races originating off the U.S. coast) the **New York Yacht Club,** 37 W. 44th St., New York, NY 10036 (© **212/382-1000;** www.nyyc.org).

May

Bermuda Heritage Day and Month. Bermuda Heritage Month culminates on **Bermuda Day,** May 24, a public holiday that's Bermuda's equivalent of Independence Day. Bermuda Day is punctuated with parades through downtown Hamilton, dinghy and cycling races, and the Bermuda Half-Day Marathon (open only to island residents). For the rest of the month, a program of cultural and sporting events is presented (the schedule will be available at the tourist office). Any hotel in town can fill you in on the events planned for the year's biggest political celebration, or contact the Bermuda Department of Tourism Office (see "Visitor Information," earlier in this chapter).

June

Queen's Birthday (first or second Mon in June; contact the Bermuda Department of Tourism Office at *(C)* **800/ BERMUDA** or www.bermudatourism. com for exact times and schedules). The Queen's birthday is celebrated with a parade down Front Street in the City of Hamilton.

Marion-to-Bermuda Race. This 1,038km (645-mile) sailboat race from Marion, Massachusetts, to Bermuda is held in mid-June. See the entry for "International Race Week," under April, above, for details on international sailing events. For more information, call *(C)* **441/296-8598,** or visit www.marionbermuda.com.

August

Cup Match and Somers Days. Also known as the Cup Match Cricket Festival, this annual event celebrates the year's bounty with Bermuda's most illustrious cricket match. It's often compared to American Thanksgiving. Cricketers from the East End (St. George's Cricket Club) play off against those from the West End (Somerset Cricket Club), with lots of attendant British-derived protocol and hoopla. Tickets cost about $10; they're available at the gate on match day. The event is held on Thursday and Friday before the first Monday in August. For more information, call *(C)* **441/297-0374.**

September

Labour Day. This public holiday, held on the first Monday in September, features a host of activities; it's also the ideal time for a picnic. The high point

is a parade from Union Square in the City of Hamilton's Bernard Park.

Marine Science Day. Lectures, hands-on demonstrations, and displays for adults and children mark this day devoted to the study of the sea. It is hosted by the **BBSR** (Bermuda Biological Station for Research, Inc.). Call *(C)* **441/297-1880** or visit www.bbsr.edu for more information. End of September.

October

Match Racing. For Match Racing, pairs of identical sailing vessels, staffed by a rotating roster of teams from throughout the world, compete in elimination-style contests throughout the month. For details on international sailing events, see the entry for "International Race Week," under April, above.

November

Guy Fawkes Day. A small annual celebration with a minifair marks this day. The celebration starts with the traditional burning of 17th-century British traitor Guy Fawkes's effigy at the Keepyard of the Bermuda Maritime Museum, Royal Naval Dockyard, at 4:30pm. November 5.

The Opening of Parliament. A traditional ceremony, with a military guard of honor, celebrates the opening of Parliament by His Excellency the governor, as the Queen's personal representative. In anticipation of the entry of the members of Parliament (MPs) at 11am, crowds begin gathering outside the Cabinet Building around 9:30 or 10am. Spectators traditionally include lots of schoolchildren being trained in civic protocol, as well as nostalgia buffs out for a whiff of British-style pomp. For more information, call *(C)* **800/ 223-6106.** November 6.

Invitation Tennis Weeks. More than 100 visiting players vie with Bermudians during 2 weeks of matches. Unlike

Wimbledon—this event's role model—virtually everyone buys tickets at the gate. For information, contact the **Bermuda Lawn Tennis Association,** P.O. Box HM 341, Hamilton HM BX, Bermuda (© **441/296-0834;** www.blta.bm). Early November.

Remembrance Day. Bermudian police, British and U.S. military units, Bermudians, and veterans' organizations participate in a small parade in remembrance of all who have given their lives in battle. November 11.

Seniors Rugby World Cup. Former international rugby players, who have recently retired from the international stage, compete with Bermudians at the

Bermuda National Sports Club (© **441/295-6574**). Mid-November.

December

Bermuda Goodwill Tournament. Pro-amateur foursomes from international golf clubs play more than 72 holes on four of Bermuda's eight courses. Anyone who wants to compete must pass the sponsors' stringent requirements and may appear only by invitation. Spectators are welcome to watch from the sidelines for free. For more information, contact the **Bermuda Goodwill Golf Tournament,** P.O. Box WK 127, Warwick WK BX, Bermuda (© **441/295-4640;** www.bermudagoodwill.org). Early December.

5 Planning an Island Wedding or Honeymoon

GETTING MARRIED IN BERMUDA

Couples who would like to get married in Bermuda must file a "Notice of Intended Marriage" with the Registry General, accompanied by a fee of $210, plus $21 for the certificate (in the form of a bank draft or money order, not a personal check). Make out the draft to "The Accountant General," and mail or deliver it in person to the **Registry General,** Government Administration Building, 30 Parliament St., Hamilton HM 12, Bermuda (© **441/297-7709;** www.registrygeneral.gov.bm). Bermuda Department of Tourism offices in Atlanta and New York (see "Visitor Information," earlier in this chapter) distribute

"Notice of Intended Marriage" forms, or you can contact the Bermuda Department of Tourism (© **800/BERMUDA**) and a form will be mailed to you. If either of the prospective marriage partners has been married before, that person must attach a photocopy of the final divorce decree to the "Notice of Intended Marriage."

Once the Registry General receives the "Notice of Intended Marriage," it will be published, including names and addresses, in any two of the island's newspapers. Assuming that there is no formal objection, the registry will issue the license 15 days after receiving the notice. Airmailing your completed notice to Bermuda takes 6 to 10 days, so plan

Fun Fact **Have Your Cake & Eat It, Too**

Custom dictates that Bermudians have two wedding cakes: a plain pound cake covered with gold leaf for the groom, and a tiered fruit cake covered with silver leaf and topped with a miniature cedar tree for the bride. The tiny tree is planted on the day of the wedding to symbolize the hope that the marriage will grow and mature like the tree. The rest of the first tier of the bride's cake is frozen until the christening of the first child.

accordingly. The marriage license will be sent to you and will be valid for 3 months.

HIRING A WEDDING CONSULTANT

Many hotels can help make wedding arrangements—reserving the church and clergy, hiring a horse and buggy, ordering the wedding cake, and securing a photographer. Bermuda weddings range from simple ceremonies on the beach to large-scale extravaganzas at the Botanical Gardens. Other popular sites include churches and yachts.

Wedding consultants can discuss your options with you and arrange all the details. **The Wedding Salon,** 76 Spanish Point Rd., Suite 10, Pembroke HM 02, Bermuda (© **919/217-4395** or 441/292-5677; www.bermudaweddingsalon.com), operates its planning office in North Carolina. After a contractual agreement is made, the office puts customers in contact with their Bermuda consultant. **The Bridal Suite,** Parkside Building, 3 Park Rd., Suite 7, Hamilton HM 09, Bermuda (© **888/253-5585,** 441/292-2025, or 905/427-1551; www.bridalsuitebermuda weddings.com), arranges wedding packages

that range in cost from $1,000 to $15,000.

Some hotels—including the Elbow Beach Hotel, the Sonesta Beach Resort, and both of the Fairmont hotels—will arrange weddings; see chapter 4, "Where to Stay," for contact information. If you're staying at a small hotel, it's better to go through a wedding consultant to plan your wedding.

HONEYMOONING IN BERMUDA

Bermuda attracts more than 23,000 honeymooners and second honeymooners each year, with good reason: It offers an ideal environment for couples, whether they prefer an active schedule or a relaxing one. Many of Bermuda's hotels, from luxurious resorts to intimate cottage colonies, offer honeymoon packages. Typically, these include airfare, accommodations, meal plans, champagne upon arrival, flowers in your room, and discounts at local attractions and restaurants. See "The Best Resorts for Lovers & Honeymooners," in chapter 1, "The Best of Bermuda." For other options, consult your travel agent or call the hotels listed in chapter 4, "Where to Stay," directly and inquire about honeymoon packages.

6 Travel Insurance

Although close to the United States, a visit to Bermuda is, in essence, "going abroad." You can encounter all the same problems in Bermuda that you would in going to a more remote foreign destination. Therefore, it's wise to review your insurance coverage, especially concerning lost luggage or medical insurance.

The cost of travel insurance varies widely, depending on the cost and length of your trip, your age and health, and the type of trip you're taking, but expect to pay between 5% and 8% of the vacation itself. You can get estimates from various providers through **InsureMyTrip.com**. Enter your trip cost and dates, your age,

and other information, for prices from more than a dozen companies.

TRIP-CANCELLATION INSURANCE

Trip-cancellation insurance will help retrieve your money if you have to back out of a trip or depart early, or if your travel supplier goes bankrupt. Permissible reasons for trip cancellation can range from sickness to natural disasters to the State Department declaring a destination unsafe for travel.

For more information, contact one of the following recommended insurers: **Access America** (© 866/807-3982;

> ## ⟨Tips⟩ Daily Life in Bermuda
>
> Here are some miscellaneous Bermuda survival tips: Know that ATMs dispense only Bermuda dollars, and that buses accept only coins. Also, don't get caught in the City of Hamilton's rush-hour traffic, which is Monday to Friday from 8:30 to 9am and 5 to 6pm.

---

www.accessamerica.com); **Travel Guard International** (© 800/826-4919; www.travelguard.com); **Travel Insured International** (© 800/243-3174; www.travelinsured.com); and **Travelex Insurance Services** (© 888/457-4602; www.travelexinsurance.com).

MEDICAL INSURANCE

For travel overseas, most U.S. health plans (including Medicare and Medicaid) do not provide coverage, and the ones that do often require you to pay for services upfront and reimburse you only after you return home. As a safety net, you may want to buy travel medical insurance, particularly if you're traveling to a remote or high-risk area where emergency evacuation might be necessary. If you require additional medical insurance, try **MEDEX Assistance** (© 410/453-6300; www.medexassist.com) or **Travel Assistance International** (© 800/821-2828; www.travelassistance.com; for general information on services, call the company's

Worldwide Assistance Services, Inc., at © **800/777-8710**).

LOST-LUGGAGE INSURANCE

On flights within the U.S., checked baggage is covered up to $2,500 per ticketed passenger. On international flights (including U.S. portions of international trips), baggage coverage is limited to approximately $9.07 per pound, up to approximately $635 per checked bag. If you plan to check items more valuable than what's covered by the standard liability, see if your homeowner's policy covers your valuables, get baggage insurance as part of your comprehensive travel-insurance package, or buy Travel Guard's "BagTrak" product.

If your luggage is lost, immediately file a lost-luggage claim at the airport, detailing the luggage contents. Most airlines require that you report delayed, damaged, or lost baggage within 4 hours of arrival. The airlines are required to deliver luggage, once found, directly to your house or destination free of charge.

7 Health & Safety

STAYING HEALTHY

Limit your exposure to the sun, especially between the hours of 11am and 2pm and during the first few days of your trip. Use a sunscreen with a high protection factor and apply it liberally. Remember that children need more protection than adults do.

As you travel around Bermuda on a scooter, on bike, or on foot, it's always wise to carry along some bottled water to prevent dehydration.

WHAT TO DO IF YOU GET SICK AWAY FROM HOME

Finding a doctor or getting a prescription filled on Bermuda is relatively simple. See "Drugstores," under "Fast Facts: Bermuda," in chapter 3, for addresses of pharmacies. In an emergency, call **King Edward VII Hospital,** 7 Point Finger Rd., Paget Parish (© **441/236-2345**), and ask for the emergency department. For less serious medical problems, ask someone at your hotel for a recommendation.

We list **hospitals** and **emergency numbers** under "Fast Facts," p. 64.

If you suffer from a chronic illness, consult your doctor before your departure. Pack **prescription medications** in your carry-on luggage, and carry them in their original containers, with pharmacy labels—otherwise they won't make it through airport security. Carry the generic name of prescription medicines, in case a local pharmacist is unfamiliar with the brand name.

For travel abroad, you may have to pay all medical costs upfront and be reimbursed later. See "Medical Insurance," under "Travel Insurance," above.

STAYING SAFE

Bermuda has a low to moderate crime rate. Incidents of serious violent crime are infrequent, but petty thefts and assaults do occur. Valuables left in hotel rooms (occupied and unoccupied) or left unattended on beaches are vulnerable to theft. Criminals often target transportation systems and popular tourist attractions. Examples of common crimes include pickpocketing, theft of unattended baggage and items from rental motorbikes, and purse snatchings (often perpetrated against pedestrians by thieves riding motorbikes).

Travelers should exercise caution when walking after dark or visiting out-of-the-way places on the island, which can be vulnerable to crime, and because narrow and dark roadways can contribute to accidents. Incidents of verbal, and sometimes physical, assault against both locals and tourists have been reported. Petty drug use is frequent and open. Gang activity, including assaults and arson, has been reported in Bermuda as well. There have been several assaults and thefts in the area of Pitts Bay Road from the Hamilton Princess Hotel into the City of Hamilton, and the back roads of Hamilton are often the setting for assaults, particularly after the bars close.

The loss or theft abroad of a U.S. passport should be reported immediately to the local police and the nearest U.S. embassy or consulate. U.S. citizens can refer to the Department of State's pamphlet *A Safe Trip Abroad* for ways to promote a more trouble-free journey. This publication and others, such as *Tips for Travelers to the Caribbean,* are available by mail from the Superintendent of Documents, U.S. Government Printing Office, Washington, DC 20402; via the Internet at www.gpoaccess.gov; or via the Bureau of Consular Affairs home page at http://travel.state.gov.

ECOTOURISM

You can find eco-friendly travel tips, statistics, and touring companies and associations—listed by destination under "Travel Choice"—at the TIES website, www.ecotourism.org. **Ecotravel.com** is part online magazine and part eco-directory that lets you search for touring companies in several categories (water-based, land-based, spiritually oriented, and so on). Also check out **Conservation International** (www.conservation.org)—which, with *National Geographic Traveler,* annually presents **World Legacy Awards**

Healthy Travels to You

The following government websites offer up-to-date health-related travel advice.

- **Australia:** www.dfat.gov.au/travel/
- **Canada:** www.hc-sc.gc.ca/index_e.html
- **U.K.:** www.dh.gov.uk/PolicyAndGuidance/HealthAdviceForTravellers/fs/en
- **U.S.:** www.cdc.gov/travel/

Avoiding "Economy Class Syndrome"

Deep vein thrombosis, or as it's know in the world of flying, "economy-class syndrome," is a blood clot that develops in a deep vein. It's a potentially deadly condition that can be caused by sitting in cramped conditions—such as an airplane cabin—for too long. During a flight (especially a long-haul flight), get up, walk around, and stretch your legs every 60 to 90 minutes to keep your blood flowing. Other preventative measures include frequent flexing of the legs while sitting, drinking lots of water, and avoiding alcohol and sleeping pills. If you have a history of deep vein thrombosis, heart disease, or another condition that puts you at high risk, some experts recommend wearing compression stockings or taking anticoagulants when you fly; always ask your physician about the best course for you. Symptoms of deep vein thrombosis include leg pain or swelling, or even shortness of breath.

(www.wlaward.org) to those travel tour operators, businesses, organizations, and places that have made a significant contribution to sustainable tourism.

For information about the ethics of swimming with dolphins and other outdoor activities, visit the **Whale and Dolphin Conservation Society** (www.wdcs.org) and **Tread Lightly** (www.treadlightly.org).

8 Specialized Travel Resources

TRAVELERS WITH DISABILITIES

Most disabilities shouldn't stop anyone from traveling. There are more options and resources out there than ever before.

However, Bermuda is not a great place for persons with disabilities who are not planning to stay on-site at a resort. Getting around the islands is a bit difficult even for the agile, who must rely on motorbikes, bicycles, and buses. It is difficult to walk with a cane outside the town of St. George and City of Hamilton, because most roads don't have sidewalks or adequate curbs. When two vehicles pass, you are often crowded off the road.

Taking taxis to everything you want to see can be very expensive. Unfortunately, the public buses are not geared for passengers in wheelchairs. However, you can ask your hotel to check on the availability of volunteer buses operated by the Bermuda Physically Handicapped Association (no phone). It occasionally runs buses with hydraulic lifts. You can also call the tourist office and request a schedule for such transportation; make arrangements as far in advance as possible.

Before you go, you can seek information from the website of the **Bermuda Physically Handicapped Association** (© 441/293-5035; www.bermuda-online. org/BPHA.htm). Visitors planning to bring a guide dog to Bermuda must obtain a permit in advance from any Bermuda Department of Tourism office.

The most accessible hotels in Bermuda are Elbow Beach Hotel, the Sonesta Beach Resort, the Fairmont Hamilton Princess, and the Fairmont Southampton (see chapter 4 for listings).

Many travel agencies offer customized tours and itineraries for travelers with disabilities. Among them are **Flying Wheels Travel** (© 507/451-5005; www.flying wheelstravel.com); **Access-Able Travel Source** (© 303/232-2979; www.access-able.com); and **Accessible Journeys** (© 800/846-4537 or 610/521-0339; www. disabilitytravel.com).

Organizations that offer assistance to disabled travelers include **MossRehab** (www.mossresourcenet.org); the **American Foundation for the Blind (AFB)** (✆ 800/232-5463; www.afb.org); and **SATH (Society for Accessible Travel & Hospitality)** (✆ 212/447-7284; www.sath.org). **AirAmbulanceCard.com** is now partnered with SATH and allows you to preselect top-notch hospitals in case of an emergency. The community website **iCan** (www.icanonline.net/channels/travel) has destination guides and several regular columns on accessible travel. Also check out the quarterly magazine *Emerging Horizons* (www.emerginghorizons.com), and *Open World* magazine, published by SATH.

GAY & LESBIAN TRAVELERS

Think twice before planning a holiday on Bermuda. Although many gays live in and visit Bermuda, the island is rather repressive to homosexuals. Displays of affection by same-sex couples will be frowned upon at public beaches and most hotel pools, restaurants, or attractions. If you want really happening gay beaches, bars, and clubs, head for South Miami Beach, Key West, Puerto Rico, or the U.S. Virgin Islands, a series of islands that are much more accepting of homosexual relationships.

For most of its existence, Bermuda had harsh penalties against male homosexuals, making sex between consenting legal-age males a crime subject to imprisonment. Lobbying against such a measure, The Bermuda Human Rights Alliance, a Bermuda gay and lesbian group, helped to bring about a repeal of the criminal code. Since an assembly vote in the Bermuda Parliament, sex between men over the age of 18 is now legal.

If you're contemplating a visit, point your browser to **www.gaybermuda.com**, a comprehensive website geared to gay travelers to Bermuda.

The International Gay and Lesbian Travel Association (IGLTA) (✆ 800/448-8550 or 954/776-2626; www.iglta.org) is the trade association for the gay and lesbian travel industry, and offers an online directory of gay- and lesbian-friendly travel businesses; go to their website and click on "Members."

Many agencies offer tours and travel itineraries specifically for gay and lesbian travelers. Among them are **Above and Beyond Tours** (✆ 800/397-2681; www.abovebeyondtours.com); **Now, Voyager** (✆ 800/255-6951; www.nowvoyager.com); and **Olivia Cruises & Resorts** (✆ 800/631-6277; www.olivia.com).

Gay.com Travel (✆ 800/929-2268 or 415/644-8044; www.gay.com/travel or www.outandabout.com) is an excellent online successor to the popular *Out & About* print magazine. It provides regularly updated information about gay-owned, gay-oriented, and gay-friendly lodging, dining, sightseeing, nightlife, and shopping establishments in every important destination worldwide.

The following travel guides are available at many bookstores, or you can order them from any online bookseller: *Frommer's Gay & Lesbian Europe* (www.frommers.com), an excellent travel resource to the top European cities and resorts; *Spartacus International Gay Guide* (Bruno Gmünder Verlag; www.spartacusworld.com/gayguide/); *Odysseus: The International Gay Travel Planner* (Odysseus Enterprises Ltd.); and the *Damron* guides (www.damron.com), with separate, annual books for gay men and lesbians.

SENIOR TRAVELERS

Though much of the island's sporting and nightlife activity is geared toward more youthful travelers, Bermuda has a lot to offer seniors. The best source of information for seniors is the Bermuda Department of Tourism (see "Visitor

Information," earlier in this chapter). If you're staying in a large resort hotel, the activities director or concierge is another excellent source.

Members of **AARP** (formerly known as the American Association of Retired Persons), 601 E St. NW, Washington, DC 20049 (© **888/687-2277;** www. aarp.org), get discounts on hotels, airfares, and car rentals. AARP offers members a wide range of benefits, including *AARP: The Magazine* and a monthly newsletter. Anyone over 50 can join.

Many reliable agencies and organizations target the 50-plus market. **Elderhostel** (© **877/426-8056;** www.elder hostel.org) arranges study programs for those age 55 and over. **ElderTreks** (© **800/741-7956;** www.eldertreks.com) offers small-group tours to off-the-beaten-path or adventure-travel locations, restricted to travelers 50 and older. **INTRAV** (© **800/456-8100;** www.intrav.com) is a high-end tour operator that caters to the mature, discerning traveler (not specifically seniors), with trips around the world that include guided safaris, polar expeditions, private-jet adventures, and small-boat cruises down jungle rivers.

Recommended publications offering travel resources and discounts for seniors include the quarterly magazine *Travel 50 & Beyond* (www.travel50andbeyond. com); *Travel Unlimited: Uncommon Adventures for the Mature Traveler* (Avalon); *101 Tips for Mature Travelers,* available from Grand Circle Travel (© **800/221-2610** or 617/350-7500; www.gct.com); and *Unbelievably Good Deals and Great Adventures That You Absolutely Can't Get Unless You're Over 50* (McGraw-Hill), by Joann Rattner Heilman.

FAMILY TRAVEL

Bermuda is one of the best vacation destinations for the entire family. Toddlers can spend blissful hours in shallow seawater or pools geared just for them, and older children can enjoy boat rides, horseback riding, hiking, and snorkeling. Most resort hotels offer advice for families with kids (including help in finding a babysitter), and many have play directors and supervised activities for various age groups.

Outside the town of St. George and City of Hamilton, walking with a baby stroller is difficult—most roads don't have sidewalks or adequate curbs. It is extremely dangerous to carry a baby on a motorbike or bike, as baby seats are not provided. Buses, taxis, and ferries are the safest ways to travel around Bermuda with a baby.

For some recommendations on where to stay and eat, refer to "Family-Friendly Accommodations," in chapter 4, and "Family-Friendly Restaurants," in chapter 5.

To locate accommodations, restaurants, and attractions that are particularly kid-friendly, refer to the "Kids" icon throughout this guide.

Familyhostel (© **800/733-9753;** www. learn.unh.edu/familyhostel) takes the whole family, including kids ages 8 to 15, on moderately priced U.S. and international learning vacations. Lectures, field trips, and sightseeing are guided by a team of academics.

Recommended family travel websites include **Family Travel Forum** (www.family travelforum.com); **Family Travel Network** (www.familytravelnetwork.com); **Traveling Internationally with Your Kids** (www.travelwithyourkids.com); and **Family Travel Files** (www.thefamilytravel files.com).

AFRICAN-AMERICAN TRAVELERS

Black Travel Online (www.blacktravel online.com) posts news on upcoming events and includes links to articles and travel-booking sites. **Soul of America** (www.soulofamerica.com) is a comprehensive website, with travel tips, event and family-reunion postings, and sections on historically black beach resorts and active vacations.

Agencies and organizations that provide resources for black travelers include **Rodgers Travel** (© 800/825-1775; www.rodgerstravel.com); the **African American Association of Innkeepers International** (© 877/422-5777; www.africanamericaninns.com); and **Henderson Travel & Tours** (© 800/327-2309 or 301/650-5700; www.hendersontravel.com), which has specialized in trips to Africa since 1957. For more information, check out the following collections and guides: *Go Girl: The Black Woman's Guide to Travel & Adventure* (Eighth Mountain Press), a compilation of travel essays by writers including Jill Nelson and Audre Lorde; *The African American*

Travel Guide by Wayne Robinson (Hunter Publishing; www.hunterpublishing.com); *Steppin' Out* by Carla Labat (Avalon); *Travel and Enjoy Magazine* (© 866/266-6211; www.travelandenjoy.com); and *Pathfinders Magazine* (© 877/977-PATH; www.pathfinderstravel.com), which includes articles on everything from Rio de Janeiro to Ghana as well as information on upcoming ski, diving, golf, and tennis trips.

STUDENT TRAVEL

The Bermuda Department of Tourism offers Spring Break programs for sports teams from the mainland, as well as Spring Break Arts Programs. Inquire with the tourism office for details (see "Visitor Information," earlier in this chapter).

9 Planning Your Trip Online

SURFING FOR AIRFARE

The most popular online travel agencies are **Travelocity** (**www.travelocity.com**, or www.travelocity.co.uk); **Expedia** (**www.expedia.com**, www.expedia.co.uk, or www.expedia.ca); and **Orbitz** (www.orbitz.com).

In addition, most airlines now offer online-only fares that even their phone agents know nothing about. For the websites of airlines that fly to and from your destination, go to "Getting There: Flying to Bermuda," p. 40.

Other helpful websites for booking airline tickets online include:

- www.biddingfortravel.com
- www.cheapflights.com
- www.hotwire.com
- www.kayak.com
- www.lastminutetravel.com
- www.opodo.co.uk
- www.priceline.com
- www.sidestep.com
- www.site59.com
- www.smartertravel.com

SURFING FOR HOTELS

In addition to **Travelocity, Expedia, Orbitz, Priceline,** and **Hotwire** (see above), the following websites will help you with booking hotel rooms online:

- www.hotels.com
- www.quickbook.com;
- www.travelaxe.net
- www.travelweb.com
- www.tripadvisor.com

It's a good idea to **get a confirmation number** and **make a printout** of any online booking transaction.

TRAVEL BLOGS & TRAVELOGUES

A few noteworthy travel blogs include:

- www.gridskipper.com
- www.salon.com/wanderlust
- www.travelblog.com
- www.travelblog.org
- www.worldhum.com
- www.writtenroad.com

Frommers.com: The Complete Travel Resource

For an excellent travel-planning resource, we highly recommend **Frommers. com** (www.frommers.com), voted Best Travel Site by *PC Magazine*. We're a little biased, of course, but we guarantee that you'll find the travel tips, reviews, monthly vacation giveaways, bookstore, and online-booking capabilities thoroughly indispensable. Among the special features are our popular **Destinations** section, where you'll get expert travel tips, hotel and dining recommendations, and advice on the sights to see for more than 3,500 destinations around the globe; the **Frommers.com Newsletter,** with the latest deals, travel trends, and money-saving secrets; our **Community** area featuring **Message Boards,** where Frommer's readers post queries and share advice (sometimes even our authors show up to answer questions); and our **Photo Center,** where you can post and share vacation tips. When your research is finished, the **Online Reservations System** (www.frommers. com/book_a_trip) takes you to Frommer's preferred online partners for booking your vacation at affordable prices.

10 The 21st-Century Traveler

INTERNET ACCESS AWAY FROM HOME
WITHOUT YOUR OWN COMPUTER

To find cybercafes in your destination check **www.cybercaptive.com** and **www. cybercafe.com**.

Aside from formal cybercafes, most **youth hostels** and **public libraries** have Internet access. Avoid **hotel business centers** unless you're willing to pay exorbitant rates.

Most major airports now have **Internet kiosks** scattered throughout their gates. These give you basic Web access for a per-minute fee that's usually higher than cybercafe prices.

WITH YOUR OWN COMPUTER

More and more hotels, cafes, and retailers are signing on as Wi-Fi (wireless fidelity) "hot spots." Mac owners have their own networking technology: Apple AirPort. **T-Mobile Hotspot** (www.t-mobile.com/hotspot) serves up wireless connections at more than 1,000 Starbucks coffee shops nationwide. **Boingo** (www.boingo.com) and **Wayport** (www.wayport.com) have set up networks in airports and high-class hotel lobbies. IPass providers (see below) also give you access to a few hundred wireless hotel lobby setups. To locate other hot spots that provide **free wireless networks** in cities around the world, go to **www.personaltelco.net/index.cgi/ WirelessCommunities**.

For dial-up access, most business-class hotels throughout the world offer dataports for laptop modems, and a few thousand hotels in the U.S. and Europe now offer free high-speed Internet access. In addition, major Internet Service Providers (ISPs) have **local access numbers** around the world, allowing you to go online by placing a local call. The **iPass** network also has dial-up numbers around the world. You'll have to sign up with an iPass provider, who will then tell you how to set up your computer for your destination(s). For a list of iPass providers, go to www. ipass.com and click on "Individuals Buy

Now." One solid provider is **i2roam** (© **866/811-6209** or 920/235-0475; www.i2roam.com).

Wherever you go, bring a **connection kit** of the right power and phone adapters, a spare phone cord, and a spare Ethernet network cable—or find out whether your hotel supplies them to guests. See "Electricity" under "Fast Facts" in chapter 3.

CELLPHONE USE

The three letters that define much of the world's wireless capabilities are GSM (Global System for Mobiles), a big, seamless network that makes for easy cross-border cellphone use throughout Europe and dozens of other countries worldwide. In the U.S., T-Mobile, AT&T Wireless, and Cingular use this quasi-universal system; in Canada, Microcell and some Rogers customers are GSM, and all Europeans and most Australians use GSM. If your cellphone is on a GSM system, and you have a world-capable multiband phone such as many Sony Ericsson, Motorola, or Samsung models, you can make and receive calls across civilized areas around much of the globe. Just call your wireless operator and ask for "international roaming" to be activated on your account. Unfortunately, per-minute charges can be high—usually $1 to $1.50.

For many, **renting** a phone is a good idea. (Even worldphone owners will have to rent new phones if they're traveling to non-GSM regions, such as Japan or Korea.) While you can rent a phone from any number of overseas sites, including kiosks at airports and at car-rental agencies, we suggest renting the phone before you leave home. North Americans can rent one before leaving home from **InTouch USA** (© 800/872-7626; www.intouchglobal.com) or **RoadPost** (© 888/290-1606 or 905/272-5665; www.roadpost.com). InTouch will also, for free, advise you on whether your existing phone will work overseas; simply call © **703/222-7161** between 9am and 4pm EST, or go to **http://intouchglobal.com/travel.htm**.

Online Traveler's Toolbox

Veteran travelers usually carry some essential items to make their trips easier. Following is a selection of handy online tools to bookmark and use.

- **Airplane Food** (www.airlinemeals.net)
- **Airplane Seating** (www.seatguru.com, and www.airlinequality.com)
- **Foreign Languages for Travelers** (www.travlang.com)
- **Maps** (www.mapquest.com)
- **Subway Navigator** (www.subwaynavigator.com)
- **Time and Date** (www.timeanddate.com)
- **Travel Warnings** (http://travel.state.gov, www.fco.gov.uk/travel, www.voyage.gc.ca, or www.dfat.gov.au/consular/advice)
- **Universal Currency Converter** (www.xe.com/ucc)
- **Visa ATM Locator** (www.visa.com), **MasterCard ATM Locator** (www.mastercard.com)
- **Weather** (www.intellicast.com, and www.weather.com)

11 Getting There: Flying to Bermuda

From North America's East Coast, you can be in Bermuda in approximately 2 hours. From London, England, the trip takes about 7 hours.

BY PLANE

American Airlines (© 800/433-7300; www.aa.com) flies nonstop, three times a day, from New York's JFK Airport and once daily from Miami. Departures coincide with dozens of connecting flights from elsewhere in North America.

Delta (© 800/221-1212; www.delta.com) offers daily nonstop service from Boston and Atlanta. The Boston flight departs in the morning (around 9am). The Atlanta flight leaves around 11am—late enough to allow connections from most of the other cities in Delta's vast network.

Continental Airlines (© 800/525-0280; www.continental.com) offers nonstop service from New Jersey's Newark Airport. Departures are daily. The low-cost carrier **JetBlue Airways** (© 800/JET-BLUE) now offers two daily nonstop flights between New York and Bermuda, with one-way fares costing from $129 per passenger. The 2-hour flights originate at Kennedy International Airport.

AmericaWest/US Airways (© 800/428-4322; www.usairways.com) offers daily nonstop flights from Philadelphia and Boston year-round, plus daily nonstop flights from New York (La Guardia). In 2004, the airline also launched nonstop service from Orlando (Florida) to Bermuda.

USA3000 Airlines, a low-fare, full-service airline, is now the newest air route to Bermuda, flying regularly scheduled services from the Baltimore/Washington International Airport. The airline offers flights that depart every Tuesday and Friday. For more information check www.USA3000.com.

Air Canada (© 888/247-2262; www.aircanada.ca) offers daily nonstop flights from Toronto, with frequent connections into Toronto from virtually every other city in Canada. The flight departs around 9am, permitting convenient connections from Montreal and Quebec City. The airline also offers a nonstop flight from Halifax on Saturday at noon.

The airline of choice from the United Kingdom is **British Airways** (© 0870/850-9850; www.britishairways.com). It flies from London's Gatwick Airport about three times a week, year-round. No other airline flies nonstop between Britain and Bermuda.

Most airlines offer the best deals on tickets booked at least 14 days in advance, with a stopover in Bermuda of at least 3 days. You might need to stay over on a Saturday night to keep fares down. Airfares fluctuate according to the season, but tend to remain competitive among the companies vying for a piece of the lucrative Bermuda run.

Peak season (summer) is the most expensive time to go; low season (usually from mid-Sept to mid-Mar) sees less expensive fares. The airlines that fly to Bermuda seldom observe a shoulder (intermediate) season. Because most aircraft flying from North America to Bermuda are medium-size, there's space

---

Tips **Packing Tip**

Bermuda is more formal than most resort destinations, so men planning to dine at upscale restaurants should be sure to pack a jacket and tie.

Tips **Getting Through the Airport**

- Arrive at the airport 2 hours before an international flight; if you show up late, tell an airline employee and he or she will probably whisk you to the front of the line.
- Beat the ticket-counter lines by using airport electronic kiosks or even online check-in from your home computers, from where you can print out boarding passes in advance. Curbside check-in is also a good way to avoid lines.
- Bring a current, government-issued photo ID such as a driver's license or passport. Children under 18 do not need government-issued photo IDs for flights within the U.S., but they do for international flights to most countries.
- Speed up security by removing your jacket and shoes before you're screened. In addition, remove metal objects such as big belt buckles. If you've got metallic body parts, a note from your doctor can prevent a long chat with the security screeners.
- Use a TSA-approved lock for your checked luggage. Look for Travel Sentry certified locks at luggage or travel shops and Brookstone stores (or online at www.brookstone.com).

---

for only two classes of service: first class and economy.

FLYING FOR LESS: TIPS FOR GETTING THE BEST AIRFARE

- Passengers who can book their ticket either **long in advance or at the last minute,** or who **fly midweek** or **at less-trafficked hours,** may pay a fraction of the full fare. If your schedule is flexible, say so, and ask if you can secure a cheaper fare by changing your flight plans.
- Search **the Internet** for cheap fares (see "Planning Your Trip Online," above).
- Keep an eye on local newspapers for **promotional specials** or **fare wars,** when airlines lower prices on their most popular routes. You rarely see fare wars offered for peak travel times, but if you can travel in the off-months, you may snag a bargain.
- **Consolidators,** also known as bucket shops, are great sources for international tickets, although they usually can't beat Internet fares within North America. Start by looking in Sunday newspaper travel sections; U.S. travelers should focus on the *New York Times, Los Angeles Times,* and *Miami Herald.* U.K. travelers should search in the *Independent, The Guardian, or The Observer.* ***Beware:*** Bucket shop tickets are usually nonrefundable or rigged with stiff cancellation penalties, often as high as 50% to 75% of the ticket price, and some put you on charter airlines, which may leave at inconvenient times and experience delays. Several reliable consolidators are worldwide and available online. **STA Travel** has been the world's lead consolidator for students since purchasing Council Travel, but their fares are competitive for travelers of all ages. **ELTExpress (Flights.com)** (*©* **800/TRAV-800;** www.eltexpress. com) has excellent fares worldwide, particularly to Europe. They also

have "local" websites in 12 countries. **FlyCheap** (© **800/FLY-CHEAP;** www.1800flycheap.com), owned by package-holiday megalith MyTravel, has especially good fares to sunny destinations. **Air Tickets Direct** (© **800/778-3447;** www.airtickets direct.com) is based in Montreal and leverages the currently weak Canadian dollar for low fares; they also book trips to places that U.S. travel agents won't touch, such as Cuba.

- Join **frequent-flier clubs.** Frequent-flier membership doesn't cost a cent, but it does entitle you to better seats, faster response to phone inquiries, and prompter service if your luggage is stolen or your flight is canceled or delayed, or if you want to change your seat. And you don't have to fly to earn points; **frequent-flier credit cards** can earn you thousands of miles for doing your everyday shopping. With more than 70 mileage awards programs on the market, consumers have never had more options. Investigate the program details of your favorite airlines before you sink

points into any one. Consider which airlines have hubs in the airport nearest you, and, of those carriers, which have the most advantageous alliances, given your most common routes. To play the frequent-flier game to your best advantage, consult Randy Petersen's **Inside Flyer** (www.insideflyer. com). Petersen and friends review all the programs in detail and post regular updates on changes in policies and trends.

LONG-HAUL FLIGHTS: HOW TO STAY COMFORTABLE

- Your choice of airline and airplane will definitely affect your leg room. Find more details about U.S. airlines at **www.seatguru.com**. For international airlines, the research firm Skytrax has posted a list of average seat pitches at **www.airlinequality.com**.
- Emergency exit seats and bulkhead seats typically have the most legroom. Emergency exit seats are usually left unassigned until the day of a flight (to ensure that someone able-bodied fills the seats); it's worth getting to the

---

Tips Ask Before You Go

Before you invest in a package deal or an escorted tour:

- Always ask about the **cancellation policy.** Can you get your money back? Is there a deposit required?
- Ask about the **accommodations choices and prices** for each. Then look up the hotels' reviews in a Frommer's guide and check their rates online for your specific dates of travel. Also find out what types of rooms are offered.
- Request a complete **schedule.** (Escorted tours only)
- Ask about the **size** and demographics of the group. (Escorted tours only)
- Discuss what is included in the **price** (transportation, meals, tips, airport transfers, and so on). (Escorted tours only)
- Finally, look for **hidden expenses.** Ask whether airport departure fees and taxes, for example, are included in the total cost—they rarely are.

ticket counter early to snag one of these spots for a long flight. Many passengers find that bulkhead seating (the row facing the wall at the front of the cabin) offers more legroom; but keep in mind that bulkheads are where airlines often put baby bassinets, so you may be sitting next to an infant.

- To have two seats for yourself in a three-seat row, try for an aisle seat in a center section toward the back of coach. If you're traveling with a companion, book an aisle and a window seat. Middle seats are usually booked last, so chances are good you'll end up with three seats to yourselves.
- Ask about entertainment options. Many airlines offer seat-back video systems where you get to choose your movies or play video games—but only on some of their planes. (Boeing 777s are your best bet.)
- To sleep, avoid the last row of any section or the row in front of an emergency exit, as these seats are the least likely to recline. Avoid seats near highly trafficked toilet areas. Avoid seats in the back of many jets—these can be narrower than those in the rest of coach. You also may want to reserve a window seat so you can rest your head and avoid being bumped in the aisle.
- Get up, walk around, and stretch every 60 to 90 minutes to keep your blood flowing. See the box "Avoiding 'Economy Class Syndrome,'" under "Health & Safety," p. 34.
- Drink water before, during, and after your flight to combat the lack of humidity in airplane cabins. Avoid alcohol, which will dehydrate you.
- If you're flying with kids, don't forget to carry on toys, books, pacifiers, and chewing gum to help them relieve ear pressure buildup during ascent and descent.

12 Packages for the Independent Traveler

Package tours are simply a way to buy the airfare, accommodations, and other elements of your trip (such as car rentals, airport transfers, and sometimes even activities) at the same time and often at discounted prices.

One good source of package deals is the airlines themselves. Most major airlines offer air/land packages, including **American Airlines Vacations** (✆ 800/321-2121; www.aavacations.com), **Delta Vacations** (✆ 800/221-6666; www.deltavacations.com), **Continental Airlines Vacations** (✆ 800/301-3800; www.co

vacations.com), and **United Vacations** (✆ 888/854-3899; www.unitedvacations.com). Several big **online travel agencies**— Expedia, Travelocity, Orbitz, Site59, and Lastminute.com—also do a brisk business in packages.

Travel packages are also listed in the travel section of your local Sunday newspaper. Or check ads in the national travel magazines such as *Arthur Frommer's Budget Travel Magazine, Travel & Leisure, National Geographic Traveler,* and *Condé Nast Traveler.*

13 Cruising to Bermuda

Cruise ships tie up at three harbors in Bermuda: St. George in the East End, the Royal Naval Dockyard in the West End, and Hamilton Harbour at the City of Hamilton. While the cruise experience isn't for everyone, it's very appealing to some people, and is certainly a carefree, all-inclusive vacation. Ships from the East Coast of the United States reach Bermuda in a little over a day. You'll spend a few full days (usually 3) moored at the island, exploring during the day and returning to the ship at night. It's convenient and comfortable—like having a luxury hotel and restaurant that travels with you.

Of course, that's also its major disadvantage. Most cruisers don't get to know the real Bermuda as well as those who stay in hotels ashore. For instance, cruise-ship passengers generally eat all their meals aboard the ship—mainly because they've already paid for the meals as part of their cruise price—and so they miss out on sampling Bermuda's cuisine. They also rarely get to meet and interact with Bermudians the way land-based visitors do.

Seven-day cruises out of New York usually include 4 days at sea, with 3 days in port. Most cruise ships arrive in the traditional port of the City of Hamilton, the capital of Bermuda and its chief commercial and shopping center. If shopping is more important to you than sightseeing, be sure that your cruise ship docks here. Once you're ashore, head to Front Street for shopping, or get your bearings by taking the walking tour that we describe in chapter 8, "Island Strolls."

If you're more interested in historic Bermuda, make sure that your ship is scheduled to anchor at St. George, at the eastern tip of the island. With its narrow lanes and old buildings and streets, St. George has been called the Bermudian equivalent of Colonial Williamsburg. Your ship will probably offer a guided tour of the town as a shore excursion; we've provided a self-guided tour in chapter 8 for those who would rather explore on their own. St. George has become more of a shopping destination than it used to be, but this still isn't the primary place to come for shopping. Depending on the cruise line, its schedules, and the current tides, some cruise ships dock at both St. George and the City of Hamilton while in Bermuda. Ships often plan to dock at St. George, but find that they cannot do so because of the tides.

It's not too likely that you'll disembark at Somerset, which is at the western end of the island and farthest from many of Bermuda's attractions. The West End has its own charm and sightseeing appeal; it is home of the Royal Naval Dockyard, one of the island's major attractions. In a shopping mall at the dockyard, you'll find craft stores and museums.

WHICH CRUISE LINE IS FOR YOU?

If you decide that a Bermuda cruise is right for you, you'll need to choose your cruise line. Some lines want their passengers to have a totally action-filled vacation—with activities from sunup to sundown. Others see time at sea as a period of tranquillity and relaxation, with less emphasis on organized activities. The cruise lines listed here offer regularly scheduled Bermuda sailings. See the section that follows for tips on getting a good deal on the price.

- **Celebrity Cruises** (© **877/202-4345** or 305/539-6000; www.celebrity.com). Noted for modern, state-of-the-art, large-but-not-mammoth cruise ships, and for exceptional cuisine and service, Celebrity is unpretentious but classy. It's several notches above mass market but still competitively priced. Cabins are roomy and well equipped, and, in general, the decor is elegantly modern, eschewing the glitz of some competitors. Celebrity attracts a broad range of passengers, including families drawn by the line's children's programs. Its *Zenith* and *Constellation* both sail 7- to 12-night Bermuda itineraries from Bayonne, New Jersey, between May and October. They spend 2 nights in St. George and 2 nights in the City of Hamilton. Runs from other East Coast cities are interspersed throughout the season.
- **Norwegian Cruise Line** (© **800/ 327-7030** or 305/436-4000; www. ncl.com). NCL offers affordable

(sometimes downright cheap) down-to-earth cruises. The *Norwegian Majesty* makes Bermuda runs from Boston between April and October, allowing 4 days of "shore leave" in St. George. The *Norwegian Majesty* was "stretched" a whole new midsection length, gaining more than 33m (110 ft.) in size with an additional 220 new cabins added. There's a lot more deck space and a casino and swimming pool, too. *Norwegian Crown* sails its ship on 6- to 7-night Bermuda round-trips from Philadelphia from April to June, followed by 7-night round-trip jaunts from New York to Bermuda from late June to October. NCL's ships offer a great roster of activities and sports, of both the active and the spectator variety. The ship even has sports bars with links to ESPN, so you won't miss the big game. NCL's innovation is what they call "Freestyle Cruising." As part of this concept, passengers are no longer assigned a dining time; instead they can eat at any time, in whichever dining room they choose, with whomever they choose, every night. Dinner dress code is "resort casual," with occasional dress-up nights that are completely optional. Not surprisingly, NCL tends to attract a somewhat younger, laid-back crowd. Most passengers are couples age 25 to 60, with a fair number of honeymooners. Families with kids tend to show up during holidays.

• **Royal Caribbean International** (✆ **800/562-7625;** www.royal caribbean.com). The atmosphere onboard these vessels is a little more high-energy than that of Celebrity's ships, and roughly comparable to that of NCL's. Stopovers include 2 days in St. George and 2½ days in Hamilton Harbour. *Grandeur of the Seas* includes Bermuda in its 5-day itineraries from Baltimore. The *Jewel* offers a 10-night Bermuda cruise that also includes ports in the Caribbean. Sailings are from Boston in September and October. Finally, *Voyager* sails from Bayonne, New Jersey, in October and November on 5-night jaunts to Bermuda. You can find all walks of life on a Royal Caribbean cruise. The common denominator: passengers looking for fun and action in an attractive setting. Most passengers are couples, but there also tend to be plenty of families and singles onboard as well. Overall, passengers are active, social, and looking for a good time, no matter what their age.

HOW TO GET THE BEST DEAL ON YOUR CRUISE

Cruise lines operate like airlines, setting rates for their cruises and then selling them in a rapid-fire series of discounts, offering almost whatever it takes to fill their ships. Because of this, great deals come and go in the blink of an eye, and most are available only through travel agents.

If you have a travel agent you trust, leave the details to him or her. If not, try contacting a travel agent who specializes in booking cruises. Some of the most likely contenders include the following: **Cruises, Inc.,** 1415 NW 62 St., Suite 205, Fort Lauderdale, FL 33009 (✆ **866/ 280-8198** or 954/958-3700; www.cruise inc.com); **Cruises.com,** 100 Sylvan Rd., Suite 600, Woburn, MA 01801 (✆ **800/ 288-6006;** www.cruises.com); **The Cruise Company,** 10760 Q St., Omaha, NE 68127 (✆ **800/289-5505** or 402/339-6800; www.thecruisecompany.com); **Kelly Cruises,** 1315 W. 22nd St., Suite 105, Oak Brook, IL 60523 (✆ **800/837-7447** or 630/990-1111; www.kelly cruises.com); **Hartford Holidays Travel,** 129 Hillside Ave., Williston Park, NY 11596 (✆ **800/828-4813** or 516/746-6670; www.hartfordholidays.com); and

Mann Travel & Cruises, 4400 Park Rd., Charlotte, NC 28209 (© **800/849-2301** or 704/556-8311; www.manntravels.com).

A FEW MONEY-SAVING TIPS

- **Book early:** You can often receive considerable savings on a 7-day cruise by booking early. Ask a travel agent or call the cruise line directly.
- **Book an inside cabin:** If you're trying to keep costs down, ask for an inside cabin (one without a window). They're often the same size and offer the same amenities as the more expensive outside cabins. If you're planning on using the space only to sleep, who needs a window?

- **Take advantage of senior discounts:** The cruise industry offers some discounts to seniors (usually defined as anyone 55 or older), so don't keep your age a secret. Membership in AARP, for example, can net you substantial discounts; always ask your travel agent about these types of discounts when you're booking.
- **Don't sail alone:** Cruise lines base their rates on double occupancy, so solo passengers usually pay between 150% and 200% of the per-person rate. If you're traveling alone, most lines have a program that allows two solo passengers to share a cabin.

14 Recommended Reading

Most of the books listed below have been printed in Bermuda. Thus, while they're readily available on the island, they may be hard to find in the United States and elsewhere.

THE MYSTERIOUS BERMUDA TRIANGLE

Many writers have attempted to explain the Bermuda Triangle. None has sufficiently done so yet, but all of these books make good reads for those of us intrigued by this tantalizing mystery.

The best of the lot is *The Bermuda Triangle Mystery Solved* (Prometheus Books) by Larry Kusche. It's a good read even though it doesn't "solve" the mystery. A mass-market paperback, *Atlantis: Bermuda Triangle* (Berkley Pub Group), by Greg Donegan, also digs into the puzzle, as does another paperback, *The Mystery of the Bermuda Triangle* (Heineman Library), by Chris Oxlade.

ART & ARCHITECTURE

For Bermuda style, both inside the house and outside, two books lead the pack:

Bermuda Antique Furniture and Silver, published by Bermuda National Trust, and *Architecture Bermuda Style,* by David R. Raine, issued by Pompano Publications.

DIVERS, HIKERS & SHIPWRECKS

Daniel Berg has written the finest book on the shipwrecks of Bermuda—a great choice for a diver to read before actually going under the water. It's called *Bermuda Shipwrecks: A Vacationing Diver's Guide to Bermuda's Shipwrecks* (Aqua Explorers).

Divers might also like to pick up a copy of *Marine Fauna and Flora of Bermuda* (Wiley Publishing, Inc.), edited by Wolfgang Sterrer. Another good book for divers is *Diving Bermuda* (AquaQuest Publications), part of the Aqua Quest Diving Series, this one authored by Jesse Concelmo and Michael Strohofer. Its second edition is the most up-to-date of all the sports guides to Bermuda.

3

Getting to Know Bermuda

Settling into Bermuda is relatively easy. First-timers soon learn that Bermuda isn't one island, as is commonly thought, but a string of islands linked by causeways and bridges—at least the 20 or so that are inhabited. The other islands can be reached by boat.

Bermuda is prosperous, characterized by neat, trim houses that are a source of great pride to their owners. There won't be a casino at your megaresort—Bermuda has no casinos—and you'd better have your fill of Big Macs before you leave home. There are some fast-food joints, but nothing like those on the U.S. mainland, or even in the Bahamas. There's a sense of order in Bermuda, and everything seems to work efficiently, even when the weather's hot.

1 Arriving

BY PLANE

Planes arrive at the **Bermuda International Airport,** Kindley Field Road, St. George (© **441/293-2470;** www.bermudaairport.com), 14.5km (9 miles) east of the City of Hamilton and about 27km (17 miles) east of Somerset at the far western end of Bermuda.

The flight from most East Coast destinations—including New York, Raleigh/Durham, Baltimore, and Boston—takes about 2 hours. Flights from Atlanta take 2½ hours; from Toronto it's less than 3 hours.

After clearing Customs (see "Entry Requirements & Customs," in chapter 2, for details), you can pick up tourist information at the airport before heading to your hotel. Because you aren't allowed to rent a car in Bermuda, and buses don't allow passengers to board with luggage, you must rely on a taxi or minivan to reach your hotel.

LEAVING THE AIRPORT
BY TAXI OR MINIVAN

More than 600 taxis are available on Bermuda, and cabbies meet all arriving flights. Taxis are allowed to carry a maximum of four passengers. If you and your traveling companion have a lot of luggage, you will need the taxi to yourselves.

Taxis in Bermuda are unduly expensive: They usually move slowly, meters seem to rise alarmingly fast, and taxi fares will inevitably represent a significant percentage of your day-to-day spending money. Regrettably, this situation can't be avoided. Nonresidents are forbidden to drive cars, and your only other option involves either walking (not practical on many of the very narrow roads) or renting either a bicycle or a small-capacity motorcycle (more on that later).

Unless the taxi has been specifically called to pick you up, in which event it will be a bit higher, the meter should read $4 when you first get in a cab. After that, expect to pay $6 for the first 1.6km (1 mile) and $2 for each additional 1.6km (1 mile) for

Did You Know?

- More than 23,000 couples honeymoon on Bermuda each year.
- Bermudians imported the idea of moon gates—large rings of stone used as garden ornaments—from Asia centuries ago. Walking through a moon gate is supposed to bring good luck.
- This mysterious island inspired William Shakespeare's 1610 play *The Tempest*.
- Somerset Bridge is the world's smallest drawbridge. At only 56cm (22 in.) wide, the opening is just large enough for a ship's mast to pass through.
- Bermuda has more golf courses per square kilometer than any other place in the world; there are eight of them on the island's approximate 138 sq. km (53 sq. miles).
- Sir Brownlow Gray, the island's former chief justice, played the first game of tennis in the Western Hemisphere on Bermuda in 1873.
- With the arrival of spring comes the blossoming of Bermuda's Easter lilies, first brought to the island from Japan in the 18th century.
- Bermuda has no billboards: There is a ban on outdoor advertising and neon signs.

up to four passengers. The following is a sample of taxi fares, including a tip of 10% to 15%, from the airport: To any point within the City of Hamilton, expect a metered fare of around $38; to points in and around St. George, around $18 to $23; to points near Tucker's Town, around $28; to such south shore beach hotels as Elbow Beach or the Sonesta, around $35 to $45; and to such far-distant points as the West End, around $55. Fares increase by 25% between midnight and 6am, as well as all day on Sundays and holidays. Luggage carries a surcharge of $1 per piece. In almost every case, a meter determines the fare, unless you ask for a general tour of the island, in which event the driver might opt to charge you and your party about $65 per hour.

There are several authorized taxi companies on the island, including **C.O.O.P.** (© **441/292-4476**), **Bermuda Taxi Radio Cabs Ltd.** (© **441/295-4141**), and **Sandys** (© **441/234-2344**).

It's cheaper for a party of four or more to call a minivan and split the cost than to take two taxis (because usually only two people with luggage can fit into each taxi). Arrange, if it's practical, for a 10-passenger minivan, or if you're conducting a large group, for a bus holding between 20 and 25 passengers, before you arrive in Bermuda by contacting **Bermuda Hosts,** 3 Cahhow Way, St. George CR 04 (© **441/293-1334;** www.bermudahosts.bm). If you're traveling in a party of only two, consider asking a waiting chartered bus at the airport if it has room to take in two extra passengers. Using that mode of transportation, trips from the airport to such nearby hotels as Grotto Bay will cost as little as $11 per person, trips to the City of Hamilton will cost around $17 per person, and trips to the island's distant West End will cost around $32 per person.

Bear in mind, however, that these fares are imposed on a per-person basis, and taxis charge their rates for a collective carload of up to four passengers, pending their ability to fit in all their luggage.

BY CRUISE SHIP

This is the easiest way to arrive in Bermuda. The staff present you with a list of tour options long before you arrive in port, and almost everything is done for you unless you choose to make your own arrangements (although an independent taxi tour is far more expensive than an organized tour). Most passengers book shore excursions when they reserve their cruise.

Depending on your ship, you will probably arrive in either the City of Hamilton (best for shopaholics) or St. George (best for architecture and history buffs). A few ships also dock at the Royal Naval Dockyard on Bermuda's West End. Whichever port you dock at, you can avail yourself of the waiting taxis near your ship, or rent a moped or bicycle (see "Getting Around," later in this chapter) and do some touring and shopping on your own. For more information about cruising to Bermuda, see p. 43.

2 Orienting Yourself: The Lay of the Land

For administrative purposes, the islands of Bermuda are divided into **parishes,** all named for shareholders of the Bermuda Company, which was formed by English investors in the early 1600s to develop Bermuda as a profit-making enterprise. From west to east, the parishes are listed below.

SANDYS PARISH

In the far western part of the archipelago, Sandys (pronounced *sands*) Parish encompasses the islands of **Ireland, Boaz,** and **Somerset.** This parish (named for Sir Edwin Sandys) centers in Somerset Village, on Somerset Island. Sandys Parish is often called Somerset.

Some visitors to Bermuda head directly for Sandys Parish and spend their entire time here; they feel that the far western tip, with its rolling hills, lush countryside, and tranquil bays, is something special and unique. (This area has always stood apart from the rest of Bermuda: During the U.S. Civil War, when most Bermudians sympathized with the Confederates, Sandys Parish supported the Union.) Sandys Parish has areas of great natural beauty, including **Somerset Long Bay,** the biggest and best public beach in the West End (which the Bermuda Audubon Society is developing into a nature preserve), and **Mangrove Bay,** a protected beach in the heart of **Somerset Village.** Take a walk around the old village; it's filled with typically Bermudian houses and shops. On Somerset Road is the **Scaur Lodge Property,** whose waterfront hillside is open daily at no charge.

If you want to be near the shops, restaurants, and pubs of the City of Hamilton, you may want to stay in a more central location and visit Sandys Parish on a day trip. However, the parish's isolation is part of its charm for those who prefer tranquillity and unspoiled nature to shopping or lingering over an extra pint in a pub. This is the perfect parish for couples seeking privacy and romance.

Tips Visitor Information on the Island

You can get answers to most of your questions at the Visitors Service Bureau locations at the **Ferry Terminal,** 8 Front St., Hamilton (© **441/295-1480**), open Monday to Saturday 9am to 5pm; **King's Square,** St. George (© **441/297-1642**); and the **Royal Naval Dockyard** (© **441/234-3824**), open daily from 9am to 5pm.

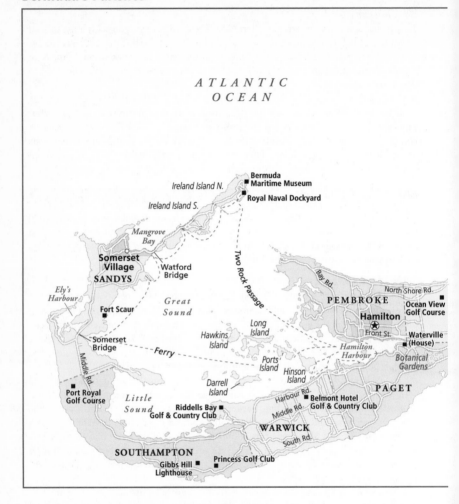

ATLANTIC
OCEAN

Ireland Island N.

Ireland Island S.

Bermuda
■ Maritime Museum
■ Royal Naval Dockyard

Mangrove
Bay

Somerset
Village
SANDYS

Watford
Bridge

Ely's
Harbour

Fort Scaur

Great
Sound

Two Rock Passage

Bay Rd.

PEMBROKE

North Shore Rd.

■ Ocean View
Golf Course

Hamilton
★
Front St.

■ Waterville
(House)

Long
Island

Hawkins
Island

Somerset
Bridge

Ferry

Ports
Island

Hamilton
Harbour

Botanical
Gardens

Darrell
Island

Hinson
Island

PAGET

Middle Rd.

Port Royal
Golf Course

Little
Sound

Riddells Bay ■
Golf & Country Club

Harbour Rd.

Middle Rd.

■ Belmont Hotel
Golf & Country Club

SOUTHAMPTON

WARWICK

South Rd.

Gibbs Hill ■
Lighthouse

■ Princess Golf Club

An advantage of staying here is that Sandys has several embarkation points for various types of sea excursions. The parish also boasts some of the most elegant places to stay in Bermuda. You can commute to the City of Hamilton by ferry, although it's a bit time-consuming and not recommended if your days on Bermuda are limited.

SOUTHAMPTON PARISH

Southampton Parish (named for the third earl of Southampton) is a narrow strip of land opening at its northern edge onto Little Sound and on its southern shore onto the Atlantic Ocean. It stretches from Riddells Bay to Tucker's Island, and is split by Middle Road.

If dining at waterfront restaurants and staying at big resort hotels is part of your Bermuda dream, then Southampton is your parish; it's the site of such famed resorts as

The Fairmont Southampton and the Sonesta Beach Resort. Southampton is also the best place to stay if you plan to spend a great deal of time on the island's fabled pink, sandy beaches. Among Southampton's jewels is **Horseshoe Bay,** one of Bermuda's most attractive public beaches, with changing rooms, a snack bar, and space for parking.

Southampton lacks the intimacy and romance of Sandys, but it has a lot of razzle-dazzle going for it. It's the top choice for a golfing holiday. If you like to sightsee, you can easily occupy 2 days just exploring the parish's many attractions. It also has more nightlife than Sandys—although not as much as the City of Hamilton.

WARWICK PARISH

Named in honor of the second earl of Warwick, this parish lies in the heart of Great Bermuda Island. Like Southampton, it is known for its long stretches of rosy sand.

Along the south shore is **Warwick Long Bay,** one of Bermuda's best public beaches. Warwick also offers parklands bordering the sea, winding country roads, two golf courses, and a number of natural attractions. This area is the best on the island for horseback riding, which is the ideal way to see pastoral Bermuda up close.

Warwick is a great choice for visitors seeking cottage or apartment rentals (where you can do some of your own cooking to cut down on the outrageous expense of food). The parish is not strong on restaurants; one of its disadvantages is that you have to travel a bit if you like to dine out. Nightlife is also spotty—just about the only action you can find after dark is in hotel lounges. This parish is for tranquillity-seekers, but because of its more central location, it doesn't offer quite the seclusion that Sandys does.

PAGET PARISH

Paget Parish lies directly south of the capital City of Hamilton, separated from it by Hamilton Harbour. Named after the fourth Lord Paget, it has many residences and historic homes and it's also the site of the 15-hectare (37-acre) **Botanical Gardens.** But the south-shore beaches—the best in the chain of islands—are what draw visitors here in droves. Paget Parish is also the site of **Chelston,** on Grape Bay Drive, the official residence of the U.S. consul general. Situated on 5.8 hectares (14 acres) of landscaped grounds, it's open only during the Garden Club's Home and Garden Tours in the spring (see "Bermuda Calendar of Events," in chapter 2, "Planning Your Trip to Bermuda," for details).

This is one of the best parishes to stay in—it has many excellent accommodations, including Elbow Beach Hotel. It's close enough to the City of Hamilton for an easy commute, but far enough away to escape the hordes. Because public transportation is all-important (you can't rent a car), Paget is a good place to situate yourself; it has some of the best and most convenient ferry connections and bus schedules. There are docks at Salt Kettle, Hodson's, and Lower Ferry; you can even "commute" by ferry to Warwick Parish or Sandys Parish, to the west. Paget's relatively flat terrain, rural lanes, and streets lined with old mansions make this an ideal place for biking. And hikers will find many small trails bordering the sea.

If you don't like big resort hotels, you can rent a cottage or one of several little guesthouses here. Unlike Warwick, Paget has a number of dining choices too. Elbow Beach offers the most, but other fine options include Fourways Inn and Paraquet Restaurant. Most of the parish's nightlife centers on Elbow Beach.

There are no major disadvantages to staying in Paget. You will find overcrowded beaches during spring break, though, and congestion in the City of Hamilton in the summer, when many cruise ships arrive.

PEMBROKE PARISH

This parish (named after the third earl of Pembroke) houses one-quarter of Bermuda's population. It is home to the **City of Hamilton,** Bermuda's capital and its only full-fledged city. The parish opens at its northern rim onto the vast Atlantic Ocean and on its southern side onto Hamilton Harbour; its western border is on Great Sound. The City of Hamilton is the first destination that most cruise-ship passengers will see.

This parish is not ideal for those seeking a tranquil holiday. Pembroke Parish, already packed with the island's greatest population density, also attracts the most visitors. The little city is especially crowded when cruise ships are in the harbor and travelers pour into the stores and restaurants. Yet for those who like to pub-crawl English

---

Tips **Finding an Address**

The island chain of Bermuda doesn't follow a rigid system of street addresses. Most hotels, even in official government listings, don't bother to include an address, although they do include post-office boxes and postal codes. Bermudians just assume that everybody knows where everything is, which is fine if you've lived on Bermuda all your life. But if you're a first-time visitor, get a good map before setting out—and don't be shy about asking directions. In general, people are very helpful.

Most of the establishments you'll be seeking are on some street plan. However, some places use numbers in their street addresses, and others—perhaps their neighbors—don't. The actual building number is not always important, because a building such as a resort hotel is likely to be set back so far from the main road that you couldn't see its number anyway. Look for signs with the name of the hotel rather than the street number. Cross streets will also aid you in finding an address.

---

style, shop until they drop, and have access to the largest concentration of dining choices, Pembroke—the City of Hamilton in particular—is without equal on Bermuda.

Whether or not you stay in Pembroke, try to fit a shopping (or window-shopping) stroll along Front Street into your itinerary. The area also boasts a number of sightseeing attractions, most of which are easily accessible on foot (a plus because you don't have to depend on taxis, bikes, or scooters—which can get to be a bit of a bore after a while). Nightlife is the finest on the island. Don't expect splashy Las Vegas–type revues, however; instead, think restaurants, pubs, and small clubs.

DEVONSHIRE PARISH

Lying east of Paget and Pembroke parishes, near the geographic center of the archipelago, Devonshire Parish (named for the first earl of Devonshire) is green and hilly. It has some housekeeping (self-catering) apartments, a cottage colony, and one of Bermuda's oldest churches, the **Old Devonshire Parish Church,** which dates from 1716. Three of Bermuda's major roads traverse the parish: the aptly named South Road (also unofficially referred to as South Shore Rd.), Middle Road, and North Shore Road. As you wander its narrow lanes, you can, with some imagination, picture yourself in the parish's namesake county of Devon, England.

Golfers flock to Devonshire to play at the **Ocean View Golf Course.** Along North Shore Road, near the border of Pembroke Parish, is **Devonshire Dock,** long a seafarer's haven. In fact, during the War of 1812, British soldiers came to Devonshire Dock to be entertained by local women. Today, fishers still bring in grouper and rockfish, so you can shop for dinner if you're staying at a nearby cottage with a kitchen.

Devonshire has a number of unspoiled nature areas. The **arboretum** on Montpelier Road is one of the most tranquil oases on Bermuda. This open space, created by the Department of Agriculture, Fisheries, and Parks, is home to a wide range of Bermudian plant and tree life, especially conifers, palms, and other subtropical trees. Along South Road, west of the junction with Collector's Hill, is the **Edmund Gibbons Nature Reserve.** This portion of marshland, owned by the National Trust, provides living space for a number of birds and rare species of Bermuda flora.

Devonshire is one of the sleepy residential parishes, known for its hilly interior, beautiful landscape, and fabulous estates bordering the sea. There's little sightseeing here; all those stunning private estates aren't open to the public, so unless you get a personal invite, you're out of luck. But the parish is right in Bermuda's geographic center, so it's an ideal place to base yourself if you'd like to explore both the West End and the East End. There are two major drawbacks: With a few notable exceptions, the parish has very few places to stay and almost no dining choices.

SMITH'S PARISH

Named for Sir Thomas Smith, this parish faces the open sea to the north and south. To the east is Harrington Sound; to the west, bucolic Devonshire Parish.

The parish encompasses **Flatts Village,** one of the island's most charming parish towns (take bus no. 10 or 11 from the City of Hamilton). It was a smugglers' port for about 200 years and served as the center of power for a coterie of successful "planter politicians" and landowners. Flatts Village's government was second in importance to that of St. George, which was Bermuda's capital at the time. People gathered at the rickety Flatts Bridge to "enjoy" such public entertainment as hangings; if the offense was serious enough, victims were drawn and quartered here. From Flatts Village, you have panoramic views of both the inlet and Harrington Sound. At the top of McGall's Hill is St. Mark's Church, based on the same designs used for the Old Devonshire Parish Church.

Most visitors view Smith's Parish as a day trip or a half-day trip, although the parish does have places to stay, such as the Pink Beach Club and Cottages. Dining choices are extremely limited, however, unless you stick to the hotels. Again, if you're seeking lots of nighttime diversion, you'll have to go to another parish. Because the **Spittal Pond Nature Reserve** is here, many nature lovers prefer Smith's to the more populated parishes. Basically, Smith's Parish is for the visitor who wants serenity and tranquillity but not at the celestial prices charged at the "cottages" of Sandys.

HAMILTON PARISH

Not to be confused with the City of Hamilton (which is in Pembroke Parish), Hamilton Parish lies directly north of Harrington Sound, opening onto the Atlantic. It's bordered on the east by St. George and on the southwest by Smith's Parish. Named for the second marquis of Hamilton, the parish surrounds Harrington Sound, a saltwater lake stretching some 10km (6¼ miles). On its eastern periphery, the parish opens onto Castle Harbour.

The big attractions here are the **Bermuda Aquarium** and the **Crystal Caves.** Scuba diving and other watersports are also very popular in the area.

Around **Harrington Sound,** the sights differ greatly from those of nearby St. George (see below). You'll find activities like fishing, swimming, sunfish sailing, and kayaking at Harrington Sound, but it doesn't offer the historical exploration that St. George does. Some experts believe that Harrington Sound was a prehistoric cave that fell in. Harrington Sound's known gateway to the ocean is an inlet at Flatts Village (see "Smith's Parish," above). However, evidence suggests that there are underwater passages as well—several deep-sea fish have been caught in the sound.

For the best panoramic view of the north shore, head for **Crawl Hill,** the highest place in Hamilton Parish, just before you come to Bailey's Bay. *Crawl* is a corruption of the word *kraal,* which is where turtles were kept before slaughter. **Shelly Bay,** named for one of the passengers of the British ship *Sea Venture* that foundered on Bermuda's reefs in 1609, is the longest beach along the north shore.

At Bailey's Bay, **Tom Moore's Jungle** consists of wild woods. The poet Tom Moore is said to have spent many hours writing verse here under a calabash tree (which is still standing). The jungle is now held in private trust, so you must obtain permission to enter it. It's much easier to pay your respects to the Romantic poet by going to Tom Moore's Tavern (see "Hamilton Parish," in chapter 5, "Where to Dine").

Although the parish has some major resorts, such as Grotto Bay Beach Hotel, most visitors come here for sightseeing only. We have to agree: Hamilton is a good place to go exploring for a day or half-day, but you're better off staying elsewhere. If you stay here, you'll spend a great deal of your holiday time commuting into the City of Hamilton or St. George. Bus no. 1 or 3 from the City of Hamilton gets you here in about an hour.

ST. GEORGE PARISH

At Bermuda's extreme eastern end, this historic parish encompasses several islands. The parish borders Castle Harbour on its western and southern edges; St. George's Harbour divides it into two major parts, **St. George's Island** and **St. David's Island.** A causeway links St. David's Island to the rest of Bermuda, and St. George's is also linked by a road. Many parish residents are longtime sailors and fishers. St. George Parish also includes **Tucker's Town** (founded in 1616 by Gov. Daniel Tucker), on the opposite shore of Castle Harbour.

Settled in 1612, the **town of St. George** was once the capital of Bermuda; the City of Hamilton succeeded it in 1815. The town was settled 3 years after Sir George Somers and his shipwrecked party of English sailors came ashore in 1609. (After Admiral Somers died in Bermuda, in 1610, his heart was buried in the St. George area, while the rest of his body was taken home to England for burial.) Founded by Richard Moore, of the newly created Bermuda Company, and a band of 60 colonists, St. George was the second English settlement in the New World, after Jamestown, Virginia. Its coat of arms depicts St. George (England's patron saint) and a dragon.

Tips **Finding Your Way**

We've included bulleted maps throughout this book to help you locate Bermuda's accommodations, restaurants, beaches, and sights.

The Bermuda Department of Tourism publishes a free *Bermuda Handy Reference Map.* The tiny pocket map, distributed by the tourist office and available at most hotels, includes an overview and orientation map of Bermuda, highlighting its major attractions, golf courses, public beaches, and hotels. (It does not, however, pinpoint individual restaurants unless they are attached to hotels.) On the other side is a detailed street plan of the City of Hamilton, indicating all its major landmarks and service facilities, such as the ferry terminal and the post office. There's also a detailed map of the Royal Naval Dockyard, the West End, and the East End, plus tips on transportation—ferries, taxis, buses—and other helpful hints, such as a depiction of various traffic signs. For exact locations of Visitors Service Bureau locations where you can pick up a copy of the *Bermuda Handy Reference Map,* see the "Visitor Information on the Island" box, earlier in this chapter.

Almost 4 centuries of history come alive here. Generations of sailors have set forth from its sheltered harbor. St. George even played a role in the American Revolution: Bermuda depended on the American colonies for food, and when war came, supplies grew dangerously low. Although Bermuda was a British colony, the loyalties of its people were divided because many Bermudians had relatives living on the American mainland. A delegation headed by Col. Henry Tucker went to Philadelphia to petition the Continental Congress to trade food and supplies for salt. George Washington had a different idea. He needed gunpowder, and a number of kegs of it were stored at St. George. Without the approval of the British Bermudian governor, the parties struck a deal. The gunpowder was trundled aboard American warships waiting in the harbor of Tobacco Bay under cover of darkness. In return, the grateful colonies supplied Bermuda with food.

Although St. George still evokes a feeling of the past, it's actively inhabited. When cruise ships are in port, it's likely to be overrun with visitors. Many people prefer to visit St. George at night, when they can walk around and enjoy it in relative peace and quiet. You won't be able to enter any of the sightseeing attractions, but they're of minor importance. After dark, a mood of enchantment settles over the place: It's like a storybook village.

Would you want to live here for a week? Probably not. Once you've seen the glories of the town of St. George—which you can do in a day—you're inconveniently isolated at the easternmost end of Bermuda for the rest of your stay. Several chains, including Club Med, have tried and failed to make a go of it here. Accommodations are extremely limited, although there are a number of restaurants (many of which, frankly, are mediocre). For history buffs, no place in Bermuda tops St. George. But as a parish to base yourself in, you might do better in the more centrally located and activity-filled Pembroke or Southampton parishes. As for nightlife in St. George, you can always go to a pub on King's Square.

3 Bermuda in a Nutshell: Suggested Itineraries for 1 to 5 Days

You may be eager to start exploring right away, especially if your time is short. Below is a suggested itinerary for the first 5 days. A week's visit will let you break up your sightseeing trips with time on the beach, boating, or engaging in some of the island's other outdoor pursuits, such as golf or scuba diving. Hitting the beach is the first priority for most visitors—but you don't need us to tell you how to schedule your time in the sun!

If You Have ❶ Day

If you have only 1 day for sightseeing, we suggest you spend it in the historic former capital of **St. George,** a maze of narrow streets with quaint names: Featherbed Alley, Duke of York Street, Petticoat Lane, Old Maid's Lane, and Duke of Kent Street. You can spend a day exploring British-style pubs, seafood restaurants, shops (several major City of Hamilton stores have branches here), old forts, museums, and churches. You can even see stocks, a ducking stool, and a pillory, all used generations ago to humiliate wrongdoers.

And what would a day in Bermuda be without time spent on the beach? **Elbow Beach** and **Warwick Long Bay** are among the most appealing spots. The no. 7 bus will take you there from St. George.

If You Have ❷ Days

Spend **Day 1** as indicated above. Devote **Day 2** to sightseeing and shopping in the City of Hamilton. If you're staying in Paget or Warwick, a ferry from either parish will take you right into the city. For many visitors, the City of Hamilton's shops are its most compelling attraction. Try to time your visit to avoid the arrival of cruise ships; on those days, the stores and restaurants in the city can really get crowded. You can obtain a schedule of cruise-ship arrivals and departures from the tourist office.

If you took our advice and went to the beach yesterday, try a different one today. After all, Bermuda isn't just about sightseeing and shopping—it's about those marvelous pink sands too.

If You Have ❸ Days

Spend **Days 1 and 2** as outlined above. On **Day 3,** take the ferry from the City of Hamilton across Great Sound to Somerset. Carry your bicycle on the boat—you'll need it later (see "Getting Around," below, for details on rentals). You'll disembark at the western end of Somerset Island in Sandys Parish, where you'll find the smallest drawbridge in the world. It's easy to spend an hour walking around Somerset Village. Then head west on foot or on bicycle until you reach Somerset Long Bay Beach, along the northern rim of the island.

Sandys Parish has several places for lunch (see chapter 5, "Where to Dine"). The **Somerset Country Squire Tavern,** a typical village inn near the Watford Bridge ferry stop at the western end of the island, is one of the best.

After lunch, hop on your bicycle and cross Watford Bridge to **Ireland Island,** home of the **Royal Naval Dockyard** and the **Maritime Museum.** On your way back to Somerset Bridge and the ferry back to the City of Hamilton, you might take the turnoff to Fort Scaur; from **Scaur Hill,** you'll have a commanding view of Ely's Harbour and Great Sound. If you don't want to go through Somerset again, the ferry at Watford Bridge will also take you back to the City of Hamilton.

If You Have ❹ or ❺ Days

Spend **Days 1 through 3** as outlined above. Make **Day 4** a beach day. Head for **Horseshoe Bay Beach,** in Southampton Parish, in the morning. Spend most of your time there, exploring hidden coves in all directions. Have lunch right on the beach at a concession stand. In the afternoon, visit **Gibbs Hill Lighthouse.** After a rest at your hotel, sample some Bermudian nightlife.

On **Day 5,** conclude your stay with an excursion to **Flatts Village,** which lies in the eastern sector of Smith's Parish. Explore the **Bermuda Aquarium, Natural History Museum & Zoo;** and consider an undersea walk (see the box "A Look Under Bermuda's Waters," in chapter 6, "Fun in the Surf & Sun").

Have lunch at the **Inlet Restaurant,** in the Palmetto Hotel, then visit **Elbow Beach.** After relaxing over afternoon tea at one of the hotels, arrange to see an evening show—if it's scheduled, make it gombey dancing, which has its roots in Africa and which remains a strong cultural symbol in Bermuda (p. 214).

4 Getting Around

Driving is on the left, and the national speed limit is 32kmph (20 mph) in the countryside, 24kmph (15 mph) in busier areas. Cars are limited to one per resident family—and visitors are not allowed to rent cars at all. You'll rely on taxis, bikes, motorized bicycles called "putt-putts," and maybe even a romantic, colorful, fringe-topped surrey.

Tips **Taxi Touring Tip**

When a taxi has a blue flag on its hood (locals call the hood the "bonnet"), the driver is qualified to serve as a **tour guide.** The government checks out and tests these drivers, so you should use them if you plan to tour Bermuda by taxi. "Blue-bonnet" drivers charge no more than regular taxi drivers.

For a radio-dispatched cab, call **C.O.O.P.** (© **441/292-4476**).

BY TAXI

Dozens of taxis roam the island, and virtually every hotel, restaurant, and shop is happy to call one for you. The hourly charge is $38 for one to four passengers. A luxury tour van accommodating up to six passengers costs $52 an hour. If you want to use one for a sightseeing tour, the minimum is 3 hours.

BY MOTORBIKE

Bermuda is the only Atlantic island that restricts car ownership to local residents. Part of the reason for this is the notoriously narrow roads, which have small or nonexistent shoulders and hundreds of blind curves. Add frequent rainfall and the British custom of driving on the left, and there would be traffic chaos if newcomers were allowed to take to the roads in rented cars.

The resulting dependence on cabs and rented motor scooters, mopeds, and bicycles is simply a fact of Bermudian life that newcomers quickly accept as part of the island's charm. Although not having a car at your disposal is inconvenient, the island's tourist brochures make it seem just wonderful: a happy couple bicycling or mopeding around Bermuda on a sunny day, slowly putt-putting across the islands.

What the brochures don't tell you is that the roads are too narrow, and Bermudians—who are likely to own cars, and pay dearly for the privilege—feel that the road is theirs. Sometimes it starts raining almost without warning; but the skies usually clear rapidly, and the roads dry quickly. During inclement weather, scooter riders are likely to be edged close—sometimes disturbingly close—to the shoulder; after rainstorms, they'll almost certainly be splattered with water or mud. Many accidents occur on slippery roads after a rain, especially involving those not accustomed to using a motor scooter.

Who should rent a moped or scooter, and who should avoid them altogether? Frankly, the answer depends on your physical fitness and the time of day. Even the most stiffly starched might find a wind-whipped morning ride from the hotel to the beach or tennis courts invigorating and fun. Dressed to the nines for a candlelit dinner, you'd find the experience horrifying. And although the putt-putters can be a lot of fun during a sunny day, the machines can be dangerous and capricious after dark—and, of course, when you've had too many daiquiris. Not everyone is fit enough, either. And visitors on mopeds have a high accident rate, with at least some of the problems related to driving on the left.

Considering the hazards, we usually recommend that reasonably adept sports enthusiasts rent a moped for a day or two. For evening outings, we firmly believe that a taxi is the way to go.

You must be 16 or older to rent a motorbike. Some vehicles are big enough to cozily accommodate two adults. Helmets are required, and rental companies must provide them. Know in advance that on a hot day, they're uncomfortable. But, what the heck—you'll be at the beach soon enough.

What's the difference between a moped and a motor scooter? Many visitors rent one or the other and never really understand the difference. They're basically alike, with equivalent maximum speeds and horsepower. Mopeds have larger wheels than scooters, and subject riders to fewer shocks as they traverse bumps in the road. Most (but not all) mopeds are designed for one rider; scooters accommodate either a single passenger or two passengers riding in tandem.

There are quite a few gas stations (called "petrol stations"). Once you "tank up" your motorbike, chances are you'll have plenty of gas to get you to your destination; for example, one tank of gas in a motorbike will take you from Somerset in the west to St. George in the east.

Among the rental companies listed below, there's a tendency toward price fixing. Rental fees across the island tend to be roughly equivalent, and shopping around for a better deal is usually a waste of time. On average, mopeds for one rider rent for $57 to $65 for the first day, $80 to $87 for 2 days, $110 for 3 days, and $147 for 5 days. Scooters for two riders cost about $75 for 1 day, $116 for 2 days, or up to $200 for 5 days. You must pay with a major credit card; it serves as a deposit in case of damage or theft. You must also purchase a one-time insurance policy for $20 to $25. The insurance is valid for the length of the rental.

You can rent mopeds and scooters at **Wheels Cycle** (© 441/292-2245; www.bermuda.com/wheels), which has two locations in the City of Hamilton: one at Flatts Village, Grotto Bay Hotel, and one in Paget Parish.

Oleander Cycles Ltd., 6 Valley Rd., Paget Parish (© 441/236-5235; www.oleandercycles.bm), rents only scooters. A first-day rental for a single-seater is $55; $65 for double. Subsequent days have price reductions depending on the length of rental. There is an additional charge of $20 for insurance. There are also locations at 15 Gorham Rd. in the City of Hamilton (© 441/295-0919), 8 Middle Rd. in Southampton (© 441/234-0629), 26 York St. in St. George's (© 441/297-0478), King's Wharf Dockyard (© 441/234-2764), and The Reefs Hotel Southampton (© 441/238-0222). Open daily 8:30am to 5:30pm, with a 24-hour emergency number (© 441/236-5235).

Eve's Cycle Ltd., 114 Middle Rd., Paget Parish (© 441/236-6247; www.evecycles.com), 1 Water St., St. George's (© 441/236-0839), and at the International Airport (© 441/293-6188), rents a variety of scooters; they cost $45 to $63 for the first day, and $120 to $160 for 5 days, depending on the model, with successively lower prices for each additional day.

A final option for motorbike rentals, with a reputation that goes back to 1947, is **Smatt's Cycle Livery, Ltd.,** 74 Pitts Bay Rd., Hamilton, Pembroke Parish (© 441/295-1180; www.smattscyclelivery.com). It's adjacent to the Hamilton Princess Hotel with two additional offices in Southampton—one at Wyndham Bermuda Resort & Spa (© 441/238-7900), the other at Fairmont Southampton (© 441/238-7800). They keep a well-maintained inventory of about 100 motorbikes, priced at $50 for a 1-day rental, $91 for a 2-day rental, and $124 for a 3-day rental. Dual-seaters, suitable for two riders, rent for about 25% to 30% more. A mandatory one-time insurance premium of $25 is added onto the rental price. Staff will give you instructions on bike safety and protocol before your rental experience begins.

BY BICYCLE

Looking for a more natural means of locomotion than a putt-putt? You can rent bikes at most cycle liveries (see "By Motorbike," above), but for cyclists who don't work out 6 hours a day, pedaling a bike up Bermuda's steep hills can be a bit of a challenge. **Eve's Cycle Ltd.,** 114 Middle Rd., Paget Parish (© **441/236-6247**), offers one of the best rental deals on the island. Named after the legendary matriarch who founded the company more than 50 years ago, Eve's rents men's and women's bicycles (usually 10- to 12-speed mountain bikes, well suited to the island's hilly terrain). Prices for 21-speed bikes are $25 for a 1-day rental, $45 for a 2-day rental, and $60 for a 3-day rental. No insurance is required. The shop is a 10-minute taxi ride (or a leisurely 20-min. cycle) west of the City of Hamilton. As with motorbiking, exercise caution because roads are narrow and often slippery, and scooter riders and left-hand driving can make things confusing. See "Biking," in chapter 6, "Fun in the Surf & Sun," for more details.

Island-Hopping on Your Own

Most first-time visitors think of Bermuda as one island, but in fact it's a small archipelago. Many of the islands that make up the chain are uninhabited. If you're a bit of a skipper, you can explore them on your own. With a little guidance and the proper maps, you can discover small islands, out-of-the-way coral reefs, and hidden coves that seem straight out of the old Brooke Shields B-movie *The Blue Lagoon.*

For this boating adventure, rent a Boston whaler with an outboard engine. The name of these small but sturdy boats reveals their origins: New Englanders once used them in their pursuit of Moby Dick. It's important to exercise caution, remembering that the English found Bermuda in 1612 only after the *Sea Venture,* en route to the Jamestown Colony, was wrecked off the Bermuda coast.

In the East End, you can explore Castle Harbour, which is almost completely surrounded by islands, forming a protected lake. If you stop to do some fishing, snapper is your likely catch. (Visitors who rent condos or apartments often take their quarry back to their kitchenette to prepare it for dinner.) To avoid the often-powerful swells, drop anchor on the west side of Castle Harbour, near Castle Harbour Golf Club and Tucker's Town. Then head across Tucker's Town Bay to Castle Island and Castle Island Nature Reserve. In 1612, Governor Moore ordered the construction of a fort on Castle Island, the ruins of which you can see today.

In the West End, begin your exploration by going under Somerset Bridge into well-protected Ely's Harbour. To the north, you can visit Cathedral Rocks before making a half-circle to Somerset Village; from here, you can explore the uninhabited islands off Mangrove Bay.

You can rent a 4m (13-ft.) Boston whaler—and pick up some local guidance—at **Blue Hole Water Sports,** Grotto Bay Beach Hotel, Hamilton Parish (© **441/293-2915**; www.blueholewater.bm). Prices begin at $75 for 2 hours, $120 for 4 hours, and $180 for 8 hours. Rates do not include gas.

BY BUS

You can't rent a car. Taxis are expensive. Horse-drawn carriages aren't really a viable option. You may not want to ride a bicycle or a motorbike. What's left for getting around Bermuda? Buses, of course.

The bus network covers all major routes, and nearly all hotels, guesthouses, and restaurants have bus stops close by. There's even a do-it-yourself sightseeing tour by bus and ferry. Regularly scheduled buses go to most of the destinations that interest visitors in Bermuda, but be prepared to wait. Some buses don't run on Sundays and holidays, so be sure you know the schedule for the trip you want to make.

Bermuda is divided into 14 zones of about 3km (1¾ miles) each. The regular cash fare for up to three zones is $3. For more than three zones, it's $4.50. Children 5 to 16 pay $2 for all zones; children under 5 ride free. *Note:* You must have the exact change or tokens ready to deposit in the fare box as you board the bus. Drivers do not make change or accept bills. On the run from the City of Hamilton to the Royal Naval Dockyard (no. 7 or 8), the fare is $4 for adults, $2 for children.

You can purchase $4 tokens at branch post offices or at the **Central Bus Terminal** on Washington Street in the City of Hamilton, where all routes, except route 6, begin and end. The terminal is just off Church Street, a few steps east of City Hall. You can get there from Front Street or Reid Street by going up Queen Street or through Walker Arcade and Washington Mall.

If you plan to travel a lot, you might want to purchase a booklet of 15 tickets. A booklet of 14-zone tickets costs $30; of 3-zone tickets, $20. For children, 15 tickets cost $7.50, regardless of the number of zones. You can buy the booklets at post offices or the central bus terminal. You can also purchase passes that allow travel in all zones for 1 day to 1 month. A 1-day pass costs $12, a 3-day pass is $28, a 1-week pass is $45, and a 1-month pass is $55.

For more information on bus service, call ℂ **441/292-3851.**

In the east, **St. George's Mini-Bus Service** (ℂ **441/297-8492** or 8199) operates a minibus service around St. George Parish and St. David's Island. The basic one-way fare is $3. Buses depart from King's Square in the center of St. George, and can be flagged down along the road. In summer, service is daily 7:30am to midnight. In the off season, service is Monday to Thursday 7:30am to 10pm, Friday and Saturday 7:30am until midnight.

Trolley-like **buses** that seat 60 serve the City of Hamilton and the Royal Naval Dockyard. Passengers can get on and off throughout the day for a single fare of $12. The City of Hamilton trolley stops at the major points of interest, including the Botanical Gardens; the dockyard bus calls at the crafts market. Tickets are sold at most hotels, the City of Hamilton train station, and the Oleander cycle shop (see "By Motorbike," above). For bus routes, see the map on the inside back cover.

BY FERRY

One of the most interesting ways of getting around Bermuda is the government-operated ferry service. Ferries crisscross Great Sound between the City of Hamilton and Somerset; the one-way fare is $4. They also take the harbor route, from the City of Hamilton to the hotel-filled parishes of Paget and Warwick. The ride from the City of Hamilton to Paget costs $2.50. On all routes, children 5 to 16 pay $2, and children under 5 ride free. Motorbikes and bicycles are allowed on the City of Hamilton to Somerset run for $4.

For ferry service information, call ☏ **441/295-4506** in the City of Hamilton. Ferry schedules are posted at each landing and are available at the Ferry Terminal, the Central Bus Terminal in the City of Hamilton, and most hotels.

BY HORSE-DRAWN CARRIAGE

Once upon a time, this was the only way a tourist could get around Bermuda. Before 1946 (when automobiles first came to the island), horses were the principal means of transportation. They're primarily available only for those into the romance and nostalgia of yesteryear.

Today, it's estimated that about 35 or so of these horse-drawn vehicles are still available in Bermuda, hiring themselves out for the tourist trade or for more unusual circumstances, such as after-wedding rides of the bride and groom to the reception hall. Their routes and destinations tend to revolve around the tried-and-true. We usually advise participants to stick to routes within the City of Hamilton (see below). Deviations from these routes—say, if you commission a horse and carriage to pick you up at your hotel for excursions outside of the city limits of Hamilton—can cost hundreds of dollars, depending on how far they are from the place where the carriages and horses are lodged.

Between March and October, drivers congregate along Front Street in the City of Hamilton, adjacent to Passenger Pier no. 1 at the cruise-ship docks. A single carriage (that is, drawn by one horse) accommodating between one and four passengers costs $40 for the first 30 minutes, with an additional 30 minutes priced at between $35 and $40. If you call the island's leading repository of horse-drawn carriages, **Terceira's Stables,** Jubilee Road, Devonshire DV 06 (☏ **441/236-3014**), they'll make arrangements to have a carriage pick you up at various points, regardless of how far-flung, for custom-designed rides.

FAST FACTS: Bermuda

American Express The representative in the City of Hamilton, **Meyer Franklin Travel,** 35 Church St. (P.O. Box 510), Hamilton HM 12 (☏ **441/295-4176**), handles travel itineraries for the company.

Banks The main offices of Bermuda's banks are in the City of Hamilton. All banks and their branches are open Monday from 9:30am to 4pm, Tuesday to Friday from 8:30am to 4:30pm. Banks are closed Saturday, Sunday, and public holidays. Many big hotels will cash traveler's checks, and there are ATMs all around the island.

The **Bank of Bermuda,** 6 Front St., Hamilton (☏ **441/295-4000**), has branches on Church Street, Hamilton; on Par-la-Ville Road, Hamilton; and in Somerset.

The **Bank of Butterfield,** 65 Front St., Hamilton (☏ **441/295-1111**), has several branches, including locations in St. George and Somerset.

The **Bermuda Commercial Bank** is at 43 Victoria St., Hamilton (☏ **441/295-5678**).

Bookstores **Bermuda Book Store (Baxters),** Queen Street, Hamilton (☏ **441/295-3698**), stocks everything that's in print about Bermuda, including titles on gardening, flowers, local characters, poets, and other topics; some books are available only through this store. There are also many English publications not easily obtainable in the United States, as well as a fine selection of children's books. You can also buy that beach novel you forgot to bring. Open Monday to Saturday from 8am to 6pm.

Business Hours Most businesses are open Monday to Friday 9am to 5pm. Stores are generally open Monday to Saturday 9am to 5pm; several shops open at 9:15am. A few shops are also open in the evening, but usually only when big cruise ships are in port.

Car Rentals There are no car-rental agencies in Bermuda because visitors are not allowed to rent cars. For transportation information, see "Getting Around," earlier in this chapter.

Climate See "When to Go," in chapter 2, "Planning Your Trip to Bermuda."

Crime See "Safety," below.

Currency Exchange Because the U.S. dollar and the Bermuda dollar are on par, both currencies can be used. It's not necessary to convert U.S. dollars into Bermuda dollars. Canadian dollars and British pounds must be converted into local currency. For more information, see "Money," in chapter 2, "Planning Your Trip to Bermuda."

Customs For details on what you can bring into Bermuda and what you can carry home, see "Entry Requirements & Customs," in chapter 2.

Dentists For dental emergencies, call **King Edward VII Memorial Hospital,** 7 Point Finger Rd., Paget Parish (*©* **441/236-2345**), and ask for the emergency department. The hospital maintains lists of dentists on emergency call.

Doctors In an emergency, call **King Edward VII Memorial Hospital,** 7 Point Finger Rd., Paget Parish (*©* **441/236-2345**), and ask for the emergency department. For non-emergencies, ask the concierge at your hotel for a recommendation.

Documents Required See "Entry Requirements & Customs," in chapter 2, "Planning Your Trip to Bermuda."

Drinking Age See "Liquor Laws," below.

Driving Rules Visitors cannot rent cars. To operate a motor-assisted cycle, you must be age 16 or over. All cycle drivers and passengers must wear securely fastened safety helmets. Driving is on the left side of the road, and the speed limit is 32kmph (20 mph) in the countryside, 24kmph (15 mph) in busy areas.

Drug Laws In Bermuda, there are heavy penalties for the importation of, possession of, or dealing of unlawful drugs (including marijuana). Customs officers, at their discretion, may conduct body searches for drugs or other contraband goods.

Drugstores Try the **Phoenix Drugstore,** 3 Reid St., Hamilton (*©* **441/295-3838**), open Monday to Saturday 8am to 6pm, Sunday noon to 6pm.

In Paget Parish, **Paget Pharmacy,** 130 Rural Hill Plaza (*©* **441/236-7275**), is open Monday to Saturday 8am to 8pm, Sunday 10am to 6pm. The **Somerset Pharmacy,** 49 Mangrove Bay, Somerset Village (*©* **441/234-2484**), is open Monday to Friday 8am to 6pm, Saturday 8am to 5pm, and Sunday noon to 2pm.

Electricity Electricity is 110 volts AC (60 cycles). North American appliances are compatible without converters or adapters. Visitors from the United Kingdom or other parts of Europe need to bring a converter.

Embassies & Consulates The **American Consulate General** is located at Crown Hill, 16 Middle Rd., Devonshire (© **441/295-1342**), and is open Monday to Friday 8am to 4:30pm. The **Canadian Consulate General** (Commission to Bermuda) is at Reid House, 31 Church St., Hamilton (© **441/294-3611**). Britain doesn't have an embassy or a consulate in Bermuda.

Emergencies To call the police, report a fire, or summon an ambulance, dial © **911**. The non-emergency police number is © **441/295-0011**. For Air-Sea Rescue, Rescue Coordination Center, dial © **441/297-1010**.

Etiquette Well-tailored Bermuda shorts are acceptable on almost any occasion, and many men wear them with jackets and ties. On formal occasions, they must be accompanied by navy blue or black knee socks. Aside from that, Bermudians are rather conservative in their attitude toward dress—bikinis, for example, are banned more than 7.5m (25 ft.) from the water. Men are usually required to wear a jacket to dinner.

Eyeglass Repair There are at least a half-dozen well-recommended opticians and optometrists operating out of storefronts in Hamilton, but two of the most visible and best are **The Bermuda Optical Company,** 12 Church St., Hamilton (© **441/295-6175**); and **Atlantic Vision Care,** 66 King St., Hamilton (© **441/295-7300**). Each is equipped to handle eyeglass repair and contact- lens replacement.

Gasoline Before you rent a moped, be very clear about what kind of fuel it runs on. Most of the mopeds available for rental by a nonresident of Bermuda have 50cc two-stroke engines that almost always require a mixture of gasoline and oil. Selling for around $6.55 per gallon, and designated locally as "mixed" fuel, it's dispensed directly from specially designated pumps at service stations throughout Bermuda. Larger bikes (including some of the newer models with 80cc engines, and virtually all of the modern-day 100cc engines), as well as all conventional automobiles (which most temporary visitors can neither rent nor drive), require unadulterated gasoline, which sells for $6.20 per gallon. The octane level of all gasoline in Bermuda is designated as "high test," and all of it, by law, is unleaded.

Holidays See "When to Go," in chapter 2, "Planning Your Trip to Bermuda."

Hospitals **King Edward VII Memorial Hospital,** 7 Point Finger Rd., Paget Parish (© **441/236-2345**), has a highly qualified staff and Canadian accreditation.

Hot Lines Call © **441/236-3770** Monday to Friday and you'll be connected to either Bermuda Psychiatric Hospital's outpatient clinic (9am–5pm) or St. Brendan's Hospital (in the evening). Both can help with life-threatening problems, personal crises, or referral to a medical specialist.

Information For information before you go, see "Visitor Information," in chapter 2, "Planning Your Trip to Bermuda"; once you're on Bermuda, see "Orienting Yourself: The Lay of the Land," earlier in this chapter. For telephone directory assistance, call © **411**.

Legal Aid The U.S. consulate will inform you of your limited rights and offer a list of attorneys. However, the consulate's office cannot interfere with Bermuda's law-enforcement officers. The **Citizens' Emergency Center** of the Office of Special Consular Services in Washington, D.C. (© **888/407-4747** or

202/501-4444), operates a hot line that's useful in an emergency for U.S. citizens arrested abroad. The staff can also tell you how to send money to U.S. citizens arrested abroad.

Liquor Laws Bermuda sternly regulates the sale of alcoholic beverages. The legal drinking age is 18, and most bars close at 3am. Some bars are closed on Sunday.

Specialty stores sell liquor, beer, and wine. Although it's legal for grocery stores to sell hard liquor, most limit their inventories to beer and wine. Alcohol can't be sold on Sunday. You can bring beer or other alcohol to the beach legally, as long as your party doesn't get too rowdy and you generally stay in one spot. The moment you actually *walk* on the beach or the streets with an open container of liquor, it's illegal. (The thinking behind this law is apparently that roaming gangs of loud, obnoxious drunks are more dangerous and disruptive than sedentary gangs of loud, obnoxious drunks.)

Mail Deposit regular mail in the red pillar boxes on the streets. You'll recognize them by the monogram of Queen Elizabeth II. The postage rates for airmail letters up to 10 grams and for postcards is 70¢ to the United States and Canada, 85¢ to the United Kingdom. Airmail letters and postcards to the North American mainland can take 5 to 7 days, to Britain possibly a little longer. Often visitors return home before their postcards arrive.

Newspapers & Magazines Bermuda has one daily newspaper, the *Royal Gazette*, a publication that's usually regarded as the newspaper of record for the island as a whole. There are two competitors providing alternative versions of the news, including the *Bermuda Sun,* which is issued every Wednesday and Friday, and the *Mid-Ocean News,* which is published every Friday. Major U.S. newspapers, including the *New York Times* and *USA Today,* and magazines such as *Time* and *Newsweek,* are delivered to Bermuda on the day of their publication on the mainland. *This Week in Bermuda* is a weekly guide for tourists.

Passports **For residents of the United States:** Whether you're applying in person or by mail, you can download passport applications from the U.S. State Department website at **http://travel.state.gov**. For general information, call the **National Passport Agency** (℃ **877/487-2778**). To find your regional passport office, either check the U.S. State Department website or call.

For Residents of Australia: You can pick up an application from your local post office or any branch of Passports Australia, but you must schedule an interview at the passport office to present your application materials. Call the **Australian Passport Information Service** at ℃ **131-232,** or visit the government website at www.passports.gov.au.

For Residents of Canada: Passport applications are available at travel agencies throughout Canada or from the central **Passport Office,** Department of Foreign Affairs and International Trade, Ottawa, ON K1A 0G3 (℃ **800/567-6868;** www.ppt.gc.ca).

For Residents of Ireland: You can apply for a 10-year passport at the **Passport Office,** Setanta Centre, Molesworth Street, Dublin 2 (℃ **01/671-1633;** www.irl gov.ie/iveagh). Those under age 18 and over 65 must apply for a 3-year passport. You can also apply at 1A South Mall, Cork (℃ **021/272-525**), or at most main post offices.

For Residents of New Zealand: You can pick up a passport application at any New Zealand Passports Office or download it from their website. Contact the **Passports Office** at ✆ **0800/225-050** in New Zealand or 04/474-8100, or log on to www.passports.govt.nz.

For Residents of the United Kingdom: To pick up an application for a standard 10-year passport (5-year passport for children under 16), visit your nearest passport office, major post office, or travel agency or contact the **United Kingdom Passport Service** at ✆ **0870/521-0410** or search its website at www.ukpa.gov.uk.

For Residents of the United States: Whether you're applying in person or by mail, you can download passport applications from the U.S. State Department website at http://travel.state.gov. To find your regional passport office, either check the U.S. State Department website or call the **National Passport Information Center** toll-free number (✆ **877/487-2778**) for automated information.

Pets To take your pet with you to Bermuda, it must be a minimum of 10 months of age. You'll need a special permit issued by the director of the **Department of Agriculture, Fisheries, and Parks,** P.O. Box HM 834, Hamilton HM CX, Bermuda (✆ **441/236-4201**). The island has no quarantine facilities, so animals arriving without proper documents will be refused entry and will be returned to the point of origin. Some guesthouses and hotels allow you to bring in small animals, but others will not; so be sure to inquire in advance. Always check to see what the latest regulations are before attempting to bring a dog or another pet—including Seeing Eye dogs—to Bermuda.

Pharmacies See "Drugstores," above.

Photographic Needs If you want to buy a camera or film, or develop Kodak or Fuji film, try the City of Hamilton's leading camera store, **Stuart's,** 5 Reid St., near the corner of Queen Street (✆ **441/295-5496**). Film can be developed in-house in about 4 hours (sometimes within 1 hr., for a surcharge). Open Monday to Saturday from 9am to 5pm.

Police In an emergency, call ✆ **911**; otherwise, call ✆ **441/295-0011.**

Post Offices The **General Post Office,** 56 Church St., Hamilton (✆ **441/297-7866**), is open Monday to Friday from 8am to 5pm, Saturday from 8am to noon. Post office branches and the Perot Post Office, Queen Street, Hamilton, are open Monday to Friday from 8am to 5pm. Some post offices close for lunch from 11:30am to 1pm. Daily airmail service for the United States and Canada closes at 9:30am in Hamilton. See also "Mail," above.

Radio & TV News is broadcast on the hour and half-hour over AM stations 1340 (ZBM), 1230 (ZFB), and 1450 (VSB). The FM stations are 89 (ZBM) and 95 (ZFB). Tourist-oriented programming, island music, and information on activities and special events air over AM station 1160 (VSB) daily from 7am to noon.

The local television channel, 9 (ZBM), is affiliated with America's Columbia Broadcasting System (CBS).

Restrooms The City of Hamilton and St. George provide public facilities, but only during business hours. In the City of Hamilton, toilets are at City Hall, in Par-la-Ville Gardens, and at Albouy's Point. In St. George, facilities are available at Town Hall, Somers Gardens, and Market Wharf. Outside of these towns, you'll find restrooms at the public beaches, at the Botanical Gardens, in several of the forts, at the airport, and at service stations. Often you'll have to use the facilities in hotels, restaurants, and wherever else you can find them.

Safety Bermudians are generally peaceful people, not given to violence. To be sure, the island has experienced racial tensions in the past, but right now relations between white and black residents seem to be harmonious, as blacks assume a greater role in Bermuda's affairs.

Crimes against tourists, violent or otherwise, are rare, but don't be lulled into a false sense of security. Crime does exist in Bermuda, as it does in any society. Take care to protect your valuables, especially when you're at the beach. Lock your moped each time you leave it. If you bring very valuable items with you (this is not advisable), place them in your hotel safe and never leave them carelessly in your room.

Smoking Tobacconists and other stores carry a wide array of tobacco products, generally from either the United States or England. Prices vary but tend to be high. At most tobacconists you can buy classic cigars from Havana, but Americans must enjoy them on the island—they can't be taken back to the United States. Smoking in public places (such as restaurants) is generally permitted, but check before lighting up. Movie theaters set aside a section for nonsmokers.

Taxes Whereas Bermuda charges visitors a Passenger Tax before they depart from the island, it's hidden within the cost of an airline or cruise-ship ticket. Frankly, you might never know that a tax has actually been imposed, but if you're interested, $25 of the cost of your airline ticket, and $60 of the cost of your cruise-ship ticket, goes to the Bermudian government. Children under 2 are exempt from paying this tax.

All room rates, regardless of the category of accommodation or the plan under which you stay, are subject to a government tax of 7.25%.

Taxis See "Getting Around," earlier in this chapter.

Telephone, Telegrams, Telexes & Faxes Worldwide direct-dial phone, fax, and cable service is available at the **Cable & Wireless Office,** 12 Burnaby St., Hamilton (© **441/297-7022**). Hours are Monday to Friday from 9am to 5pm. Prepaid phone cards may be purchased and used island-wide, and calling cards may be used from selected call boxes.

Cable & Wireless, in conjunction with the Bermuda Telephone Co., provides international direct dialing (IDD) to more than 150 countries. Country codes and calling charges may be found in the Bermuda telephone directory. Telephone booths are available at the Cable & Wireless office, and customers can either prepay or buy cash cards in $10, $20, and $50 denominations. Cash-card phone booths are available at numerous locations around the island. Making international calls with cash cards can be a lot cheaper than using the phone at your hotel, which might impose stiff surcharges. To make a local call, deposit 20¢ (Bermudian or U.S.). Hotels often charge between 20¢ and $1 for local calls.

Special phones at passenger piers in the City of Hamilton, St. George, and the dockyard will connect you directly with an AT&T, Sprint, or MCI operator in the United States, permitting you to make collect or calling-card calls.

Telephone Directory All Bermuda telephone numbers appear in one phone book, revised annually. The Yellow Pages (www.bermudayp.com) in the back list all the goods and services you are likely to need.

Time Bermuda is 1 hour ahead of Eastern Standard Time (EST). Daylight saving time is in effect from the first Sunday in April until the last Sunday in October, as it is in the United States.

Tipping In most cases, a service charge is added to hotel and restaurant bills. In hotels, the charge is in lieu of tipping various individuals, such as bellhops, maids, and restaurant staffers (for meals included in a package or in the daily rate). Check for this carefully to avoid double tipping. Otherwise, a 15% tip for service is customary. Taxi drivers usually get 10% to 15%.

Tourist Offices See "Visitor Information," in chapter 2, and the "Visitor Information on the Island" box, earlier in this chapter.

Transit Information For information about ferry service, call ✆ **441/295-4506.** For bus information, call ✆ **441/292-3854.**

Useful Telephone Numbers On Bermuda, for time and temperature, call ✆ **909.** To learn "What's On in Bermuda," dial ✆ **974.** For medical emergencies or the police, dial ✆ **911.** If in doubt during any other emergency, dial ✆ **0** (zero), which will connect you with your hotel's switchboard or the Bermuda telephone operator.

Water Tap water is generally safe to drink.

Weather Call ✆ **977** at any time for a forecast covering the next 24-hour period or go to www.weather.bm.

Where to Stay

Bermuda offers a wide choice of lodg- ings, from small, casual guesthouses to large, luxurious resorts. Facilities vary greatly in size and amenities within each category.

CHOOSING THE PLACE THAT'S RIGHT FOR YOU

Accommodations in Bermuda basically fall into five categories:

- **Resort Hotels:** These generally large properties are Bermuda's most lavish, offer- ing many facilities, services, and luxuries—but also charging the highest prices, especially in summer. The lowest rates, usually discounted about 20%, are in effect from mid-November to March. The large resorts usually have their own beaches or beach clubs, along with swimming pools; some have their own golf courses. It's cheaper to choose the Modified American Plan (MAP) dining option (explained below under "Rates & Reservation Policies"), which includes breakfast and dinner, than to order all your meals a la carte. However, if you go the MAP route, you'll be confined to the same dining room every night and miss the oppor- tunity to sample different restaurants.

- **Cottage Colonies:** This uniquely Bermudian option typically consists of a series of bungalows constructed around a clubhouse, which is the center of social life, drinking, and dining. The cottages, usually scenically arranged on landscaped grounds, are designed to provide maximum privacy and are typically equipped with kitchenettes for preparing light meals. In many of the cottage colonies, breakfast isn't available; you can go out, or buy supplies the night before and pre- pare your own meal. Most colonies have their own beaches or swimming pools.

- **Small Hotels:** This option might be just the right fit for those who hate mega- resorts. Bermuda's small hotels offer the intimacy of upscale bed-and-breakfasts, but with considerably more facilities. At a small hotel, you might feel more connected to the island and its people. Another plus? They're often cheaper than the big resorts.

- **Housekeeping Units:** These cottage or apartment-style accommodations (often called efficiencies in the U.S.) usually occupy landscaped estates surrounding a main clubhouse. All of them offer kitchen facilities—perhaps a full, well-equipped kitchen, but at least a kitchenette where you can whip up snacks and breakfast. Most offer minimal daily maid service. Generally, housekeeping units are simpler and less expensive than cottage colonies.

- **Guesthouses:** These are Bermuda's least expensive accommodations. The larger guesthouses are old Bermuda homes in garden settings. Generally, they've been mod- ernized and have comfortable guest rooms. Some have their own swimming pools. A number of guesthouses are small, modest places, offering breakfast only; you may share a bathroom with other guests. Also, you may have to "commute" to the beach.

Another option is renting a **villa** or vacation home. Villa rentals are like renting someone's home. At some, you're entirely on your own; others provide maid service. Most are on or near a beach. This is generally an expensive option.

Private **apartments** offer fewer frills than villas or condos; the building housing the apartment may not have a swimming pool or even a front desk. Apartments are available with or without maid service.

Cottages, or cabanas, offer the most independent lifestyle in the category of vacation accommodations—they're entirely self-catering. Some open onto a beach, and others surround a communal swimming pool. Most of them are fairly basic, consisting of a simple bedroom plus a small kitchen and bathroom. For the peak summer season, make cabana reservations at least 5 or 6 months in advance.

Several United States and Canadian agents can arrange these types of rentals. **Bermuda Realty,** Atlantic House, 11 Par-la-Ville Rd., Hamilton (✆ **441/292-1793;** www.bermudarealty.com), specializes in condos and villas. It can arrange bookings for a week or longer.

RATES & RESERVATION POLICIES

The rates that we've listed throughout this chapter are "rack rates"—the rates you'd be quoted if you walked in off the street. These are helpful largely for purposes of comparison. Especially at the big resorts, almost no one ever pays the rack rate. By booking a package deal that includes airfare, or just by asking for packages and discounts at the hotel when you make your reservation, you can usually do much better. At small hotels and guesthouses, the rates quoted here are much more likely to be accurate. Before you book anything, read the "Packages for the Independent Traveler" section in chapter 2.

All room rates, regardless of meal plan, are subject to a 7.5% tax, which will be tacked onto your bill. A service charge (10%–15%) is also added to your room rate in lieu of tips; remember that the service charge does not cover bar tabs. Third-person rates (for those occupying a room with two other people) are lower, and children's rates vary according to their age.

Note: The rack rates we've listed in this chapter include tax and service charge unless otherwise noted. However, we strongly encourage you to confirm what the rates include when you reserve, to avoid any misunderstanding. Hotels usually quote you the full rate you'll pay upon checkout; they don't want misunderstandings either.

Bermuda's high season is spring and summer—the opposite of the Bahamian and Caribbean high season. Most of Bermuda's hotels charge high-season rates from March (Easter is the peak period) through mid-November. A few hotels have year-round rates, and others charge in-between, or "shoulder," prices in spring and autumn. If business is slow, many smaller places shut down in winter.

You may see some unfamiliar terms and abbreviations used to describe rate plans. **AP** (American Plan), sometimes called "full board," includes three meals a day. **MAP** (Modified American Plan), sometimes called "half-board," includes breakfast and dinner. **BP** (Bermuda Plan) includes full American or English breakfast. **CP** (Continental Plan) includes only continental breakfast (basically bread, jam, and coffee). **EP** (European Plan) is always cheapest—it includes only the room, no meals.

Note that prices aren't uniform in several of the larger, older resorts, which offer a wide range of rooms. For instance, one guest at the Elbow Beach Hotel might be paying a price that can be categorized as "moderate," whereas another might be booked

> ⟨*Tips*⟩ **Dining at Your Hotel**
>
> Chances are, you'll take more meals at your hotel in Bermuda than you would
> in other sunny destinations, such as Florida. Although you're generally out and
> about for lunch, many visitors don't like to hire an expensive taxi or take a bike
> or motorbike along Bermuda's narrow roads in search of a spot for dinner. Taxis
> are expensive and motorbikes can be a bit hazardous at night. Since you can't
> rent a car, you are often stuck for meals at your hotel, and therefore you might
> want to consider food options when deciding where to stay.
>
> In many destinations, hotel restaurants aren't a big factor in selecting accom-
> modations. But because of transportation difficulties in Bermuda, especially at
> night, consider the cuisine served at a hotel before checking in. To help you
> out, we've added more details about hotel dining than you can find in most
> other guidebooks.

at a "very expensive" rate—it all depends on your room assignment. So even if you
can't pay $200 a night, it might be worth a call to see if a cheaper room is available.

Accommodations that are members of the Bermuda Hotel Association require 2
nights' deposit within 14 days of confirming a reservation; full payment 30 days
before arrival; and notice of cancellation 15 days before scheduled arrival to avoid for-
feiting your deposit. Some smaller hotels and other accommodations levy an energy
surcharge; inquire about this when you make your reservations.

TIPS FOR SAVING ON YOUR HOTEL ROOM

- **Don't be afraid to bargain:** Get in the habit of asking for a lower price than the
first one quoted. Most rack rates include commissions of 10% to 25% or more for
travel agents, which many hotels will cut if you make your own reservations and
haggle a bit. Always ask politely whether a less-expensive room is available, or
whether any special rates apply to you. You may qualify for corporate, student,
military, senior, or other discounts. Be sure to mention membership in AAA,
AARP, frequent-flier programs, or trade unions, which may entitle you to special
deals as well.

- **Rely on a qualified professional:** Certain hotels give travel agents discounts in
exchange for steering business their way, so if you're shy about bargaining, an
agent may be better equipped to negotiate discounts.

- **Dial direct:** When booking a room in a chain hotel, call the hotel's local line, as
well as the toll-free number, and see where you get the best deal. A hotel makes
nothing on a room that stays empty. The clerk who runs the place is more likely
to know about vacancies than the person at the toll-free number, and will often
grant deep discounts in order to fill rooms.

- **Consider a suite:** If you are traveling with your family or another couple, you can
pack more people into a suite (which usually comes with a sofa bed) and thereby
reduce your per-person rate. Remember that some places charge for extra guests
and some don't.

- **Book an efficiency:** A room with a kitchenette allows you to grocery shop and
eat some meals in. Especially during long stays with families, you're bound to save
money on food this way.

LANDING THE BEST ROOM

Somebody has to get the best room in the house, and it might as well be you.

Always ask for a corner room. They're usually larger, quieter, and closer to the elevator. They often have more windows and light than standard rooms, and they don't always cost more.

When you make your reservation, ask if the hotel is renovating; if it is, request a room away from the renovation work. Many hotels now offer nonsmoking rooms, which you should ask for if smoke bothers you. Inquire, too, about the location of the restaurants, bars, and discos, which could all be sources of irritating noise. If you aren't happy with your room when you arrive, talk to the front desk. If the hotel has another room, the staff should be happy to accommodate you, within reason.

1 Resort Hotels

With their wealth of amenities, the big resort hotels can keep you so well occupied that you may not feel the need to leave the premises (but make sure you resist the pull of the resort and venture out). The large hotels typically have their own beaches or beach clubs and swimming pools; some have their own golf courses too. Most of these hotels also boast such luxury services and facilities as porters, room service, planned activities, sports facilities (such as tennis courts), shops (including bike shops), beauty salons, bars, nightclubs, entertainment, and taxi stands.

VERY EXPENSIVE

SOUTHAMPTON PARISH

The Fairmont Southampton ⭐⭐⭐ *Kids* Sitting atop Bermuda's highest point, this resort is the largest and most luxurious property on the island. It overlooks the ocean, the bay, and its own good beach, located in front of the hotel. The hotel's beach is sheltered in a jagged cove, flanked by cliffs, and studded with rocky outcroppings lashed by the tides. The bedrooms were revitalized with a modern, English-inspired decor, and a spiffy new glossiness was added to the cavernous-looking lobby. The atmosphere is mahogany-trimmed conservatism, glowing and rich-looking and perhaps a little uptight and stuffy to the party-loving Carnival cruise crowd. This mammoth resort stands on 40 hectares (99 acres) of undulating and verdant land that looks gloriously manicured.

Often compared to its sibling in the City of Hamilton, the Fairmont Hamilton Princess, the Fairmont Southampton is located on the beach, whereas the Fairmont Hamilton is situated close to shops and attractions. We don't think it's the place for those who want an intimate, romantic hideaway; in fact, its biggest drawback is that it's a favorite with conventions and tour groups. Nonetheless, it and Elbow Beach (see below) are the finest choices for the well-heeled family who want to stay at a place where virtually everything is on-site—from sports to beaches to a wide selection of dining.

The Fairmont Southampton is decorated in 18th-century English style, with well-upholstered furnishings. Baronial staircases connect the public rooms, situated on three floors. The plush guest rooms are arranged in wings that radiate more or less symmetrically from a central core. This design gives each luxurious room a private veranda with a sweeping view of the water. Rooms are generally spacious, with one king or two double beds. Bathrooms, which come with tub/shower combinations, tend to be modest. For those who can afford it, the choice spot here is the Fairmont

Gold floor, a hotel-within-a-hotel, pampering its guests in ultimate luxury on the top floor, offering an array of services from shoeshines to private check-ins. The Gold Floor offers complimentary continental breakfast, newspapers, and the use of a fax and VCR.

The cuisine is among the island's finest—we recommend several of the resort's restaurants even if you're not staying here (see chapter 5, "Where to Dine"). In a place this large, it's hard to keep an eye on quality, but the Fairmont Southampton does admirably well. This is a mammoth operation, but the hotel has wisely split its dining into smaller enclaves. The dining rooms include Windows on the Sound, a three-tiered palace reminiscent of Mayfair in the 1930s and New York's Rainbow Room; through 6m-high (20-ft.) arched windows, you can see the islands of Great Sound. Other choices include Wickets, Newport Room, the Whaler Inn, and the Waterlot Inn. Nightlife is more staid here than at the Wyndham, and not every restaurant has a bar that's open to nondiners (the Waterlot Inn and the Whaler Inn do). Jasmine's Lounge has live music, usually a jazz combo, beginning at 8pm. Some of the island's finest Italian cuisine is served in the on-site Bacci.

Guests who don't want to leave the premises enjoy a self-contained village of bars, restaurants, shops, and athletic facilities that are among the island's finest. Everyone's favorite pool is a re-creation of a Polynesian waterfall, with streams of heated water spilling from an artificial limestone cliff. You can swim here even during cold weather, thanks to the greenhouse above. A trolley carries guests around the sprawling acreage of the Fairmont Southampton grounds; and a ferry boat reserved for guests only goes from the Waterlot Inn to the piers of the Fairmont Hamilton.

101 South Rd. (P.O. Box HM 1379), Southampton Parish HM FX, Bermuda. © **800/441-1414** in the U.S., 800/268-7176 in Canada, or 441/238-8000. Fax 441/238-8968. www.fairmont.com. 593 units. Winter $259–$389 double, from $619 suite; summer $549–$699 double, from $849 suite. Children 17 and under stay free in a room with 1 or 2 adults. AE, DC, DISC, MC, V. Free private ferry to the Fairmont Hamilton Princess. **Amenities:** 7 restaurants; 2 bars; private beach club; 1 pool (outdoor); par-3 18-hole golf course; 6 tennis courts; health club; spa; sauna; dive shop; moped rental; children's program in summer; business center; 24-hr. room service; massage; babysitting; laundry service; dry cleaning; nonsmoking rooms; rooms for those w/limited mobility. *In room:* A/C, TV, dataport, minibar, coffeemaker, hair dryer, iron, safe.

Wyndham Bermuda Resort & Spa ⊛ *Kids*

Guests still arrive looking for the once-famous Sonesta Beach Resort, but it is "Gone with the Wind." Wyndham has taken over the property, which is now better than it was before, following a massive renovation in 2005. All the bedrooms have been redone in a tasteful, first-rate styling. The main restaurant is now the Chameleon, serving exceptional international and American cuisine, and the lobby-level Sazanami serves Japanese specialties such as sushi, sashimi, tempura, and other fare.

This is the only major luxury resort on Bermuda with access to three beaches, including Church Bay, 5 minutes away by bike. Among full-service hotels, only Elbow Beach (see below) and the Fairmont Southampton (see above) outclass it. Built in the shape of a crescent, the resort sits on 13 hectares (32 acres) of prime seafront property, curving along the spine of a rocky peninsula whose jagged edges provide ocean views. The resort features ample lengths of oceanside walkways. Those who seek Bermudian charm and character would probably prefer the Cambridge Beaches resort (p. 86), but spa-goers, honeymooners, and watersports and beach buffs like this resort a lot. The Wyndham also caters to families, who gravitate to its wide selection of activities, including beaches, spacious rooms with private terraces, a large swimming pool, and even first-rate babysitters.

Where to Stay in Bermuda

ATLANTIC
OCEAN

Ireland Island N.
Ireland Island S.

Mangrove Bay
2 **1**
Somerset Village
SANDYS Watford Bridge

Ely's Harbour

Two Rock Passage

Bay Rd. **37** **38** **PEMBROKE** North Shore Rd.

36
35
33 **34** **Hamilton**
32 **31** Front St.
30

Great Sound

Long Island

Hawkins Island

Somerset Bridge — Ferry —

Hamilton Harbour **26**

Ports Island **29** **28** **27** Botanical Gardens
Hinson Island **17** **PAGET** **25** **24** **23**

Darrell Island

Little Sound

Harbour Rd. **16** **15**

Middle Rd.

19 **20**
18 **21** **22**

3

4

5

WARWICK
11 **12** **13**
10 **14**

SOUTHAMPTON **8** **9**

South Rd.

6 **7**

Ariel Sands Beach Club **39**
Astwood Cove **10**
Aunt Nea's Inn at Hillcrest **44**
Cambridge Beaches **1**
Clear View Suites & Villa **41**
Coco Reef Resort **22**
Dawkins Manor **19**
Edgehill Manor Guest House **35**
Elbow Beach Hotel **21**

The Fairmont Hamilton
  Princess **32**
The Fairmont
  Southampton **9**
Fourways Inn **17**
Granaway Guest House
  & Cottage **16**
Grape Bay Beach Hotel **24**
Grape Bay Cottages **23**
Greene's Guest House **5**

Grotto Bay Beach Resort **42**
Hamiltonian Hotel
  & Island Club **38**
Harmony Club **25**
Horizons and Cottages **18**
Little Pomander Guest House **26**
Marley Beach Cottages **11**
Munro Beach Cottages **4**

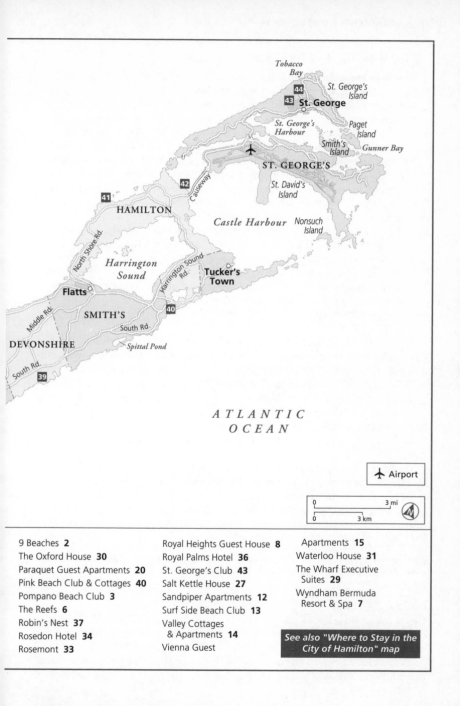

9 Beaches **2**
The Oxford House **30**
Paraquet Guest Apartments **20**
Pink Beach Club & Cottages **40**
Pompano Beach Club **3**
The Reefs **6**
Robin's Nest **37**
Rosedon Hotel **34**
Rosemont **33**

Royal Heights Guest House **8**
Royal Palms Hotel **36**
St. George's Club **43**
Salt Kettle House **27**
Sandpiper Apartments **12**
Surf Side Beach Club **13**
Valley Cottages
 & Apartments **14**
Vienna Guest

Apartments **15**
Waterloo House **31**
The Wharf Executive
 Suites **29**
Wyndham Bermuda
 Resort & Spa **7**

See also "Where to Stay in the
City of Hamilton" map

Moments **The Spa Treatment**

Wyndham Bermuda Resort & Spa, Southampton (© **877/999-3223** in the U.S., or 441/238-8122; www.wyndham.com), has some of the island's most comprehensive spa facilities. Designed in the European style, it offers health and fitness programs you'd find in an American spa, including a "Bermuda Shorts Cellulite Treatment"; deluxe facial care from Paris; and ancient forms of therapeutic and relaxing massage such as aromatherapy, reflexology, and Swedish massage. Some people check into the hotel as part of a 3-night, 4-day spa program. The program, which is jointly operated with **Cedars Spa,** includes access to low-fat, low-calorie, and low-sodium menu items, and a daily regime, as loosely or as rigidly structured as you want, of aerobics, massage, skin and body care, supervised exercise, mud treatments, and so on.

The facilities are also available to hotel guests and nonguests who want selected treatments (priced separately) rather than the full spa experience. The up-to-date accouterments include Universal gym equipment, saunas, steam baths, and massage rooms. The staff conducts daily exercise classes. Half- and full-day packages are available to nonguests. For after-workout pick-me-ups, there's a beauty salon adjacent to the health spa.

The circular bay in front, flanked by limestone cliffs and sandy beaches, was used long ago by gunpowder smugglers, and later by rumrunners, who loved its well-camouflaged entrance. Circled with palm-shaded cabanas and bars, the bay has a soft, sandy bottom and looks like a small corner of Polynesia transported to the Atlantic.

At a multimillion-dollar cost, the resort renovated its guest rooms and public areas. Rooms have private terraces, thick carpeting, high-quality light wood, louvered closets, and electronic locks. Bathrooms are generous in size, with tiled tub/shower areas. Some units open onto garden views, while more expensive units boast ocean or beach views.

The hotel has three restaurants. Overall, the food here is perfectly good, if not truly gourmet, nor as excellent as that at the Southampton Princess. You'll never go thirsty at the Wyndham—each restaurant has a bar.

6 Sonesta Dr., Southampton Parish (P.O. Box HM 1070), Hamilton HM EX, Bermuda. © **877/999-3223** in the U.S. or Canada, or 441/238-8122. Fax 441/238-8463. www.wyndham.com. 508 units. May–Aug $192–$221 double, $364–$462 suite; Apr and Sept–Nov 15 $372–$422 double, $463–$522 suite; Nov 16–Mar $211–$242 double, $310–$352 suite. AE, MC, V. Bus: 7. **Amenities:** 3 restaurants; 2 bars; 2 pools (1 indoor, 1 outdoor); golf course; health club; spa; dive shop; children's program (May 1 to Labor Day); business center; limited room service; babysitting; laundry service; dry cleaning; nonsmoking rooms; rooms for those w/limited mobility. *In room:* A/C, TV, minibar, hair dryer, iron, safe.

PAGET PARISH

Elbow Beach Hotel *★★★ (Kids)*   Elegant and commanding, this is the best full-service resort on Bermuda, though it lacks the intimacy and local charm you'd find at a smaller place like the Reefs (p. 82). Today it's become part of Mandarin Oriental's portfolio of luxury hotels. The canary yellow hotel complex opens onto Elbow Beach, where a prime strand of sand is reserved for hotel guests. In its latest $20-million

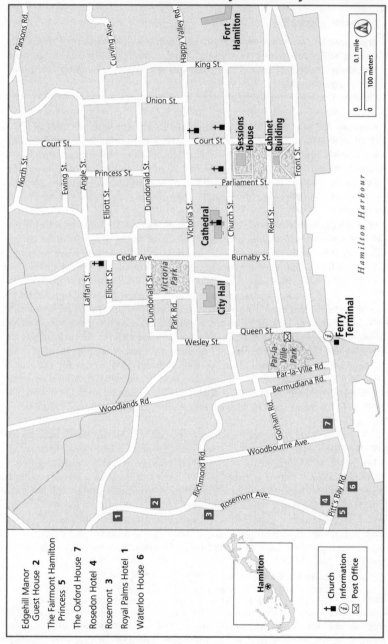

Where to Stay in the City of Hamilton

Edgehill Manor
Guest House **2**
The Fairmont Hamilton
Princess **5**
The Oxford House **7**
Rosedon Hotel **4**
Rosemont **3**
Royal Palms Hotel **1**
Waterloo House **6**

Church
Information
Post Office

Hamilton

⟨Tips⟩ Package Deals

Refer to the "Packages for the Independent Traveler" section of chapter 2 before you call these resorts yourself. Buying a package is the way to go; you can save hundreds of dollars over what you would pay by booking your hotel and airfare separately.

---

restoration, the now-chic hotel has abandoned its chintzy florals in favor of a more Zen approach. Built in 1908, Elbow Beach appeals to vacationers, especially families, who like everything under one roof (or at least on-site). Another advantage is the proximity to the City of Hamilton, which is 10 minutes away by taxi. The resort sits on 20 hectares (49 acres) of gardens with its own .5km (⅓-mile) pink-sand beach on the south shore. Long gone are the days when rowdy college students descended at Easter.

You can choose from a wide array of accommodations, from rooms with balconies overlooking the water to duplex cottages; from lanai rooms overlooking the pool and the Atlantic to others that are surfside. Many guest rooms feature Asian furnishings, hardwood floors, and exposed ceiling beams. Bathrooms are Italian marble, with tub/shower combinations, up-to-date plumbing, and touches of luxury such as robes. The most spacious units are in low-rise buildings on terraces leading to the sands; the least desirable rooms open onto a heavily trafficked corridor on the lobby floor. The pale yellow core was built in 1908, but since then, it has been expanded massively and frequently. No other hotel in Bermuda offers as wide a choice of outbuildings from the main one. There are as many as 17 of these, each scattered across the steeply slop-ing and landscaped grounds. Families with children tend to opt for some of the low-slung accommodations in the gardens; and business travelers tend to opt for accommodations within the stately looking main building. In fact, the hotel's site map evokes a theme park by Disney, meandering as it does through a labyrinth of walkways.

The cuisine here has never been better; the culinary "dream team" includes chefs who have worked at some of the grandest dining rooms of the world, from Atlanta's Ritz-Carlton to Wolfgang Puck's California restaurants. All guests, including those on MAP, may choose dinner at either of the hotel's two oceanview restaurants or at a nightly outdoor theme party. The main dining room, the Seahorse Grill, is the most formal of the restaurants. At the beachfront Cafe Lido, the kitchen focuses on seafood with a Mediterranean accent. The resort also participates in a "dine around" program with several City of Hamilton restaurants; hotel guests can eat at participating restau-rants and charge their meals to the resort. The Veranda Bar is Bermuda's first rum bar, featuring a lively Latino beat.

60 South Rd. (P.O. Box HM 455), Paget Parish HM BX, Bermuda. ℂ **441/236-3535.** Fax 441/236-8043. www. mandarinoriental.com/bermuda. 235 units. Summer $395–$615 double, from $960 suite; off season $285–$460 dou-ble, from $450 suite. Children 17 and under stay free in parent's room. Packages available. AE, DC, MC, V. Bus: 1, 2, or 7. **Amenities:** 6 restaurants; 2 bars; nightclub; outdoor pool; putting green; 5 all-weather tennis courts (2 lit for night play); health spa with whirlpool; sauna; watersports equipment/rental (including deep-sea fishing, scuba div-ing, kayaking, and windsurfing); summer children's program (the best on island); business center; 24-hr. room serv-ice; babysitting; laundry service; dry cleaning; nonsmoking rooms; executive suites; rooms for those w/limited mobility; nearby horseback riding. *In room:* A/C, TV, dataport, minibar, hair dryer, iron, safe.

PEMBROKE PARISH (CITY OF HAMILTON)

The Fairmont Hamilton Princess 🐦🐦 This landmark luxury hotel launched Bermuda's tourist industry and is still going strong. Following a multimillion-dollar renovation, it is brighter and better than ever. Its sibling, the Fairmont Southampton, has better dining, grander facilities, and the advantage of being on a beach, but it is somewhat remote; the Fairmont Hamilton earns fans and devotees because it is more conveniently positioned for shopping and sightseeing. The hotel, which evokes a wedding cake, is near downtown Hamilton, on the edge of Hamilton Harbour. Elbow Beach (the closest beach) is a 20-minute taxi ride or 45-minute bicycle ride from the hotel. The easily accessible ferry delivers guests to the Fairmont Southampton (see above), and sun lovers can get their fill at the sandy stretch there. The lack of a beach here doesn't keep the glitterati away: This is the hotel of choice for Hollywood and European movie stars, as well as the yachting set. Past visitors have included everyone from Mark Twain to Michael Jackson (quite a range!).

Opened in 1884 and named for Princess Louise (Queen Victoria's daughter), this princess is far more staid than the Fairmont Southampton. It doesn't even attempt to offer the roster of activities available at Elbow Beach, so the young and the restless might want to book elsewhere. This is the flagship of the Fairmont hotel chain, and it's certainly the one with the most history: British intelligence officers stationed here during World War II worked to crack secret Nazi codes.

Modern wings, pierced with row upon row of balconied loggias, surround the hotel's colonial core. The property was designed around a concrete pier that extends into the harbor, near a Japanese-style floating garden. Many of the spacious rooms have private balconies, which were designed "to create the feeling that you'd choose the same kind of bedroom if you owned a home here." Most of the tiled bathrooms are generous in size. Some 40% of the guests are repeat visitors.

The hotel has a wide array of bars and restaurants. For a review of Harley's, see chapter 5, "Where to Dine."

76 Pittsbay Rd., Pembroke Parish HM CX, Bermuda. ℂ **800/441-1414** in the U.S., or 441/295-3000. Fax 441/ 295-1914. www.fairmont.com. 410 units. Apr–Nov $399–$499 double, from $609 suite; off season $319–$419 double, from $529 suite. AE, DC, MC, V. Frequent ferry service to and from the Fairmont Southampton, weather permitting. **Amenities:** 2 restaurants; 2 bars; heated freshwater swimming pool, unheated saltwater swimming pool; access to golf, tennis, horseback riding, sailing, and white-sand beaches at the Fairmont Southampton; world-class health club; saunas; moped rentals; watersports equipment/rentals; business center; salon; limited room service; massage area; babysitting; laundry service; dry cleaning; nonsmoking rooms; rooms for those w/limited mobility; executive suites. *In room:* A/C, TV, dataport, minibar, coffeemaker, hair dryer, iron, safe.

EXPENSIVE
HAMILTON PARISH

Grotto Bay Beach Resort 🐦 *Kids* This resort (named after its subterranean caves) is lushly planted with tropical fruit trees. A sandy but mediocre beach nearby offers a view of an unused series of railroad pylons, leading onto forested Coney Island across the bay. The beach is narrow, with rocky outcroppings, and unfortunately there are not a lot of other good beaches nearby. However, the nearby coastline is enchanting, with many natural caves and intimate coves. From the seaside, the airy public areas look like a modern version of a mogul's palace, with big windows, thick white walls, and three peaked roofs with curved eaves.

This restored resort appeals to young couples and families who don't need all the hustle and bustle and central location of a resort like Elbow Beach (see above).

A Preview of Coming Attractions

One of Bermuda's most visible real-estate developments has occurred within two separate plots of land in Paget Parish. The venue involves a "marriage" between a once-lackluster hotel, formerly known as Newstead, and one of the island's most appealing golf courses, Belmont Hills. The resulting entity is known as **The Newstead Belmont Hills Golf Resort & Spa** (27 Harbour Rd., Paget, Bermuda PG 02; © **441/236-5367**; fax 441/236-2296; www.newsteadbelmonthills.com). Though separated by a drive of at least 10 minutes, they were united into a coherent whole in 2003, and immediately began the painful process of reinvention.

The resulting resort includes a radically reconfigured par-70 golf course, The Belmont Hills, which was up and open for business in 2005, at least 2 years in advance of the rest of the now-unified whole. Accommodations associated with this course are expected to be operational early in 2007.

Everything is expected to be plush, five-star, and intimate. With a total of only 46 units, that means posh, boutiquey, and stylish, but in a tastefully understated way that evokes the genuine conservatism of Bermuda. Think of it as a miniature and vastly more intimate version of the Fairmont Southampton, which is also dependent for part of its allure on its golf course.

Don't expect a conventional hotel. Investors buy a one-sixth ("fractional") interest in one of the resort's available accommodations, in return for which they're granted 8 weeks per year access to that unit. Those weeks are scattered strategically on a rotating basis throughout the year (2 weeks per season). Whenever the investors don't want access to their units, the resort's management will rent it out to short-term renters. Hotel guests can opt for studios, one-bedroom, and two-bedroom units. These lie within a low-rise compound of buildings close to the sea, but within a 10-minute drive of the golf course.

Also on-site will be a full-service spa, a gym, a swimming pool, a restaurant and bar, and water taxi service that makes several runs a day across the Sound to the commercial center of Hamilton.

Although it's unattractively located across from the airport, noise from planes is not a problem. The sprawling, 8.5-hectare (21-acre) property contains 11 three-story buildings with balconies and sea views (but no elevators). If your room is far from the main building, you may think you've been sentenced to Siberia (though there are secluded units that appeal to honeymooners). All accommodations are well furnished; the bathrooms are equipped with tub/shower combinations and are well maintained. The children's programs and playground make this a good bet for families. There are also a lot of activities offered, including nature walks, twice-weekly "cave crawls," daily cave swims, organized activities for teenagers, scavenger hunts, communal croquet near the bar, fish feeding, and bridge competitions. The best rooms are directly on the beach, but they're at the bottom of a serpentine flight of about 30 masonry steps. That's no big deal for guests of average fitness, but those with limited mobility might opt for oceanview, not oceanfront, rooms.

The on-site restaurants serve fair if unremarkable Continental cuisine, enlivened by fresh seafood. A multimillion-dollar renovation has perked up the look of all food and beverage outlets, including the Bayside Bar & Grill, the Rumhouse Bar, the Palm Court, and the Hibiscus dining room, which now offers an outside patio allowing guests to dine alfresco. The lounge books live entertainment nightly, and there are a handful of other bars on the property. Afternoon tea is served every day, and there's a daily happy hour. Blasted out of natural rock, the swimming pool has a swim-up bar. Solitude, tranquillity, and friendly, personal service are the draws here.

11 Blue Hole Hill, Hamilton Parish CR 04, Bermuda. ⓒ 800/582-3190 in the U.S., 800/463-0851 in Canada, or 441/293-0188. Fax 441/293-2306. www.grottobay.com. 201 units. Nov 1–27 and Dec 24–Jan 2 $185–$195 double; Jan 3–Mar 8 $165–$175 double; Mar 9–Apr 5 $205–$215 double; Apr 6–Apr 28 $238–$259; Apr 29–Oct 31 $315–$330 double; from $350 suites year-round. MAP (breakfast and dinner) $53 per person. AE, MC, V. Bus: 1, 3, 10, or 11. **Amenities:** 2 restaurants; 2 bars; outdoor freshwater pool; nearby golf course; 4 tennis courts (2 lit for night play), frequent tennis clinics; small health club; daily Jazzercise in Rum House Lounge before breakfast; Jacuzzi; watersports/equipment rentals; excursion boat; moped rentals; summer children's program; game room; limited room service; babysitting; coin-operated laundry; nonsmoking rooms; rooms for those w/limited mobility. *In room:* A/C, TV, dataport, minifridge, coffeemaker, hair dryer, iron, safe.

2 Small Hotels

In direct contrast to the sprawling resorts are Bermuda's more intimate, informal, small hotels. Many have their own dining rooms and bars, and some even have their own beaches or beach clubs; all offer pools and patios.

VERY EXPENSIVE
SOUTHAMPTON PARISH
Pompano Beach Club ⚜   Right next to the Port Royal Golf Course, this seaside hotel is perched on a limestone hill, above a cove beach fringed with rocky outcroppings. From the terraced beach above the hotel's clubhouse, waist-deep water covers the clean, sandy bottom for the length of 2½ football fields before the deep water begins. It would be hard to imagine a more dramatic building site than what was selected for this hotel. Anchored to a bluff that rises directly above the sea, the hotel features windows that seem to take in the full expanse of the wide blue ocean. The Atlantic is so close that from the public areas, you'll get the illusion that you're onboard a cruise ship headed out to sea; the water sparkles turquoise or gray, depending on the weather, in attractive contrast to the color scheme that the hotel's architects labeled, in its honor, Pompano pink. It attracts couples of all ages who want privacy and tranquillity; golfers especially like this place.

The hillside villas scattered over the landscaped property have a balcony or terrace to take advantage of the ocean views. If you can afford it, request the deluxe rooms at the top of the price scale (see below), as these accommodations often have wet bars and showers with oversize tubs. Some units are more spacious than others.

If you don't want to dine around at night, you can order meals on-site in the dining room, with alfresco tables on a terrace. The hotel offers a complimentary shuttle to and from the local Rockaway ferry stop, making it easier for guests to commute back and forth from Hamilton.

36 Pompano Beach Rd., Southampton Parish SB 03, Bermuda. ⓒ **800/343-4155** in the U.S. and Canada, or 441/234-0222. Fax 441/234-1694. www.pompano.bm. 74 units. May–Sept 5 $475–$545 double; off-season $270–$495 double. Rates include MAP (breakfast and dinner). Packages available. AE, MC, V. Hamilton ferry to Somerset. Bus: 7 or 8. **Amenities:** 2 restaurants; cafe, 2 bars; freshwater heated swimming pool; access to government-owned Port Royal Golf Course; 4 all-weather tennis courts (2 lit for night play); oceanfront health club; ocean- and poolside Jacuzzis; watersports equipment/rentals; moped rentals; game room; salon; massage; babysitting with 24-hr. notice; laundry service. *In room:* A/C, TV, dataport, minifridge, coffeemaker, hair dryer, iron, safe.

The Reefs 👁👁 Not as refined, but also not as stuffy, as Horizons or Cambridge Beaches (p. 87 and 86 respectively), this is one of the island's state-of-the-art inns, opening onto a private beach of pink-flecked sand surrounded by palm trees and jutting rocks.

This inn boasts top-notch maintenance, first-class personal service, and unmatched ocean views. This "lanai colony" of salmon-pink cottages on Christian Bay spreads along a low coral ridge. The lanais are cheerfully decorated in rattan and bright island colors. All have private sun decks and ocean views. These midsize accommodations have tasteful furnishings and small bathrooms with tub/shower combinations, separate dressing areas, and dual basins. The hotel offers eight "Cottage Suites by the Reefs," and these are the most desirable; they come in one-, two-, or three-bedroom units built along the cliffs and hillside of the resort and featuring the privacy of a home with the luxuries and services of a resort. If you're looking for action, head over to the Wyndham, or even consider checking into the Elbow Beach Hotel or the Fairmont Southampton (see above). But if you want a smaller place and more tranquillity, consider one of the Reefs's relaxing pink lanais.

The attentive staff of the plant-filled Ocean Echo, the more formal dining option, serves Continental and North American cuisine. The chefs concentrate on bringing out the food's natural flavors; they don't overpower your taste buds with extra sauces and gimmicks. If you want to let your hair down a bit, opt for Coconuts; there's no finer or more romantic spot in Bermuda for an alfresco sunset dinner than this beach terrace. The chefs draw inspiration from around the world—Thailand to the United States. The kidney-shaped swimming pool sits on a ledge with an ocean view. The latest improvement here is a spa, La Serena (serenity), offering, among other services, the only authentic Thai massage on island. There is also an array of other services ranging from reflexology to facials, and even a nonsurgical facelift.

56 South Shore Rd., Southampton Parish SN 02, Bermuda. ⓒ **800/742-2008** in the U.S. and Canada, or 441/238-0222. Fax 441/238-8372. www.thereefs.com. 65 units. Apr 1–13 and Nov $368–$438 double, $724–$754 junior suite, $784–$854 suite, $548–$1,398 cottage; Apr 14–Oct double, $488–558, junior suite, $738–758, suite, $798–868, cottage, $564–$1434; Dec–Mar $294–$364 double, $444–$474 junior suite, $525–$534 suite, $340–$860 cottage. Rates include MAP (breakfast and dinner). AE, MC, V. Bus: 7. **Amenities:** 3 restaurants; 2 bars; outdoor pool; 3 golf courses nearby; 2 all-weather tennis courts; health club; complimentary kayaks and snorkeling equipment; moped and mountain-bike rentals; babysitting; laundry service; dry cleaning; nonsmoking rooms; rooms for those w/limited mobility; croquet; shuffleboard. *In room:* A/C, TV, dataport, fridge, coffeemaker, hair dryer, iron, safe.

PAGET PARISH

Coco Reef Resort 👁 Pink sands lie just a few steps from your room at this reincarnation of the old Stonington Beach Hotel, previously owned by the government of Bermuda. Opening onto the island's South Shore Beach, the restored property is inviting with its Caribbean-style fabrics and wicker furnishings, reflecting the island's pastels. In each room there are original paintings of scenes of Bermudian life. Redevelopment involved the creation of a dramatic atrium lobby, improved dining, the refurbishment of all public rooms, and the complete restoration of all the guest bedrooms, which are midsize and comfortably furnished. The large bathrooms have tub/shower combinations. At La Vista Bar, you can enjoy a panoramic view of the ocean while sitting in an antique rattan chair. The on-site restaurant, Juanito's, is named after Bermuda's first visitor, Juan de Bermudez. The eclectic menu roams the world for inspiration.

3 Stonington Circle, Paget Parish PG BX, Bermuda. ℂ **800/648-0799** in the U.S. and Canada, or 441/236-5416. Fax 441/236-0371. www.cocoreefbermuda.com. 62 units. Apr 16–Oct $443–$498 double, from $654 suite; Nov–Apr 15 $294–$349 double, from $517 suite. Rates include full breakfast. AE, MC, V. Bus: **7. Amenities:** 2 restaurants; bar; heated freshwater swimming pool; 2 tennis courts; access to a nearby health club; business services; babysitting with advance notice; laundry service; dry cleaning; complimentary afternoon tea; rooms for those w/limited mobility. *In room:* A/C, TV, dataport, kitchenette, minifridge, coffeemaker, hair dryer, iron, safe.

Grape Bay Beach Hotel ℛ *Finds*

This is the incarnation of a well-respected middle-bracket hotel that was, until a reconfiguration early in the millennium, known as White Sands Hotel. The core of this place is a shell-pink two-story Bermuda-style house. The hotel is a 3-minute walk from the white sands of Grape Bay Beach. In the 1980s, a concrete-sided annex was shoehorned into the narrow space that until then had been a lawn. The result is simple and completely unpretentious motel-style lodgings, most of which have access to a private balcony, a respectable amount of space, and a simple but serviceable decor that represents good value on an otherwise expensive island. One of the best aspects of the place is its location within a neighborhood of otherwise private homes, each set either on the crest of a hill or on the side of a hill, with views of the wide Atlantic. The on-site restaurant, Sapori, presents a curve-sided coral wall to the force of the Atlantic winds, and offers a sun terrace and large-windowed views of the sea.

White Sands Rd. (P.O. Box PG 174), Paget Parish PG BX, Bermuda. ℂ **800/548-0547** in the U.S., or 441/236-2023. Fax 441/236-2486. 32 units. Apr–Oct $220–$250 double; off season $155–$177 double. AE, DC, MC, V. Bus: 2, 7, or 8. **Amenities:** Restaurant; 2 bars; limited room service; babysitting; nonsmoking rooms. *In room:* A/C, TV, dataport, fridge, coffeemaker, hair dryer, iron, safe.

Harmony Club ℛ

This hotel is for couples only. However, the couple can be any combination of gender or age (over 18). Elbow Beach, the closest beachfront, is a 15-minute walk or a 5-minute scooter ride away. Named after the 1830s home of a 19th-century merchant that stood on the site, this hotel retains only a few vestiges of its original historic core, but tries to keep the friendly informality of a private home.

The accommodations, furnished in Queen Anne style, occupy a series of rambling pink-sided wings that encircle formal gardens with gazebos. Rooms near the road tend to be somewhat noisy. Units are generous in size, with sitting areas, double or king beds, oversize closets, and well-maintained private bathrooms with tub/shower combinations.

The property's chefs are competent, if not dazzling. However, there's such a wealth and variety of food that you're almost certain to find something you like. Evening meals are served by candlelight on fine china and crystal in the Casuarina. A full English tea is served every afternoon; there are also weekly cocktail parties and entertainment 6 nights a week.

109 South Rd. (P.O. Box PG 299), Paget Parish PG BX, Bermuda. (© 888/427-6664 in the U.S., or 441/236-3500. Fax 441/236-2624. www.harmonyclub.com. 68 units. Jan–Apr 15 $155 double, with full breakfast $185, with MAP $275; Apr 16–Dec $210 double, with breakfast $225–$240, with MAP $270–$330. AE, MC, V. Bus: 7 or 8. No children 17 and under accepted. **Amenities:** 2 restaurants; 2 bars; freshwater swimming pool; putting green; 2 tennis courts; health club; whirlpool; Jacuzzis; sauna; nearby access to moped rental; laundry service; dry cleaning; nonsmoking rooms; rooms for those w/limited mobility. *In room:* A/C, TV, dataport, minibar, coffeemaker, hair dryer, iron, safe.

The Wharf Executive Suites ⊕   One of Bermuda's most modern accommodations, this boutique hotel opened in 2002. It caters to the business traveler and the extended-stay visitor. The location is on the harbor overlooking the City of Hamilton, which is reached by taking a 7-minute ferry ride. The management, with some justification, bills its offering as a "home away from home." No hotel can be that, but this one tries admirably. The hotel is in a pale-yellow-painted building offering studio suites equipped with kitchenettes and full suites with full kitchens. All bedrooms have executive work centers, including a desk and ergonomic chair, a two-line speakerphone, a high-speed Internet connection, and a fax machine/printer/copier. Personalized concierge service is also provided. Rooms are spacious and furnished in a conservative, traditional style, each unit with a balcony overlooking Hamilton Bay. There is no restaurant on-site, but a continental breakfast is served. The property was totally renovated and refurbished in 2002, including sparkling bathrooms with tub/shower combinations.

1 Harbour Rd., Paget Parish PG BX, Bermuda. (© 441/232-5700. Fax 441/232-4008. www.wharfexecutivesuites. com. 15 units. Nov–Mar $225 double, $310 suite; Apr $235 double, $310 suite; May–Oct $245 double, $400 suite. Rates include continental breakfast. AE, MC, V. **Amenities:** 2 pools (1 indoor, 1 outdoor); babysitting; laundry service; nonsmoking rooms; rooms for those w/limited mobility. *In room:* A/C, TV, dataport, kitchenette (studios), full kitchen (suites), coffeemaker, hair dryer, iron, safe.

PEMBROKE PARISH (CITY OF HAMILTON)

Waterloo House ⊕   This is the favorite of businesspeople in the City of Hamilton who appreciate the convenience of its location—on the harbor, not on a beach. Sandwiched between the City of Hamilton and its bigger and more anonymous-looking rival, the Fairmont Hamilton Princess, the Waterloo is one of the most British of the Bermuda hotels, with just a whiff of the majesty of Lord Nelson after his victory at Waterloo. It was established as a hotel in the 1930s, on a site that had been occupied by the private mansion of the Wainwright family, merchants who had built it in 1812, and named it after that year's most decisive military victory, Waterloo. Today, only a few vestiges of the original home remain, within a pink-walled compound that's wrapped around a trio of enclosed courtyards that culminate in a waterfront terrace overlooking a marina and the water cargoes of Hamilton Harbour. The venue is posh, plush, small-scale, boutiquey, and charming. The inn has its devotees—two guests told us they stay here every year and wouldn't think of checking into another hotel.

On the edge of Hamilton Harbour (on the outskirts of town), this enlarged and remodeled private home was built around 1910. Terraced gardens descend to the water in the Italian Riviera style; behind salmon-colored walls, the gardens contain palms, magnolias, poinsettias, urns overflowing with ivy, a splashing fountain, and white wrought-iron garden furniture shaded with fringed parasols. There are nooks for drinks and sunbathing around the property, and shade trees surround the swimming pool.

Inside, the drawing room has antique English furnishings and decorative tile floors. Rooms vary in size and decor; each evokes the feeling of a country-house guest room. A newer wing offers small studios and twin-bedded units, though accommodations in the main unit have more character. The highest prices are for the five cottages, which have living and dining areas and refrigerators (though no kitchens). They also have spacious, well-kept bathrooms. Although the bathrooms in the hotel's newer wing are larger and better maintained, we still prefer the older units for their quaint charm. All bathrooms feature tub/shower combinations. This is a pet-friendly facility.

The main dining room (reviewed in chapter 5, "Where to Dine") overlooks the terrace and harbor. On the lower terrace level is a bar lounge with Moorish arches, English armchairs, and hand-woven pillow covers. You can enjoy afternoon tea on the lawn at the water's edge.

100 Pitts Bay Rd. (P.O. Box HM 333), City of Hamilton, Pembroke Parish HM BX, Bermuda. (C) **800/468-4100** in the U.S. and Canada, or 441/295-4480. Fax 441/295-2585. www.waterloohouse.com. 29 units. Apr–Nov $380–$465 double, $460–$780 suite; Dec–Mar $285–$380 double, $360–$650 suite. Rates include full breakfast and afternoon tea; MAP (breakfast and dinner) $50 per person. AE, MC, V. Bus: 1, 7, or 8. **Amenities:** 2 restaurants; bar; freshwater outdoor swimming pool; private dock; reciprocal relationship with Bermuda's best golf courses; privileges at the members-only Coral Beach & Tennis Club (tennis and squash) 6.5km (4 miles) from Hamilton; small health club; spa; business center; limited room service; laundry service; dry cleaning; nonsmoking rooms; rooms for those w/limited mobility, waterside barbecue area. *In room:* A/C, TV, fax, dataport, hair dryer, iron.

EXPENSIVE
PEMBROKE PARISH (CITY OF HAMILTON)
Rosedon Hotel ★ *Finds*   If you'd like a small local hotel with charm and character in the City of Hamilton, Rosedon is for you. (Those who want a megahotel with lots of facilities can check into the Hamilton Princess across the street.) The staff at this stately 1906 mansion are helpful, polite, and personable. Although its rates are rather high for what it is—basically, an overblown guesthouse—it has its fans. Business travelers often stay here because of its proximity to the City of Hamilton.

Rosedon resembles a colonial-era plantation great house, with a pristine white exterior and royal blue shutters. Extensive gardens and lawns encircle the property. Look for the loquat tree (a small evergreen), a Bermuda trademark; other shrubs include hibiscus, banana plants, and bird of paradise. Once occupied by an English family, this was the first house in Bermuda with gaslights. The building has a formal entry hall and two antiques-filled lounges. A flagstone terrace with parasol-shaded tables surrounds the large, temperature-controlled pool.

The individually decorated, midsize bedrooms have balconies or patios, along with small but neat bathrooms containing tub/shower combinations. The modern veranda accommodations in the rear are often preferred over rooms in the main house. The modern accommodations open onto the pool. The colonial-style bedrooms in the main house, however, have more island flavor and character. All but six of the accommodations lie within a rambling two-story contemporary-looking annex that encircles a garden and a swimming pool in back. The main house, which is a white-sided, blue-shuttered neoclassical building built in the early 1900s, is mostly used as a reception area and office, and site of the above-mentioned six upstairs bedrooms.

The honor system prevails at the self-service bar. The full breakfast included in the rates is good and plentiful, with plenty of variety even if you stay a week. It can also be delivered to your room. There's afternoon tea, but no restaurant.

61 Pitts Bay Rd. (P.O. Box HM 290), City of Hamilton, Pembroke Parish HM AX, Bermuda. © **800/742-5008** in the U.S. and Canada, or 441/295-1640. Fax 441/295-5904. www.rosedonbermuda.com. 47 units. Apr–Nov $228–$336 double; off season $180–$284 double. Extra person $35. Rates include full breakfast and afternoon tea. AE, MC, V. Free round-trip shuttle service to Stonington Beach, 10 min. away. **Amenities:** Bar; heated outdoor swimming pool; access to tennis courts at South Shore Beach & Tennis Club; limited room service; babysitting; same-day laundry service. *In room:* A/C, TV, dataport, fridge, coffeemaker, hair dryer, iron, safe.

MODERATE
PEMBROKE PARISH (CITY OF HAMILTON)
Hamiltonian Hotel & Island Club　Set on a hill less than 1.5km (1 mile) north-west of the City of Hamilton, this is a quiet, relatively simple hotel that markets its rooms as timeshare units. Don't expect a particularly cozy reception—think of it as an anonymous getaway from the pressures of urban life, with no particular facilities for dining or partying. The one-bedroom accommodations are in four pink-sided, stone-roofed, apartment-style buildings. They're comfortable and well maintained, with average-size bathrooms equipped with tub/shower combinations. Units don't have a full kitchen, but you can heat up food and make toast or coffee—in other words, prepare yourself a snack.

Langton Hill (P.O. Box HM 1738), City of Hamilton, Pembroke Parish HM GX, Bermuda. © **441/295-5608**. Fax 441/295-7481. 32 units. Apr–Nov $189 double; off season $106 double. AE, MC, V. **Amenities:** Outdoor pool; 3 tennis courts (2 lit for night play). *In room:* A/C, TV, fridge, coffeemaker, microwave.

3 Cottage Colonies

These accommodations are uniquely Bermudian. Each colony has a main clubhouse with a dining room, lounge, and bar, plus its own beach or pool. The cottage units, spread throughout landscaped grounds, offer privacy and sometimes luxury. Most have kitchenettes suitable for preparing beverages and light snacks, but not for full-scale cooking.

If you were a travel agent working for Brooke Astor, Barbara Walters, and Goldie Hawn, you'd book them as follows: the aristocratic Astor into Cambridge Beaches, the media star Walters into Horizons, and the actress and producer Hawn into Ariel Sands. That should help you to distinguish one colony from the next.

VERY EXPENSIVE
SANDYS PARISH
Cambridge Beaches 🏨🏨🏨　The restored Cambridge Beaches—the most westerly resort in Bermuda—attracts rich honeymooners, old-money families, and *Vanity Fair* couples who seek privacy, pampering, and plenty of facilities. The ambience is even more refined than that of the Horizons (reviewed below), and guests have access to five private palm-fringed beaches. If you're a first-time visitor, the clubby atmosphere may make you feel like an outsider. For snob appeal, Cambridge Beaches is numero uno in Bermuda (followed by Horizons). It's the natural choice for Saudi royalty. Children 4 and under are not allowed.

On a peninsula overlooking Mangrove Bay in Somerset, the colony's 10 hectares (25 acres) of semitropical gardens and green lawns occupy the entire western tip of the island. The colony centers on an old sea captain's house. The main lounges are taste-fully furnished with antiques; the dominant feeling here is that of a country estate. Scattered throughout the gardens are nicely furnished cottages, some of which are nearly 300 years old. They have distinct Bermudian architectural features, with an added British starchiness. All of the cottages (some of which were once private homes) are conservatively furnished and come with sun-and-breakfast terraces, generally with unobstructed views of the bay and gardens. A cottage can comfortably house four. The least expensive units have land rather than ocean vistas. Clad in marble, the bathrooms contain dual basin sinks and whirlpool tubs along with showers.

Dining is in the excellent and very pricey Tamarisk Dining Room (reviewed in chapter 5, "Where to Dine"), or on the terrace, where barbecues are sometimes held. There's also an informal lounge, the Port O' Call Pub, with nightly entertainment during the high season.

30 Kings Point Rd., Sandys Parish MA 02, Bermuda. ℭ **800/468-7300** in the U.S., or 441/234-0331. Fax 441/ 234-3352. www.cambridgebeaches.com. 94 units. Apr 16–Oct $415–$650 double and $690–$1,535 suite (rates include full breakfast and afternoon tea), $495–$730 double and $790–$1,615 suite with MAP and afternoon tea; off season $340–$540 double and $570–$1,295 suite (rates include breakfast and afternoon tea), $420–$620 double and $650–$1,375 suite with MAP and afternoon tea. AE, MC, V. Bus: 7 or 8. **Amenities:** 2 restaurants; 3 bars; 2 heated outdoor pools; access to all golf courses of Bermuda, including nearby Robert Trent Jones–designed golf course, Port Royal; putting green; 3 tennis courts (1 lit for night play); health club; spa; Jacuzzi; sauna; watersports equipment/rental (windsurfing, canoeing, kayaking, snorkeling, fishing, sailing, boating, glass-bottom-boat excursions, and more); 2 bonefishing flats adjacent to the colony; bicycle and moped rentals; salon; limited room service; babysitting; laundry service; nonsmoking rooms. *In room:* A/C, TV, dataport, fridge, hair dryer, iron, safe.

PAGET PARISH
Horizons and Cottages ★★★   This deluxe cottage colony sits atop a hill overlooking Coral Beach, a 10-minute walk away. The lack of a beach on the premises might be a serious drawback for some visitors, especially at these prices. Otherwise, you'll be a pampered darling here. Bermuda's top cottage colonies—Cambridge Beaches and Horizons—are both popular with a well-heeled crowd. Subdued sophistication characterizes both, though Horizons is perhaps a touch less snobbish. At Horizons, families with big bank accounts predominate in summer, and there's a mature repeat clientele in winter; trust-fund honeymooners show up year-round. Sometimes the atmosphere evokes a discreet house party, with fellow guests regularly being introduced. You might find more privacy, anonymity, and seclusion at Cambridge Beaches.

Horizons and Cottages has at its core a converted manor farm (ca. 1690), where the traditional ambience remains. A Relais & Châteaux member, Horizons is situated on a 10-hectare (25-acre) estate with terraced gardens and lawns. The reception rooms of the manor house have old Bermudian architectural details, as well as antiques from England and the Continent; several drawing rooms have open fireplaces.

All guest units are handsomely furnished with Italian terra-cotta tile floors, scatter rugs, traditional tray ceilings, and ceiling fans. They have separate dressing areas and private terraces overlooking the ocean. Some units are split-level. The generous tiled bathrooms come with oversize mirrors, and tub/shower combinations.

The main dining room, the Middleton Room (reviewed in chapter 5, "Where to Dine"), serves French *cuisine naturelle,* using all fresh products. The food, especially the tender steak and fresh seafood dishes, is exceptional for Bermuda, although the chefs at Cambridge Beaches seem to work more magic. Lunch is served on the terrace, which is transformed into an entertainment area in the evenings, with informal dancing and, at times, calypso music. Guests can also have lunch and dinner, by reservation, at Coral Beach & Tennis Club and Waterloo House.

33 South Rd., Paget Parish PG 04, Bermuda. **℗ 800/468-0022** in the U.S. and Canada, or 441/236-0048. Fax 441/236-1981. www.horizonscottages.com. 48 units. High season $330–$410 double, $450–$510 suite (rates include full breakfast); off season $230–$290 double, $320–$365 suite (rates include breakfast). MAP $35 per day extra. AE, MC, V. Bus: 2 or 7. **Amenities:** Restaurant; bar; heated freshwater swimming pool; 9-hole golf course, 18-hole putting green; croquet; 3 tennis courts; access to nearby Coral Beach & Tennis Club for more tennis, squash, snorkeling gear, health club, and spa; access to nearby bike and scooter rentals; massage; babysitting; laundry service; nonsmoking rooms. *In room:* A/C, fax, dataport, kitchenette (in some), hair dryer, safe; TV or minibar upon request.

DEVONSHIRE PARISH

Ariel Sands Beach Club ✦✦   At the ocean's edge, with a sandy beach just a 2-minute walk away, secluded Ariel Sands is one of the best cottage colonies in Bermuda, though not quite in the platinum class of Cambridge Beaches and Horizons. This is a quiet place, popular with well-heeled families looking for a summer retreat. The grounds are nicely landscaped, with flowering trees, coconut palms, and one of the most original sculptures on the island—Seward Johnson Jr.'s stainless-steel statue of Ariel, who dances like a water sprite on the surf.

One of Ariel's part-owners is Diana Darrid, the mother of actor Michael Douglas (and ex-wife of film legend Kirk Douglas), and the family has contributed $5 million to the resort's recent refurbishment. It looks fresh, bright, and new—better than it has in years. In chilly weather, a double-hearth fireplace warms a reception lounge and bar area. The smallish rooms have private entrances. They're attractively decorated, with white walls, cool pastels, Bermudian flower paintings, straw matting on terra-cotta floors, and bentwood furniture; most have private porches. The art in many of the private and public rooms is based on themes from *The Tempest,* and guest rooms have names such as Miranda's Cabana, Sea Nymph, and Prospero. The midsize bathrooms with tub/shower combinations are handsomely tiled and well maintained.

The first-class health spa offers such services as beachside massages, aromatherapy, skin and hair treatments, and a full exercise facility. Complete health and fitness appraisals are available, including programs devoted to nutrition, cardiac risk, and lifestyle health issues.

34 Shore Rd. (P.O. Box HM 334), Devonshire Parish HM BX, Bermuda. **℗ 800/468-6610** in the U.S., or 441/236-1010; call collect from Canada. Fax 441/236-0087. www.arielsands.com. 47 units. May–Oct $340–$900 double; Nov–Apr $230–$650 double. Rates include full breakfast. AE, DC, MC, V. Bus: 1. **Amenities:** Restaurant; 2 bars; 1 heated freshwater and 2 saltwater pools; 2 tennis courts (both lit for night games); health club; spa; outdoor hot tub; snorkeling equipment rental; moped rentals; limited room service; babysitting with 24-hr. notice; laundry service; private beach. *In room:* A/C, TV, dataport, fridge, coffeemaker, hair dryer, iron, safe.

SMITH'S PARISH

Pink Beach Club & Cottages ✦✦✦   Two pretty beaches surround this complex of pink-sided, white-roofed cottages, and bay grape trees and hibiscus bushes grace its 6.5-hectare (16-acre) oceanfront setting. Away from the congestion of Hamilton, this is the largest cottage colony on Bermuda, attracting an affluent international crowd. The staff, among the best on the island, includes people who have been with Pink Beach since it opened for the first time in 1947.

Major improvements, completed after Hurricane Fabian in 2003, have made this hotel sparkle anew. Rooms are each configured as either a suite or a junior suite, and include restyled marble bathrooms fitted with cherry-wood cabinetry, tub/shower combinations, Italian tile floors, and plantation-style furnishings. All units have a generously proportioned bedroom/sitting area, a fully equipped kitchen, a good-size bathroom, a patio, and an outdoor terrace or veranda. The most luxurious

⌢Kids Family-Friendly Accommodations

Elbow Beach Hotel (p. 76)   Children stay free in their parent's room at this hotel, one of the finest full-service resorts on the island. Your best bet is the "Family Value Package," which includes accommodations, transfers, daily breakfast buffet, and a host of activities and extras; inquire about it when you book.

The Fairmont Southampton (p. 72)   This giant resort offers the best children's program on the island, including parties and reliable babysitting. Children 18 and under stay free in a room with one or two adults.

Grotto Bay Beach Resort (p. 79)   A longtime family favorite, this hotel features a heavily discounted "Family Special" for two adults and two children 15 and under spending at least 4 nights.

Rosemont (p. 95)   Rosemont caters to families, and each of its units contains a kitchen. Some rooms can be joined together to accommodate larger broods. Babysitting can be arranged.

Royal Palms Hotel (p. 96)   Although it can't compete with the big resorts in facilities, this longtime family favorite extends a cordial welcome. It's within walking distance of the City of Hamilton, so families can save on transportation. There's a freshwater pool, but the beach is a 10-minute ride or 30-minute walk away.

Sandpiper Apartments (p. 94)   Families looking for a moderately priced vacation might check in here. Some units have living/dining areas with two double pullout sofa beds. Each unit has a kitchen where Mom and Dad can prepare simple meals to cut down on the high cost of dining out in Bermuda.

Wyndham Bermuda Resort & Spa (p. 73)   Try to book into this stellar resort on a family package plan (consult a travel agent). Most rooms accommodate two parents and two kids, and there are plenty of activities and diversions for children, including unlimited free ice cream and pizza parties.

accommodations include a quartet of oceanfront suites. These are ideal for honeymooners or other couples, or even families seeking spacious accommodations. The Pink Beach Club's public areas have working fireplaces that take the chill off some Bermuda evenings.

The heart of the colony is the limestone clubhouse, with a dining room that's sheathed in wood paneling. Vegetables, many of them grown nearby, and fresh seafood go into the international cuisine. Every table provides a view of the ocean, and occasionally of a celebrity diner (often an off-the-record actor or rock star) on discreet getaway from the madding crowds. The food is nicely prepared, and served indoors, except during clement weather and when business warrants, in which case an additional outdoor dining terrace is available, in effect creating a second restaurant with an entirely separate set of menus. Breakfast here is a treat; request it the night before and a maid will serve you on your private terrace.

116 South Shore Rd., Tucker's Town, Smith's Parish (P.O. Box HM 1017, Hamilton HM DX, Bermuda). ℭ 800/ 355-6161 in the U.S. and Canada, or 441/293-1666. Fax 441/293-8935. www.pinkbeach.com. 94 units. Summer $475–$875 double, from $635 suite. Off-season $320–$500 double, from $420 suite. Rates include MAP (breakfast and dinner). AE, MC, V. Bus: 1. **Amenities:** Restaurant; bar; large heated freshwater outdoor pool; sun terrace; nearby access to 2 championship golf courses; 2 tennis courts; health club; spa; watersports equipment/rentals; moped rentals; massage; babysitting; laundry service; dry cleaning; nonsmoking rooms; rooms for those w/limited mobility. *In room:* A/C, dataport, coffeemaker, hair dryer, iron, safe.

ST. GEORGE PARISH
St. George's Club ⚘   Far less stuffy than the cottage colonies listed above, this resort encompasses 7 hectares (17 acres) atop Rose Hill (off York St.). It features clusters of traditionally designed Bermudian one- and two-bedroom cottages; all were completely renovated in 1996. For a family or for two or three couples traveling together and sharing a cottage, the price is reasonable. A shuttle bus takes guests to the beach club at Achilles Bay, about a 2-minute ride away, where the beach is sandy with some rocky outcroppings. The Atlantic waters are a bit turbulent in autumn and spring, but they calm during the summer. The complex functions primarily as a time-share property; units are rented to the public when the owners are not using them. Cottages have private balconies or patios, comfortable living and dining areas, fully equipped kitchens, and bathrooms with sunken tubs (and showers) and marble vanities. Views are of the ocean, the pool, or the golf course.

The colony's elegant restaurant, Griffin's (reviewed in chapter 5, "Where to Dine), is open to the public, and is among the finest dining rooms in the East End. Blackbeard's Hideout restaurant is also a popular spot.

6 Rose Hill (P.O. Box GE 92), St. George Parish GE BX, Bermuda. ℭ 441/297-1200. Fax 441/297-8003. www. stgeorgeclub.com. 71 units. Apr–Nov $360 cottage for up to 4 people, $425 cottage for up to 6; Dec–Mar $205 cottage for up to 4, $240 cottage for up to 6. AE, DC, MC, V. Bus: 1, 3, 6, 10, or 11. **Amenities:** 2 restaurants; 2 bars; 3 freshwater swimming pools (1 heated); adjacent Robert Trent Jones–designed 18-hole golf course (guests receive preferential tee times and reduced rates); 3 all-weather tennis courts (2 lit for night play); watersports equipment/rentals; moped rentals; babysitting upon request; coin-operated laundry; convenience store; nonsmoking rooms; rooms for those w/limited mobility. *In room:* A/C, TV, dataport, fully equipped kitchen (most units), kitchenette (remaining units), coffeemaker, iron.

MODERATE
HAMILTON PARISH
Clear View Suites & Villas   Adjacent to a grassy, rock-strewn patch of seafront, Clear View offers units that feature kitchenettes and a good deal of privacy. Midway between the City of Hamilton and St. George, it's a cluster of one- and two-story pink concrete buildings erected during the 1970s. Each holds two to six units decorated with pastel upholstery, tiled surfaces, and big windows. Units with sea views are more expensive. Bathrooms are tiled and well kept with tub/shower combinations.

The centerpiece of the resort is a white-sided farmhouse that holds the restaurant, Landfall, which offers Bermudian cuisine, and a bar. You can swim in the ocean, but there's no beach—most guests head 1.5km (1 mile) west to the sands of Shelly Bay Beach. A small art gallery displays the works of local painters. Ruth Paynter (and her husband, Gerald) arrange art classes that are popular among the island's community of retirees.

Sandy Lane, Hamilton Parish CR 02, Bermuda. ℭ 800/468-9600 in the U.S. or Canada, or 441/293-0484. Fax 441/293-0267. 45 units. Year-round $182–$352 double. MAP (breakfast and dinner) $55 per person. AE, DC, MC, V. Bus: 10 or 11. **Amenities:** Restaurant; bar; 2 outdoor saltwater pools; tennis court; moped rentals; coin-operated laundry; nonsmoking rooms; rooms for those w/limited mobility; conference facility. *In room:* A/C, TV, kitchenette, fridge, coffeemaker, hair dryer, iron.

SANDYS PARISH

9 Beaches This is Bermuda's newest and most casual getaway, though it's far from luxurious and may seem a bit spartan for some visitors, appealing to younger and more active adults. It opened in May 2005, and offers bungalow-style living. Accommodations are perched on stilts, some overlooking the ocean, with glass floors "spying" on the sea creatures below—a rather novel twist, evocative of a glass-bottom boat. You can select from these simply decorated cabanas spread across 7.3 waterfront hectares (18 acres). True to its name, the resort opens onto nine beaches, but only at high tide.

It's built on a long peninsula with numerous coves and limestone grottos in addition to those beaches. Picnic tables, chaise longues, benches, and hammocks are spread around the property, and aquatic options abound, including Hobie catamarans and sea kayaks. The cabanas, with ocean vistas, have ample windows and double doors opening onto verandas. *Tip:* Opt for one of eight cabanas aptly named "Top Banana." Each cabana offers a small bathroom with shower (no tub). The living area has a queen bed, a futon sofa that doubles as a place to sleep, a table, and two chairs. The Hi Tide restaurant serves a full menu as well as tapas. The chefs are also known for their gourmet picnic packages. The laid-back beach bar and grill, Dark 'n Stormy, overlooks the sea.

4 Daniel's Head Lane, Sandys Parish MA 238, Bermuda. ✆ **866/841-9009** in the U.S., or 441/232-6655. www.9Beaches.com. 84 units. Apr 29–June 9 $125–$245 double; June 10–Oct 10 $240–$350; off-season $170–$295. Rates include continental breakfast. AE, MC, V. Bus: 7 or 8. **Amenities:** Restaurant; bar; outdoor pool; bikes and scooters; laundry service; dry cleaning; babysitting; dive shop. *In room:* A/C, hair dryer.

4 Housekeeping Units

Housekeeping apartments, Bermuda's efficiency units, vary from modest to superior. Most have kitchens or kitchenettes and provide minimal daily maid service. Housekeeping cottages, which are air-conditioned and have fully equipped kitchens or kitchenettes, offer privacy and casual living on or close to a beach.

VERY EXPENSIVE
PAGET PARISH

Fourways Inn ⚘ This posh little place feels like a secret hideaway. Pink-sided, airy, and stylish, the Bermudian cottages occupy well-maintained gardens. The sands of Elbow Beach and Mermaid Beach lie within a 15-minute walk or 5-minute scooter ride. The main building is a former private home dating from 1727. Each two-bedroom cottage has a patio and a fully equipped kitchenette, plus a good-size tile bathroom with a tub/shower combination. Rooms contain conservatively comfortable furniture. The kitchenettes are better suited for sandwich and snack preparation than for making a feast. There's a medium-size grocery store across the road.

1 Middle Rd. (P.O. Box PG 294), Paget Parish PG BX, Bermuda. ✆ **800/962-7654** in the U.S. and Canada, or 441/236-6517. Fax 441/236-5528. www.fourwaysinn.com. 6 units, 5 cottages. Apr–Oct $195–$$285 double, $395–$595 suite; off season $130–$165 double, $195–$320 suite. Extra person $40. Rates include continental breakfast; MAP (breakfast and dinner) $50 per person. AE, MC, V. Bus: 8. **Amenities:** Restaurant; bar; heated swimming pool; limited room service; laundry service. *In room:* A/C, TV, kitchenette, minibar, coffeemaker, hair dryer, iron, safe.

EXPENSIVE
WARWICK PARISH

Marley Beach Cottages ⚘ *Value* For two couples traveling together, this may be your best bargain. The pink-walled cottages sit on a steep, beautifully landscaped plot of land. Atop a low cliff on the south shore, near Astwood Park, the resort was used for scenes in *The Deep* and *Chapter Two*. Part of another film, *Bermuda Grace,* was also shot there. Three narrow beaches lie at the bottom of the slope that leads to the sea. It's not an ideal place for children, because there's little for them to do other than swim in the pool or at the beach. Parents who do bring the kids are warned to keep a close eye on them because of the steep drop-off to the beaches below. We wouldn't recommend this place for anyone who might have a problem with the steps leading down the cliff to the ocean, but reasonably fit guests won't mind the walk.

The spacious cottages have fully equipped bathrooms with tub/shower combinations, kitchens, hibachis, and sea views from the patio. Floor plans within each cottage can be adapted, depending on the preferences of guests, by either opening or closing of doors, thereby configuring them as either studio apartments or suites. If you're cooking in, you can phone in an order to a local grocery that delivers, or give a list to the staff, who'll phone in your order. There's no delivery charge for orders over $20.

South Rd. (P.O. Box PG 278), Paget Parish PG BX, Bermuda. (℃ **800/637-4116** in the U.S., or 441/236-1143. Fax 441/236-1984. 13 units. Apr–Oct $230–$295 double; Nov–Mar $135–$180 double. Extra person $40 in summer, $25 off season. AE, MC, V. Bus: 7. **Amenities:** Heated freshwater swimming pool; whirlpool; nonsmoking rooms. *In room:* A/C, TV, kitchen, fridge, coffeemaker, iron/ironing board.

Surf Side Beach Club ✎   This club occupies a steeply sloping hillside that descends through gardens to a crescent-shaped sweep of private beachfront. (The steps down to the beach may be hard for mobility-impaired guests to manage.) Flowering trees and panoramic walkways adorn the terraced property. From lookout points in the garden, visitors can see grouper and other fish swimming near the rocks of the shallow sea.

Accommodations consist of one-bedroom apartments near the terrace pool, and other lodgings in hillside buildings. The self-contained units are simple and sunny, outfitted in bright colors with comfortable accessories. Each has a fully equipped kitchenette (including English china, wineglasses, and even salt and pepper shakers). The small tiled bathrooms are neatly kept and contain showers. This is a pet-friendly facility. A local grocery accepts phone orders and will deliver to your unit, with no delivery charge for orders over $20. The apartments also have private balconies or patios; some have sitting rooms as well. The restaurant and bar, Palms, offers American and international cuisine; the menu changes daily.

South Rd. (P.O. Box WK 101), Warwick Parish WK BX, Bermuda. (℃ **800/553-9990** in the U.S., or 441/236-7100. Fax 441/236-9765. www.surfsidebermuda.com. 43 units, 10 with shower only. Apr–Oct $275–$325 double, $500–$975

Your Own Private Villa

Bermuda Accommodations (℃ **416/232-2243**; www.bermudarentals.com) offers more than 40 privately owned cottages, apartments, and villas for rent in Bermuda, at prices beginning at $50 per person per day. Most rentals for two guests range from $90 to $150 daily for a well-equipped and fully furnished unit, with private garden entrances, kitchens, and bathrooms (mainly with shower). Many accommodations also have pools on-site as well as easy access to the ocean. The homes are owned by Bermudians for the most part, and are rented when they are not occupied by the owners. If you call her, Fiona T. Campbell (see number above) will answer all your questions.

up to 6 people; off season $150–$195 double, $300–$800 up to 6 people. Extra person $50. MAP $65 per person. Off-season extended-stay discounts available. AE, MC, V. Bus: 7. **Amenities:** Restaurant; bar; pool; tennis; minispa; hot tub; sauna; salon; limited room service; babysitting; coin-operated laundry; dry cleaning; rooms for those w/limited mobility. *In room:* A/C, TV, kitchen w/microwave, fridge, coffeemaker, hair dryer, iron, safe.

MODERATE
SOUTHAMPTON PARISH
Grape Bay Cottages This "resort" consists of two cozy saltbox-style cottages directly beside the sea. Each has comfortably unpretentious furniture and lots of reminders of Bermuda's maritime traditions, as well as a nice bathroom containing a tub/shower combination, a fully equipped kitchen, a wide front veranda, and family-friendly ambience. Maid service is provided for the bedrooms and living rooms (but not for the kitchens) every Monday to Saturday. The venue, which is often booked 6 months in advance, is about as laissez-faire as you're likely to find anywhere in Bermuda, but it's usually well suited to the many clients who prefer self-catered holidays in a simple cottage by the beach.

Grape Bay Dr., off Middle Rd., Southampton Parish (P.O. Box HM 1851, Hamilton HM HX, Bermuda). **€ 800/637-4116** in the U.S., or 441/295-7017. Fax 441/236-1662. Two 2-bedroom units. Apr–Oct $315 1–4 persons; Nov–Mar $210 1–4 persons. Extra person $35 in summer, $20 off season. AE, MC, V. Bus: 7 or 8. **Amenities:** Nonsmoking rooms; rooms for those w/limited mobility. *In room:* A/C, TV, kitchen, coffeemaker, iron.

Munro Beach Cottages At a secluded seaside resort overlooking a private beach at Whitney Bay, this cottage complex borders the Port Royal Golf Course and its tennis courts. It sits at the western end of the south shore and opens onto Munro Beach, which boasts some of the best bonefishing and snorkeling in Bermuda. Each spacious unit has a fully equipped kitchen; a combination dining, living, and bedroom area; and a separate tiled bathroom equipped with a tub/shower combination. Nonsmoking accommodations are available. All cottages provide homelike comforts, and there is daily maid service. If you don't feel like cooking, several first-class restaurants are within a 10- to 15-minute taxi ride. Snorkeling, sailing, and scuba diving are also close at hand.

2 Port Royal Golf Course Rd., Southampton Parish SN BX, Bermuda. **€ 800/637-4116** in the U.S., or 441/234-1175. Fax 441/234-3528. www.munrobeach.com. 17 units. May–Oct $235–$250 double; off season $135–$155 double. MC, V. **Amenities:** Nonsmoking rooms; rooms for those w/limited mobility. *In room:* A/C, TV, kitchen w/microwave, coffeemaker, hair dryer, iron, safe, toaster, ceiling fan, grill.

WARWICK PARISH
Astwood Cove 🏠 Cameron and Deirdre Hill own this homestead, which was built in 1720 on a dairy farm. (Sisters Maude, Ada, and Mary Astwood stipulated in their will that the house should always carry their name.) The white-sided apartment complex occupies a peaceful setting, overlooking lightly wooded meadows and the south shore. The closest large beach, Long Bay, is .5km (⅓ mile) away; Astwood Beach is only a 3-minute stroll from the complex.

Each self-contained apartment has a ceiling fan and a terrace or porch. Local phone calls are free. Some units have sitting rooms, and all have kitchens or kitchenettes equipped with English china. Most of the kitchens are generously proportioned units with stoves, microwaves, and enough basic accessories to prepare a real meal. A few smaller units have just microwaves and stovetop burners. Each unit has a small tiled bathroom, with a shower.

There's a minimart less than 3km (1¾ miles) away. A grocery store somewhat farther away delivers orders over $20. A building added in 1985 has a communal terrace, pavilion, and TV.

49 South Shore Rd., Warwick Parish WK 07, Bermuda. © **800/637-4116** in the U.S., or 441/236-0984. Fax 441/236-1164. 20 units, all with shower only. Apr–Nov 15 $155–$190 double; Nov 16–Mar $115–$130 double. AE, MC, V. Bus: 7. **Amenities:** Outdoor pool; sauna; bike rentals; babysitting; coin-operated laundry; rooms for those w/limited mobility; gas-fired barbecue grills. *In room:* A/C, kitchenette w/microwave, minibar, fridge, coffeemaker, iron, ceiling fans.

Sandpiper Apartments *(Kids)*   Built in 1979 and frequently upgraded, this apartment complex is a bargain, attracting self-sufficient families who like the spacious accommodations and who often shop for groceries to prepare some of their own meals—helpful in cutting down on the pricey restaurant bills in Bermuda. Nine units are studios for one or two people, with two double beds, a small tiled bathroom, and a fully equipped kitchenette that's sufficient for simple meals. Five units contain a bedroom (with king-size or twin beds), a kitchen, and a living/dining area with two double pullout sofa beds. Every apartment has a bathroom equipped with a tub/shower combination and balcony. There's daily maid service. The Sandpiper is minutes away from restaurants and the supermarket. The closest beach is 457m (1,500 ft.) away, and the property has gardens for lounging.

South Shore Rd., Warwick Parish (P.O. Box HM 685, Hamilton HM CX, Bermuda). © **441/236-7093.** Fax 441/236-3898. www.bermuda.com/sandpiper. 14 units. Apr–Oct $150 double, $190–$220 suite for 3 or 4; off season $110 double, $150–$180 suite for 3 or 4. Children 11 and under stay free in parent's room; for children 12 and older, add $20 per child. AE, MC, V. Bus: 7. **Amenities:** Outdoor pool; outdoor Jacuzzi; babysitting; coin-operated laundry; dry cleaning; barbecue grills. *In room:* A/C, TV, dataport, kitchenette, minibar, fridge, coffeemaker, hair dryer, iron, safe.

Vienna Guest Apartments   This apartment complex lies on attractively landscaped grounds, with panoramic views of Forest Hills, Gibbs Hill Lighthouse, and Great Sound. It opened in the early 1990s. Informality is definitely the theme—you're even welcomed with beer or wine. Five units can accommodate up to four guests each, and one unit holds two people comfortably. Each good-size apartment has one queen-size bed and one double bed, a clock radio, a combined living and dining room with a ceiling fan, a fully equipped kitchen with a patio, and a small tiled bathroom with a tub/shower combination.

63 Cedar Hill (P.O. Box WK 761), Warwick Parish WK BX, Bermuda. © **441/236-3300.** Fax 441/236-6100. www. bermuda.com/vienna/ 6 units. Apr–Nov $130–$140 double, extra adult $30, child 4–12 $20; off season $85–$105 double, extra adult $25, child $20. AE, MC, V. Bus: 8C. **Amenities:** Outdoor pool; can arrange for watersports; coin-operated laundry; barbecue grills; sun deck; airport transfer. *In room:* A/C, TV, kitchen, coffeemaker, hair dryer, safe.

PAGET PARISH

Paraquet Guest Apartments *(Value)*   If you're looking for a bargain and are happy with rather motel-like accommodations, this is the place for you. This buff-colored collection of Bermudian houses sits in a gentle knoll, a 5-minute walk from Elbow Beach and a 10-minute bus ride from the City of Hamilton. Built in the mid-1970s, the complex is owned by the Portuguese-born Correia family. Nine units have kitchenettes that are attractive and compact but efficient, filled with the basic equipment you'd need to prepare a meal. All the units (which range from small to midsize) contain functional but comfortable modern furniture, plus a small tiled bathroom with shower. The apartment groupings also operate a decently priced restaurant, Paraquet (reviewed in chapter 5, "Where to Dine"). In addition, a grocery store is a mere 45m (148 ft.) from the hotel.

South Rd. (P.O. Box PG 173), Paget Parish PG BX, Bermuda. © **441/236-5842.** Fax 441/236-1665. www.paraquet apartments.com. 12 units. Apr–Oct $155 double without kitchen, $195 double with kitchen; Nov–Mar $115–$138 double without kitchen, $166 double with kitchen. Extra person $42. Children 13 and under stay $32. MC, V. Bus: 7.

Amenities: Restaurant; outdoor pool; coin-operated laundry; rooms for those w/limited mobility. *In room:* A/C, TV, kitchenette, coffeemaker, iron, phone (in some).

Valley Cottages & Apartments

In a semitropical setting in the center of the island, this is a good choice for self-sufficient types, although we think you get a better deal at the Paraquet Guest Apartments. The complex of typically pink Bermuda buildings lies a short walk from Elbow Beach and a number of food markets and tennis courts. Ferry and bus connections to the rest of Bermuda are easily accessible. These midsize cottages and studios are in a garden, and contain kitchens, living rooms, and private balconies, along with small tiled bathrooms with tub/shower combinations. The decor is minimalist but comfortable, with good beds.

Valley Rd. (P.O. Box PG 214), Paget Parish PG BX, Bermuda. © **441/236-0628.** Fax 441/236-3895. www.valley cottages.com. 9 units. Summer $95–$130 studio double, $155–$180 cottage up to 4 people; off season $85–$100 studio double, $120–$150 cottage up to 4 people. AE, MC, V. Bus: 8. **Amenities:** Spa pool and sun terrace in a secluded area; nonsmoking rooms. *In room:* A/C, TV, kitchen w/microwave, coffeemaker, iron.

PEMBROKE PARISH (CITY OF HAMILTON)

Robin's Nest

Consider Robin's Nest if you'd like a snug little apartment in a family-managed compound in a residential neighborhood. It consists of three separate buildings, each painted terra cotta, scattered amid a small but well-maintained garden that's supervised by Milt and Renée Robinson. Units are spacious and have a summery-looking decor that includes lots of wicker. Each unit contains a fully equipped kitchen and a bathroom with a tub/shower combination. Hibachis are available in case you want to expand your cooking facilities into the great outdoors. Two coves, suitable for swimming, lie within a 10-minute walk of the compound.

10 Vale Close, North Shore, Pembroke Parish HM 04 Bermuda. © **800/637-4116** in the U.S., or 441/292-4347. Fax 441/292-4347. rob@bspl.bm. 4 units. Year-round $130 double; $180 triple; $205 quad. Children 11 and under $10 each. No credit cards. Bus: 4. **Amenities:** Large freshwater swimming pool; nonsmoking rooms; 1 room for those w/limited mobility; hibachis. *In room:* A/C, TV, kitchen, fridge, coffeemaker, hair dryer, iron, safe.

Rosemont ✪ *Kids*

Possessing more character and island charm than Valley Cottages, Rosemont is a cluster of gray-walled cottages, each with a large veranda, on a flowered hillside near the Hamilton Princess. Two of the cottages are former private homes, built in the 1940s; the rest are more modern structures constructed within the past 2 decades. The harbor is visible from the raised terrace. Business travelers, "subdued" families, and older couples frequent Rosemont, attracted by its peace and tranquillity. There is a policy here to "keep it quiet," so the hotel usually doesn't accept college students or large groups.

Each well-furnished room has a kitchen. We find some units a little on the dark side. As many as three rooms can be joined together to accommodate families. The hotel also has three suites with private entrances and better furnishings. Each accommodation comes with a small but neat private tiled bathroom.

There's no restaurant on the premises; everybody cooks in. A grocery store is close by, downtown City of Hamilton is 10 minutes away, and Elbow Beach is a 15-minute scooter or taxi ride away.

41 Rosemont Ave. (P.O. Box HM 37), City of Hamilton, Pembroke Parish HM AX, Bermuda. © **800/367-0040** in the U.S., 800/267-0040 in Canada, or 441/292-1055. Fax 441/295-3913. www.rosemont.bm. 47 units. Apr–Nov $180–$220 double; Dec–Mar $170–$200 double. For children 2–12, add $25 per child. Rates do not include service and taxes. AE, MC, V. **Amenities:** Outdoor pool; scooter rentals arranged; babysitting; coin-operated laundry; nonsmoking rooms; rooms for those w/limited mobility. *In room:* A/C, TV, dataport, kitchen, fridge, coffeemaker, hair dryer, iron.

5 Guesthouses

Bermuda's guesthouses are usually comfortable, old, converted manor houses in garden settings. Some have pools and terraces. The smaller ones are much more casual. They offer fewer facilities than other types of accommodations and are often outfitted with simple, lived-in furniture. Most guesthouses serve breakfast only. Those accommodating fewer than 12 guests are usually private homes. Some have housekeeping units, and others offer shared kitchen facilities for guests to prepare snacks. The vast majority of guesthouse hosts will happily arrange for bicycling, golf, tennis, watersports, or any other activity that you may want to participate in but the guesthouse does not directly offer.

EXPENSIVE
PEMBROKE PARISH (CITY OF HAMILTON)
Royal Palms Hotel 🌟 *Kids*   Just a 5-minute walk from the City of Hamilton, the Royal Palms is one of the most sought-after small hotels on the island, thanks to the care and restoration work of brother-and-sister owners Richard Smith and Susan Weare. Built in 1903, and transformed into a hotel in the late 1940s, it's a fine example of Bermudian architecture, with coral-colored walls, white shutters, a white roof, and a wraparound front porch with rocking chairs and armchairs. Local residents often walk by the garden to admire the marigolds and zinnias. The closest beach is Elbow Beach, a 10-minute taxi or scooter ride or a 30-minute walk away.

The guest rooms were once the living rooms, parlors, and bedrooms of the grand private house. All are spacious, sunny, and comfortably furnished, with rich fabrics throughout. Most units have high ceilings and tall windows, and each comes with a small, well-maintained private bathroom equipped with a tub/shower combination. In the mid-1990s, the mews house associated with this place was radically upgraded into some of the most charming minisuites in the hotel. It's connected via a brick-paved walkway and a formal courtyard with a fountain to the original (main) house. This guesthouse is an excellent choice for budget-minded families traveling together. Family travelers generally request one of the units that come with kitchen facilities.

Cozy public areas include Ascots (reviewed in chapter 5, "Where to Dine"), which serves European and Bermudian cuisine.

24 Rosemont Ave. (P.O. Box HM 499), City of Hamilton, Pembroke Parish HM CX, Bermuda. © **800/678-0783** in the U.S., 800/799-0824 in Canada, or 441/292-1854. Fax 441/292-1946. www.royalpalms.bm. 25 units. Apr–Dec 1 $200–$290 double; $300–$340 suite. Off season $185–$265 double, $260–$305 suite. Extra person $40. Children 15 and under $25; children 2 and under stay free in parent's room. Rates include continental breakfast. AE, MC, V. **Amenities:** Restaurant; bar; outdoor pool; babysitting; laundry service. *In room:* A/C, TV, dataport, kitchen (some units), coffeemaker, hair dryer, iron, safe.

MODERATE
SOUTHAMPTON PARISH
Royal Heights Guest House   At the top of a steep driveway near the summit of Lighthouse Hill, this guesthouse is convenient to the Southampton Princess, with its varied nightlife and dining options. It's a modern, turquoise-trimmed building with two wings that embrace the front entryway. Guests are welcome to gather in the living room of the owners, Russel and Jean Richardson, who are happy to suggest activities. Each tidy but small room has a balcony and comfortable furniture, plus a tiled bathroom with shower. Horseshoe Bay, the closest beach, is a 5-minute taxi or scooter

ride or 15-minute walk away. You can watch ships passing by on the Great Sound as you float in the guesthouse's swimming pool.

Lighthouse Hill (P.O. Box SN 144), Southampton Parish SN BX, Bermuda. © **441/238-0043.** Fax 441/238-8445. www.bermudatourism.com/house9.html. 7 units. Apr–Nov $165 double, $215 triple; off season $145 double, $195 triple. Rates include continental breakfast. AE, MC, V. Closed Feb. Bus: 7 or 8. **Amenities:** Saltwater pool, babysitting. *In room:* A/C, TV, fridge, coffeemaker, microwave, no phone.

PAGET PARISH

Dawkins Manor   In a quiet residential neighborhood, a 5-minute walk from Elbow Beach, this inn offers simple, unpretentious accommodations. Originally built in the 1930s, it has expanded massively since Jamaican-born Celia Dawkins bought the place in the early 1990s. Off-island lecturers conducting short-term classes at nearby Bermuda College sometimes stay here. Even the simplest rooms contain microwaves and coffeemakers; more elaborate accommodations contain kitchens that are bigger than those in lots of other rental properties, suitable for bona fide cooking. Each unit comes with a small but tidy tiled bathroom with a tub/shower combination. A grocery store can be found 2 minutes from the Manor.

29 St. Michael's Rd. (P.O. Box PG 34), Paget Parish PG BX, Bermuda. © **441/236-7419.** Fax 441/236-7088. www. bermuda-charm.com. 8 units. Summer $150 double without kitchenette, $175 double with kitchenette, $195–$225 suite for 2 with kitchenette, $390 2-bedroom suite, extra person $50; off season $100 double without kitchenette, $110 double with kitchenette, $130–$140 suite for 2 with kitchenette, $260 2-bedroom suite, extra person $50. No credit cards. Bus: 7. **Amenities:** Pool; bike rentals; babysitting; coin-operated laundry; nonsmoking rooms. *In room:* A/C, TV, kitchen w/microwave (some units), fridge, coffeemaker, hair dryer, iron, safe.

PEMBROKE PARISH (CITY OF HAMILTON)

Edgehill Manor Guest House   Just outside the city limits and a 15-minute walk from the nearest beach, Edgehill Manor is in a quiet residential area that's convenient to the City of Hamilton's restaurants and shopping. It was built around the time of the American Civil War, exudes an old-fashioned, homey quality, and attracts a rather middle-age clientele. British-born proprietor Bridget Marshall continues the tradition of serving English tea in the afternoon. Although each unit has its own style, all have small balconies or patios; three have kitchenettes, and all come with small tiled bathrooms with shower units. Ms. Marshall's continental breakfast, she is proud to say, is "all home baked."

Rosemont Ave. (P.O. Box HM 1048), City of Hamilton, Pembroke Parish HM EX, Bermuda. © **441/295-7124.** Fax 441/ 295-3850. www.bermuda.com/edgehill. 9 units. Apr–Dec 1 $184–$192 double; off season $156–$166 double. Extra person $26–$36. Children 11 and under in adult's room $22. Rates include continental breakfast. No credit cards. Bus: 7 or 8. **Amenities:** Freshwater pool; limited room service; babysitting; nonsmoking rooms. *In room:* A/C, TV, dataport, kitchen w/microwave (some units), fridge, iron/ironing board, safe.

The Oxford House ⋆ The Oxford House is one of the best and most centrally located guesthouses in the City of Hamilton, about a 10-minute scooter ride or a 30-minute walk from Elbow Beach. The only property in Bermuda constructed specifically as a guesthouse, it's on a side street that leads to Front Street, near the Bermudiana Hotel.

The guesthouse was built in 1938 by a doctor and his French wife, who requested that some of the architectural features follow French designs. Doric columns, corner mullions, and urn-shaped balustrades flank the white- and cream-colored entrance portico. Inside, a curved stairwell sweeps up to spacious, well-furnished guest rooms, each named after one of Bermuda's parishes. They have high ceilings and dressing areas. Two accommodations are equipped with full bathrooms; the rest contain shower units. There's also a sunny upstairs sitting room. Breakfast might include a fresh fruit salad made with oranges and grapefruit grown in the yard. The gracious hostess is Welsh-born Ann Smith.

Woodbourne Ave. (P.O. Box HM 374), City of Hamilton, Pembroke Parish HM BX, Bermuda. ✆ 800/548-7758 in the U.S., 800/272-2306 in Canada, or 441/295-0503. Fax 441/295-0250. www.oxfordhouse.bm. 12 units. Mar 16–Nov $199 double, $252 triple, $286 quad; off season $185 double, $243 triple, $280 quad. Rates include continental breakfast. AE, MC, V. *In room:* A/C, TV, coffeemaker, hair dryer.

ST. GEORGE PARISH

Aunt Nea's Inn at Hillcrest 🌟 *Value*   The only true B&B inn in historic St. George, this inviting place is now better than ever following a major overhaul, in 1998, and annual improvements since then. The early-18th-century house stands on a hill off Old Maid's Lane. Three beaches with great watersports are within 10 minutes on foot. In 1804, the Irish poet Thomas Moore roomed here for several weeks. He developed a passion for Nea Tucker next door and wrote several romantic verses for her.

Each room is uniquely furnished, with four-poster beds constructed of tropical hardwoods or wrought iron, and complementary armoires and accent pieces. Four rooms have whirlpools; the others come with shower units. Owners Delaey Robinson and Andrea Dismont have given the rooms names such as "Green Turtle" and "Queen Conch," which represent many of the natural treasures of Bermuda. Smoking is not allowed.

1 Nea's Alley (P.O. Box GE 96), St. George Parish GE BX, Bermuda. ✆ 441/297-1630. Fax 441/297-1908. www.aunt neas.com. 15 units. $190–$250 double; $190–$350 suite. Rates include continental breakfast. AE, MC, V. Bus: 1, 3, 6, 10, or 11. **Amenities:** Nonsmoking rooms. *In room:* A/C (in 10 units), dataport, kitchenette, fridge, coffeemaker, hair dryer, iron, safe.

INEXPENSIVE
SOUTHAMPTON PARISH

Greene's Guest House   From the outside, this guesthouse overlooking Great Sound is well maintained and unpretentious. A look on the inside reveals pleasant, conservatively furnished rooms that are more impressive than you might have supposed. A pair of lions resting on stone columns flanks the entry. The tables in the dining room, which adjoins the kitchen, are set with full formal dinner service throughout the day. Owner Jane Greene welcomes guests to use the spacious, well-furnished living room and the sun-washed terraces in back. Bedrooms are small to medium, each comfortably furnished with a tidily kept compact private bathroom with a tub/shower combination.

There's a swimming pool in the back garden, and Whale Bay Beach lies 3 minutes away by bus or 10 minutes by foot. Dinner is available in the dining room if requested in advance. Facing the sea is a cozy lounge where guests record their drinks on the honor system. The bus to and from the City of Hamilton stops right in front of the house.

71 Middle Rd. (P.O. Box SN 395), Southampton Parish SN BX, Bermuda. ✆ 441/238-0834. Fax 441/238-8980. www. greenesguesthouse.com. 7 units. $130 double. Rates include full breakfast. No credit cards (2-night deposit required with personal check). Bus: 7 or 8. **Amenities:** Outdoor pool; nonsmoking rooms. *In room:* A/C, TV, dataport, fridge, coffeemaker, hair dryer, iron/ironing board.

PAGET PARISH

Greenbank Guest House   This guesthouse stands at the water's edge in Salt Kettle, just across the bay—a 10-minute ferry ride—from the City of Hamilton. It's an old home (the oldest section dates from the 1700s), hidden under pine and palm trees, with shady lawns and flower gardens. The manager welcomes guests in an antiques-filled drawing room. The atmosphere is relaxed, and the service, by the Ashton family, personal.

Greenbank offers accommodations with private entrances and kitchens in waterside and garden-view cottages. Rooms vary in size and shape, but most are small, with small bathrooms as well, each with a shower unit. The furnishings are rather plain but comfortable. The four units in the main house afford less privacy than the cottages. The guesthouse has a private dock for swimming; the charter operation on the property rents motorboats and sailboats. The nearest beach is Elbow Beach, a 15-minute taxi or moped ride away.

17 Salt Kettle Rd. (P.O. Box PG 201), Paget Parish PG BX, Bermuda. © 800/637-4116 in the U.S., or 441/236-3615. Fax 441/236-2427. www.greenbankbermuda.com. 11 units. Apr–Nov $165–$185 waterside cottage for 2, $300 waterside apt with 2 bathrooms for 4, $145 garden apt for 2; off season $145–$165 waterside cottage for 2, $280 waterside apt with 2 bathrooms for 4, $125 garden apt for 2. Extra person $25 year-round. AE, MC, V. Ferry from Hamilton. *In room:* A/C, kitchen, fridge, coffeemaker, iron.

Little Pomander Guest House ⭐ *Finds*   This guesthouse is a pink-sided home that once served as the annex to what is now a privately operated tennis club across the street. Little Pomander can trace its history and foundations to the 1630s. The grassy lawn stretches a short distance down to the rocky shoreline, where you can see cruise ships anchored in Hamilton Harbour. The small rooms are tastefully outfitted with floral prints and alpine-style curtains designed by decorator Irene Trott, who owns the inn with her daughters. There are five apartments, each with a full kitchenette. All rooms come with a small bathroom with a combo tub/shower. The closest beach is Elbow Beach; it's a 5-minute scooter ride or 15-minute walk away.

16 Pomander Rd., Paget Parish (P.O. Box HM 384, Hamilton HM BX, Bermuda). © 441/236-7635. Fax 441/236-8332. www.littlepomander.com. 5 units. Apr–Oct $140 double; off season $110 double. Extra person $30. Rates include continental breakfast. AE, MC, V. Bus: 1, 7, or 8. **Amenities:** Nonsmoking rooms. *In room:* A/C, TV, kitchenette w/microwave, fridge, coffeemaker, hair dryer.

Salt Kettle House ⭐⭐ *Finds*   Informal and secluded, this little charmer sits on a narrow peninsula jutting into Hamilton Harbour. You can swim in a cove and watch ships going in and out of the harbor. The core of this guesthouse is a 200-year-old cottage that has been enlarged over the years. In the late 1970s, another cottage was custom built on the lot's only remaining space. Today, the compound is a cheerful architectural hodgepodge that's popular with boaters. Rooms are generally small, but comfortably furnished; they evoke a traditional Bermuda compound without the glitz of the resort hotels. Four waterside cottages have sitting rooms, shaded patios, and kitchens. The Starboard, the best cottage, can comfortably accommodate four guests. All units have private bathrooms mostly with tub/shower combinations. Guests in the main house also have use of a fully equipped kitchen, and cottages have full kitchens. The owner-manager is Mrs. Hazel Lowe.

10 Salt Kettle Rd., Paget Parish PG 01, Bermuda. © 441/236-0407. Fax 441/236-8639. 11 units. Mar–Dec 1 $120 double, $140 cottage for 2; Dec 2–Feb $100 double, $110 cottage for 2. Additional guests pay an extra 50% of initial rate ($50–$70). Rates include full breakfast. No credit cards. Hamilton ferry to Salt Kettle, then 3-min. walk. **Amenities:** Nonsmoking rooms; kitchen; cable TV. *In room:* A/C, kitchen (cottages), iron/ironing board upon request, safe, no phone (pay phone on premises).

WARWICK PARISH
Granaway Guest House & Cottage ⭐ *Finds*   A cliché of pink-walled, white-washed-roofed Bermudian charm, Granaway is a home built in 1734 with guest rooms and a garden cottage. The property opens onto views of Great Sound and its sparsely inhabited islands. This was once prime anchorage for the privateers of the

18th and 19th centuries. Granaway was one of the stately waterfront homes used as a storeroom for the "booty." The old cedar beams of the original house are still maintained, although modern conveniences have been added. The bedrooms are handsomely furnished and comfortable, each with a small private bathroom with a combination tub/shower. Four of the rooms are in the main house, although the most romantic retreat is the separate Granaway Cottage. This former slave quarters has been completely refurbished with a full kitchen, hand-painted Italian floor tiles, and a fireplace. The most scenic way to reach the City of Hamilton is by taking a short walk to Harbour Road, where you can board one of the ferryboats. In fair weather, guests are served breakfast in the garden, by a pool surrounded by lush foliage.

Harbour Rd. (P.O. Box WK 533), Warwick Parish, Bermuda. © **441/236-3747.** Fax 441/236-3749. www.granaway. com. 5 units. Summer $130–$180 double, $200–$280 double in cottage; off season $100–$160 double, $150–$200 double in cottage. Extra person $25. Rates include continental breakfast (cottages excluded). MC, V. Bus: 8. **Amenities:** Outdoor pool. *In room:* A/C, TV, fridge, no phone.

Where to Dine

Wahoo steak, shark hash, mussel pie, fish chowder laced with rum and sherry peppers, Hoppin' John (black-eyed peas and rice), and the succulent spiny Bermuda lobster (called "guinea chick") await you in Bermuda. Of course, you won't find these dishes on all menus, as many resorts and mainstream restaurants specialize in a more Continental or international cuisine. But for a true taste of Bermuda, you might want to search the menu for local grub.

Bermudian food has improved in recent years, but dining out is still not a major reason to visit the island. American and British dishes are common. Truly innovative gourmet fare often isn't—although the prices would make you think you're getting something special. Dining in Bermuda is generally more expensive than it is in the United States and Canada. Because virtually everything except fish must be imported, restaurant prices are closer to those in Europe.

In general, it's not a good idea to order meat very often; it's flown in, and you can't be sure how long it has been in storage. Whenever possible, stick to local food; for a main course, that usually means fish. The seafood, especially Bermuda rockfish, is generally excellent—that is, when local fishers have caught something that day. Sometimes the waters are too rough for fishing. A lot of fish is imported frozen from the United States; you may want to ask before you order. To find the dishes that are truly worthy, you'll have to pick and choose your way carefully through the menu—and that's where we come in.

Most restaurants, at least the better ones, prefer that men wear a jacket and tie after 6pm; women usually wear casual, chic clothing in the evening. Of course, as most of the world dresses more and more casually, Bermuda's dress codes have loosened up a bit—but this is still a more formal destination than many other islands. It's always wise to ask about required dress when you're reserving a table. During the day, no matter what the establishment, be sure to wear a coverup—don't arrive for lunch sporting a bikini.

Because of the absence of inexpensive transportation, many travelers on a budget eat dinner at their hotels. If you like to dine around and you're concerned about cost, find a hotel that offers a variety of dining options, or stay in or near the City of Hamilton.

BERMUDA'S BEST DINING BETS

You'll find Bermuda's best sushi at **The Harbourfront** in the City of Hamilton; the best Chinese and Thai at **Chopsticks Restaurant** in the City of Hamilton; the best sandwiches at **Paradiso Cafe** in the City of Hamilton; the best British pub grub at **Hog Penny** in the City of Hamilton; the best Bermudian cuisine at **M. R. Onions** in the City of Hamilton; the best ice cream at **Bailey's Ice Cream & Food D'Lites Restaurant** in Hamilton Parish; and the best pizza at **Portofino** in the City of Hamilton. For a wide sampling of Bermuda seafood, go to the **Whaler Inn,** in the Fairmont

Southampton. Here you can enjoy the best of the day's catch, preceded, of course, with a bowl of Bermuda fish chowder. For a romantic dinner, head for **Tom Moore's Tavern** in Hamilton Parish, which was built as a private home in 1652. It once housed Thomas Moore, the Irish romantic poet, and the sense of romance still lingers in a refined setting with a classic French and Mediterranean menu.

1 From Rockfish to Island Rum: Dining, Bermuda Style

For years, Bermuda wasn't known for its cuisine; the food was too often bland and lacking in flavor. However, the culinary scene has notably changed. Chefs seem better trained, and many top-notch (albeit expensive) restaurants dot the archipelago. Italian food is in vogue, as is Chinese. (On the other side of the coin, fast food, including KFC, has arrived, too.)

In recent years, some Bermudians have shown an increased interest in their heritage. They've revived many traditional dishes and published the recipes in books devoted to Bermudian cooking (not a bad idea for a souvenir).

Bermuda imports most of its food from the United States. As the population grows, less and less farmland is available on the island. But lots of people still tend their own gardens; at one home, we were amazed at the variety of vegetables grown on a small plot of land, including sorrel, oyster plants, and Jerusalem artichokes.

WHAT'S COOKING?

SEAFOOD   Any local fisherman will be happy to tell you that more species of shore and ocean fish—including grunt, angelfish, yellowtail, gray snapper, and the ubiquitous rockfish—are found off Bermuda's coastline than in any other place.

Rockfish, which is similar to Bahamian grouper, appears on nearly every menu. From the ocean, it weighs anywhere from 15 to 135 pounds (or even more). Steamed, broiled, baked, fried, or grilled, rockfish is a challenge to any chef. There's even a dish known as "rockfish maw," which we understand only the most old-fashioned cooks (there are still a handful on St. David's Island) know how to prepare. It's the maw, or stomach, of a rockfish, stuffed with a dressing of forcemeat (seasoned chopped fish) and simmered slowly on the stove. If you view dining as an adventure, you may want to try it.

The most popular dish on the island is **Bermuda fish chowder,** made with a variety of white fish (often rockfish). Waiters usually pass around a bottle of sherry peppers

---

Fun Fact **Local Dining Customs**

One of Bermuda's most delightful traditions is the English ritual of **afternoon tea,** which many local homes and hotels maintain.

In hotels, the typical afternoon tea is served daily from 3 to 5pm. Adding a contemporary touch, it's often served around a swimming pool, with guests partaking in their bathing suits—a tolerated lapse from the usual formal social and dress code.

At some places, more formal tea is served at a table laid with silver, crisp white linens, and fine china, often imported from Britain. The usual accompaniments include finger sandwiches made with thinly sliced cucumber or watercress, and scones served with strawberry jam.

Tips A Note on Reservations

Nearly all major restaurants prefer that you make a reservation; many popular places require that you do so as far in advance as possible. Weekends in summer can be especially crowded. Some repeat visitors make their reservations for the most popular spots before they leave home.

---

and some black rum, which you add to your soup; these lend a distinctive Bermudian flavor.

Shark isn't as popular on Bermuda as it used to be, but many traditional dishes, including hash, are made from shark. Some people use shark-liver oil to forecast the weather; it's said to be more reliable than the nightly TV report. The oil is left in the sun in a small bottle. If it lies still, fair weather is ahead; if droplets form on the sides of the bottle, expect foul weather.

The great game fish in Bermuda is **wahoo,** a sweet fish that tastes like albacore. If it's on the menu, go for a wahoo steak. Properly prepared, it's superb.

The **Bermuda lobster** (or "guinea chick," as it's known locally) has been called a first cousin of the Maine lobster. It's in season from September to March. Its high price tag has led to overfishing, forcing the government to issue periodic bans on its harvesting. In those instances, lobster is imported.

You can occasionally get good **conch stew** at a local restaurant. **Sea scallops,** though still available, have become increasingly rare. **Mussels** are cherished in Bermuda; one of the most popular traditional dishes is Bermuda-style mussel pie, with a filling of papaya, onions, potatoes, bacon, curry powder, lemon juice, thyme, and, of course, steamed mussels.

FRUITS & VEGETABLES   In restaurants and homes, **Portuguese red-bean soup**—the culinary contribution of the Portuguese farmers who were brought to the island to till the land—precedes many a meal.

The **Bermuda onion** figures in many recipes, including onion pie. Bermuda-onion soup, an island favorite, is usually flavored with Outerbridge's Original Sherry Peppers.

Bermudians grow more **potatoes** than any other vegetable; the principal varieties are Pontiac red and Kennebec white. The traditional Sunday breakfast of codfish and bananas cooked with potatoes is still served in some homes.

"**Peas and plenty**" is a Bermudian tradition. Black-eyed peas are cooked with onions, salt pork, and sometimes rice. Dumplings or boiled sweet potatoes may also be added to the mix at the last minute. Another peas-and-rice dish, **Hoppin' John,** is eaten as a main dish or as a side dish with meat or poultry.

Both Bermudians and Bahamians share the tradition of **Johnny Bread,** or **Johnnycake,** a simple pan-cooked cornmeal bread. Fishermen would make it at sea over a fire in a box filled with sand to keep the flames from spreading to the boat.

The **cassava** (a starchy root), once an important food on Bermuda, is now used chiefly as an ingredient in the traditional Christmas cassava pie. Another dish with a festive holiday connection is **sweet-potato pudding,** traditionally eaten on Guy Fawkes Day (on Nov 5).

Bermuda grows many **fresh fruits,** including strawberries, Surinam cherries, guavas, avocados, and, of course, bananas. Guavas are made into jelly, which in turn often goes into making the famous Bermuda syllabub, traditionally accompanied by Johnnycake.

WHAT TO WASH IT ALL DOWN WITH

For some 300 years, **rum** has been the drink of Bermuda. Especially popular are Bacardi (the company's headquarters are in Bermuda) and Demerara rum (also known as black rum). The rum swizzle (with rum, citrus juices, and club soda) is the most famous cocktail in Bermuda.

For decades, the true Bermudian has preferred a drink called **"Dark and Stormy."** Prepared with black rum and ginger beer (pronounced *burr*), it has been called the national drink of the island.

An interesting drink is **loquat liqueur.** It can be made with loquats (a small plumlike local fruit), rock candy, and gin, or more elaborately with brandy instead of gin and the addition of such spices as cinnamon, nutmeg, cloves, and allspice.

You'll find all the usual name-brand alcoholic beverages in Bermuda, but prices on mixed drinks can run high, depending on the brand.

Like the British, Bermudians often enjoy a sociable **pub lunch.** There are several pubs in the City of Hamilton, St. George, and elsewhere on the island. For the visitor, a pub lunch—say, fish and chips or shepherd's pie, a pint or two of ale, and an animated discussion about politics, sports, or the most recent royal visit—is an experience to be cherished as truly Bermudian.

2 Restaurants by Cuisine

AMERICAN

Heritage Court (City of Hamilton, $$, p. 124)

M. R. Onions (City of Hamilton, $$, p. 126)

Palms Restaurant ✸ (Warwick Parish, $$$, p. 116)

ASIAN

L'Oriental ✸ (City of Hamilton, $$, p. 125)

BERMUDIAN

Aqua ✸✸ (Devonshire Parish, $$$, p. 132)

The Beach (City of Hamilton, $, p. 128)

Black Horse Tavern ✸✸ (St. George Parish, $$, p. 136)

Grill 56 ✸ (Southampton Parish, $$$, p 113)

Heritage Court (City of Hamilton, $$, p. 124)

Hog Penny (City of Hamilton, $, p. 129)

Landfall ✸ (Hamilton Parish, $$$, p. 134)

M. R. Onions (City of Hamilton, $$, p. 126)

North Rock Brewing Company ✸ (Smith's Parish, $$, p. 133)

Paraquet Restaurant (Paget Parish, $, p. 118)

Pawpaws Restaurant & Bar (Warwick Parish, $$, p. 116)

Sapori ✸ (Paget Parish, $$$, p. 117)

The Spot Restaurant (City of Hamilton, $, p. 132)

Swizzle Inn South Shore (Hamilton Parish, $, p. 136)

Waterloo House ✸ (City of Hamilton, $$$$, p. 120)

White Horse Tavern (St. George Parish, $$, p. 138)

BRITISH

The Beach (City of Hamilton, $, p. 128)

The Frog & Onion Pub (Sandys Parish, $, p. 111)

Henry VIII (Southampton Parish, $$, p. 114)

Key to Abbreviations: $$$$ = Very Expensive $$$ = Expensive $$ = Moderate $ = Inexpensive

Hog Penny (City of Hamilton, $, p. 129)

Lighthouse Tea Room (Southampton Parish, $, p. 115)

Mrs. Tea's Victorian Tearoom ⊛ (Southampton Parish, $, p. 115)

Somerset Country Squire Pub & Restaurant (Sandys Parish, $$, p. 110)

Swizzle Inn South Shore (Hamilton Parish, $, p. 136)

CARIBBEAN

Coconuts ⊛ (Southampton Parish, $$$, p. 113)

Jamaican Grill (City of Hamilton, $, p. 130)

CHINESE

Chopsticks Restaurant ⊛ (City of Hamilton, $, p. 128)

East Meets West ⊛ (City of Hamilton, $$, p. 123)

CONTINENTAL

Bistro J (City of Hamilton, $$, p. 123)

Lemon Tree Café (City of Hamilton, $, p. 130)

Lighthouse Tea Room (Southampton Parish, $, p. 115)

Little Venice (City of Hamilton, $$$$, p. 118)

Monte Carlo ⊛ (City of Hamilton, $$$, p. 122)

Palm Court ⊛ (Hamilton Parish, $$, p. 135)

Pawpaws Restaurant & Bar (Warwick Parish, $$, p. 116)

Tom Moore's Tavern ⊛⊛ (Hamilton Parish, $$$$, p. 134)

Waterloo House ⊛ (City of Hamilton, $$$$, p. 120)

DELI/LIGHT BITES

Bailey's Ice Cream & Food D'Lites Restaurant (Hamilton Parish, $, p. 135)

The Hickory Stick (City of Hamilton, $, p. 129)

Paradiso Cafe (City of Hamilton, $, p. 131)

EGYPTIAN

Café Cairo (City of Hamilton, $$$, p. 121)

FRENCH

Ascots ⊛ (City of Hamilton, $$$, p. 120)

Newport Room ⊛⊛⊛ (Southampton Parish, $$$$, p. 111)

Red Carpet Bar & Restaurant (City of Hamilton, $$, p. 127)

Tom Moore's Tavern ⊛⊛ (Hamilton Parish, $$$$, p. 134)

ICE CREAM

Bailey's Ice Cream & Food D'Lites Restaurant (Hamilton Parish, $, p. 135)

INDIAN

East Meets West ⊛ (City of Hamilton, $$, p. 123)

House of India ⊛ (City of Hamilton, $, p. 130)

INTERNATIONAL

Aqua ⊛⊛ (Devonshire Parish, $$$, p. 132)

Black Horse Tavern ⊛⊛ (St. George Parish, $$, p. 136)

The Breakers Ocean Terrace Café ⊛ (Smith's Parish, $$$, p. 133)

Café Cairo (City of Hamilton, $$$, p. 121)

Café Gio (St. George Parish, $$, p. 136)

Coconut Rock (City of Hamilton, $, p. 129)

Coconuts ⊛ (Southampton Parish, $$$, p. 113)

Flanagan's Irish Pub & Restaurant (City of Hamilton, $$, p. 123)

Freddie's Pub on the Square (St. George Parish, $$, p. 137)

Green Lantern (City of Hamilton, $, p. 129)

Grill 56 ✿ (Southampton Parish, $$$, p. 113)

The Middleton Room ✿ (Paget Parish, $$$, p. 117)

Monty's (City of Hamilton, $, p. 131)

North Rock Brewing Company ✿ (Smith's Parish, $$, p. 133)

Palms Restaurant ✿ (Warwick Parish, $$$, p. 116)

The Pickled Onion ✿✿ (City of Hamilton, $$$, p. 122)

Pirates Landing (Sandys Parish, $$, p. 110)

The Porch (City of Hamilton, $$, p. 126)

Red Carpet Bar & Restaurant (City of Hamilton, $$, p. 127)

The Robin Hood (City of Hamilton, $, p. 132)

Sapori ✿ (Paget Parish, $$$, p. 117)

Specialty Inn (Smith's Parish, $, p. 134)

Tamarisk Dining Room ✿✿ (Sandys Parish, $$$, p. 107)

Tavern by the Sea (St. George Parish, $$, p. 138)

Waterlot Inn ✿✿ (Southampton Parish, $$$$, p. 112)

Wickets Brasserie (Southampton Parish, $, p. 116)

ITALIAN

Aqua ✿✿ (Devonshire Parish, $$$, p. 132)

Ascots ✿ (City of Hamilton, $$$, p. 120)

Bacci (Southampton Parish, $$$, p. 112)

The Harbourfront ✿✿ (City of Hamilton, $$$, p. 121)

La Trattoria (City of Hamilton, $$, p. 125)

Little Venice (City of Hamilton, $$$$, p. 118)

Monte Carlo ✿ (City of Hamilton, $$$, p. 122)

Pasta Basta (City of Hamilton, $, p. 131)

Portofino (City of Hamilton, $, p. 131)

Primavera (City of Hamilton, $$, p. 127)

Red Carpet Bar & Restaurant (City of Hamilton, $$, p. 127)

Rustico (Hamilton Parish, $$, p. 135)

Tio Pepe (Southampton Parish, $$, p. 115)

Tuscany ✿ (City of Hamilton, $$, p. 127)

JAMAICAN

Jamaican Grill (City of Hamilton, $, p. 130)

LEBANESE

Café Cairo (City of Hamilton, $$$, p. 121)

MEDITERRANEAN

Beethoven's (Sandys Parish, $$, p. 110)

Cafe Lido ✿ (Paget Parish, $$$, p. 117)

East Meets West ✿ (City of Hamilton, $$, p. 123)

Fresco's Restaurant & Wine Bar ✿ (City of Hamilton, $$, p. 124)

Harley's (City of Hamilton, $$, p. 124)

La Coquille ✿ (City of Hamilton, $$$$, p. 118)

Mediterraneo Bar & Ristorante ✿✿ (City of Hamilton, $$$, p 122)

Monte Carlo ✿ (City of Hamilton, $$$, p. 122)

MOROCCAN

Café Cairo (City of Hamilton, $$$, p. 121)

PASTRIES

Paradiso Cafe (City of Hamilton, $, p. 131)

PIZZERIA

Rustico (Hamilton Parish, $$, p. 135)

SEAFOOD

Barracuda Grill ✿ (City of Hamilton, $$$, p. 121)

The Harbourfront ✿✿ (City of Hamilton, $$$, p. 121)

Lobster Pot & Boat House Bar ✿✿ (City of Hamilton, $$, p. 125)

Somerset Country Squire Pub & Restaurant (Sandys Parish, $$, p. 110)

Whaler Inn ✿ (Southampton Parish, $$$, p. 114)

SPANISH

Tio Pepe (Southampton Parish, $$, p. 115)

STEAK & SEAFOOD

Freeport Seafood Restaurant ✿ (Sandys Parish, $, p. 111)

Greg's Steakhouse ✿ (Southampton Parish, $$, p. 114)

Griffin's ✿ (St. George Parish, $$, p. 137)

Mickey's Beach Bistro & Bar ✿ (Hamilton Parish, $$$, p. 135)

Port O'Call (City of Hamilton, $$, p. 127)

Waterlot Inn ✿✿ (Southampton Parish, $$$$, p. 112)

SUSHI

Coconut Rock (City of Hamilton, $, p. 129)

The Harbourfront ✿✿ (City of Hamilton, $$$, p. 121)

SWISS

Beethoven's (Sandys Parish, $$, p. 110)

TEX-MEX

Rosa's Cantina (City of Hamilton, $, p. 132)

THAI

Chopsticks Restaurant ✿ (City of Hamilton, $, p. 128)

Silk ✿✿✿ (City of Hamilton, $$, p. 127)

WEST INDIAN

The Spot Restaurant (City of Hamilton, $, p. 132)

3 Sandys Parish

The following restaurants are all on Somerset Island.

EXPENSIVE

Tamarisk Dining Room ✿✿ INTERNATIONAL   This elegant cottage colony is the top dining spot in the parish for classic cuisine and also for innovative fare. Tamarisk boasts impeccable service. A dress-up place, it makes local eateries such as Pirates Landing and the Frog & Onion look publike.

The formal dining room has a new color decor of salmon and lime green, limed wood, impressive columns, and beamed ceilings, evoking an upscale country club. In warm weather, sliding glass doors extend the dining area onto a rambling, east-facing terrace that overlooks the bay.

At lunch, you're likely to come across platters of chicken-macadamia salad, a signature pita-bread sandwich (stuffed, California-style, with chicken salad, avocado slices, and bean sprouts), and some of the best cheeseburgers in the parish. The dinner menu changes every night. It nearly always includes snails in garlic butter; chargrilled vegetables fashioned into a spicy terrine; pan-seared sea scallops with mango, pineapple, sweet chile salsa, and saffron oil; and a rack of lamb with mustard and garden-herb crust.

Live entertainment is provided April to October.

At Cambridge Beaches Hotel, 30 Kings Point Rd. © **441/234-0331**. Reservations required. Jacket suggested for men dining inside, not for dining on the terrace. Lunch main courses $12–$20; dinner main courses $35–$50. MC, V. Daily 12:30–2:30pm and 7–9pm. Bus: 7 or 8 (each marked "Dockyards").

Where to Dine in Bermuda

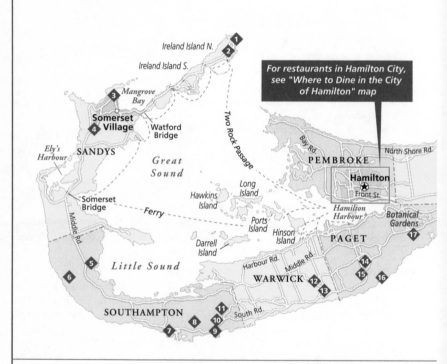

For restaurants in Hamilton City, see "Where to Dine in the City of Hamilton" map

Aqua **19**	Coconuts **7**	Mickey's Beach Bistro & Bar **16**
Bacci **11**	Freeport Seafood	The Middleton Room **15**
Bailey's Ice Cream &	Restaurant **2**	Mrs. Tea's Victorian Tearoom **5**
Food D'Lites Restaurant **25**	The Frog & Onion Pub **1**	Newport Room **11**
Beethoven's **1**	Greg's Steakhouse **6**	North Rock Brewing Company **21**
Black Horse Tavern **28**	Grill 56 **7**	Palm Court **27**
The Breakers	Henry VIII **9**	Palms Restaurant **12**
Ocean Terrace Café **18**	Landfall **23**	Paraquet Restaurant **14**
Cafe Lido **16**	Lighthouse Tea Room **8**	Pawpaws Restaurant & Bar **13**

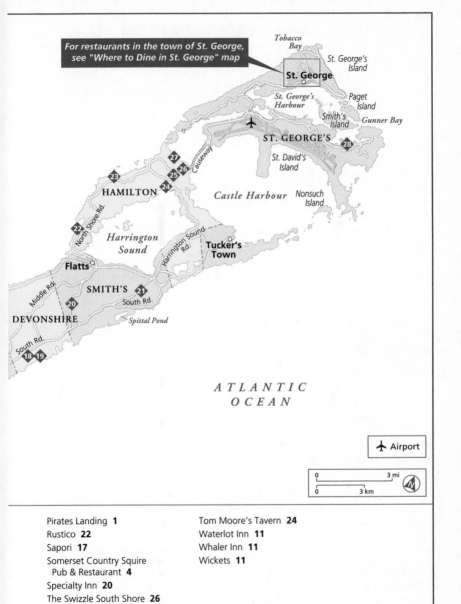

For restaurants in the town of St. George, see "Where to Dine in St. George" map

Tobacco Bay

St. George's Island

St. George

St. George's Harbour

Paget Island

Smith's Island

Gunner Bay

ST. GEORGE'S

28

St. David's Island

27

26

25

24

23

HAMILTON

22

Castle Harbour

Nonsuch Island

Harrington Sound

North Shore Rd.

Harrington Sound Rd.

Causeway

Tucker's Town

Flatts

21

SMITH'S

South Rd.

20

Middle Rd.

DEVONSHIRE

Spittal Pond

South Rd.

18 19

ATLANTIC OCEAN

✈ Airport

0   3 mi
0   3 km

Pirates Landing **1**
Rustico **22**
Sapori **17**
Somerset Country Squire
  Pub & Restaurant **4**
Specialty Inn **20**
The Swizzle South Shore **26**
Tamarisk Dining Room **3**
Tio Pepe **10**

Tom Moore's Tavern **24**
Waterlot Inn **11**
Whaler Inn **11**
Wickets **11**

MODERATE

Beethoven's MEDITERRANEAN/SWISS   A pub-cum-restaurant, this eatery lies within the Clocktower Building at the historic Royal Dockyards. It's owned and operated by two Swiss chefs who feature a formal menu of beautifully presented and well-prepared dishes. There is al fresco dining in the courtyard. The setting is casual and intimate, and the restaurant is a good choice for meals throughout the day and evening. It even serves afternoon tea. A large lunch menu involves fish chowder, burgers, sandwiches, and daily specials such as fiery jerk chicken, along with about 10 main courses such as fish of the day or onion quiche with goat cheese and sun-dried tomatoes. At night, the fare is more elaborate, with a fine selection of appetizers, including some especially savory tempura snails with a roasted garlic and teriyaki sauce. Well-crafted main courses range from corn-breaded Maryland crab cakes served on mesclun salad with balsamic dressing to Oriental chicken in an Asian ginger wrap. This otherwise moderately priced restaurant becomes super expensive only if you order the shellfish dishes such as lobster.

Clocktower Building, Royal Naval Dockyard. ℭ **441/234-5009.** Reservations recommended for dinner. Lunch main courses $9–$50; dinner main courses $24–$70. AE, MC, V. May–Oct Sun–Wed 9am–6pm; Thurs–Sat 11am–9pm; Nov–Apr daily 9am–5pm. Bus: 7 or 8, or ferry from the City of Hamilton.

Pirates Landing INTERNATIONAL   Overlooking the Great Sound, this restaurant offers a diverse menu that pleases diners who aren't too demanding. If you want filling and satisfying food, it's a suitable choice, though it's not quite as fun a spot as the Frog & Onion Pub (p. 111). The seating, at pine tables and chairs, is comfortable, and the serving staff (costumed as pirates) is helpful. It's a little hokey, but everyone seems to get into the "pirate-esque" spirit, especially after a rum punch or two. For the most part, the standard lunch fare—soups, burgers, pastas, and grilled specialties—is adequate, but not special. However, the gyros on pita bread are spicy delights, especially the 7-inch gyro pizza made with fresh vegetables, pepperoni, and mozzarella.

At night the kitchen shines more brightly, as the chefs look abroad for inspiration. Two of the finest dishes are beef tenderloin with porcini mushrooms and chicken cacciatore. Pastas, made fresh daily, are quite delicious. We are less devoted to the garlic shrimp and fresh fisherman's grill.

Royal Naval Dockyard. ℭ **441/234-5151.** Lunch main courses $9–$12; dinner main courses $27–$31. AE, MC, V. Daily 11:30am–4pm and 6–10pm. Closed Jan–Mar. Bus: 7 or 8, or ferry from the City of Hamilton.

Somerset Country Squire Pub & Restaurant BRITISH/SEAFOOD   You'll pass through a moon-gate arch to reach the raised terrace of this waterside restaurant in the center of the village. Limestone blocks and hedges ring the terrace; inside, the dining

---

Tips **Check, Please! A Note on Service Charges**

Although a service charge (typically 10%–15%) is added to most restaurant bills, it's customary to leave something extra if the service has been good. However, it isn't necessary—in fact, many diners find 15% too generous. Be on the lookout for this scam: Some restaurants include the basic 15% service charge in the bill, but leave the service charge line blank. Many diners unknowingly add another 10% to 15%, without realizing they've already paid for service. Scrutinize your bill, and don't be shy about asking if you're not sure what's included.

room is located downstairs. The bill of fare ranges from British pub grub to fresh local fish to traditional roast beef with Yorkshire pudding. Local Bermudian favorites and the specialties of the day, including curried mussel pie and fresh Bermuda tuna or wahoo, are your best bets. Most of the food is fairly routine, but the chef is especially proud of his Bermuda fish chowder, a tomato-based soup that some locals consider the best in the West End.

10 Mangrove Bay Rd., Somerset Village. ✆ 441/234-0105. Lunch main courses $10–$29; dinner main courses $16–$29. AE, MC, V. Daily 11:30am–4pm and 6:30-10pm. Bus: 7 or 8.

INEXPENSIVE

Freeport Seafood Restaurant ✦ *Value* STEAK & SEAFOOD   Come here for the best locally caught seafood. Somehow this old favorite manages to turn up a fresher catch than its Somerset competitors, and broils it to perfection, a welcome change from the greasy "fish and chips" grub served at the other dockyard spots. There is no great presentation or dramatic flourish to the platters served, but the taste is often delectable, especially the fish platter or one of the broiled Bermuda rockfish dishes, our particular favorite. The menu is less formal—and somewhat less expensive—at lunch than at dinner. During the day, you get the regular chow you'd find almost anywhere, including burgers, salads, pizzas, and steak on the grill. The tasty fish sandwich is usually the star of the lunch menu. In the evening, the fish selection might feature tuna or wahoo. For those who want a good old T-bone, those are on the menu, too. We found the lobster a bit overpriced and overcooked. This restaurant is also an Internet cafe with computers for patrons to use.

At the Royal Naval Dockyard, 1 Freeport Rd. ✆ 441/234-1692. Lunch main courses $9–$27; dinner main courses $14–$35. AE, MC, V. Daily 11:30am–1am. Bus: 7 or 8.

The Frog & Onion Pub BRITISH   In the former 18th-century cooperage (barrel-making factory) of the Royal Naval Dockyard, Frog & Onion is the most traditional British pub in Bermuda. It's "named" for the owners, French-born Jean-Paul Magnin (the Frog) and Bermuda-born Carol West (the Onion). You can sit back with a pint of English lager in the shadows of the cooperage's enormous fireplace. Many folks stay to dine: At lunch there are standard sandwiches, salads, lasagna, and some tasty bar pies. We especially like the beef barley pie with Guinness for a real taste of Bermuda, although you might opt for the shepherd's pie. The dinner menu includes all of the lunchtime choices plus some more delicious European dishes. Your best bet for the evening might be the featured local fish plate. The food is not spectacular, but it is well-prepared and rather hearty fare. Since portions are large, no one leaves hungry.

The Cooperage, at the Royal Naval Dockyard. ✆ 441/234-2900. Lunch sandwiches, salads, and platters $10–$19; dinner main courses $13–$30. MC, V. Mon–Sat 11:30am–4pm and 6–9:30pm; Sun noon–4pm and 5:30–9pm. Bar daily noon–midnight. Closed Mon Dec–Feb. Bus: 7 or 8, or ferry from the City of Hamilton.

4 Southampton Parish

VERY EXPENSIVE

Newport Room ✦✦✦ FRENCH   The Newport Room is unequaled in its sumptuous but subtle decor and succulent French cuisine—it's among the best restaurants in Bermuda. The only local establishment that can compete with it is the Waterlot Inn (which is even more famous than the Newport Room). The Newport, however, is much more formal. The dining room, entirely paneled in teak and rosewood with nautical brass touches, suggests the interior of a yacht. A maitre d' stationed beside a ship's compass greets diners at the entrance, and the service is attentive. In the center of the room are exact miniature replicas of two of the former winning sailboats from the Newport-Bermuda Race.

Settle into a leather armchair and prepare yourself for what just might be your most memorable meal in Bermuda. The regularly changing menu reads like a textbook of modern gourmet cuisine; it might include duck breast with cinnamon-and-fig sauce, or baby veal chops. The kitchen uses the freshest and best ingredients in its carefully prepared, artfully presented dishes. The wine list includes a wide array of international selections, all served in Irish crystal.

At the Fairmont Southampton, 101 South Shore Rd. © **441/238-8000.** Reservations required. Jacket required, tie recommended. Main courses $35–$45. Fixed-price menus $75 for 3 courses, $85 for 4 courses. AE, DC, MC, V. Daily 6:30–10pm. Usually closed Dec to mid-Jan. Bus: 7.

Waterlot Inn ☆☆ INTERNATIONAL/STEAK & SEAFOOD   Less rigidly formal than the Newport, and with a more welcoming staff, this is one of our all-time favorites for a special night out in Bermuda. The service is impeccable, and the culinary repertoire is inventive—doubly impressive given the large number of diners every evening.

About 300 years ago, merchant sailors unloaded their cargo directly into the basement of this historic inn and warehouse. Today, the best way to approach the inn is still by water, and that's precisely what many Bermudians do, mooring their sailing craft in its sheltered cove. Over the years, the inn has attracted such guests as Mark Twain, James Thurber, Eleanor Roosevelt, and Eugene O'Neill. You can enjoy a drink in an upstairs bar, where a classical pianist entertains. After descending a colonial staircase with a white balustrade, you'll be seated in one of three conservatively nautical dining rooms. Each is filled with captain's or Windsor chairs, oil paintings of old clipper ships, and lots of exposed wood. Menu items include well-prepared steaks and beef dishes, each of them grilled and served according to your wishes, along with tasty meals such as foie gras of duck and a savory version of coq au vin simmered in red wine. If none of these meaty entrees appeals to you, many kinds of fresh fish can be grilled, broiled, or blackened, according to your requests.

At the Fairmont Southampton, 101 South Shore Rd. © **441/238-8000.** Reservations recommended. Jacket required for men. Main courses $32–$61. AE, MC, V. Daily 6–10pm. Closed Jan–Feb. Bus: 7.

EXPENSIVE

Bacci ITALIAN   Set on the upper floor of the golf clubhouse, on the manicured grounds of the also-recommended hotel, this restaurant became one of the most vibrant and talked-about Italian restaurants in Bermuda shortly after its inauguration during the post–Hurricane Fabian rebuilding of the Fairmont Southampton Hotel. Its staff describes it as "Italian with passion," thanks to excellent food and a decor that incorporates striking tones of red, black, yellow, and pastels; a bar that's especially busy with espresso and after-dinner-drink lovers late in the evening; and a view that sweeps down over the golf course to the sea. One of the most appealing aspects of this place is the antipasto buffet, which can be approached either as an appetizer ($9 per person) or as a main course ($18 per person). Chef Kim Dean prepares some of the best and most raved-about spaghetti carbonara and lasagna on the island, a sumptuous version of osso buco, several types of simply grilled fresh fish, and her acclaimed versions of rib-eye steaks that are served over beds of risotto. The restaurant's name, incidentally, translates from the Piemontese dialect as "quick and friendly kisses."

Moments Where to Put Together the Perfect Picnic & Where to Enjoy It

The kitchens of many major hotels will prepare a picnic lunch for you, but you need to request it at least a day in advance. On Front Street in the City of Hamilton, you can order sandwiches at a cafe and pick up a bottle of wine or mineral water. If it's a weekday, the best place to buy picnic supplies is the **Hickory Stick** (p. 129).

If you enjoy picnicking and biking, you can do both in Sandys Parish. Start by crossing Somerset Bridge (heading in the direction of Somerset Village), and continue along Somerset Road to **Fort Scaur Park**, where you'll enjoy a panoramic view of Ely's Harbour.

Another ideal picnic location is **Spanish Point Park** in Pembroke, where you will find a series of little coves and beaches. You don't need to go to the trouble of packing a picnic basket—in warm weather, a lunch wagon rolls around every day at noontime. We also love to picnic at one of the island's best beaches, **Warwick Long Bay**.

In the golf clubhouse of the Fairmont Southampton. 101 South Shore Rd. ℂ 441/238-8000. Reservations required. Main courses $21–$26. AE, DC, MC, V. Daily 6-10pm. Bus: 7.

Coconuts *Finds* CARIBBEAN/INTERNATIONAL   If view is important to you, we recommend Coconuts, not only for its scenic vista, but also for its cuisine. It lies between high cliff rocks and a sandy pink beach on the south coast. Alfresco dining here is most romantic, although those breezy nights tend to cool your food before you've finished it.

The restaurant is set in an open-sided dining room, richly paneled with varnished cedar, that's positioned within a few steps of the beach. If you prefer a table directly on the sand, the staff can set one up for you, at a net fee of $85 per person with food and wine included, although sand invariably gets into your shoes. Lunch is nothing special—the usual, burgers, salads, sandwiches, and the like. But at night, the chefs strut their stuff, offering a set menu (which changes daily) full of variety, flavor, taste, and scope, and presented with flair. Freshly grown produce is served with Cajun and West Indian spices, for a "taste of the islands." We can't guarantee what you'll get on any given night here, but the scope is wide enough to appeal to most diners—if you have very obscure food tastes, you'd better call and check.

In the Reefs Hotel, 56 South Rd. ℂ 441/238-0222. Reservations recommended. Lunch main courses $12–$16; set-price 4-course dinner $61 per person. AE, MC, V. Daily noon–3pm and 7–9pm. Bus 7.

Grill 56 BERMUDIAN/INTERNATIONAL   This is the main dining room of the Reefs (p. 82), and is open to nonguests as well. Against a backdrop of typical Bermudian architecture, including solid limestone walls, a finely honed cuisine is presented. The entire menu changes daily, but many dishes, at least the most popular ones, are regularly repeated. This rather formal restaurant opens onto a private beach. Tantalizing appetizers include five-spice roasted duck breast with a ginger-flavored noodle salad, Caribbean shrimp with mango salsa, or a selection from the chilled seafood and sushi raw bar. Fresh soups are made daily, not just the standard Bermuda fish chowder, but such favorites as Tuscan mushroom soup. For your main course, the chefs fly in fresh steamed Maine lobster, or you might opt for the oven-roasted prime rib of beef au jus, truly succulent, and served with buttermilk-mashed potatoes. For dessert, no one can top the blueberry cheesecake with a fruit coulis. You can also order the "world's smallest chocolate mousse parfait."

In the Reefs Hotel, 56 South Rd. (C) **441/238-0222.** Reservations required. Main 4-course fixed-price dinner $55. AE, DC, MC, V. Daily 6:30–8:30pm. Bus: 7.

Whaler Inn ₰ SEAFOOD   This oceanfront restaurant, perched atop a low cliff overlooking rocks and pink sands, is justifiably famous for its seafood. Clusters of sea grapes, Norfolk Island pines, and padded iron armchairs dot its landscaped terraces; and you can watch the sun set over one of the island's most secluded beaches. The panoramic view through the huge windows is the airy restaurant's most prominent feature.

You might begin with baked oysters Rockefeller, Bermuda fish chowder, or something as exotic as roasted pumpkin–potato gnocchi served with roasted sunflower seeds. The special main courses are well-seasoned portions of the daily catch—game fish such as yellowfin tuna, barracuda, shark, wahoo, or dolphin fish (mahimahi). All are excellently prepared, either broiled or sautéed in butter. We like to come here for the hearty pasta and seafood combination served in a zesty tomato-basil sauce. The chef can also cook you a savory platter of mussels marinière that beats out the deep-fried fisherman's platter any day. Desserts are good. Two popular favorites—Key lime cheesecake and a passion fruit tart—will make you want to come back for a second visit.

Live entertainment is provided Tuesday to Sunday.

In the Fairmont Southampton, 101 South Rd. (C) **441/238-8000.** Reservations required. Lunch main courses $12–$19; dinner main courses $26–$42. AE, MC, V. Daily 11am–4pm and 6–10pm. Bus: 7.

MODERATE

Greg's Steakhouse ₰ STEAK & SEAFOOD   This is the island's only real steakhouse, although the chefs prepare other dishes as well, including seafood. They feature only certified Angus beef, and it's not only aged to perfection but also well flavored, perfectly cooked, and tender—the best steaks on the island. The chefs also prepare a delectable rack of lamb. Other dishes likely to please are fresh Bermuda rockfish or pasta primavera. Only the shellfish is exorbitant. All the dishes come with fresh vegetables and a choice of potatoes.

Port Royal Golf Course, Middle Rd., Port Royal. (C) **441/234-6092.** Reservations recommended Sat–Sun. Lunch main courses $14–$33; dinner main courses $25–$80. AE, MC, V. Daily 8–11am, 11:30am–5pm, and 6:30–10pm. Bus 7 or 8.

Henry VIII BRITISH   Set within a stucco-sided, russet-colored building that sits in a prominent position between two of the island's biggest resort hotels, this restaurant feeds and entertains a clientele that's about equally divided between local residents and dining-room refugees from the relatively expensive hotels nearby. There's something that's just a bit cloying about the Tudor theme of the place—waitresses, some of them Scottish, in long dresses of royal purple, a menu that makes bemused references to Henry VIII's ongoing and oft-changing marriage vows, and a timbered and oak-paneled decor with lots of polished brass. But despite any drawbacks (and indeed, many locals appreciate the venue's warmth and the way it emulates an old-fashioned pub in Merrie Olde England), the food is straightforward and a wee bit less expensive than what you'd find within the more glamorous dining rooms of some nearby hotels. The menu is strong on beef dishes, especially steaks, with some pork and fish choices thrown in for variety. Burgers are available at lunch but not at dinner. Some kind of entertainment, usually a vocalist with a keyboard, begins at 9:45pm every night of the week except Tuesday.

52 South Shore Rd. (between the Fairmont Southampton and the Wyndham Bermuda Resort & Spa). ℂ **441/238-1977.** Reservations recommended for dinner. Lunch main courses $7.75–$23; dinner main courses $19–$40; Sun brunch $25 per person. AE, DC, MC, V. Mon–Sat noon–2:30pm and 6–10pm; Sun noon–2:30pm and 6:30–10pm. Bus: 7.

Tio Pepe ITALIAN/SPANISH   Don't let the Spanish name fool you—the cuisine here is predominantly traditional Italian. A few Spanish dishes do appear on the menu, including roast suckling pig. It's fairly straightforward fare: pizzas, pastas, and classic Italian cuisine in generous portions, all with a bit of Mediterranean pizzazz. The kitchen also prepares local fish, plus salmon and lobster, with subtle Italian flavors. We especially like the huge range of hot Bermuda appetizers; the clams steamed in white wine, garlic, and parsley; and the chef's *penne o solo mio,* which is made with pasta, cauliflower, saffron, raisins, anchovies, capers, garlic, and red pepper in a white-wine sauce. Seating is on a wide garden-view terrace and in three indoor dining rooms. The restaurant is convenient to the Fairmont Southampton and Horseshoe Bay Beach. The friendly atmosphere, bountiful food, and prices are right on target.

117 South Rd., Horseshoe Bay. ℂ **441/238-1897.** Reservations recommended. Lunch $13–$25; pizzas and pastas $19–$31; main courses $24–$32. AE, MC, V. May–Sept daily 11:30am–10pm; Oct–Apr daily noon–10pm. Bus 7.

INEXPENSIVE

Lighthouse Tea Room *Finds* BRITISH/CONTINENTAL   Step inside this lace-curtained room for a taste of an old-fashioned tearoom. It's a handy place if you're touring in the Southampton area on the south shore. After you've climbed the winding steps to the famous Gibbs Hill Lighthouse, you'll have worked up an appetite. If you're lunching here, begin with such starters as warm Camembert cheese topped with a mix of wild berries or salmon-stuffed crepes. A vegetable grill is served with fettuccini noodles in a light hoisin dressing, or else you can order a mango, mozzarella, and walnut salad on a bed of fresh greens. Sandwiches include the amusingly named "Bermuda Triangle" (slices of smoked salmon, tuna, and baby shrimp). More substantial dishes include curried lamb pie and codfish croquettes. In the afternoon you can enjoy any number of specialty teas, including mango apple and strawberry. The new owner, Heidi Cowen, is the granddaughter of the last lighthouse keeper who lived here in the 1960s. She too lived in the lighthouse with her grandparents. Ms. Cowen also runs Little Steps Bakery, which produces a range of special gluten-free cakes and breads now available to customers of the Lighthouse.

Gibbs Hill Lighthouse, 68 St. Anne's Rd. ℂ **441/238-8679.** Breakfast $5.25–$12; lunch $5.95–$13. AE, MC, V. Daily 9am–5pm. Bus: 7 or 8.

Mrs. Tea's Victorian Tearoom ⊛ *Finds* BRITISH   Opposite the Port Royal Golf Course, this much-loved tearoom offers the island's most traditional English tea. The tearoom occupies a small white house with black shutters that was originally conceived as a private home. The authentic and somewhat cluttered Victorian decor is prissy enough that you could even invite the Queen of England here for a cuppa. The dainty china goes perfectly with the floral tablecloths. Locals come here for shepherd's pie at lunch—how British can you get? You can also enjoy stuffed sandwiches such as smoked turkey, or a selection of pastries and scones, with your tea. The tearoom is in a Bermuda National Trust property off the Railway Trail. To reach it, turn off Middle Road by the Esso station.

25 Middle Rd. © **441/234-1374.** Lunch $11–$12; afternoon tea with sandwiches and sweets from $16. No credit cards. Tues–Sun noon–5pm. Bus: 7 or 8.

Wickets Brasserie *Kids* INTERNATIONAL   Outfitted like a British cricket club, this brasserie and bistro features a health-conscious breakfast buffet with low-sodium and high-fiber offerings, as well as one of the most comprehensive lunch menus on the island. It's good food—nothing more. You'll probably be satisfied with it if your expectations don't run too high. Standard "family fare" includes deli-style sandwiches, soups, chowders, pastas, salads, and platters such as grilled steaks and veal. The most popular fish dish is grilled grouper with citrus-butter sauce, which has more flavor than the routine steaks and chops on the menu.

The restaurant, on the lower lobby level of the Fairmont Southampton, overlooks the swimming pool and the ocean beyond. Many Bermudians, with kids in tow, come here for a late lunch or a light supper. The informal but traditional restaurant requests only that guests cover their bathing suits with a shirt. A children's menu is available.

In the Fairmont Southampton, 101 South Rd. © **441/238-8000.** Breakfast buffet $14–$20; lunch main courses $12–$18; dinner main courses $18–$20. AE, DC, MC, V. Daily 7am–6pm. Ferry from the City of Hamilton.

5 Warwick Parish

EXPENSIVE

Palms Restaurant *⊛ Moments* AMERICAN/INTERNATIONAL   At the Surf Side Beach Club, one of the best places to be on a summer night in Bermuda is this undeniably romantic spot overlooking the ocean. The Palms serves a delicious menu, and has one of the most user-friendly set of hours on the island, open for breakfast, lunch, and dinner, as well as for afternoon tea and bar snacks. The daily happy hour is 5:30 to 7pm when drink prices are reduced. Breakfast has all the standard choices, but we enjoy the omelets and the buttermilk pancakes. A large choice of appetizers, soups, and salads is offered—everything from oysters Rockefeller to spiny lobster bisque flavored with cognac. When available, poached wahoo is delectably served with a white-wine sauce, capers, and grapes; and the roast baby rack of lamb wafts an enticing aroma of fresh thyme and rosemary. Two classic desserts are the bittersweet chocolate mousse with a raspberry sauce and the bread-and-butter pudding with a spicy rum sauce.

At Surf Side Beach Club, South Rd. © **441/236-7100.** Reservations required. Breakfast main courses $6.50–$7.50; lunch and dinner main courses $27–$42. AE, MC, V. Daily 8–10am, noon–3pm, and 6–9:30pm. Closed Jan to mid-Mar. Bus: 7.

MODERATE

Pawpaws Restaurant & Bar *Value Kids* BERMUDIAN/CONTINENTAL   This family favorite, located about 5km (3 miles) west of the City of Hamilton, offers a varied and unusual menu at reasonable prices. With the aura and ambience of a European bistro, Pawpaws attracts everybody from couples seeking an upscale dinner to

---

Tips **Dressing the Part**

Some of the upscale restaurants in Bermuda ask that men wear a jacket and tie for dinner; some restaurants require a jacket but not a tie. When making reservations, always ask what the dress code is. "Casual but elegant" dress is preferred at most Sunday buffets.

parents with kids. On the walls are murals of papaya trees and other scenes, along with trelliswork and paintings by local artists.

The lunch menu features sandwiches, salads, and the restaurant's signature dish, Pawpaw Montespan (made from green papaya [pawpaws], ground beef, and herbs). In the evening, one of the most popular dishes (and deservedly so) is lobster ravioli in basil-cream sauce with strips of smoked salmon. If you're yearning for island cuisine, sample the red snapper in banana sauce. You'll also find more classic and ordinary dishes, including tender pepper steak in cognac-cream sauce, and lamb kabobs served with mushroom, raisin, and pineapple couscous, topped with a tomato basil sauce.

87 South Rd. ⓒ **441/236-7459.** Reservations recommended. Lunch main courses $10–$21; dinner main courses $18–$30. MC, V. Daily 11:30am-9:45pm. Bar open until 1am. Bus: 7.

6 Paget Parish

EXPENSIVE

Cafe Lido ⓐ MEDITERRANEAN This well-recommended beachfront restaurant consists of an outdoor terrace and an indoor dining room with big windows that fill the room with light. Come here for the location and convenience to Elbow Beach. If you're a serious foodie, you'll find the vittles at Horizons and Cottages tastier. Shades of pale yellow and red predominate, the chairs are comfortable enough to linger in, and the menu is one of the most diverse on the island. We strongly recommend trying the cassoulet of calamari with wine-based red sauce; lobster medallions with lime sauce; seafood casserole with Mediterranean-style red sauce and garlic; a very upscale version of surf and turf (filet steak with half a Bermuda lobster); Angus rib-eye steak (grilled); and roasted lamb. Cafe Lido patrons are also admitted free to the on-site club, The Deep (see "Bermuda After Dark," chapter 10).

In the Elbow Beach Hotel Sea Terrace, 60 South Rd. ⓒ **441/236-9884.** Reservations recommended. Dinner main courses $26–$52. AE, MC, V. Daily 6:30–10:30pm. Bar open until 1am. Bus: 1, 2, or 7.

The Middleton Room ⓐ INTERNATIONAL On a hilltop overlooking 12 hectares (30 acres) of carefully landscaped grounds and a golf course, this popular restaurant lies in a much-expanded building that was originally constructed as a private home in the 17th century. It's a member of the prestigious Relais & Châteaux association of international hotels and restaurants, and it's associated with the clubby and very expensive cottage colony Horizons.

The eclectic cuisine often encompasses influences from France and the Far East. Menus, served only as fixed-price meals, change daily. They depend on the chef's whim and on whatever fish, produce, and meats are fresh and available that day. Artfully arranged sushi might serve as a foil for the European-style main courses. Examples from past (and memorable) meals include osso buco of ostrich, curried lamb in phyllo pastry, venison in port wine sauce, and filets of marlin, snapper, or tuna. Midsummer diners usually appreciate the medley of chilled soups that is one of the restaurant's trademarks. The cellar has won the *Wine Spectator* international award 8 years in a row.

In Horizons and Cottages, South Shore Rd. ⓒ **441/236-0048.** Reservations required. Jacket and tie required. Lunch main courses $14–$20. Fixed-price menu $60. AE, MC, V. Daily 12:30–3pm and 7–9:30pm. Bus: 7.

Sapori ⓐ BERMUDIAN/INTERNATIONAL Casual elegance prevails with alfresco dining offered at Grape Bay Beach Hotel's (p. 83) poolside terrace overlooking the ocean. The name Sapori means "flavor," which you'll find in abundance in its dishes: fresh fish from Bermuda, spicy hot Thai curries, Japanese sushi, and succulent

Italian pastas and pizzas. The bar also serves light meals and sushi. For starters, sample the twice-baked crab soufflé on a bed of mesclun or the pepper-seared salmon flavored with balsamic and avocado oil. Among the main courses, you will rarely go wrong with the pan-fried catch of the day served with shellfish sauce and a saffron risotto. Our pasta favorite is ravioli aragosta (filled with lobster meat and served in a creamy pink sauce). For dessert, try the sticky fig pudding with a butterscotch sauce and vanilla ice cream, or the more sophisticated chocolate mocha tart with caramel sauce and a white chocolate sorbet.

At Grape Bay Beach Hotel, White Sands Rd. (℃ **441/236-7201.** Reservations recommended. Lunch main courses $18–$25; dinner main courses $26–$37. AE, MC, V. Thurs–Sat 11:45am–2:30pm, Sun 11:45am–4pm; Mon–Sat 6–10pm. Bus: 2, 7, or 8.

INEXPENSIVE

Paraquet Restaurant _Value_ BERMUDIAN   This restaurant doesn't even pretend to offer a cuisine as fine as those restaurants already recommended in the parish, but in high-priced Bermuda, it's a bargain. Near a major south-shore traffic junction, this unpretentious restaurant is at the center of an apartment cluster of the same name. From your table, you can see a circular formal flower garden created by the Portuguese owners. The coffee-shop setting—complete with lime-colored Formica—and the menu of substantial home-style Bermudian fare are straight out of the '50s. You'll find one of the island's largest sandwich menus (both hot and cold), as well as omelets, homemade soups (there's always a fish chowder of the day), and salads. You can order mixed platters, which feature various dishes such as turkey breast and crabmeat; grilled dishes like T-bone steak; fried liver and onions; or a roast half-chicken. A main course platter is a meal in itself.

South Rd. (near the Elbow Beach Hotel). (℃ **441/236-9742.** Breakfast special (until 11am) $10; sandwiches $4–$12; main courses $18–$30. MC, V. Daily 9:30am–1:30am. Closed Feb. Bus: 2 or 7.

7 City of Hamilton (Pembroke Parish)

VERY EXPENSIVE

La Coquille 𝒻 MEDITERRANEAN   Set on the eastern edge of downtown Hamilton, on the ground floor of the Underwater Exploration Institute, this is a stylish and occasionally sought-after enclave of fine Mediterranean dining with a Provençal accent. Inside, you'll find two wide-open and airy-looking dining rooms, one positioned just a step or two above the other, a big-windowed view of the sea, a theatrical-looking bar near the entrance, and an expensive-looking mahogany and cherrywood trim. Menu items are the kind of thing that food and dining magazines like to feature. Food varies with the season and the availability of ingredients but might include pan-seared scallops with beechwood-flavored vinaigrette; teriyaki-marinated salmon with pomegranate dressing; mussels flavored with Pernod and five herbs; and seared breast of duck served with duck-meat-stuffed cannelloni. Dessert might include a warm, partially melted chocolate pudding _("fondant au chocolat")_.

19 Crown Lane. (℃ **441/296-6122.** Reservations recommended. Main courses $25–$45. AE, MC, V. Mon–Fri noon–2:15pm; Mon–Sat 6:30–10pm. Bus: Any, to city of Hamilton.

Little Venice CONTINENTAL/ITALIAN   This is one of the most prominent Italian restaurants in Bermuda, a staple that has been here as long as anyone can remember. The owner, Emilio Barberrio (originally from Capri), is justly proud of his

Where to Dine in the City of Hamilton

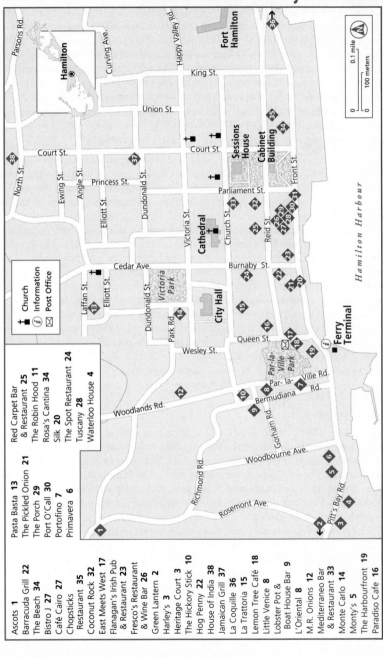

Ascots **1**
Barracuda Grill **22**
The Beach **34**
Bistro J **27**
Café Cairo **27**
Chopsticks
Restaurant **35**
Coconut Rock **32**
East Meets West **17**
Flanagan's Irish Pub
& Restaurant **23**
Fresco's Restaurant
& Wine Bar **26**
Green Lantern **2**
Harley's **3**
Heritage Court **3**
The Hickory Stick **10**
Hog Penny **22**
House of India **38**
Jamaican Grill **37**
La Coquille **36**
La Trattoria **15**
Lemon Tree Café **18**
Little Venice **8**
Lobster Pot &
Boat House Bar **9**
L'Oriental **8**
M.R. Onions **12**
Mediterraneo Bar
& Restaurant **33**
Monte Carlo **14**
Monty's **5**
The Harbourfront **19**
Paradiso Cafe **16**

Pasta Basta **13**
The Pickled Onion **21**
The Porch **29**
Port O'Call **30**
Portofino **7**
Primavera **6**

Red Carpet Bar
& Restaurant **25**
The Robin Hood **11**
Rosa's Cantina **34**
Silk **20**
The Spot Restaurant **24**
Tuscany **28**
Waterloo House **4**

specialties. One star is a savory *casseruola di pesce dello chef,* which consists of a medley of local seafood—including lobster, shrimp, mussels, clams, and several kinds of fish—cooked together with white wine, herbs, and tomatoes. Other choices include flavorful fish chowder, spaghetti with seafood, several veal dishes, and an array of pastas, including superb homemade ravioli stuffed with tomatoes and ricotta. Italian wines are featured, in bottles and (less expensively) in carafes. An abbreviated menu is offered at lunchtime. The downside? Service here leaves much to be desired.

Bermudiana Rd. (between Par-la-Ville Rd. and Woodbourne Ave.). © **441/295-3503.** Reservations recommended. Lunch main courses $14–$27; dinner main courses $42–$65. AE, MC, V. Daily 11:30am–2pm and 6–10pm. Bus: 1, 2, 10, or 11.

Waterloo House ☆ BERMUDIAN/CONTINENTAL

At the edge of Hamilton Harbour, this former private home—now the most famous inn on Bermuda—is a Relais & Châteaux property. Terraced gardens, which descend to the water, are often the setting for waterside buffets. Guests dine by candlelight on the harborfront terrace or in the elegantly appointed, English-style dining room, where a fire roars in the fireplace on nippy evenings.

Some reports suggest that the food has declined in quality, but that's not what we found on recent visits. A discriminating reader from Virginia agreed, saying she found the food "absolutely fantastic—though somewhat expensive." Portions at lunch were so large that she skipped dinner. Waterloo has a dramatic and elegant setting.

You might begin with such appetizers as poached lobster in season or else crusted salmon with a black-olive stuffing. For a main course, opt for such delights as a rack of lamb (perfectly roasted), or else the baked rockfish with real island flavor when an almond and banana crust is added. Another specialty is beef tenderloin in a port wine sauce. You can also order Bermuda lobster as a main course; it's served with jumbo prawns and comes in a white-wine sauce.

100 Pitts Bay Rd. © **441/295-4480.** Reservations required at dinner. Jacket welcomed, tie optional. Lunch main courses $15–$18; dinner main courses $32–$36. Afternoon tea $16. AE, MC, V. Daily 7am–2:30pm (tea 4–5pm), and 7–9:30pm. Bus: 7 or 8.

EXPENSIVE

Ascots ☆ FRENCH/ITALIAN

This restaurant and its tempting Continental menu are relatively undiscovered—but they deserve to be better known. Ascots is set in a spacious house originally built in 1903, and located in a residential neighborhood at the end of a country lane at the edge of the City of Hamilton. The antique porcelain, Queen Anne armchairs, and Welsh pine evoke a chintz-filled English country house. In the summer, diners sit at candlelit tables on the front porch, and sometimes beneath a tent in the garden.

The menu relies on classic techniques and first-rate ingredients. It includes one of the best selections of hot and cold appetizers in the City of Hamilton, ranging from Mediterranean chicken salad with goat cheese, to fresh homemade ravioli filled with crabmeat and served in smoked-salmon-and-spinach cream sauce. Vegetarian dishes are available. Count on the chef's catch of the day, prepared as you like it, or try blackened mahimahi with tomato, pineapple, and lemon compote. If you prefer more traditional dishes, you might find the grilled sirloin steak with port glaze and roasted thyme polenta more to your taste. For dessert, the crepe Garibaldi (warm crepes filled with strawberries and a chocolate-hazelnut sauce, served with fresh berries and crème chantilly) is a good choice. Even more exciting are seasonal berries with Frangelico and chocolate ice cream.

THE TRAVELOCITY GUARANTEE

...THAT SAYS EVERYTHING YOU BOOK WILL BE RIGHT, OR WE'LL WORK WITH OUR TRAVEL PARTNERS TO MAKE IT RIGHT, RIGHT AWAY.

*To drive home the point,
we're going to use the word "right" in every single sentence.*

Let's get right to it. Right to the meat! Only Travelocity guarantees everything about your booking will be right, or we'll work with our travel partners to make it right, right away. Right on!

Here's a picture taken smack dab right in the middle of Antigua, where the Guarantee also covers you.

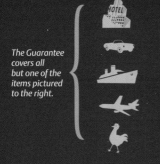

The Guarantee covers all but one of the items pictured to the right.

For example, what if the ocean view you booked actually looks out at a downright ugly parking lot? You'd be right to call – we're there for you. And no one in their right mind would be pleased to learn the rental car place has closed and left them stranded. Call Travelocity and we'll help get you back on the right track.

Now, you may be thinking, "Yeah, right, I'm so sure." That's OK; you have the right to remain skeptical. That is until we mention help is always right around the corner. Call us right off the bat, knowing our customer service reps are there for you 24/7. Righting wrongs. Left and right.

Now if you're guessing there are some things we can't control, like the weather, well you're right. But we can help you with most things – to get all the details in righting,* visit travelocity.com/guarantee.

*Sorry, spelling things right is one of the few things not covered under the Guarantee.

I'd give my right arm for a guarantee like this, although I'm glad I don't have to.

travelocity
You'll never roam alone.

©2006 Travelocity.com LP. GST# 2056372-50.

> **⸤Tips⸥ A Note on Hotel Dining**
>
> In high season (Apr–Nov), many resort hotels require guests to take the Modified American Plan (MAP), or half-board arrangement of breakfast and dinner. To spare guests the routine of eating in the same dining room every night, some hotels offer a "dine around" program. It allows you to dine at other hotels on your own meal plan or at somewhat reduced prices. Ask about dine-around arrangements when booking your room.

In the Royal Palms Hotel, 24 Rosemont Ave. ℂ 441/295-9644. Reservations recommended. Lunch main courses $17–$24; dinner main courses $34–$38. AE, MC, V. Sun–Fri noon–2:30pm; daily 6:30–10pm. Bus: 1, 2, 10, or 11.

Barracuda Grill ⸙ SEAFOOD   One of Hamilton's more stylish and contemporary-looking restaurants occupies a pair of dining rooms one floor above street level of a building in downtown Hamilton. Established in April 2002, it boasts an ultracontemporary lighting design, with dozens of hanging lamps that shed the kind of light that makes virtually everyone look attractive. Amid walls sheathed with unusual modern paintings, you can order a roster of mostly fish-based dishes that change with whatever comes in from local fishermen on the day of your arrival. The best examples include a shrimp "sundae," composed of jumbo prawns arranged in a martini glass and layered with vegetarian chili, Monterey Jack cheese, and olives; tartare of tuna with spicy mango slices; oysters Rockefeller; grilled rack of lamb with wild mushroom risotto; and a platter piled high with grilled rockfish and steamed lobster served with braised fennel and beurre blanc or "white butter" sauce. The most expensive and elegant item on the menu is the "ultra exclusive" Kobe beef and foie gras burger.

5 Burnaby Hill. ℂ **441/292-1609.** Reservations recommended. Lunch main courses $15–$21; dinner main courses $25–$43. AE, MC, V. Mon–Fri noon–2:30pm; daily 5:30–10pm. Bus: 1, 2, 10, or 11.

Café Cairo EGYPTIAN/INTERNATIONAL/LEBANESE/MOROCCAN   This restaurant's success is proof of Bermuda's appreciation of well-prepared, exotic food and its flair for drama. It's the best venue on the island for the savory, sometimes spicy food of the Middle East, with a decor that evokes Arabian nights. That includes elaborately carved doors and window screens imported from the souks of Egypt, a valuable collection of early-19th-century antiques hauled in from Cairo, copper tables whose reflective surfaces are mirrors, and the kind of diffused lighting that seems to well up from behind the chairs, tables, and chests. Enjoy beer from Egypt or wine from Lebanon as accompaniments for good-tasting food such as grilled shrimp salads; whole red snapper prepared with Moroccan spices; tagines loaded with savory chunks of marinated lamb; harira soup; vegetable or lamb-stocked versions of couscous; baba ghanouj and hummus; and shish kebabs that are cooked on charcoal braziers placed directly on your table. There might occasionally be entertainment from one or a trio of Middle Eastern dancers, each veiled, charming, and evocative of the harem of a desert lord.

95 Front St. ℂ **441/295-5155.** Reservations recommended. Main courses $19–$49. AE, MC, V. Daily noon–3am. Lunch daily noon–4pm; dinner daily 6pm–midnight.

The Harbourfront ⸙⸙ ITALIAN/SEAFOOD/SUSHI   Front Street was once known only for pubs and fish and chips shops, but this restaurant has challenged its neighbors. It offers innovative Continental dishes and the town's best selection of sushi—no longer does fish have to be deep-fried in oil left over from last week. The cuisine fairly bursts with flavors and aromas. Even if some dishes aren't as successful as others, the kitchen should be applauded for trying to wake up the City of Hamilton's sleepy taste buds.

For starters, the inevitable Bermudian fish chowder appears, but miso soup is also available. Of the pasta specialties, our pick is lobster and crab served open-faced with a garlic white-wine sauce. Fresh fish comes in a variety of ways, including pan-fried, broiled, baked, or Cajun style. You might also try the shrimp and vegetable tower— vegetable ragout surrounded by grilled jumbo shrimp served in champagne-leek sauce. Shellfish, such as lobster, will make your bill soar. The restaurant also offers poultry and meat, including a well-prepared sliced breast of duck served in foie gras tempura. Pastries and cakes are prepared daily, and a wide variety of homemade Italian ice cream is always available.

The spacious restaurant is on the second floor of an old building across from the ferry terminal in the center of town. There's limited seating on the balcony, which juts out over the street and is quite popular in fair weather.

21 Front St. ℂ **441/295-4207.** Reservations recommended. Lunch main courses $15–$23; dinner main courses $23–$80; Mon sushi buffet $24. AE, MC, V. Mon–Sat 11:45am–4pm and 6–10pm. Bus: 1, 2, 10, or 11.

Mediterraneo Bar & Ristorante 🍴🍴 MEDITERRANEAN   The island's hottest restaurant, Mediterraneo, is a chic dining enclave and fashionable meeting place for those who enjoy fine food and wine. Franco Caparra is the mastermind behind this eatery, where flavor is paramount, and chefs take inspiration from Italy, the Middle East, the Greek Islands, and everything in between. Winning appetizers include a chilled Andalusian gazpacho or baked scallops with apple-wood smoked bacon. Our favorite pasta is linguine with an array of shellfish simmered in white wine and fresh parsley. Also try the seared duck breast with apple, Cointreau, and foie gras. The atmosphere is inviting—golden yellow walls, wooden furniture, and blue accents— and the upstairs outdoor dining area is a prized setting for a tasty meal.

39 Church St. ℂ **441/296-5277.** Reservations required. Lunch main courses $9–$18; dinner main courses $15–$29. AE, MC, V. Mon–Fri 11am–3pm and 5–11:45pm; Sat 5pm–midnight; Sun 5–11pm. Bus: 7 or 8.

Monte Carlo 🍴 CONTINENTAL/ITALIAN/MEDITERRANEAN   This cheery restaurant celebrates the cuisine of southern France and Italy. Booths and banquettes in the outer dining room sit beneath a local artist's impressions of the countryside around Monaco; seating in the main dining room centers on a brick-sided fireplace. The chefs prepare the best bouillabaisse in the City of Hamilton; using Atlantic seafood, they achieve the savory style that's typical of Marseilles. One of the better dishes is filet of tuna marinated in oil and herbs and grilled over charcoal. The rack of lamb is tender and well seasoned with Provençal herbs. Classic lamb chops appear with the flavoring of the Côte d'Azur, and veal scaloppini is sautéed and served with sun-dried tomatoes and peppers on angel-hair pasta.

9 Victoria St. (behind City Hall). ℂ **441/295-5453.** Reservations recommended. Lunch main courses $10–$23; dinner main courses $21–$36. AE, MC, V. Mon–Fri noon–2:30pm; daily 6–11pm. Bus: 1, 2, 10, or 11.

The Pickled Onion 🍴🍴 INTERNATIONAL   In a former liquor warehouse overlooking Hamilton Harbour, this is a good, reasonably priced dining choice and after-dark venue. The menu is satisfying, though not memorable. You might begin with Caribbean seafood salad, loaded with calamari, shrimp, fresh mussels, and other local fish, all in a basil vinaigrette. Angus beef, cut and trimmed in-house, is the chef's signature dish; it's tender and cooked to your specifications, accompanied by steak-cut potatoes and zesty peppercorn sauce. Prime rib, sizzling pizza, and some of the island's best fish chowder are regularly featured.

The balcony opens onto Front Street. On Wednesday, Harbor Night, the busiest night of the week, the street is closed off and the scene becomes a festive minicelebration, with street performers and vendors setting the tone (May–Oct). There is live entertainment 7 nights a week during high season.

53 Front St. ℂ **441/295-2263**. Reservations recommended Wed and Fri–Sat. Lunch main courses $13–$26; dinner main courses $15–$30. AE, DC, MC, V. Sun–Thurs 11am–1am; Fri–Sat 11am–2am. Closed Christmas Day. Bus: 1, 2, 10, or 11.

MODERATE

Bistro J CONTINENTAL   Set on a narrow, steeply sloping alleyway (Chancery Lane) that runs uphill from Front Street, and outfitted in cozy tones of ocher and mustard, this restaurant's tavern-like setting somehow evokes the Middle Ages. The menu is posted on an oversized chalkboard at one end of the establishment's only room. Depending on the season and the whims of the chef, it might include herb-crusted salmon with wasabi mash, beef kebabs with jasmine rice and béarnaise sauce, and penne with shrimp, spinach, chile powder, and blue cheese. The chef's specialty is marinated, char-grilled loin of pork with crisp potato pancakes and caramelized Bermuda onions. The kitchen also does savory pastas, and there is a large wine selection, most of it reasonably priced.

102 Chancery Lane. ℂ **441/296-8546**. Reservations recommended. Main courses $10–$21. DC, MC, V. Mon–Fri noon–2:30pm; daily 6–10pm. Bus: 1, 2, 10, or 11.

East Meets West ✧ CHINESE/INDIAN/MEDITERRANEAN   At this restaurant and bistro, the East truly meets the West—the cuisine is globally inspired. Culinary influences range from Asia to California. An appetizer such as cold Mediterranean tuna with potato salad sounds simple but is a well-flavored entry into a meal. From the Bayou country of Louisiana comes a savory jambalaya served atop Cajun rice. The kettle of spicy rice noodles, with a Malaysian accent, is stir-fried. Indian rotis are filled with lamb curry, and chicken breast is well seasoned and served with fresh broccoli. The chef relies heavily on such ingredients as lime juice, coconut milk, jalapeños, coriander, garlic, and, of course, lemon grass.

27 Bermudiana Arcade. ℂ **441/295-8580**. Reservations recommended. Main courses $8–$16. MC, V. Mon–Sat 7:30am–10pm. Bus: 2, 8, 10, or 11.

Flanagan's Irish Pub & Restaurant INTERNATIONAL   Flanagan's occupies a prime position on Front Street, immediately across the street from the spot where cruise ships float at anchor during their Bermuda sojourns. Don't judge the place by what you'll find on the street level, where pool tables and at least seven big-screen TVs broadcast up to three different international sporting events at a time, as pinball and automated poker games blare away in the corners. Try to get a seat in the upstairs dining room or on the panoramic veranda. Flanagan's is not known for culinary distinction except in one category: It serves the best fish chowder in Bermuda. At other places, fish chowder is sometimes a bland dish, tasting like boiled fish in milk, but at Flanagan's, the dish has zest and flavor.

That charbroiled 8-ounce sirloin that appears on your plate tastes even more delectable when served with a zesty peppercorn sauce. If you're not a meat eater, opt for the daily changing menu of fresh fish, which will be grilled to perfection.

In the Emporium Building, 69 Front St. ℂ **441/295-8299**. Main courses $11–$23. AE, MC, V. Daily 11:30am–10pm; bar 11am–1am (happy hour 5–7pm). Bus: 7 or 11.

Fresco's Restaurant & Wine Bar ☞ MEDITERRANEAN   Nestled in an early-1900s building with a vaulted ceiling and thick stone walls, this cozy spot feels very much like a European wine cellar. We find dining and drinking wine here to be less boisterous and more satisfying than at the Hog Penny or the Pickled Onion. A trellis-covered courtyard in back holds a handful of tables for alfresco dining. Oenophiles will appreciate the selection of more than 160 different wines from around the world. The dress code is casual and the atmosphere is relaxed. The menu changes monthly. The specialty is the fresh catch of the day—perhaps mahimahi, tuna, or wahoo—which can be seared, grilled, or pan-fried. Another delectable option is sea scallops framed with potato and basil dumplings. Whenever possible, local flavors such as papaya, cassava, and loquats are used. One of the best desserts on Bermuda is Fresco's chocolate mousse cake, freshly baked and served warm with vanilla ice cream and fresh-mint custard sauce.

Chancery Lane (between Reid and Front sts.). ℂ **441/295-5058**. Reservations recommended. Lunch main courses $10–$18; dinner main courses $19–$29. AE, MC, V. Mon–Fri noon–2:30pm; Mon–Sat 6:30–10:30pm; wine cellar 5pm–1am. Bus: 1, 2, 10, or 11.

Harley's MEDITERRANEAN   The food at this popular place used to be merely safe and predictable, but now it exhibits some flair, making this restaurant a worth-while choice even if you aren't a Hamilton Princess hotel guest. In warm weather, out-door tables sit near the swimming pool, creating the effect of a flowering terrace on the Italian Riviera.

People who are shopping in the City of Hamilton for the day often drop by for lunch, when there's a large selection of salads. Our favorite is the classic Caesar with grilled *goujons* (slices) of grouper. The catch of the day is available grilled, and there are burgers galore, including one served "topless." Pizzas are also featured, and one part of the menu is designed just for kids. The dinner menu is significantly better, with a choice of pastas—the best is grilled salmon filets on linguine. We also recom-mend the prime rib, tuna, salmon, and rockfish. Many of the main dishes conjure up thoughts of sunny Italy. Also delicious are the beef tenderloin with shrimp, stuffed chicken breast served with shiitake mushrooms, and rack of lamb.

In the Fairmont Hamilton, 76 Pitts Bay Rd. ℂ **441/295-3000**. Reservations recommended at dinner. Lunch main courses $17–$27; dinner main courses $22–$45. AE, MC, V. Daily 7:30–10:30am; Mon–Sat noon–2:30pm; Sun 12:30–3:30pm; daily 6–10pm. Bus: 7 or 8.

Heritage Court AMERICAN/BERMUDIAN   Inside the Fairmount Hamilton, this is a good choice for anything from a late breakfast to a light lunch, perhaps after-noon tea or a rib-sticking dinner. It gets rather festive in the evening, when live piano music is a feature (4:30–6:30pm), and the skilled bartender cranks out rum punches. There's also an excellent selection of single-malt whiskies along with both wine and champagne sold by the glass. Most people come here for the food, though, which includes such specialties as charbroiled filet of beef with a sweet butter and chipotle glaze with arugula-stuffed potatoes. Perhaps you'll opt for the chef's daily pasta spe-cial, or else pan-roasted salmon with a tomato mushroom ragout with a brandy lob-ster and brandy reduction. Appetizers are tangy and tasty, especially the Bloody Mary prawn cocktail or the sweet chile and garlic-flavored pork ribs. Every day a different special is featured at lunch, perhaps tandoori rockfish with saffron Basmati rice and banana chutney. At lunch you can also enjoy Bermuda fish chowder, delicious club sandwiches, and even spiny lobster burgers.

76 Pitts Bay Rd. (C) **441/295-3000.** Breakfast $16; salads and sandwiches $11–$21; afternoon teas $6; dinner main courses $17–$32. AE, DC, MC, V. Daily 10:30am–1am. Bus: 7 or 8.

La Trattoria ITALIAN   This family-oriented restaurant is tucked away in a narrow alley 2 blocks north of the City of Hamilton's harborfront. There's not a single cutting-edge or glamorous thing about it, and that's just what the loyal regulars like. The decor is straight out of old Naples, with a wood-burning pizza oven (the only one in Hamilton) and hanging Chianti bottles. The attentive, if somewhat harried, waitstaff serves generous portions of rather standard, well-flavored Italian food. You'll find 14 kinds of pizza, and the kitchen is happy to create variations for you. Pastas include lasagna, spaghetti *pescatore,* and angel hair with shrimp, pesto, and sun-dried tomatoes. Veal can be ordered parmigiana style or as scaloppine *al limone,* and there's a revolving array of fresh fish. If you're very demanding of your Italian cuisine, you'll fare better at Little Venice (p. 118).

23 Washington Lane (in the middle of the block bordered by Reid, Church, Burnaby, and Queen sts.). (C) **441/295-1877.** Reservations recommended. Pizzas $14–$16; lunch main courses $9.50–$20; dinner main courses $16–$28. AE, MC, V. Mon–Sat 11:30am–3:30pm and 5:30–10pm (to 10:30pm in summer). Bus: 1, 2, 10, or 11.

Lobster Pot & Boat House Bar 🐟🐟 SEAFOOD   For standard island dishes, this traditional favorite one-ups its neighbors M. R. Onions and Hog Penny. Near the Hamilton Princess Hotel, within a 5-minute drive of the heart of the City of Hamilton, this is one of the most consistently popular restaurants on the island—a fixture since 1973. The Lobster Pot's cedar plank walls sport brass and bamboo trim, and such underwater touches as fishing nets, branches of coral, and sea fans. There's a bar near the entrance if you want a before-dinner drink, and a dining room behind it. Menu items include both Maine and spiny Caribbean lobster, each prepared seven different ways. Fish sandwiches and platters of hogfish, wahoo, tuna, and rockfish are prepared any way you want; we prefer them grilled with amandine, banana, or lemon-butter sauce. The best starter is a cup or bowl of steaming Bermuda fish chowder. It's savory brown and enhanced with sherry peppers and shots of black rum. If you like it, you won't be alone—visitors haul quarts of the stuff (frozen) back to North America.

6 Bermudiana Rd. (C) **441/292-6898.** Reservations recommended. Lunch main courses $15–$32; dinner main courses $24–$45; lobster $27–$72. MC, V. Mon–Fri 11:30am–3pm; Mon–Sat 5:30–11pm; Sun 6–11pm (closing time can vary). Bus: 1, 2, 10, or 11.

L'Oriental 🌟 ASIAN   Located in the same building as Little Venice (p. 118), L'Oriental is a pan-Asian restaurant with a penchant for gracefully mixing cuisines as diverse as those of Malaysia, Thailand, Japan, and China. The restaurant is situated in a mahogany-and-stone-lined room with bridges, a pagoda, and lots of Oriental art. Within the efficiently organized space, you'll find an oyster, salmon, sushi, and caviar bar; and a teppanyaki table where a team of Japan-trained chefs prepares food on a super-hot grill right in front of you. Since L'Oriental prides itself on the variety of its all-Asian cuisine, no one will mind if you "fuse" together a meal from the far corners of the world's biggest continent. Tuesday night features a winning all-Chinese sampler menu, with tastings from most of the selections on the menu, available for $28 per person. The cuisine is reliable and good, without ever rising to the ranks of sublime. L'Oriental is a good choice for vegetarians and the health conscious. Most dishes are at the lower end of the price range listed below.

32 Bermudiana Rd. (above Little Venice restaurant). ℭ **441/296-4477**. Reservations recommended. Lunch main courses $7–$28; dinner main courses $19–$44. AE, MC, V. Mon–Fri 11:30am–2pm; daily 6–10pm. Bus: 7 or 11.

M. R. Onions *(Kids)* AMERICAN/BERMUDIAN   The name of this popular restaurant and bar, a chicken-and-ribs kind of place, is a colloquialism: Bermudians are known as onions, and "M. R." stands for "'em are," or "they are." The restaurant resembles an Edwardian-era bar, with potted palms, leaf-green walls, and brass and oak trim. Caricatures of many Bermudians hang on the walls. If you go early, plan to have a drink at the large, rectangular bar that fills most of the front room. During happy hour (daily 5–7pm), it's a favorite rendezvous for local office workers. The bar has a cybercafe where you can surf the Web or check e-mail while enjoying a drink. The charge is $10 for the first hour and $5 for each additional hour.

Both the bar and the dining room serve well-prepared meals that are favorites with locals and visitors alike (especially families). Specialties include the house onion soup and fresh fish—including tuna, wahoo, rockfish, and mahimahi—that can be charbroiled, pan-fried, or served with slivered almonds or spicy Cajun seasoning. Tasty barbecued chicken, ribs, burgers, and steak (no-fuss meals popular with kids) are also available. Maybe you'll even have enough room left for mud pie, cheesecake, "fudgy-wudgy" chocolate cake, or another creation from the dessert trolley. Meals here are generally satisfying but hardly memorable. There's a nonsmoking dining room, much appreciated by families because smoking is allowed in many of Bermuda's restaurants.

11 Par-la-Ville Rd. ℭ **441/292-5012**. Lunch $11–$25; dinner main courses $18–$28, 3-course early-bird dinner (5–6:15pm) $25. AE, MC, V. Daily lunch noon–5pm; dinner 5–10pm. Bar daily 11:30am–1am (happy hour daily 5–7pm). Bus: 1, 2, 10, or 11.

The Porch INTERNATIONAL   Lined with bricks and aged paneling, this warmly decorated restaurant occupies a century-old building. As the restaurant's name implies, it boasts a porch with a sweeping view over the City of Hamilton's harbor, plus a wide outdoor terrace for dining in nice weather. There's also an English-style pub. Food is available throughout, even in the pub-style areas.

The menu offers routine fare, with an emphasis on meat, including prime sirloin steak (10 oz.), prime roast rib of beef with Yorkshire pudding, and steak with shrimp. Lunch features sandwiches, salads, fresh fish, crab cakes, burgers, and oysters. It's all quite competently prepared and straightforward. This is a nice place to just drop by for a drink and soak up the atmosphere, but don't expect too much. Navigate the stairs carefully as you climb up from Front Street, and be even more careful as you come down after having a drink or two.

93 Front St. (between Burnaby and Parliament sts.). ℭ **441/292-4737**. Reservations recommended. Lunch main courses $12–$21; dinner main courses $23–$31. AE, MC, V. Mon–Sat 11am–10:30pm. Bus: 1, 2, 10, or 11.

Port O'Call STEAK & SEAFOOD   Housed in a cedar- and brass-trimmed room reminiscent of an old-fashioned yacht, this restaurant specializes in fresh local fish, four different preparations of lobster, and steaks. If you're fond of lobster, consider the curried version. Other seafood choices include grilled shrimp and blackened scallops, and Bermuda yellowfin tuna with salsa. New menu items include rack of lamb. A molten chocolate cake is the dessert specialty. During the off season, if business is slow, the place might close early, so call ahead to check if you're dining late. Port O'Call is more intimate and cozy than Primavera and Red Carpet (see below), and we prefer it for that reason. The food is also slightly better.

87 Front St. ℂ **441/295-5373**. Reservations recommended at dinner. Lunch main courses $10–$19; dinner main courses $22–$30. Lobster $29–$58. AE, MC, V. Mon–Fri noon–2:30pm; daily 6–11pm. Bus: 1, 2, 10, or 11.

Primavera ITALIAN   Tired of the traditional steak and seafood served at most City of Hamilton restaurants? Long a staple on the dining scene, Primavera offers the zesty flavors of Italy, from regions ranging from Rome to Sicily, and even some Sardinian dishes. We won't say that this has the best Italian food in the City of Hamilton, because many diners prefer Little Venice or Tuscany. But what you get here is retro fare that would have suited the Rat Pack. Savory appetizers come hot or cold and range from fresh oysters to fresh mussels served in a zesty marinara sauce. For your main course, opt for the penne sautéed with Gorgonzola cheese and walnuts, or the tenderloin of beef in a peppercorn sauce. Our favorite main dish is the *zuppa di pesce alla Livornese,* a savory kettle of clams, mussels, jumbo shrimp, and fish filets with fresh tomatoes, wine, and garlic sauce served in a sizzling cast-iron pan. Top off your meal with an espresso or a frothy cappuccino. The service is impeccable.

In Hamilton West, 69 Pitts Bay Rd. (between Front St. and the Fairmont Hamilton). ℂ **441/295-2167**. Reservations recommended. Lunch main courses $9–$23; dinner main courses $17–$30. AE, MC, V. Mon–Fri 11:45am–3pm; daily 6:30–10pm. Bus: 7 or 8.

Red Carpet Bar & Restaurant FRENCH/INTERNATIONAL/ITALIAN   In a 150-year-old building, Red Carpet serves up French and Italian dishes despite its English pub–style ambience. This place does a thriving lunch business, thanks to the many offices nearby. After work, the dimly lit bar is a popular place for people to relax with a beer. Lunch offerings include sandwiches, cold platters, and a few hot dishes such as pan-fried fish (including Bermuda tuna and wahoo). Dinners feature a wider array—veal scaloppine, veal Marsala, seafood kettle, filet mignon, New York strip sirloin, and a variety of pasta dishes. Primavera, Little Venice, and especially Tuscany serve better Italian food, but at slightly higher prices. What you get here is quite good, familiar fare.

In the Armoury Building, 37 Reid St. ℂ **441/292-6195**. Reservations recommended. Lunch main courses $12–$26; dinner main courses $15–$28. AE, DC, MC, V. Mon–Sat 11:30am–3pm and 6:30–9:45pm; bar to 1am. Bus: 1, 2, 10, or 11.

Silk ✸✸✸ THAI   With an authentic cuisine sometimes based on recipes from the old Kingdom of Siam, a team of chefs from the Shangri-La Hotel in Bangkok dazzle local palates with the stormy flavors of their home country. Evocative aromas and subtle blends of herbs and spices characterize the cuisine. Start with a prawns and coconut wrap or a duck and mango salad. The curries, especially one made with chicken breast in a green curry coconut milk sauce, are exceptional. In addition to a number of spicy rice and noodle dishes, you can order such delights as stir-fried duck breast with baby corn chili and basil sauce or else marinated pan-fried quail in a soy sauce laced with cilantro and garlic. Our favorite specialty is the spicy steamed filet of red snapper served on a banana leaf and topped with a ginger and chile sauce.

Master Building, 55 Front St. ℂ **441/295-0449**. Reservations recommended. Main courses $17–$26. AE, MC, V. Mon–Fri noon–2:30pm; daily 6–10pm. Bus: 1, 2, 10, or 11.

Tuscany ✸ ITALIAN   When local chefs have a night off, they often dine at this popular local eatery, which serves the best pizzas and the best Italian food in the City of Hamilton—and that's including Little Venice (p. 118). The decor is upscale with an air of sophistication. If the weather's right, there's seating on the balcony, with panoramic views of the main street and its harbor. The friendly waiters always seem willing to advise about what's good that evening. Try the grilled portobello mushroom with garlic, olive oil, parsley, and zucchini; or veal scaloppine sautéed with ginger, white wine, and artichokes. Fish specialties are *pesce del giorno* (served grilled, pan-fried, or sautéed in white-wine sauce). Veal is imported frozen and available almost any way you like it. Other tempting selections include the succulent homemade pastas.

95 Front St. ✆ 441/292-4507. Reservations recommended. Lunch main courses $13–$22; dinner main courses $14–$28. AE, MC, V. Mon–Fri 11:45am–2:30pm; Mon–Sat 6:30–10:30pm. Bus: 1, 2, or 10.

INEXPENSIVE

The Beach BERMUDIAN/BRITISH   To escape the routine of dining aboard ship, an international crowd of visitors flocks to this eatery across from the cruise-ship docks. Because of the wild party atmosphere often generated here, its self-proclaimed motto is "The Shame of Front Street." It's one of the most casual and laid-back places in the City of Hamilton. Sports fans watch the giant TV, others enjoy the gaming machines, and others dine at picnic tables. From Monday to Thursday, there is happy hour (4–7pm). Pub fare is the order of the day, and most patrons seem to order big, juicy hamburgers. Local fish is available seared in a pan or deep-fried. Sandwiches and tacos round out the bill of fare. At the bar you can sample Bermuda's famous "Dark and Stormy" (black rum and ginger beer). This is a food pit stop—nothing special— but because of its location, it attracts a lot of attention.

103 Front St. ✆ 441/292-0219. Main courses $8–$17. MC, V. Daily 10am–3am. Bus: 1 or 2.

Chopsticks Restaurant ⊛ CHINESE/THAI   Sooner or later, that craving for Chinese food rears its head. Although it's off the beaten track at the eastern end of the City of Hamilton, Chopsticks offers Bermuda's best Chinese and Thai food, including spicy soup, tangy pork ribs, and seafood. The chef specializes in Szechuan, Hunan,

---

⸨Kids⸩ Family-Friendly Restaurants

Bailey's Ice Cream & Food D'Lites Restaurant (p. 135)   Bailey's is a great place to take the kids for some all-natural ice cream on a hot, sunny day. They also serve sandwiches if you're looking for more than just a snack.

Café Gio (p. 136)   What kid wouldn't be drawn to this colorful cafe with its selection of pizzas *and* an ice-cream parlor on the premises?

M. R. Onions (p. 126)   M. R. Onions is one of the best family restaurants in the City of Hamilton. Everybody loves the barbecued chicken, ribs, and steak, and the array of burgers will please even the fussiest kids.

Rosa's Cantina (p. 132)   This house of chili, burritos, fajitas, nachos, tacos, and enchiladas in the City of Hamilton has no equal on the island. The kids get balloons, as well as paper and crayons to keep them busy once they're seated.

Wickets Brasserie (p. 116)   The children's menu at this popular spot in the Fairmont Southampton makes this a great place to take the kids. If you arrive before 6:30pm, kids can order dinner from the lower-priced lunch menu.

Thai, and Cantonese dishes, with an emphasis on fresh vegetables and delicate sauces. We love the excellent jade chicken, with spears of broccoli, mushrooms, and water chestnuts in a mild Peking wine sauce. Peking duck (served only for two) must be ordered 24 hours in advance. The best Thai dish is green curry chicken (chicken breast strips simmered with onions and bamboo shoots and served with fresh basil, coconut milk, and green-curry paste); it can be prepared mild, spicy, or hot. Most of the dishes are the standard ones you'd find in any North American Chinese restaurant, including sweet-and-sour chicken, beef in oyster sauce, and shrimp in lobster sauce. Some dishes, including the duck in red curry, have real flair. Vegetarians will find a haven here.

88 Reid St. ☎ **441/292-0791.** Reservations recommended. Lunch main courses $6–$13; dinner main courses $13–$30. AE, MC, V. Mon–Fri noon–2:30pm; daily 5–11pm. Bus: 1, 2, 10, or 11.

Coconut Rock INTERNATIONAL/SUSHI   This lively, informal eatery in the center of the City of Hamilton is both a drinking and a dining destination. German-born Christian Herzog presides over a main restaurant and two popular bars where music videos play. The place is a bit of a discovery and not likely to be overrun. Your best bet for dinner is the fish of the day, most often pan-seared and served in lemon-butter sauce with potatoes and vegetables. Spicy linguine and tiger shrimp in spicy tomato sauce are two of our favorites. Chicken quesadillas are a fast-moving item, as are Buffalo chicken wings in honey and hot sauce. Drinks are discounted during the daily happy hour (5–7pm).

The restaurant recently added a sushi bar, Yashi, with one of the widest and best selections in Bermuda, including such exotica as flying-fish eggs and wahoo.

13 Reid St. ☎ **441/292-1043.** Reservations recommended Sat–Sun. Lunch main courses $11–$22; dinner main courses $13–$25. AE, MC, V. Mon–Sat 11:30am–2:30pm; daily 6–10:30pm. Bus: 1, 2, 10, or 11.

Green Lantern *(Value* INTERNATIONAL   This unpretentious restaurant resembles an upscale diner and is a great value in the often-expensive City of Hamilton; it is a good place to fill up, but not a prime spot for collecting recipes for *Gourmet* magazine. The limited menu changes every day, but you'll always find fresh fish, roasted chicken, and roast beef. The menu might also feature meatloaf and pork chops, lamb chops and stewed oxtail, or curried chicken and steak. No liquor is served, but you can bring your own bottle. The setting is a century-old house about a mile west of the city limits of Hamilton; the outside is painted—you guessed it—a pale shade of green.

Serpentine Rd. (at Pitts Bay Rd.). ☎ **441/295-6995.** Main courses $11–$19. MC, V. Mon–Tues and Thurs–Sat 6am–9pm; Wed 9am–3pm. Closed 1st 2 weeks in Mar. Bus: 1, 2, 10, or 11.

The Hickory Stick DELI/LIGHT BITES   Near the Hamilton Princess, The Hickory Stick is the most popular delicatessen and takeout restaurant in the city. It serves 1,000 customers a day, including lots of office workers. Although one section seems like a coffee shop (with scones, doughnuts, and morning coffee), most customers come here for overstuffed sandwiches and takeout meals. Offerings include steaming portions of chicken Parmesan and fish cakes. Even more popular are the salads, sandwiches, and hot dogs, all of which can be wrapped up for a picnic—the staff provides paper napkins and plastic cutlery on request. The restaurant has added a sushi bar. Advance telephone orders are accepted—a good idea if you don't want to wait.

2 Church St. (at Bermudiana Rd.). ☎ **441/292-1781.** Salads $4–$6; sandwiches and platters $4–$9. No credit cards. Mon–Fri 6:30am–4pm (closing times vary). Bus: 1, 2, 10, or 11.

Hog Penny BERMUDIAN/BRITISH   A bit tired these days, Hog Penny remains Bermuda's most famous and enduring pub, serving draft beer and ale to each new generation of mainlanders who head here, probably on the advice of their grandparents. The dark paneled rooms are decorated in the British style, with old fishing and farm tools, bentwood chairs, and antique mirrors. At lunch you can order pub specials (including shepherd's pie) or tuna salad and the like. The kitchen prepares a number of passable curries, including chicken and lamb. Fish and chips, and steak-and-kidney pie are the perennial favorites, and they are comparable to what you'd find in a London pub. Dinner is more elaborate; the menu might include a whole lobster, a fresh fish of the day (perhaps Bermuda yellowfin tuna), and excellent Angus beef. The food is better upstairs at the Barracuda Grill (p. 121). There's nightly entertainment from 9:30pm to 1am; dress is casual.

5 Burnaby Hill. © 441/292-2534. Reservations recommended. Lunch main courses $12–$21; dinner main courses $15–$28; early-bird dinner (5:30–7pm) $27. AE, MC, V. Mon–Sat 11:30am–3pm; daily 5:30–10pm; pub hours daily 11:30am–1am. Bus: 1, 2, 10, or 11.

House of India ⟨R⟩ *(Finds)* INDIAN   This is the only Indian restaurant in Bermuda, and the only one in the City of Hamilton itself. As such, it's viewed as something of a dining oddity. Within a dining room that's decorated with Indian paintings and woodcarvings, on the northern edge of the City of Hamilton, you'll enjoy a menu that specializes in the slow-cooked, often-spicy cuisine of Northern India. There are a wide variety of vegetarian, beef, lamb, and chicken dishes, prepared to whatever degree of spiciness you request. Our favorite dishes on the menu are lamb maas (lamb simmered in an array of spices) and beef rogan josh (Indian curry with a variety of spices, plus yogurt and tomatoes). A buffet lunch is served weekdays, including a wide selection of vegetarian dishes. The chefs point out that except for breads and pastries, all dishes are free of gluten and wheat.

Park View Plaza, 57 North St. © 441/295-6450. Main courses $9.50–$18. MC, V. Mon–Fri 11:30am–2:30pm; daily 5:30–10pm. Bus: 7 or 8.

Jamaican Grill CARIBBEAN/JAMAICAN   This casual, family-run eatery specializes in the spicy cookery of Jamaica and also serves other West Indian specialties. It's geared mostly to the takeout crowd who place their orders downstairs. You can also sit at tables upstairs. No alcohol is offered, but customers consume natural juices or else ice tea at their meals. Many of the juices are of the health-bar variety, including mango, carrot, or a ginger-flavored pineapple concoction. The Jamaican national dish, ackee and salt fish, is served here with peas and rice. You can also order such classics as jerk chicken, curried goat, or oxtail stew. We are especially fond of the pineapple-glazed chicken, and there are also such old favorites as macaroni and cheese or roast beef in a mushroom sauce. Unless you order lobster, most main dishes are priced at the lower end of the range listed below.

32 Court St. © 441/296-6577. Reservations recommended Sat–Sun. Main courses $8.50–$30. AE, MC, V. Mon–Thurs 7am–10pm; Fri–Sat 7am–11pm; Sun 3–9pm. Bus: 7 or 8.

Lemon Tree Café CONTINENTAL   Right in the center of Hamilton, this cafe is being discovered by more and more visitors. You can drop in here for breakfast, ordering some unusual concoctions in addition to the standard scrambled eggs and bacon. Try, for example, a Bermuda fish cake served on a raisin bun. For lunch you might opt for one of their freshly made sandwiches, our favorite being the Parma ham with Brie cheese. Ask Lee or Jean Claude about the daily specials—perhaps chilled fresh salmon with a garlic blue cheese dressing or one of the "wraps," such as one filled with crabmeat and avocado. The chicken salad is arguably the best in Hamilton.

7 Queen St. ℂ **441/292-0235.** Breakfast main courses $4–$8. Sandwiches $6.50–$8.50. Main courses $6.50–$14. MC, V. Mon–Fri 7am–4pm, Sat 7am–2pm. Bus: 1, 2, 10, or 11.

Monty's INTERNATIONAL   On the western waterfront road leading to the most congested part of the City of Hamilton, this family-style choice is a simple, friendly place to sit down for a meal. The atmosphere is bright, airy, and casual; many guests of the nearby Hamilton Princess head here.

Monty's serves a variety of international dishes, with an emphasis on English and classic Bermudian fare. Hot dishes include bangers and mash, Angus beef with mashed potatoes, and curried chicken, plus more exotic choices like smoked salmon with mango sauce and pumpernickel bread. There's a selection of hot and cold sandwiches and burgers. This is a great choice for breakfast if you're in the mood to venture out. Stop by on Sunday morning for a traditional Bermudian breakfast of codfish and potatoes. The food—solid, reliable fare—rises above mediocre without ever becoming superlative.

75 Pitts Bay Rd. ℂ **441/295-5759.** Reservations recommended Fri–Sat. Sandwiches and burgers $9; lunch $7.50–$15; main courses $19–$28. AE, DC, MC, V. Daily 7:30am–2:30pm; Mon–Sat 6–10pm. Bus: 7 or 8.

Paradiso Cafe DELI/LIGHT BITES/PASTRIES   One of the City of Hamilton's most consistently crowded lunch spots, the Paradiso Cafe serves hundreds of office workers every day. The most popular choices are pastries, sandwiches, and endless cups of tea and coffee, and the platters of the day are full meals in themselves. Depending on what's available at the market, daily specials might include lasagna with a side salad, savory breast of chicken with greens, or a platter of "deep-fried rice" with minced beef or pork.

In the Washington Mall, Reid St. (at Queen St.). ℂ **441/295-3263.** Reservations not accepted. Tea or coffee $1.50; sandwiches $6–$8.50; daily specials $8.50. AE, DC, MC, V (for purchases of $25 or more). Mon–Fri 7am–5pm; Sat 8am–5pm. Bus: 1, 2, 10, or 11.

Pasta Basta ITALIAN   This is the larger of two Bermuda restaurants that serve the same cafeteria-style pasta-and-salad combination. Pasta Basta's Italian cuisine ranks far below those restaurants already recommended, but its prices are very low.

In a summery setting, customers are offered two kinds of salad (tossed and Caesar) and about a dozen varieties of pasta. Served in full or half portions, they include two kinds of lasagna (one is meatless), plus a frequently changing array of pastas topped with a choice of meat, seafood, and vegetarian sauces. The daily special is likely to be shells with sausage and onions, in a pink sauce. This restaurant is a great place to fill up on decent food at a reasonable price. **Note:** No wine, beer, or alcohol is served, and local licensing laws do not permit you to bring your own drinks.

1 Elliott St. ℂ **441/295-9785.** Reservations not accepted. Pastas $7 (half portion) or $14 (full portion). No credit cards. Mon–Sat 11:45am–11pm; Sun 5–11pm. Bus: 1, 2, 10, or 11.

Portofino ITALIAN   The warm and inviting decor of this trattoria, complete with hanging lamps, evokes northern Italy. We think Tuscany, La Trattoria, and Little Venice will feed you better, but this place has its devotees.

You'll find well-prepared, reasonably priced specialties, including classic minestrone; three kinds of spaghetti; freshly made pastas, including lasagna, ravioli, and cannelloni; and 18 varieties of 9-inch pizzas. There are also familiar Italian dishes such as Venetian-style liver, veal parmigiana, chicken cacciatore, and beefsteak pizzaiola. Your best bet is one of the freshly made daily specials. There's a limited selection of Italian wines.

20 Bermudiana Rd. ℭ **441/292-2375**. Reservations recommended. Pizzas $13–$18; main courses $10–$40. AE, MC, V. Mon–Fri 11:30am–3pm; daily 6pm–midnight. Bus: 1, 2, 10, or 11.

The Robin Hood INTERNATIONAL   Woodsy-looking, and percolating in a sense of nostalgia for Merrie Olde England, this is a comfortably rustic tavern that has evolved into the local watering hole for many of Pembroke Parish's nearby residents. No one will mind if you drop in just for a drink or two, and many of your fellow elbow-benders traditionally do that many nights until the closing bell. But if you're in the mood for food as well, you'll find the kind of fare (pizzas, burgers, steaks, and curries) that goes well with liquor and suds. Menu items include jalapeño nachos, spicy buffalo wings, Caesar salads with shrimp or grilled chicken, and pizzas (including a "porker" that's topped with bacon, ham, ground sausage, pepperoni, and hamburger meat). Main-course platters include sweet-and-sour chicken, pastas of the day, and curried versions of chicken, beef, and shrimp.

25 Richmond Rd. ℭ **441/295-3314**. Lunch salads and sandwiches $4–$9.50; platters $8.25–$16. Dinner pizzas $7.75–$22, main courses $7.50–$19. AE, MC, V. Daily noon–11pm; bar Mon–Sat 11am–1am and Sun noon–1am. Bus: 6 or 7.

Rosa's Cantina *Kids* TEX-MEX   Head here for your Tex-Mex fix, especially if you're a traveling frugal family who likes South-of-the-Border food. You can fill up on beef and chicken fajitas, zesty chili, nachos, tacos, enchiladas, and burritos (the largest on the island), accompanied by frozen margaritas to put the fire out. While mariachi music plays in the background, you might begin with hearty black-bean soup, then move on to *carne asada* (mesquite-grilled rib-eye steak)—a chef's specialty. The prices are reasonable, and the best place to sit is on the balcony.

121 Front St. ℭ **441/295-1912**. Reservations required Fri–Sat. Main courses $10–$24. AE, MC, V. Daily 11:30am–11pm. Bus: 1, 2, 10, or 11.

The Spot Restaurant *Value* BERMUDIAN/WEST INDIAN   Set on a street running downhill into downtown Hamilton's harbor, this well-managed local diner is a welcome alternative to the high prices you're likely to find in many other nearby restaurants. Originally established in the 1930s, it attracts a clientele of off-duty police officers, construction workers, nurses from the local hospital, residents of nearby self-catering vacation apartments, and all kinds of local residents who appreciate the low prices and plentiful portions. You'll find breakfast platters that range from international (all kinds of bacon, egg, pancake, and waffle dishes) to West Indian (codfish with potato fritters) breakfast dishes. Lunches and dinners focus on burgers, salads, sandwiches, and daily specials such as roast turkey or chicken platters, oxtail stew, lamb or pork chops, or curried chicken. No alcoholic drinks of any kind are served, but since there are no shortages of bars within the neighborhood for a before-dinner drink, no one seems to mind.

6 Burnaby St. ℭ **441/292-6293**. Reservations accepted only for parties of 6 or more. Breakfast platters $6.50–$11; burgers, sandwiches, and salads $6.50–$13; main-course platters $8.50–$21. No credit cards. Mon–Sat 6:30am–10pm. Bus: 1, 2, 10, or 11.

8 Devonshire Parish

EXPENSIVE

Aqua *⋆⋆* BERMUDIAN/INTERNATIONAL/ITALIAN   With a maritime theme, this is a rather exciting new dining choice in the Ariel Sands Hotel. Sometimes, one of the resort's owners, actor Michael Douglas, might drop in with one of his vacationing pals such as Jack Nicholson. You're in for even more of a treat if it's his wife, Catherine Zeta-Jones. Try for a table overlooking the sea, an al fresco setting popular with those who like moonlight dining. This is one of the few restaurants in Bermuda that offers a dining experience literally steps from the water.

On our most recent visit in 2005, we feasted on such dishes as a Cajun-styled mahimahi, jerk snapper, and a ceviche of mixed seafood, all of which were quite tasty. At night the chefs get more elaborate, tempting you with their tandoori spiced lamb rack, or their loin of fresh tuna with chile mole on beer-battered eggplant. Or else you might opt for the roast quail on an eggplant "pickle," with fresh spinach and a spicy shiitake sauce.

34 South Rd. (℃) 441/236-2332. Reservations required. Lunch $14–$27; main courses $28–$39. AE, MC, V. Daily 8–10am, 12:30–2:30pm, and 6:30–9:30pm. Bus: 1.

9 Smith's Parish

EXPENSIVE

The Breakers Ocean Terrace Café ⭑ INTERNATIONAL   A team of European chefs work to please you at the exclusive cottage cluster of Pink Beach Club & Cottages (p. 88), where tables are placed outdoors on the renovated pool terrace overlooking the Atlantic. Chef Joanne Bainbridge takes her inspiration from many light and healthy contemporary styles of cooking and prepares traditional dishes with less fat. Her aim is to produce good-tasting food with first-rate ingredients, light textures, and natural flavors. She uses fresh herbs from the garden nearby and builds her menu around the fishermen's daily catch. Appetizers include classics such as Bermuda fish chowder and Caesar salad, as well as more imaginative fare such as wild mushroom strudel or Scottish smoked salmon scented with ricotta cheese and truffles.

At the Pink Beach Club & Cottages. South Rd. (℃) 441/293-1666. Reservations required for dinner, recommended for lunch. Main courses $29–$40. AE, MC, V. Daily noon–2:30pm and 6:30-9:30pm. Closed Jan–Feb. Bus: 1.

MODERATE

North Rock Brewing Company ⭑ *Finds* BERMUDIAN/INTERNATIONAL Although beer is brewed by other enterprises in Bermuda, this is the only brewery on the island that serves most, if not all, of its product on the premises. The setting is a smoky, and sometimes rowdy, replica of an English pub, complete with ceiling beams and paneling, plus a tony and casually upscale dining room outfitted in shades of burgundy and forest green. Most patrons tend to gravitate to the dining room, but died-in-the-wool locals sometimes opt to spend their entire time, meal and all, in the pub section, where views of copper-sided fermentation vats are visible through plate-glass windows.

If you come here to drink the local brew, that's fine, but we suggest you stick around for the cuisine too. This is not the typical pub grub dished up at one of those Front Street drinking emporiums in the City of Hamilton. Dishes here have flair, like the Brewmaster's veal chop, grilled and served with grain and Dijon mustard sauce. You can also order pub classics such as steak-and-ale pie, or perhaps beef and mushrooms simmered in porter ale. The fish and chips aren't bad either, and we like the luscious pork tenderloin and the codfish cakes. Unless you order expensive shellfish, most dishes are inexpensively priced.

10 South Rd. (℃) 441/236-6633. Lunch main courses $12–$22; dinner main courses $18–$29. AE, MC, V. Daily 11:30am–3pm and 6–10pm. Bus: 1.

INEXPENSIVE

Specialty Inn INTERNATIONAL   This south-shore restaurant's international menu revolves around Bermudian cuisine with Italian zest. Seating 35 to 40 (mostly locals, not visitors), the inn is known for its good value, generous portions, and fine cooking. Red bean soup, an ideal starter, reflects the island's Portuguese influence; and the Bermuda fish chowder is particularly good. The fresh catch of the day is usually delectable. Pasta dishes, including lasagna, are homemade. Poultry and meat, though frozen, are generally excellent—the roast lamb and barbecued chicken are especially tasty. Many other dishes display influences that run from Chinese and Indian to Mexican, Spanish, and Portuguese.

Collectors Hill, 4 South Rd. ✆ 441/236-3133. Lunch main courses $11–$17; dinner main courses $16–$26. MC, V. Mon–Sat 6am–10pm. Bus: 1.

10 Hamilton Parish

VERY EXPENSIVE

Tom Moore's Tavern ✹✹ CONTINENTAL/FRENCH   Bermuda's oldest restaurant, built in 1652 as a private home, is on Walsingham Bay, near the Crystal Caves. The Irish romantic poet Thomas Moore visited in 1804 and wrote some of his verses here; he referred to a calabash tree that still stands some 180m (590 ft.) from the tavern. The most famous dining room in Bermuda has gone through many incarnations. When Bologna-born Bruno Fiocca and his Venetian partner, Franco Bortoli, opened the present tavern in 1985, it quickly became one of the island's most popular upscale restaurants. With its four fireplaces and darkened cedar walls, this landmark establishment serves classic French and Italian cuisine.

Seafood is a specialty. During the summer, there's usually a tank of Bermuda lobsters outside. Local fish selections are likely to include rockfish and yellowtail, which may be your best bet. One reader wrote that he found the place "very expensive, but worth the price, as the service and atmosphere are both top-notch." He also noted, "The cuisine is not light, however. Extremely well-prepared meals contain very rich sauces." He's right. But if you're in the mood for a rich dinner, we recommend the chef's specialty: quail filled with goose liver, morels, and truffles, then baked in puff pastry. Two other recommendations are roasted duck in a raspberry vinaigrette and Latino-style jambalaya. The setting, English silver, German crystal, Luxembourg china, and general ambience contribute to a memorable visit.

Walsingham Lane (in Bailey's Bay). ✆ 441/293-8020. Reservations required. Jacket preferred. Main dishes $23–$36. AE, V. Daily 6:30–10pm. Closed Jan 5–Feb 14. Bus: 1 or 3.

EXPENSIVE

Landfall ✹ BERMUDIAN   Landfall has thrived in the district near the airport for almost as long as anyone can remember. It's set within a white-sided antique home that's at least 200 years old, with a view that some locals claim is the best in Bermuda. Though far from the sea, the view encompasses large stretches of seacoast, as well as faraway St. David's Island. One of the island's best-known chefs, Sean Ming, took over a few years ago. An expert on Bermuda's cuisine, Ming brings many island specialties to the menu, incorporating fresh local foodstuffs whenever he can. Try his rockfish in orange sauce, Bermuda lobster, fish chowder, pumpkin soup, and cassava cake.

At Clearview Suites and Villas, Sandy Lane. ✆ 441/293-1322. Lunch main courses $12–$15; dinner main courses $20–$35; Sun buffet $35. AE, DC, MC, V. Daily 11:30am–3pm; 6-11pm. Bus: 10 or 11.

Mickey's Beach Bistro & Bar ⚜ STEAK & SEAFOOD   In Bermuda's most famous hotel, the Elbow Beach Hotel (p. 76), this terrace dining room under the stars is Bermuda's only bistro-on-the-beach. Protected by a large custom-made tent, this is one of the island's best venues for summer dining and it's also ideal for a sundowner cocktail. The cooking is light and inventive and never overdresses the fresh ingredients. For a Caribbean touch, you might opt for a skewer of scallops and pineapple grilled with a light lemon sauce. Salmon is grilled to perfection and comes with a lemon sauce. The crab cakes are well flavored and contain lots of crab, and Bermuda lobster is featured almost daily. Meat eaters may prefer the grilled Angus sirloin steak with a grainy mustard sauce. For dessert, nothing tops the mango cheesecake with orange sauce.

At the Elbow Beach Hotel, 60 South Rd. © 441/236-9107. Reservations recommended. Lunch main courses $14–$25; dinner main courses $16–$60. AE, MC, V. Daily noon–4pm and 6-11pm. Closed Nov-Apr. Bus: 1, 2, or 7.

MODERATE

Palm Court ⚜ CONTINENTAL   At the Grotto Bay Beach Resort (p. 79), this restaurant has undergone a major redecoration and renovation, and is better than ever, though it still maintains its casual ambience. The setting features terra-cotta tiles, mahogany, and decor with a tropical theme. The chefs focus on Bermuda itself for their culinary inspiration: Oven-roasted salmon is served, along with succulent steaks. You can also dine on light fare in the evening, including a beef dip sandwich or juicy burgers and pizzas. You can arrive early for an island cocktail at the elegant bar.

At the Grotto Bay Beach Resort, 11 Blue Hole Hill. © 441/293-8333. Reservations recommended. AE, MC, V. Main courses $13–$31. Daily 6:30–9pm. Bus: 1, 3, 10, or 11.

Rustico ITALIAN/PIZZERIA   This is a local favorite known for its thin-crust pizzas and other dishes such as tempura-fried soft-shell crab or rockfish with a Black Sea ginger sauce. It is casual and quite a bit of fun. You can stop in during the day for sandwiches (often made from fish) or else a homemade burger. At night the pizza oven is going strong, with the Rustico special topping being Parma ham, arugula salad, and shaved Parmesan cheese. Pastas are succulent, especially the rigatoni with a sweet Italian sausage, roasted red pepper, broccoli, and cherry tomatoes in a wine sauce. Each day a freshly made fish chowder is presented to get you going. Main meat or poultry courses are limited but quite good, especially the roast lamb chops with a shallot-laced tarragon sauce.

8 N. Shore Rd. (in Flatts Village). © 441/295-5212. Reservations recommended. Lunch main courses $9–$21; dinner main courses $14–$26. AE, MC, V. Daily 11:45am–2:30pm and 6–10pm. Bus: 10 or 11.

INEXPENSIVE

Bailey's Ice Cream & Food D'Lites Restaurant ᴷⁱᵈˢ DELI/LIGHT BITES/ICE CREAM   This ice-cream parlor occupies a small cottage across from the Swizzle Inn South Shore (see below). For all-natural, homemade ice cream, there's no comparable spot in Bermuda—the staff concocts at least 30 flavors in the shop's 40-quart ice-cream maker. You can enjoy Bermuda banana, coconut, white-chocolate cherries and chips, or other exotic flavors at one of the outdoor tables. The popular sandwiches are served on fresh-baked bread. Also featured are fresh fruit ices, frozen yogurt, and bottled juices—perfect on a hot, sunny day.

At Wilkinson Ave. and Blue Hole Hill (in Bailey's Bay). © 441/293-8605. Sandwiches $4–$7; ice cream $2.75 per scoop. No credit cards. Daily 11am–6pm. Closed Dec–Feb. Bus: 1, 3, 10, or 11.

Swizzle Inn South Shore BERMUDIAN/BRITISH   The oldest pub in Bermuda—some 300 years old—is also the home of the famous Bermuda rum swizzle drink (made with sugar and citrus juice). The pub lies west of the airport, near the Crystal Caves. Thousands of business cards and reams of graffiti cover the walls. *The Bermudian* magazine voted the meaty Swizzleburger best in Bermuda; other freshly prepared pub favorites include fish and chips, conch fritters, and shepherd's pie. These dishes are at least a notch above typical Bermudian pub grub. At lunch, the Bailey's Bay fish sandwich and onion rings are popular with both locals and visitors. The larger, more varied dinner menu appeals to many tastes and diets. Pub grub is available for dinner, as is a seafood medley (rockfish, mussels, and shrimp in marinara sauce), catch of the day, and some tasty Asian curries. Seating is available inside and on the upper and lower patios; upstairs there are also a nonsmoking room and a gift shop.

3 Blue Hole Hill (in Bailey's Bay). ⓒ **441/293-1854.** Reservations accepted only for parties of 8 or more. Lunch main courses $10–$22; dinner main courses $10–$30. AE, MC, V. June–Sept daily 11am–1am; Oct–May daily 11am–midnight. Closed 1st 2 weeks of Jan. Bus: 1, 3, or 11.

11 St. George Parish

MODERATE

Black Horse Tavern ✿✿ BERMUDIAN/INTERNATIONAL   If you should land here, in a section of the island that Bermudians call "the country," you'll dine with the locals, many of whom maintain (with some justification) that this is the best place for "an authentic taste of Bermuda." Black Horse Tavern looks like a private home—it boasts a dusty rose exterior with green shutters and a glassed-in porch in the rear that looks over Smith's Sound. Over the years, the tavern has attracted many celebrities; some diners arrive in yachts. You can begin your meal with curried conch stew, shark hash (made with minced puppy shark), fish chowder, or curried mussels. Other choices include sandwiches, burgers, and platters of fish and chips. The chef also prepares good sirloin steak. If your luck holds, the only Bermuda Triangle you'll encounter is Black Horse's delicious drink—pineapple juice, orange juice, black rum, and Bermuda Gold liqueur.

101 St. David's Rd. (on St. David's Island). ⓒ **441/297-1991.** Reservations recommended for parties of 4 or more. Main courses $21–$40. AE, MC, V. Tues–Sat 11am–1am; Sun noon–1am. Bus: 6.

Café Gio *(Kids)* INTERNATIONAL   This restaurant occupies a narrow but brightly colored storefront whose rear opens onto an outdoor terrace with a view out over St. George's historic harbor. The cafe is an all-purpose family-friendly venue that includes a cubbyhole-size ice-cream parlor near the entrance, and a tutti-frutti–colored dining room with a menu of pizzas and tried-and-true international specialties. No one will mind if you opt just for a pizza or some ice cream, but if you're in the mood for a full meal, starters include firecracker shrimp wrapped in a wonton skin, served with chile-flavored lime sauce; Vietnamese-style vegetarian rolls wrapped in a rice skin; and old-fashioned Bermuda chowder. Main courses include grilled veal chops; artichoke-crusted roasted loin of lamb; braised beef bourguignon; brochettes of shrimp and scallops on a sugarcane skewer, and—as mentioned—pizzas. The vibe here is informal.

36 Water St. ⓒ **441/297-1307.** Reservations recommended on weekends. Pizzas, pastas, salads, and sandwiches $13–$19; main-course platters $17–$33. AE, MC, V. Mon–Sat 11:30am–2:30pm; daily 6:30–9:30pm. Bus: 3, 10, or 11.

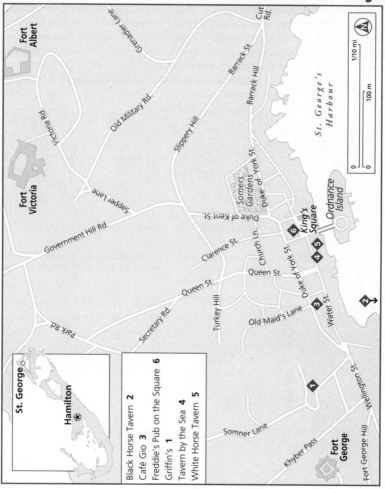

Freddie's Pub on the Square INTERNATIONAL   In a restored 18th-century building with a balcony overlooking King's Square, this popular local hangout suits diners on a variety of budgets. You can come for sandwiches and English pub fare, such as fish and chips or shepherd's pie. The more formal areas serve some very expensive fish dishes, mostly based on the catch of the day. Linen tablecloths and subdued lighting at night enhance the elegant atmosphere. Portions are very large, judging from our Angus beef and rack of lamb. The salads, including avocado, Caesar, chef's, Greek, Mexican, and seafood, are among the best in St. George.

3 King's Sq. ℂ **441/297-1717.** Reservations recommended. Sandwiches $8–$18; vegetarian dishes $9–$17; meat dishes $21–$40; seafood $20–$36. AE, MC, V. Daily 11am–3am. Bus: 7.

Griffin's ⊛ STEAK & SEAFOOD   Just off York Street, this first-class restaurant opens onto panoramic views of the harbor at St. George's. Dishes are robust with a strong emphasis on fresh seafood and succulent pastas, including fresh snow crab, Alaskan king crab legs, and scallops in a white-wine sauce. Carnivores will also be pleased by the quality of the beef dishes—the best in the east end—including succulent T-bone steaks, juicy prime rib, and melt-in-your-mouth beef tenderloin. Desserts are usually sumptuous and are prepared fresh daily.

6 Rose Hill. ℭ **441/297-4235.** Reservations recommended. Main courses $16–$30. AE, MC, V. Tues–Sat noon–2:30pm; Mon–Sat 6:30–9:30pm. Bus: 3, 10, or 11.

Tavern by the Sea INTERNATIONAL   This restaurant prides itself on its sweeping view of St. George's Harbour, and if there's a cruise ship anchored offshore (perhaps the one you're riding on), you'll have a full view of its exterior as you drink and/or dine. During clement weather, most visitors opt for a seat beneath brightly striped parasols on its wraparound veranda; otherwise, an air-conditioned interior provides nautical nostalgia. The menu here includes pastas, burgers, salads, shepherd's pie, and a short list of German dishes such as Wiener schnitzels and bratwursts. Fish and chips are always reliable, as are the steaks. Pizzas bear names of local monuments, including a version known as "The Stocks," made with pepperoni, onions, green peppers, mushrooms, and cheese.

14 Water St. ℭ **441/297-3305.** Reservations not necessary. Sandwiches, salads, pastas, and burgers $7–$18; main courses $16–$36. AE, MC, V. Daily 11:30am–10pm; bar daily 11:30am–midnight (Fri–Sat until 1:30 or 2am). Bus: 3, 10, or 11.

White Horse Tavern BERMUDIAN   The oldest tavern in St. George is the most popular in Bermuda; it's always jammed with visitors. This white building with green shutters has a restaurant and cedar bar with a terrace jutting into St. George's Harbour. The most popular item on the menu is fish and chips, in a seasoned flour batter and often overdone. The fish chowder is good, as are the pork chops and grilled wahoo (the local catch). At lunch, there are burgers and fresh salads. The food is passable, but not special. Another horsy tavern, the Black Horse Tavern (see above), serves a more authentic Bermudian cuisine. Dress is smart casual, and there's often enjoyable entertainment.

King's Sq. ℭ **441/297-1838.** Reservations accepted only for groups. Breakfast $3.25–$15; lunch main courses $17–$25; dinner main courses $21–$40. AE, MC, V. Daily 8am–10pm; bar daily 10am–1am. Bus: 3, 10, or 11.

6

Fun in the Surf & Sun

Although people visit Bermuda mainly to relax on its spectacular pink sand beaches, the island also offers a wealth of activities, both onshore and off. In fact, Bermuda's sports facilities are better than those on most Caribbean and Bahamian islands.

The most popular outdoor pursuits in Bermuda are tennis and golf, but sailing ranks high, too. You'll find a fair number of tennis courts and renowned golf courses around the island. If you hesitate to pick up a racket or golf club because you've neglected your game, fear not: Your Bermudian partner, on the court or on the links, would deem it quite improper to remark that your play was anything but superb. If a word of friendly criticism is ever offered, be assured that it will be as gentle as the island's ocean breezes.

Bermuda's waters are the clearest in the western Atlantic. Reefs, shipwrecks (many in such shallow water that they're even accessible to snorkelers), a variety of marine life and coral formations, and underwater grottoes make Bermuda ideal for scuba diving and snorkeling. For locations of many of these activities, see the maps throughout this chapter, plus the color map "The Best of Outdoor Bermuda" at the front of this book.

1 Beaches

Bermuda is one of the world's leading beach resorts. It boasts kilometers of pink shoreline, broken only now and then by cliffs that form sheltered coves. Many stretches have shallow, sandy bottoms for some distance out, making them safe for children and nonswimmers. Some beaches (usually the larger ones) have lifeguards; others do not. The Parks Division of the Department for Agriculture and Fisheries supervises public facilities. Hotels and private clubs often have their own beaches and facilities. Even if you're not registered at a hotel or resort, you can often use their beach and facilities if you become a customer by having lunch there.

You'll find dozens of spots for sunbathing, swimming, and beachcombing; here's a list of the island's most famous sands, arranged clockwise beginning with the south-shore beaches closest to the City of Hamilton.

ELBOW BEACH

One of the most consistently popular beaches in Bermuda, Paget Parish's Elbow Beach incorporates almost 1.5km (1 mile) of (occasionally interrupted) pale pink sand. Private homes and resort hotels dot the edges. Because protective coral reefs surround it, Elbow Beach is one of the safest beaches on the island—and it's the family favorite. This is also the beach of choice for college students on spring break.

Bermuda's government provides lifeguards as a public service. The **Elbow Beach Hotel** (© **441/236-3535**) offers a variety of facilities and amenities free to hotel guests, but they're off-limits to others. Amenities and facilities include sun chairs,

Bermuda's Best Public Beaches & Snorkel Sites

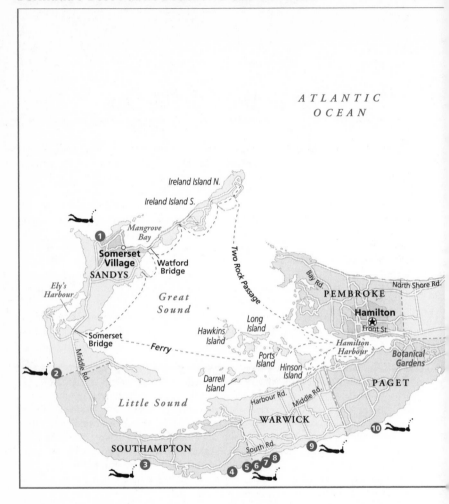

cabanas, changing rooms, showers, restrooms, and beach towels distributed three times a day by beach attendants who are trained in water safety and lifeguard techniques. The hotel also rents paddle boats, sea kayaks (around $20 per hour for one kayak, $25 per hour for two), and snorkeling equipment ($12 per hour) to anyone on the beach. Take bus no. 2 or 7 from the City of Hamilton.

ASTWOOD COVE

This Warwick Parish public beach has no problem with overcrowding during most of the year—it's in a remote location, at the bottom of a steep, winding road that intersects with South Road. Many single travelers and couples head here to escape the families that tend to overrun beaches like Elbow Beach in the high season. We like this beach for many reasons, one of them being that its cliffs are home to nesting Bermuda

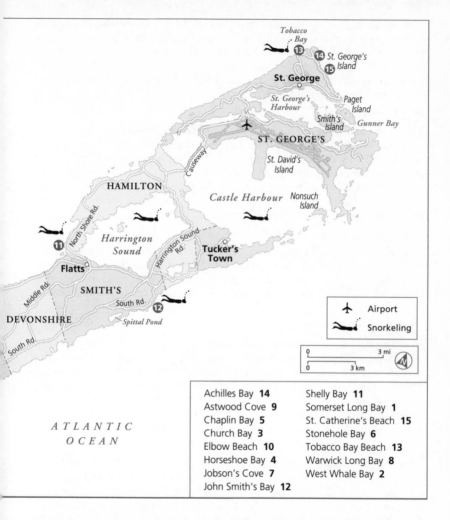

Airport ✈

Snorkeling

| 0 | 3 mi |
| 0 | 3 km |

Achilles Bay **14**
Astwood Cove **9**
Chaplin Bay **5**
Church Bay **3**
Elbow Beach **10**
Horseshoe Bay **4**
Jobson's Cove **7**
John Smith's Bay **12**

Shelly Bay **11**
Somerset Long Bay **1**
St. Catherine's Beach **15**
Stonehole Bay **6**
Tobacco Bay Beach **13**
Warwick Long Bay **8**
West Whale Bay **2**

longtails, also known as white-tailed tropic birds. Astwood Beach has public restrooms but not many other facilities. An added advantage is nearby Astwood Park, a favorite picnic and hiking area. If you like your beaches small and secluded, head here. Take bus no. 2 or 7 from Southampton.

WARWICK LONG BAY

Like Astwood Cove, this is one of the best places for people who want to escape the family crowds and find solitude. Unlike the sheltered coves of nearby Chaplin and Horseshoe bays (see below), this popular beach features a 1km (⅔-mile) stretch of sand, the longest on the island. This expanse is conducive to social interaction, but also offers plenty of space to stretch out solo—it all depends on what you prefer. Against a backdrop of scrubland and low grasses, the beach lies on the southern side of South Shore Park, in Warwick Parish. Despite the frequent winds, the waves are surprisingly small thanks to an offshore reef. Jutting above the water less than 60m (197 ft.) from the shore is a jagged coral island that, because of its contoured shape, appears to be floating above the water's foam. There are restrooms at the beach's western end, plus lots of parking, but no other facilities. There are no lifeguards because the undertow is not very strong. Take bus no. 7.

JOBSON'S COVE

This Warwick Parish beach has the feel of a secret hideaway, thanks to pink sands, gentle waves, and calm waters. Where the horseshoe-shaped bay opens to the ocean, it's only 9m (30 ft.) wide. Adjacent to the much larger and more popular Warwick Long Bay, it's excellent for snorkeling—the water is about 2m (6½ ft.) deep for a long way out into the bay. There are no buildings along the water, adding to the feeling of seclusion and peace. There are no facilities here, but it's close enough to Warwick Long Bay to walk over and use their restrooms if necessary. Take bus no. 7.

STONEHOLE BAY

Near Jobson's Cove in Warwick Parish, Stonehole Bay is more open and less sheltered than Jobson's, with a sandy shoreline that's studded with big rocks. It's almost never crowded, and wading is safe even though strong waves sometimes make the waters cloudy (so they're less than ideal for snorkeling). There are no facilities at Stonehole Bay. Take bus no. 7.

CHAPLIN BAY

Straddling the boundary between Warwick and Southampton parishes, this small but secluded beach disappears almost completely during storms and exceptionally high tides. Geologists come here to admire the open-air coral barrier that partially separates one half of the beach from the other. Chaplin Bay, like its more famous neighbor, Horseshoe Bay (see below), lies at the southern extremity of South Shore Park. From Chaplin, you can walk over to use the facilities and equipment at Horseshoe, but you'll enjoy more solitude here than at the more active Horseshoe Bay. Take bus no. 7.

HORSESHOE BAY BEACH

With its long, curved strip of pink sand, Horseshoe Bay, on South Road in Southampton Parish, is one of Bermuda's most famous beaches. That means it's likely to be crowded, especially if cruise ships are in port. Although families flock here, Horseshoe Bay isn't the safest beach on Bermuda. Don't be fooled by the seemingly smooth surface; there can be dangerous undercurrents. If you're using the beach after a storm, be especially careful that you don't encounter a Portuguese man-of-war—they often wash up here in greater numbers than elsewhere on Bermuda.

One advantage this beach has over others is the **Horseshoe Bay Beach Cafe** (© 441/ 238-2651), which offers changing rooms, toilets, beach-gear rentals, and showers. It also serves snacks and sandwiches from 9am to 5pm daily. A lifeguard is on duty from May to September. *Insider's tip:* When you tire of the crowds at Horseshoe Bay, take one of the little trails that wind through the park nearby; they'll lead you to secluded cove beaches that afford more privacy. Our favorites are Port Royal Cove to the west, and Peel Rock Cove and Wafer Rocks Beach to the east. You might also sneak over to Chaplin Bay to the east (see above). Take bus no. 7.

CHURCH BAY

This beach off West Side Road lies along Bermuda's southwestern edge, at the point in Southampton Parish where the island hooks off to the northeast. The waves pound much of the shore mercilessly, but rows of offshore reefs shelter Church Bay. Marine life abounds in the relatively calm waters, much to the delight of snorkelers. If you're just planning to lounge in the sun, this is a great place: The beach offers unusually deep pink sands. There are toilets at the top of the hill near the parking area, but don't expect much in the way of facilities (unless a concession has opened by the time you visit). Rent your snorkeling equipment before you get here. Take bus no. 7 or 8.

SOMERSET LONG BAY

When offshore storms stir up the waters northwest of Bermuda, the water here is unsafe for swimming. Because its bottom isn't always sandy or of a consistent depth, many people find Somerset Long Bay better suited to beachcombing or long walks than to swimming. Nevertheless, many single travelers favor this beach when they're looking for seclusion. The undeveloped parkland of Sandys Parish shelters it from the rest of the island, and the beach's crescent shape and length—about .5km (⅓ mile)—make it unusual by Bermudian standards. It has restrooms and changing facilities. We think this is one of the best places on Bermuda to watch the sunset. A plus is the beach's proximity to the **Bermuda Audubon Society Nature Reserve** (© 441/236-7410), where you can go for long walks and enjoy moments of solitude—except on weekends, when family picnics abound. Take bus no. 7 or 8.

SHELLY BAY

This beach of abundant pink sand is suitable for both families and those seeking solitude. Because it's not well-known, it's unlikely to be crowded, and its calm, shallow basin makes it safe for swimming. Off North Shore Road in Hamilton Parish, Shelly Bay lies in a cove whose encircling peninsula partially shelters it from mid-Atlantic waves. There are trees to sit under when the beach gets too hot, and the beach house rents snorkeling equipment, lounge chairs, beach towels, and other items; there are also public restrooms. Buses from the City of Hamilton heading east along the north shore, primarily no. 11, stop here.

TOBACCO BAY, ACHILLES BAY & ST. CATHERINE'S BEACH

St. George's Island's beaches include Achilles Bay, Tobacco Bay, and St. Catherine's Beach (formerly known as the Club Med beach), all of which are sandy, with clean bottoms. The water on the south shore is a bit rougher than the north shore's.

Lovely Tobacco Bay is an East End family favorite. It's the most popular beach on St. George's Island, especially among those who come for the day to visit the historic town of St. George. With its broad sands, Tobacco Bay resembles a south-shore beach. Its pale pink sand lies within a sheltering coral-sided cove just a short walk west of Fort St. Catherine and St. Catherine's Beach. The major disadvantage here is that the beach is likely to be overrun with cruise-ship passengers; when they're in port, you may want to seek more secluded beaches such as St. Catherine's. You can sunbathe here and even go for a swim, but don't venture out too far; the currents are dangerously strong, and a lot of seaweed washes up on the shore.

Look for the **Tobacco Bay Beach House** (© 441/297-2756), Naval Tanks Hill, St. George, which has toilets, changing rooms, showers, and a snack bar. At beachfront kiosks, you can rent flotation devices and snorkeling gear by the hour from May to September. Stands also sell cold sodas and sandwiches (tuna, grilled cheese, hamburgers, hot dogs, and the like). Take bus no. 10 or 11.

JOHN SMITH'S BAY

This is the only public beach in Smith's Parish. It's more popular with residents of Bermuda's eastern end than with visitors, who often don't know about it. It's ideal for those seeking solitude. Long, flat, wide, and rich with pale pink sand, this beach has a lifeguard from May to September. Some shallow areas are perfect for snorkeling; however, the Bay occasionally experiences rip currents. There are toilet and changing facilities. Take bus no. 1.

2 Snorkeling

Bermuda is known for the gin-clear purity of its waters and for its vast array of coral reefs. If you're ready to explore, all you need are a snorkel, mask, and fins—if you can swim, you can snorkel. A handful of companies can help you; otherwise, you can hit the water on your own.

The best places to go snorkeling are public beaches (see "Beaches," above). Many hotels that are right on the beach will lend or rent you fins, masks, and snorkels, and will advise you of the best sites in your area. You almost never have to travel far.

Die-hard snorkelers, some of whom visit Bermuda every year, prefer **Church Bay** above all other snorkeling spots on Bermuda. It lies on the south shore, west of the Fairmont Southampton Golf Club and Gibbs Hill Lighthouse. The little cove, which seems to be waiting for a movie camera, is carved out of coral cliffs. It's well protected and filled with snug little nooks. Another advantage is that the reefs are fairly close to land. But remember, the seas can be rough (as is true anywhere in Bermuda); use caution.

At the eastern end of the south shore, **John Smith's Bay,** east of Spittal Pond Nature Reserve and Watch Hill Park, is another top spot, especially if your hotel is nearby. Even more convenient, especially for snorkelers staying at St. George or at a hotel near the airport, is **Tobacco Bay,** north of St. George's Golf Club. Another good small snorkeling spot is **West Whale Bay;** it lies along the south shore at the west end of Southampton, west of the Port Royal Golf Course.

Although snorkeling is a year-round pursuit, it's best from May to October. Snorkelers usually wear wet suits in winter, when the water temperature dips into the 60s. The waters of the Atlantic, which can be tempestuous at any time of the year, can be especially rough in winter.

Some of the best snorkeling sites are accessible only by boat. If you want to head out on your own, and you have a knowledge of Bermuda's waters, we suggest renting a small boat (see "Sailing," under "More Fun in the Water," later in this chapter), some of which have glass bottoms. If you rent a boat, the rental company will advise you on where to go and not to go. Countless wrecked boats lie on the many reefs that surround Bermuda. If you're not familiar with Bermuda's waters, you should stay in the sounds, harbors, and bays, especially in Castle Harbour and Harrington Sound. If you want to visit the reefs, it's better and easier to take one of the snorkeling cruises recommended below than to captain your own boat. The use of snorkeling equipment is included in the prices listed.

Also see "Scuba Diving," below.

Bermuda Water Sports Friendly captains offer glass-bottom snorkel cruises aboard an 18m (59-ft.) motorized catamaran. The design allows the boat to anchor in

Moments **A Look Under Bermuda's Waters**

The Ocean Discovery Centre at the Bermuda Underwater Exploration Institute, East Broadway (© **441/297-7314**; www.buei.bm), hopes to give visitors an underwater adventure. The highlight of a visit is a simulated dive 3,600m (11,811 ft.) to the bottom of the Atlantic. Author Peter Benchley's videotaped commentary adds to the fun of exploring Bermuda's reefs. You'll learn about newly discovered ocean animals that live in the murky depths. Displays include large murals of sea creatures, artifacts rescued from long-sunken vessels off the coast, and even a scale model of a ship that wrecked centuries ago. On-site facilities include gift shops, a theater showing films, and La Coquille, a French bistro that specializes, of course, in seafood. Admission is $11 for adults, $5.50 for children 7–17, free for children 6 and under; hours are Monday to Friday from 9am to 4:15pm, Saturday and Sunday 10am to 5pm.

very shallow waters, which is ideal for novices or unsure swimmers. The cost—around $60 per person for a 3½-hour cruise—includes free use of snorkeling equipment and the expertise of a crew that really knows the marine life of Bermuda's offshore reefs. There are a cash bar and a shower onboard. Cruises are at 9am on Monday, 9am and 1pm on Tuesday and Thursday, and Friday at 9am.

36 Market Wharf, St. George Parish. © **441/293-2640**. Booking mid-Apr to Oct daily 9am–9pm. Bus: 10 or 11.

Bermuda Water Tours Ltd. Bermuda Water Tour's Captain Butch offers two options: The shorter cruise, 2 hours on a glass-bottom boat, costs $35 per person and departs daily at 10am. The 3-hour glass-bottom-boat cruise includes time for snorkeling; it costs $50 and departs daily at 1:15pm.

Tours leave from the docks near the City of Hamilton's Ferry Terminal. © **441/236-1500**. Bus: 1, 2, 10, or 11.

Salt Kettle Yacht Charters Salt Kettle offers private sailing/snorkeling charters on a 17m (56-ft.) sloop, the luxury yacht *Bright Star.* The outfitter also books charters on its 11m (36-ft.) motorized *Magic Carpet* for sightseeing or snorkeling among the wrecks and reefs. Charters for up to eight people cost $425 for 3 hours, $535 for 4 hours, and $750 for 6 hours, with a $22 charge for each additional person, up to a maximum of 18 passengers.

Salt Kettle, Paget Parish. © **441/236-4863**. Ferry from the City of Hamilton every 30 min.

3 Scuba Diving

Bermuda is a world-class dive site, known for its evocative and often eerie shipwrecks, teeming with marine life. All scuba diving outfitters go to all sites. If you're diving, talk to the dive master about what you'd like to see, including any or all of the various wrecks that are accessible off the coast and not viewed as dangerous. For the locations of many of these sites, see the map on p. 140.

THE DIVING SITES

The Constellation   When Peter Benchley was writing *The Deep* (later made into a film), he came here to study the wreck of *The Constellation* for inspiration. Lying in 9m (30 ft.) of water, this wreck is 13km (8 miles) northwest of the Royal Naval Dockyard. Built in 1918, *The Constellation* is a four-masted, wooden-hulled schooner. During World War II, it was the last wooden cargo vessel to leave New York harbor. She wrecked off the coast of Bermuda on July 31, 1943, and all the crew survived. Today, her hull, broken apart, can be seen on a coral and sand bottom. You can see the 36,287kg (80,000 pounds) of cement she was carrying, and morphine ampoules are still found at this site. Large populations of parrotfish, trumpet fish, barracuda, grouper, speckled eels, and octopus inhabit the wreck today.

The *Cristóbal Colón*   Bermuda's largest shipwreck is the ***Cristóbal Colón,*** a Spanish luxury liner that went down on October 25, 1936, between North Rock and North Breaker. A transatlantic liner, it weighed in excess of 10,000 tons. She was traveling to Mexico to load arms for the Spanish Civil War when she crashed into a coral reef at a speed of 15 knots. During World War II, the U.S. Air Force used the ship as target practice before it eventually settled beneath the waves. Its wreckage is scattered over a wide area on both sides of the reef. It is recommended that you take two dives to see this wreck. Most of the wreck is in 9 to 17m (30–56 ft.) of water, but the range is actually from 4.5m (15 ft.) at the bow to 24m (79 ft.) at the stern. Some artillery shells from WWII remain unexploded, so don't have a blast, please.

The *Hermes*   This 1984 American freighter rests in some 24m (79 ft.) of water about 1.5km (1 mile) off Warwick Long Bay on the south shore. The 825-ton, 50m (164-ft.) freighter is popular with divers because its U.S. Coast Guard buoy tender is almost intact. The crew abandoned this vessel (they hadn't been paid in 6 months), and the Bermuda government claimed it for $1, letting the dive association deliberately sink it to make a colorful wreck. The visibility at the wreck is generally the finest in Bermuda, and you can see her galley, cargo hold, propeller, and engines.

L'Herminie   This 1838 French frigate lies in 6 to 9m (20–30 ft.) of water off the west side of Bermuda, with 25 of its cannons still visible. A large wooden keel remains, but the wreck has rotted badly. The marine life here is among the most spectacular of any shipwreck off Bermuda's coast: brittle starfish, spiny lobster, crabs, grouper, banded coral shrimp, queen angels, and tons of sponges.

Marie Celeste   This is one of the most historic wrecks in the Atlantic, a 207-ton paddle-wheel steamer from the Confederacy. The steamer was a blockade runner during the Civil War. In exchange for guns, this vessel would return to Bermuda with cotton and cash. Evading capture for most of the war, she was wrecked off the coast of Bermuda on September 25, 1864. The ship sank in 17m (56 ft.) of water, where its ruins lie like a skeleton today. The location is off the coast from the Wyndham Bermuda. This is not a great dive site for observing marine life, but the wreck is evocative and offers many caves and tunnels to explore.

North Carolina   This iron-hulled English bark lies in 7.5 to 12m (25–39 ft.) of water off Bermuda's western coast. While en route to England, it went down on New Year's Day in 1879 when it struck the reefs. The bow and stern remain fairly intact. There is often poor visibility here, making the wreck appear almost like a ghost ship. Hogfish, often reaching huge sizes, inhabit the site, along with schools of porgies and snapper.

Rita Zovetta   This Italian cargo steamer was built in 1919 in Glasgow and went aground off St. David's Island in 1924. The ship lies in 6 to 21m (21–69 ft.) of water just off St. David's Head. The wreck measures 120m long (394 ft.), and its stern is relatively intact. Divers go through the shaft housings to see the large boilers. Stunning schools of rainbow-hued fish inhabit the site.

Tauton   This Norwegian coastal steamer ran afoul on Bermuda's treacherous reefs on November 24, 1920. The 68m (228-ft.) steel-hulled vessel sank in 3 to 12m (10–40 ft.) of water off the northern end of Bermuda. Her boilers and steam engines are still visible. This is a favorite dive for beginners, as the wreck lies in shallow water. Because of its breathtaking varieties of fish, it's a favorite site for photographers.

South West Breaker   Some 2.5km (1½ miles) off Church Bay, this was the location chosen for the famous Jacqueline Bisset scene in Peter Benchley's movie *The Deep.* The breaker was supposed to be a hideout for a man-eating squid. In reality, the breaker was created from fossilized prehistoric worms (believe it or not). It has an average depth of 8.5m (28 ft.), and on most days a visibility of 30m (98 ft.). New divers prefer this site, because it's not considered dangerous and it has a large variety of hard and soft coral. It's also a good place for snorkelers. A large tunnel split through the center of the breaker provides a protective cover for green moray eels and spiny lobsters. Schools of barracuda are also encountered here.

Tarpon Hole   This series of large breakers lies directly off the western extremity of Elbow Beach. The site is named Tarpon Hole because of the large schools of tarpon that often cluster here, some in excess of 2m (6½ ft.) long. It is a sea world of lush fans and soft corals, made all the more intriguing with its tunnels, caves, and overhangs.

Moments Walking Underwater

Helmet diving enjoys great popularity in Bermuda. Underwater walkers— clad in helmets equipped with air hoses connected to the surface—stroll along the sandy sea floor in water to depths of 3 to 4m (10–13 ft.).

Anybody can take part in this adventure. Undersea walks among the coral reefs are safe for anyone from age 5 to 89, even nonswimmers. You can walk underwater wearing your contact lenses or glasses, and you won't even get your hair wet. A guide places a helmet on your shoulders as you climb down the ladder of the boat to begin your walk. An experienced guide conducts the tours, and it's as simple as walking through a garden. On your helmet dive, you can feed dozens of rainbow-hued fish, which take food right from your hands. You can also see sponges breathing and coral feeding.

You can arrange your walk with Bermuda's original helmet-diving company by contacting **Bermuda Bell Diving**, 5 N. Shore Rd. (P.O. Box FL 281), Flatts FL BX, Bermuda (© **441/535-8707**). From April to November, a 12m (39-ft.) boat, *Cameron,* leaves Flatts Village daily at 10am and 2pm. Your underwater wonderland walk lasts about 30 minutes and costs $65 per person (adults and children). Children under 5 aren't allowed. Take bus no. 10 or 11. For more information, visit www.helmetdive.com.

DIVING SCHOOLS & OUTFITTERS

Diving in Bermuda is great for novices, who can learn the fundamentals and go diving in 6 to 7.5m (20–25 ft.) of water on the same day as their first lesson. In general, Bermuda's reefs are still healthy, despite talk about dwindling fish and dying coral formations. On occasion, in addition to the rainbow-hued schools of fish, you may even find yourself swimming with a barracuda.

Although scuba fanatics dive all year, the best diving months are May to October. The sea is the most tranquil at that time, and the water temperature is moderate—it averages 62°F (17°C) in the spring and fall, 83°F (28°C) in the summer.

Weather permitting, scuba schools function daily. Fully licensed scuba instructors oversee all dives. Most dives are conducted from a 12m (39-ft.) boat, and outfitters cover a wide range of dive sites. Night dives and certifications are also available.

All dive shops display a map of wreck sites that you can visit—there are nearly 40 in all, the oldest of which dates to the 17th century. Although locals believe there may be some 300 wrecks, the mapped sites are the best known and in the best condition. Dive depths at these sites run 7.5 to 26m (25–85 ft.). Inexperienced divers may want to stick to the wreck sites off the western coast, which tend to be in shallower waters—about 9.5m (31 ft.) or less. These shallow wreck sites are popular with snorkelers as well.

Many hotels have their own watersports equipment. If yours doesn't, the outfitters below rent equipment.

Note: Spearfishing is not allowed within 1.5km (1 mile) of any shore, and spear guns are not permitted in Bermuda.

Blue Water Divers & Watersports Ltd.   Bermuda's oldest and largest full-service scuba-diving operation offers introductory lessons and half-day dives for between $105 and $135. Daily one- and two-tank dive trips cost $65 and $90, respectively. Snorkeling trips are $44 per half-day. Full certification courses are available through PADI, NAUI, and SSI. Equipment costs extra, and reservations are required. The outfitter offers underwater scooters called DPVs or "diver propulsion vehicles." This exciting vehicle takes adventurers through underwater caves and canyons. Who knows? You may even discover a shipwreck from long ago.

Robinson's Marina, Southampton Parish. ✆ 441/234-1034. www.divebermuda.com. Daily 9am–5pm. Bus: 7 or 8.

Fantasea Diving   This outfitter is known for its daily two-tank wreck and reef dives, costing $95, although you can also go out on a one-tank dive for $65. It's also possible to go along just to snorkel off the boat, costing $40. A one-tank night dive, increasing in popularity, costs $90. A resort course lesson plus dive is $100 and includes all of the equipment. The company has two fully equipped, custom-built fiberglass dive boats with the latest approved safety gear. This is a NAUI- and PADI-affiliated dive center. Prices do not include equipment rentals, which are $20 for snorkel gear, $25 for tank, $10 for mask and fins, and $15 for a wet suit.

At the Wyndham Bermuda Resort & Spa, South Rd., Southampton Parish. ✆ 441/238-1833. www.fantasea.bm. Call a day in advance. Daily 8:30am–5pm. Closed Jan–Feb. Bus: 7.

Nautilus Diving Ltd.   This is one of the island's leading dive operators. It offers a popular "Discover Scuba" resort course ($135 for 3 hr.) that begins daily at 10:15am at Hamilton and 1:15pm at Southampton. Course participants get to complete a shallow-water scuba dive by the end of the day. All dives are from a 12m (39-ft.) boat. A two-tank dive, including a view of a shipwreck and the exploration of a reef in 7.5 to

9m (25–30 ft.) of water, costs $110 (equipment not included). This is a PADI, five-star center.

At the Fairmont Southampton, 101 South Rd., Southampton Parish; and the Fairmont Hamilton Princess, 76 Pitts Bay Rd., Pembroke Parish. ☎ **441/238-2332** or 441/295-9485. Daily 8:30am–4:30pm. Bus: 8.

4 More Fun in the Water
FISHING

Bermuda is one of the world's finest destinations for anglers, especially in light-tackle fishing. Blue marlin catches have increased dramatically in recent years, and Bermuda can add bill fishing (for marlin, swordfish, and sailfish) to its already enviable reputation. Fishing is a year-round sport, but it's best from May to November. No license is required.

You can obtain fishing information from the International Game Fish Association's representative for Bermuda, **Keith Winter,** at ☎ **441/292-7131.** He can only be reached at home in the evening.

DEEP-SEA FISHING

Wahoo, amberjack, blue marlin, white marlin, dolphin, tuna, and many other varieties of fish call Bermuda's warm waters home. A number of island outfitters offer the equipment to help you fish for them; these are our favorites:

Bermuda Sportsfishing   The De Silva family runs Bermuda Sportsfishing, which has been in business for many years. They charge $750 for a half-day of fishing and $950 to $1,000 for a full day, depending on the size of the boat. Boats range from 11 to 14m (36–46 ft.), and all equipment is provided.

Creek View House, 8 Tulo Lane, Pembroke Parish HM 02, Bermuda. ☎ **441/295-2370.** Daily 7am–10pm. Bus: 1, 2, 10, or 11.

Sea Wolfe Sportsfishing   This father-and-son business is the largest running charter operation in Bermuda. The crew here will lead you to such catches as blue marlin, white marlin, wahoo, yellowfin tuna, blackfin tuna, shark, and barracuda. Fishermen are taken out on a custom-built sportsfishing boat with three "fighting chairs." The 43-foot Sportfisher was built in Key West. Six fishermen can sign up for a full day of fishing—that is, 8 to 9 hours—costing $1,250, or else $850 per half-day.

28 Long Bay Lane, Somerset Parish. ☎ **441/234-1832.** www.sportfishbermuda.com. Bus 7 or 8.

⟨Tips⟩ Anglers Aweigh: How to Make Your Big Catch a Winning One

The **Bermuda Game Fishing Tournament** is open to any angler who takes the time and trouble to fill out the tournament application when he or she catches a really big fish. No special license is required, but your catch must be weighed and three witnesses must sign an affidavit attesting to its weight. Special prizes are awarded each year for top catches of 17 species of game fish. For more information on registering the ones that didn't get away, contact the **Bermuda Department of Tourism,** Global House, 43 Church St., Hamilton HM 12, Bermuda (☎ **441/292-0023**; www.bermudatourism.com). Open daily 9am to 5pm.

REEF FISHING

Three major reef banks lie off Bermuda, and they're likely to yield such catches as greater amberjack, almaco jack, great barracuda, little tunny, Bermuda chub, gray snapper, yellowtail snapper, and assorted bottom fish. The closest one begins about 1km (⅔ mile) offshore and stretches for nearly 8km (5 miles). The Challenger Bank is about 23km (14 miles) offshore, and the Argus Bank is about 50km (31 miles) distant. The farther out you go, the more likely you are to turn up larger fish.

Several companies offer half- or full-day charters. Arrangements can also be made through Bermuda Sportsfishing (see "Deep-Sea Fishing," above).

SHORE FISHING

Shore fishing turns up such catches as bonefish, palometa (pompano), gray snapper, and great barracuda. Locals and most visitors prefer shore fishing at Spring Benny's Bay or West Whale Bay; Great Sound and St. George's Harbour are other promising grounds. The activities director at your hotel can help make fishing arrangements for you.

PARASAILING

Skyrider Bermuda Ltd.　Skyrider takes a maximum of eight passengers into the Great Sound and north-shore area for two-person chair parasail rides. The 8- to 10-minute ride costs $50 for adults, $35 for children under 12. Boat passengers who do not parasail pay $15.

Royal Naval Dockyard, Sandys Parish. © 441/234-3019. May–Oct daily 10am–6pm. Bus 7 or 8.

SAILING

Bermuda is one of the world's sailing capitals. Sail-yourself boats are available to rent for 2, 4 (half-day), and 8 (full-day) hours. A number of places charter yachts with licensed skippers.

Blue Hole Water Sports　This outfitter rents sail-yourself Windsurfers or Sunfish for $25 per hour. A wide range of other equipment is on hand, including single and double kayaks. Kayaks are $20 for two, $15 for one.

Grotto Bay Beach Hotel, 11 Blue Hole Hill, Hamilton Parish. © 441/293-2915. www.blueholewater.bm. Daily 8:30am–5:30pm. Bus: 1, 3, 10, or 11.

Pompano Beach Club Watersports Centre　This is one of the island's best outfitters, mainly because of its variety of modern boats. Windsurfers, which hold one novice or experienced passenger, rent for $30 per hour. One or two people can rent a Sunfish sailboat for $40 per hour. Single-person kayaks go for $25 for 1 hour; double kayaks, $35 for 1 hour. Two-person Sun Cats, which travel 9.5kmph (6 mph) and look like motorized lawn chairs, go for $60 per hour.

36 Pompano Beach Rd., Southampton Parish. © 441/234-0222. www.pompano.bm. Mid-May to Oct daily 10am–6pm. Bus: 7 or 8.

Somerset Bridge Watersports　Somerset Bridge is the best outlet for renting Boston whalers for island-hopping on your own. A 4m (13-ft.) Boston whaler (25 or 30 hp) carries four and costs $65 for 2 hours, $105 for 4 hours, and $165 for 8 hours. Somerset provides lots of extras, such as canopies, special maps, a ladder, a viewing box, and a fish and coral ID card. "Jet Ski Adventures" cost $90 for 1¼ hours for one person, $115 for two persons, and $135 for three. The jet ski reaches speeds of up to 81kmph (50 mph). There may be an additional fee for gas ($10–$20).

Somerset Bridge, Ely's Harbour, Sandys Parish. © 441/234-0914. Daily 8am–sunset. Bus 7 or 8.

(Moments) Hanging Out with the Dolphins

The well-publicized **Dolphin Quest Experience**, at the Bermuda Maritime Museum in the Royal Naval Dockyard (ⓒ **441/234-4464**; www.dolphinquest. org), offers in-the-water encounters with Atlantic bottlenose dolphins. In a holding pen that's 1 to 3.5m (31/4–11 ft.) deep and separated from the open sea with underwater netting, the hotel keeps seven dolphins. Four "Dolphin Experiences" are scheduled daily at 11:30am, and also at 10:45am and 3pm Wednesday and Saturday. Up to 10 swimmers (wearing bathing suits in summer, wet suits in winter) cavort in the water with the dolphins for 30 minutes. The price is $150. In winter, it's easy to get a slot, but in summer, there's so much demand that the hotel has a lottery.

Is all this cruel to the dolphins? The staff is rigorous about protecting and caring for them; the overall atmosphere is playful and lighthearted; and the dolphins have a fairly large area to swim in. But we can't help worrying that continued contact with hordes of people and separation from their natural habitat must have something of a traumatizing effect on these beautiful animals. For more (mostly troubling) information, check out the Whale and Dolphin Conservation Society's website at **www.wdcs.org**. For more information about responsible travel in general, check out these websites: Tread Lightly (www.treadlightly.org) and the International Ecotourism Society (www.ecotourism.org).

WATER-SKIING

You can water-ski in the protected waters of Hamilton Harbour, Great Sound, Castle Harbour, Mangrove Bay, Spanish Point, Ferry Reach, Ely's Harbour, Riddells Bay, and Harrington Sound. May to September, when the waters are usually calm, is the best time for water-skiing. Bermuda law requires that a licensed skipper take water-skiers out. Only a few boat operators handle this sport, and charges fluctuate with fuel costs. Rates include the boat, skis, safety belts, and usually an instructor. Hotels and guesthouses can assist with arrangements.

Bermuda Waterski Centre   Up to five people can water-ski at the same time from a specially designed Ski Nautique. Lessons are also available. The charge for a party of any size (not per person) is $50 for a 15-minute session, $75 for a 30-minute session, and $150 for a 60-minute session. The driver is included in the price.

Robinson's Marina, Somerset Bridge, Sandys Parish. ⓒ **441/234-3354.** May–Sept daily 8am–7:30pm. Bus: 6 or 7.

5 Where to Play Some of the World's Best Golf

Since the island's first course was laid out in 1922, golf has been one of Bermuda's most popular sports. You can play year-round, but spring, fall, and early winter offer the best seaside conditions. You must arrange tee times at any of the island's eight courses in advance through your guesthouse or hotel. Women's and men's clubs (right- and left-handed) are available at each course, and most leading stores in Bermuda sell golf balls. Generally speaking, children are not welcome on golf courses; definitely check in advance if you have any underage duffers in your party.

Bermuda's Best Golf Courses

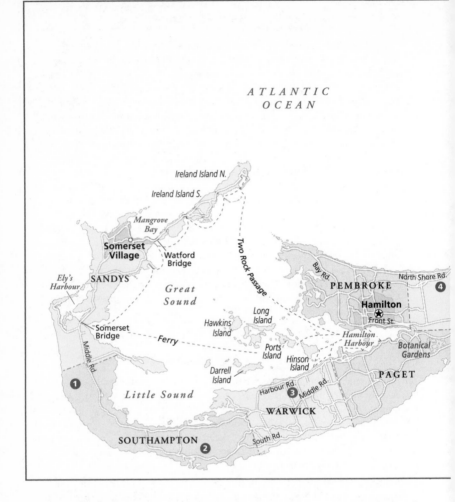

The **Tucker's Point Club** is one of the most scenic courses on the island (though it is a private club), while the **Port Royal** course, designed by Robert Trent Jones, Sr., is a challenge. Two famous courses—the **Mid Ocean Club** at Tucker's Town and the **Riddells Bay Golf and Country Club**—are private, and require introduction by a member before you can play. Certain luxury hotels can sometimes secure playing privileges at the Riddells Bay course. One of the most photographed courses on Bermuda is the **Fairmont Southampton Golf Club,** where a landscape of rolling hills and flowering shrubs adds to the players' enjoyment.

The golf courses listed below that are part of hotel complexes permit nonguests to use their facilities. All of these golf courses have pros and offer lessons.

Top players participate in tournaments throughout the year. For information, contact the **Bermuda Golf Association,** P.O. Box HM 433, Hamilton HM BX, Bermuda (✆ 441/295-9972; www.bermudagolf.org).

Tobacco
Bay

5

*St. George's
Island*

St. George

*Paget
Island*

*St. George's
Harbour*

*Smith's
Island*

Gunner Bay

✈

ST. GEORGE'S

*St. David's
Island*

Castle Harbour

*Nonsuch
Island*

HAMILTON

North Shore Rd.

*Harrington
Sound*

Harrington Sound Rd.

**Tucker's
Town**

Flatts

Middle Rd.

SMITH'S

South Rd.

DEVONSHIRE

South Rd.

Spittal Pond

Causeway

*ATLANTIC
OCEAN*

✈ Airport

| 0 | | 3 mi |
| 0 | | 3 km |

Belmont Golf & Country Club **3**
Ocean View Golf Course **4**
Port Royal Golf Course **1**
Fairmont Southampton Golf Course **2**
St. George's Golf Club **5**

Belmont Golf & Country Club Scotsman Emmett Devereux designed this course in 1923, and its layout has long been a challenge to golfers. The golfing magazines write of its par-5 11th hole, with a severe dogleg left and blind tee shot. It's sometimes difficult to finish uphill at number 18. Crystal caves under the turf sometimes cause the ball to roll unpredictably. In spite of these disadvantages, golf pros recommend the Belmont for beginners; the first hole is said to be "confidence building." It's estimated that with a 9 or 10 handicap, golfers will shoot in the 70s at Belmont—but there aren't any guarantees. Most of the course is inland, so unlike many golf courses in Bermuda, this one provides few views of the Atlantic.

Greens fees (which include golf carts) are $95 Monday to Friday, $105 weekends. A full set of clubs rents for $35.

Between Harbour Rd. and Middle Rd., Warwick Parish. ✆ 441/236-1301. www.belmonthills.com. Daily 6am–5pm. Holes: 18. Par: 70. Length: 5,199m (5,686 yd.). Ferry from the City of Hamilton. Bus: 8.

(Tips) **The Golfer's Dress Code**

Remember to dress appropriately for your golf game. Most courses have strict dress codes that require shirts with collars, Bermuda-length shorts or slacks, and soft-spiked golf shoes or tennis shoes. No bathing suits, cutoffs, short shorts, or jeans.

Fairmont Southampton Golf Club   On the grounds of one of the most luxurious hotels on Bermuda, this course occupies not only the loftiest but also one of the most scenic settings on the island. Elevated tees, strategically placed bunkers, and plenty of water hazards make it a challenge, and golfers have been known to use every club in their bags when the wind blows in from the Atlantic. Against the backdrop of the Gibbs Hill Lighthouse, the 16th hole sits in a cup ringed by flowering bushes. The vertical drop on the 1st and 2nd holes is almost 60m (200 ft.). Even experienced golfers like to "break in" on this course before taking on some of Bermuda's more challenging ones. This well-irrigated course is often green when some other courses suffer a summer brownout.

Greens fees and cart are $70 for 18 holes for both hotel guests and visitors. There are also "Sunset Rates" if you begin playing in the afternoon. You will need to contact the course to get the "Sunset Rates" times (usually 2:30 or 3:30 pm). Adults can walk the course for $25 or add a cart for an additional $20. There are no caddies, and club rental is $25.

101 South Rd., Southampton Parish. © **441/239-6952**. www.fairmont.com/southampton. Daily 7am–sunset. Holes: 18. Par: 54. Length: 2,454m (2,684 yd.). Bus: 7 or 8.

Ocean View Golf Course   In the 1950s, this was a club for African Bermudians. Later, as other clubs started to admit black players, the course was neglected and fell into disrepair. Ocean View's reputation for spotty maintenance lives on despite a $2-million renovation that vastly improved the course. However, the course is nicer than many people expect. In the center of Bermuda, in Devonshire Parish, the course offers panoramic views of the ocean from many of its elevated tees. Many golfers consider the terrain unpredictable; that, combined with rambling hills, makes the course more challenging than it appears. A few holes have as many as six tees. Winds from the Great Sound can have a greater effect on your score than you might think. The green on the 162m (177-yd.), par-3 5th hole has been cut into the coral hillside. Because the hole is draped with semitropical vines, golfers sometimes have the eerie feeling that they're hitting the ball into a cave.

On weekdays, this course tends to be the least crowded on Bermuda. Greens fees are $65 for 9 or 18 holes. Carts rent for $15 per person for 9 holes, $28 for 18 holes; clubs rent for $25. Golf shoes (soft spikes) are mandatory and can be rented for $8.

2 Barkers Hill Rd., Devonshire Parish. © **441/295-9092**. Daily 7:30am–6:30pm. Holes: 9 (18 tee positions). Par: 35. Length: 2,697m (2,949 yd.). Bus: 2, 10, or 11.

Port Royal Golf Course   Famed golf architect Robert Trent Jones, Sr., designed this government-owned and -operated course, which lies along the ocean. Jack Nicklaus might be found at the famous 16th hole, a favorite for photo layouts in golf magazines. The 15th and 16th holes ring the craggy cliffs around Whale Bay; sometimes winds from the Atlantic taunt the golf balls hit from these tees. The 7th and 8th holes are a dogleg par-5 and a windy par-3, respectively.

Port Royal is so popular that some avid golfers reserve starting times a year in advance. Greens fees for 18 holes are $132 (which includes cart). There are no caddies. A full set of clubs rents for $30, and handcarts rent for $10. The clubhouse, which overlooks the ocean and the 9th and 18th greens, contains a bar and a restaurant, Greg's Steakhouse (p. 114), which serves lunch and dinner.

5 Middle Rd., Southampton Parish. © 441/234-0974. Mon–Fri 7:30am–5pm; Sat–Sun 7am–5pm. Holes: 18. Par: 71. Length: 6,003m (6,565 yd.). Bus: 7 or 8.

St. George's Golf Club   Redesigned by Robert Trent Jones, Sr., this is the newest of the Bermuda government's courses. On a headland at the northeastern tip of the island, it's within walking distance of St. George. Links run along the hillsides, providing panoramic vistas of the ocean. The winds off the water will significantly affect your game. On some par-3s, players need everything from a 9 iron to a driver to reach the green. The greens are the smallest on the island; some no more than 7m (23 ft.) across. The abundant salt air makes them slick.

This course isn't usually crowded at midweek. Greens fees for 18 holes are $60. There are no caddies. A full set of clubs rents for $35; gas golf carts go for $28 per person, handcarts for $12.

1 Park Rd., St. George Parish. © 441/297-8067. Apr–Oct Mon–Fri 7:45am–6pm; off season Mon–Fri 8am–5pm. Holes: 18. Par: 62. Length: 3,697m (4,043 yd.). Bus: 3, 6, 8, 10, or 11.

6 Other Outdoor Pursuits: Biking, Horseback Riding & Tennis

BIKING

With a year-round average temperature of 70°F (21°C), Bermuda offers ideal weather for bicycling. Plus, biking is a great way to have fun and stay in shape, and it allows you to take a hands-on approach to your sightseeing. But be forewarned: Most roads aren't suitable for beginners. Think carefully and ask around when you're deciding where you or your children can ride safely and comfortably.

In general, roadways are well paved and maintained. The island's speed limit is 32kmph (20 mph) for all vehicles, but the roads are narrow and winding, and car traffic, especially during the day, tends to be heavy. *Always* exercise caution when riding a bike or scooter. Most drivers are considerate of cyclists, but a car may approach without warning because the government discourages unnecessary horn honking. Fellow cyclists might even overtake you—bicycle racing is one of the most popular local sports.

Bermuda on Bionic Legs

The first tour of its kind, **EZ Rider Electric Bike'n'Hike Sightseeing Excursions,** 38 Main Rd., Somerset (© **441/777-3500**), offers 2½-hour escorted tours for $65 per person. After departing from the Royal Naval Dockyard, you'll ride on easy-to-pedal, electric seven-speed mountain bikes through the West End. You have to pedal to make your bike go, but once you're moving, an electric motor assists you. As you ride almost effortlessly over country roads and through villages, you'll feel like you have bionic legs. When you reach the end of the tour, you can return to the Dockyard on a 20-minute ferry ride.

Much of the island's terrain consists of flat stretches, although the hills provide what the locals call "challenges." Some climbs are steep, especially on roads that run north and south. South Road, through Southampton and Warwick parishes, often leaves bikers huffing and puffing.

RENTING A BIKE

Push bikes or pedal bikes, the terms Bermudians use to distinguish bicycles from mopeds, are a popular form of transportation. You can rent a bicycle by the hour, by the day, or for your entire stay. For information about bicycle and scooter rentals, see "Getting Around," in chapter 3, "Getting to Know Bermuda." All of the recommended shops rent bicycles. Many hotels have bicycles for guests' use, with or without a fee. Rentals generally cost $20 for the first day, plus $5 for each additional day. Three- and 10-speed bikes are usually available. It's always a good idea to call as far in advance as possible, because demand is great, especially from April to October.

WHERE TO BIKE ON BERMUDA

Only the hardiest cyclists set out to traverse the 34km (21-mile) length of Bermuda in 1 day. For most people, it's far better to focus on smaller sections at different times. So, decide what interests you parish by parish, and proceed from there. To save time, you can take your bike aboard various ferries (they're free), and then begin cycling.

A good choice for beginning riders is the **Bermuda Railway Trail** (see below). Some of the most interesting cycling trails are in **Devonshire** and **Smith's parishes.** The hills throughout these areas guarantee that you'll get your exercise for the day, and the beautiful landscapes make your effort worthwhile. **Spittal Pond,** a wildlife sanctuary with bike paths running along seaside cliffs, is one of the most rewarding destinations. Stop by a cycle shop for a trail map and some advice. Nearly all bike shop owners know Bermuda intimately and will mark up a map for you or give you any special guidance you need.

If you're a real demon on a bike, you can go farther west for the challenge of pumping up to **Gibbs Hill Lighthouse,** the oldest cast-iron lighthouse in the world. The panoramic view from the foot of the lighthouse is well worth the effort.

If you'd like to combine a picnic with your bicycle outing, head for **Sandys Parish.** First cross Somerset Bridge, the smallest drawbridge in the world, then pedal along Somerset Road to Fort Scaur Park. There you can relax and admire the view of Ely's Harbour while enjoying your picnic.

THE BERMUDA RAILWAY TRAIL   An interesting bicycle option is the **Bermuda Railway Trail** (see the box "Rattle & Shake: The Bermuda Railway Trail," in chapter 8, "Island Strolls," for more information), which is restricted to bicyclists and pedestrians. The Railway Trail consists of seven sections, each with its own character. You can decide how much of the trail you'd like to cover in 1 day, and which sections to focus on. Pick up a copy of the *Bermuda Railway Trail Guide,* available at the Bermuda Department of Tourism in the City of Hamilton, or the Visitors Service Bureaus in the City of Hamilton and St. George, to help you plan your route.

HORSEBACK RIDING

Spicelands Riding Centre   This stable offers group trail rides for $65 per person hourly. The regularly scheduled 1-hour jaunts begin at 7:30, 9, and 11am daily, year-round. On spring, summer, and fall weekends, there are also rides at 3 and 5pm. Book at least 1 day ahead, calling between 6am and 7pm. *2, 4, 6pm*

Middle Rd., Warwick Parish. ⓒ 441/238-8212. www.spicelandsriding.com. Bus: 8.

TENNIS

Nearly all the big hotels, and many of the smaller ones, have courts, most of which can be lit for night play. Pack your tennis clothing and sneakers, because a tennis outfit (though it no longer needs to be white) may be required.

Each of the facilities listed below has a tennis pro on duty, and lessons can be arranged. All rent racquets and sell balls.

Elbow Beach Hotel   The Elbow Beach Hotel has five Laykold courts (one for lessons only). Lessons cost $35 for 30 minutes, $70 for 1 hour. Racquets can be rented for $5 per hour, and balls are $6 per can of three.

60 South Rd., Paget Parish. ℭ 441/236-3535. Call for bookings mid-Oct to mid-Apr daily 8am–5:30pm; mid-Apr to mid-Oct 8am–7pm. Bus: 1, 2, or 7.

The Fairmont Southampton   This resort has Bermuda's largest tennis court layout, with six Plexipave courts, three of which are lit for night play. The price for guests is $12 per hour; nonguests, $15. Evening rates for guests are $18; nonguests, $25. Racquets rent for $8 per hour, balls cost $7 per can. Lessons are $80 for 1 hour.

101 South Rd., Southampton Parish. ℭ 441/238-8000. Daily 8am–7pm (until 6pm in winter). Bus: 7 or 8.

Government Tennis Stadium   There are three clay and five Plexicushion courts here. Charges to play are $8 per hour for adults, $4 per hour for juniors (12 and under). Playing at night on one of the three lit courts costs $8 extra. Tennis attire is mandatory. Racquets rent for $5 per hour; balls cost $6 per can.

Cedar Ave., Pembroke Parish. ℭ 441/292-0105 to reserve a court or arrange lessons. Winter Mon–Fri 8am–10pm, Sat–Sun 8am–5pm; summer Mon–Fri 8am–10pm, Sat–Sun 8am–7pm. Bus: 1, 2, 10, or 11.

Grotto Bay Beach Club   This resort across from the airport has some of the best tennis courts on the island. The 8.5-hectare (21-acre) property offers four courts, two of which are well-lit for night games. Guests play for $10, nonguests $12 during the

---

Finds Exploring Bermuda's Natural Wonderlands

The National Trust in Bermuda has wisely protected the island's nature reserves. If you play by the rules—that is, don't disturb animal life or take plant life as a souvenir—you can explore many of these natural wonderlands. If you enjoy nature trails, they're one of the most rewarding reasons to visit Bermuda.

The best and largest sanctuary is **Spittal Pond Nature Reserve** in Smith's Parish. Birders visit the reserve—especially from September to April—to see herons, ducks, flamingos, terns, and many migratory fowl (which can't be seen after Mar). This 24-hectare (59-acre) untamed seaside park is always open to the public with no admission charge. **The Department of Parks (ℭ 441/ 236-5902)** offers free guided tours. Tours are offered primarily from November to May; call for schedules and additional information.

The island abounds with other places of natural wonder. Craggy formations shaped over the centuries out of limestone and coral dot the beaches along the southern coast, with towering cliffs forming a backdrop.

day. At night guests pay $25, nonguests $27. The hotel also rents rackets ($4) and tennis balls ($6) at the on-site pro shop.

11 Blue Hole Hill, Hamilton Parish. (C) 441/293-8333. Daily 24 hr. Bus: 1, 3, 10, or 11.

7 Spectator Sports

In this tradition-bound British colony, the most popular spectator sports are cricket, soccer, field hockey, and the not-terribly-genteel game of rugby. As you might expect, boating, yachting, and sailing are also popular. The Bermuda Department of Tourism can provide dates and venues for upcoming events; see "Visitor Information," in chapter 2, for contact information before you go, and "Orienting Yourself: The Lay of the Land," in chapter 3, for information once you've arrived. Also see the "Bermuda Calendar of Events," in chapter 2.

CRICKET

Far more Bermudians than you might suspect have memorized this terribly British sport's arcane rules. If you arrive in midsummer (the game's high season), you'll probably see several regional teams practicing on cricket fields throughout the island. Each match includes enough pageantry to remind participants of the game's imperial antecedents and enough conviviality (picnics, socializing, and chitchat among the spectators) to give you a real feel for Bermuda.

The **Cup Match Cricket Festival** is Bermuda's most passionately watched cricket event, with hundreds of viewers turning out to cheer on family members and friends. Conducted during late July or early August, it pairs Bermuda-based teams against one another. The event usually occurs at the headquarters of two of the island's approximately 30 cricket teams, either the **St. George's Cricket Club,** Willington Slip Road ((C) 441/297-0374), or the **Somerset Cricket Club,** Broome Street off Somerset Road ((C) 441/234-0327). Buy your tickets at the gate on the day of each event, and expect to pay between $12 and $15 per ticket for entrance to this long-standing Bermuda tradition.

GOLF TOURNAMENTS

Bermuda offers some of the finest golfing terrain in the world, partly due to the climate, which supports lush driving ranges and putting greens. In addition, the ever-present golfers play at surprisingly high levels. Golf tournaments are held throughout the year, culminating in the annual, much-publicized **Bermuda Open** at the Port Royal Golf Course in early October. Amateurs and professionals are welcome to vie for one of the most sought-after golfing prizes in the world. For information or an application, contact the secretary of the **Bermuda Golf Association** ((C) 441/238-1367; fax 441/295-0304; www.bermudagolf.org).

HORSE RACING & EQUESTRIAN COMPETITIONS

Contact the **National Equestrian Centre,** Vesey Street, Devonshire Parish ((C) 441/291-7223), for information about upcoming events. From September to Easter, harness races take place about twice a month.

A major equestrian event is in October: the FEI/Samsung Dressage Competition and Show-Jumping. Details are available from the **Bermuda Equestrian Federation,** P.O. Box DV 583, Devonshire DV BX, Bermuda ((C) 441/234-0485; fax 441/234-3010; www.bef.bm). If you can't reach the federation on the phone, which is quite likely, ask for information at the tourist office, or check the local newspaper.

SOCCER

Bermudians view soccer as an important part of elementary education and actively encourage children and teenagers to participate. In early April, teams from countries around the Atlantic and Caribbean compete in three age divisions for the Diadora Youth Soccer Cup. Games are held on various fields throughout the island. More accessible to spectators at other times are the many high-school games held regularly throughout the year. Contact the tourist office for a schedule.

YACHTING

Bermuda capitalizes on its geographical position in the mid-Atlantic to lure the yachting crowd. The racing season runs from March to November, with most races scheduled on weekends in the relatively calm waters of Bermuda's Great Sound. The best land vantage points include Spanish Point, the islands northeast of Somerset, and Hamilton Harbour. Shifting sightlines can make it confusing to watch races from land. Better views are available from the decks of privately owned boats that anchor near the edge of the racecourse, so it's good to befriend a private boat owner. Although the carefully choreographed regattas might be confusing to newcomers, the sight of a fleet of racing craft with spinnakers and pennants aloft is always exciting.

Bermuda is the final destination in two of the most important annual yacht races: the **Annapolis–Bermuda Race** and the even more prestigious **Newport–Bermuda Race,** both held in late June. Both provide enough visual distraction and maritime pageantry to keep you enthralled. Participating yachts range from 9 to 30m (30–98 ft.) in length, and their skippers are said to be among the most dedicated in the world.

Around Halloween, the autumn winds propel dozens of less exotic racing craft through the waters of the Great Sound. They compete in a series of one-on-one playoffs for the **King Edward VII Gold Cup International Match Racing Tournament.**

The island's yachting events are by no means limited to international competitions. Bermuda's sheltered bays and windswept open seas provide year-round enticement for anyone who has ever wanted to experience the thrill of a snapping jib and taut mainsail. See "Sailing," under "More Fun in the Water," earlier in this chapter, for details on yacht charters.

7

Seeing the Sights

Even though a large number of people live on this small island, you should never feel crowded. There are no billboards or neon signs, and relatively few cars to spoil the rolling countryside. Most houses seem to fit quite naturally into the landscape.

Bermuda consists of nine parishes (or counties). From west to east, they are Sandys (pronounced *sands*), Southampton, Warwick, Paget (which has the greatest concentration of hotels), Pembroke (home to the City of Hamilton), Devonshire, Smith's, Hamilton (not to be confused with the City of Hamilton), and St. George, which includes the U.S. naval air base and the little island of St. David's. Pembroke, which contains the capital City of Hamilton, is the largest parish in population; St. George has the largest land area.

Because of Bermuda's small size, it's easy to get to know the island parish by parish. There's much to see, whether you travel by bike, ferry, bus, or taxi. You'll need plenty of time, though, because the pace is slow. Cars and other motorized vehicles, such as mopeds, must observe the maximum speed of 24kmph (15 mph) in the City of Hamilton and St. George, and 32kmph (20 mph) in the countryside. The speed limits are rigidly enforced, and there are severe penalties for violations.

If you're visiting for the first time, you may want to follow the traditional tourist route, basically the equivalent of visiting New York and seeing the Statue of Liberty and the Empire State Building. The Aquarium, Devil's Hole, and cruise-boat outings are all popular for first-time visitors. For travelers on a second, third, or fourth visit to Bermuda, a different experience unfolds. Once you've done all the "must-sees," you'll want to walk around and make discoveries on your own. The best parishes for walking are Somerset, St. George, and the City of Hamilton.

But don't fill your days with too much structured sightseeing. You'll also want time to lounge on the beach, play in the water, or hit the links; and to enjoy moments like sitting by the harbor in the late afternoon, enjoying the views as the yachts glide by. Absorbing Bermuda's

---

Tips **The Fun of Getting Lost**

Many guidebooks contend that you can't get lost in Bermuda. Don't believe them! As you travel along the narrow, winding roads, originally designed for the horse and carriage, you may go astray—several times—especially if you're looking for an obscure guesthouse on some long-forgotten lane. But don't worry, you won't stay lost for long. Bermuda is so narrow—only about 3km (1¾ miles) wide at its broadest point—that if you keep going east or west, you'll eventually come to a main road. The principal arteries are North Shore Road, Middle Road, and South Road (also unofficially referred to as South Shore Rd.), so you'll usually have at least some sense of what part of the island you're in.

beauty at your own pace and stopping to chat with the occasional islander will give you a real taste of Bermuda.

In this chapter, we'll go on a do-it-yourself tour, parish by parish. Also consider taking one or more of the walking tours that we describe in chapter 8, "Island Strolls."

1 Island Highlights

THE TOP ATTRACTIONS

Although Bermuda is small, you really can't see much of it in a day or two. If you have more time, you may want to explore it methodically, parish by parish. That's what we'll do in this chapter—visit each parish's attractions in detail, from west to east. If your time is limited, however, you may want to consider heading straight for the following highlights. For details, see the appropriate section in this book.

- A walking tour of historic St. George Town (see chapter 8, "Island Strolls").
- A walking tour of the City of Hamilton, Bermuda's largest city and the seat of its government. (See chapter 8, "Island Strolls," if you want to combine shopping and sightseeing; also check out chapter 9, "Shopping.")
- A fascinating ode to Bermuda's nautical heritage housed in a 19th-century fortress: the Bermuda Maritime Museum, at the Royal Naval Dockyard on Ireland Island in Sandys Parish.
- The Bermuda Aquarium, Museum & Zoo, a wonderful complex along North Shore Road across Flatts Bridge in Hamilton Parish.
- A guided tour of spectacular Crystal Caves, including crystal-clear Cahow Lake, in Hamilton Parish.
- The 18th-century mansion known as Verdmont in Smith's Parish. It stands on property once owned by the man who left Bermuda to found South Carolina.
- Fort Hamilton, a massive Victorian fortification overlooking the City of Hamilton and its harbor. (See "Walking Tour 1: The City of Hamilton," in chapter 8, "Island Strolls.")
- The Botanical Gardens, a Shangri-La in the mid-Atlantic, on South Road in Paget Parish.
- Gibbs Hill Lighthouse in Southampton Parish, the oldest cast-iron lighthouse in the world.
- Southampton Parish's Horseshoe Bay Beach, the most photographed of the island's pink sandy beaches. (See "Horseshoe Bay Beach," in chapter 6, "Fun in the Surf & Sun.")
- Paget Parish's Elbow Beach, Bermuda's top stretch of sand for beach activities. (See "Elbow Beach," in chapter 6, "Fun in the Surf & Sun.")

HIGHLIGHTS FOR ARCHITECTURE LOVERS

All of Bermuda interests architecture aficionados. Mark Twain wrote of the color of Bermudian houses and roofs: "It is exactly the white of the icing of a cake, and has the same emphasized and scarcely perceptible polish. The white of marble is modest and retiring compared with it . . . clean-cut fanciful chimneys—too pure and white for this world—that will charm one's gaze by the hour." For more details and lore, see the appendix, in addition to the rest of this chapter.

THE TOWN OF ST. GEORGE

The oldest and most historic settlement on the island is likely to hold the greatest fascination for architecture buffs. Also see chapter 8, "Island Strolls," for a walking tour.

The **Old State House,** constructed in 1620, is the oldest stone house on Bermuda. The governor at the time, Nathaniel Butler, had the house built in an Italianate style. He ordered the workmen to use a combination of turtle oil and lime as mortar, a convention seen in many other buildings in Bermuda. You can view the inside of the house on Wednesdays only, from 10am to 4pm. Admission is free.

Many architects have wanted to finish the **Unfinished Church,** which you can reach using Blockade Alley. Construction began in 1874, but a schism developed in the church, and there was no money to continue the project. To this day, true to its name, it remains unfinished.

The **Old Rectory,** now a private residence, was built by a former pirate in 1705. Located on Broad Alley, it's distinguished by its Dutch doors, chimneys, shutters, and what's called a "welcoming arms" staircase, which widens in an "embrace" toward the ground level. The rectory is open for visitors November to March only, Wednesday from 1 to 5pm. Admission is free.

From an architectural point of view, one of the most intriguing structures in St. George is **St. Peter's Church,** on Duke of York Street. This is the oldest Anglican Church in the Western Hemisphere, dating from 1620. It was built to replace an even older structure (from 1612) that had been poorly constructed from posts and palmetto leaves. A storm destroyed the 1620 church in 1712. The present St. Peter's was rebuilt and enlarged in 1713; galleries were added to each side of the church in 1833. The section around the triple-tiered pulpit is believed to be the oldest part of the structure, dating from the 1600s. The first governor of the island, Richard Moore, ordered construction of the dark red Bermuda cedar altar in 1615. It's the oldest surviving piece of woodwork from Bermuda's colonial period.

Tucker House, on Water Street, was built of native limestone. The house is furnished in an interesting manner, mostly with pieces from the mid-1700s and early 1800s. It's open Monday to Saturday from 10am to 4pm. Admission is $3 for adults, $2 for children 6 to 18, free for children 5 and under.

SMITH'S PARISH

Another notable architectural structure is **Verdmont,** a mansion on Verdmont Lane. Dating from around 1710, it was owned by a wealthy shipowner, and also by the founder of the colony of South Carolina. Other owners included an American Loyalist, John Green, who fled from Philadelphia to Bermuda at the end of the Revolutionary War. Built to resemble an English manor house, Verdmont has a striking double roof and a quartet of large chimneys. Each room has a fireplace. The style of the sash windows was once fashionable in English manor houses.

2 Organized Tours

It's relatively easy to explore Bermuda on your own. But, if you prefer help from island-born and -bred residents, it's available.

OFFSHORE TOURS

Bermuda Island Cruises   This outfitter offers the best sojourns at sea. You can book over the phone or through various hotel tour desks.

Moments   **Frommer's Favorite Bermuda Experiences**

Strolling Bermuda's Pink Sands   The pink sand beaches are reason enough to come to Bermuda. Find your favorite cove (perhaps Whale Bay, Astwood Cove, or Jobson's Cove) and stroll aimlessly at dawn, at twilight, or whenever your fancy dictates. See the map "Bermuda's Best Public Beaches & Snorkel Sites," in chapter 6, "Fun in the Surf & Sun."

Cycling   On a rented bicycle, or maybe a moped built for two, explore Bermuda from end to end. Start in St. George in the East End and go all the way to the Royal Naval Dockyard in the West End, or vice versa. You can do this in 1 day or stretch it out. See "Other Outdoor Pursuits: Biking, Horseback Riding & Tennis," in chapter 6, "Fun in the Surf & Sun."

Following the Bermuda Railway Trail   As you follow this intermittent trail from one end of the island to the other, you'll take in panoramic seascapes, see exotic flora and fauna, hear the soothing sounds of the island's bird life, and often have long stretches of trail completely to yourself. See "Rattle & Shake: The Bermuda Railway Trail," in chapter 8, "Island Strolls."

Touring by Horse & Buggy   No one has ever improved on this old-fashioned method of sightseeing and shopping along the City of Hamilton's Front Street. Better yet, go on a 2-hour shopping tour of Somerset Village in the West End. See "By Horse-Drawn Carriage," under "Getting Around," in chapter 3, "Getting to Know Bermuda."

Viewing Bermuda from Gibbs Hill Lighthouse (p. 171)   Climb the 185 steps of the oldest cast-iron lighthouse in the world for one of the greatest views of the Atlantic Ocean. Springtime visitors may be lucky enough to see migrating whales beyond the shore reefs.

Two-hour glass-bottom-boat tours will take you to Bermuda's famous reefs and shipwrecks. The cruises, which include commentary by a knowledgeable guide, leave Monday to Friday at 10am and 1:30pm, and Sunday at 1:30pm, only from Hamilton Harbour. The cost is $40 for adults, $20 for children 6 to 12, free for children 5 and under.

The "Don't Stop the Carnival" evening cruise at Hawkins Island includes a barbecue dinner, music from a "Tropical Heat" band, a "Hot Spice Limbo" show, and an open bar. The cost is $95 per adult, $55 for children 7 to 14, $35 for children 6 and under. A parent must accompany children 17 and under. The cruise runs from 7 to 10:30pm on Tuesday, Wednesday, Friday, and Saturday.

E. Broadway Marina, Pembroke Parish. (441/292-8652.

Bermuda Water Tours Ltd.   This company offers 2- and 3½-hour trips for $35 and $50, respectively; children 5 to 12 are half-price, 4 and under are free. Most tours include a visit to the sea gardens, where you can see the wonders of coral reefs and fish through the boat's glass bottom. Other water trips, including snorkeling expeditions, are also available.

P.O. Box 1572, City of Hamilton. (441/236-1500.

Attractions Around the Island

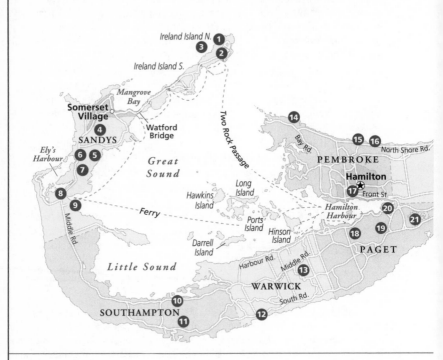

ATLANTIC OCEAN

Ireland Island N.
Ireland Island S.
Mangrove Bay
Somerset Village
Watford Bridge
SANDYS
Ely's Harbour
Great Sound
Two Rock Passage
Bay Rd.
North Shore Rd.
PEMBROKE
Hamilton
Front St.
Hawkins Island
Long Island
Ports Island
Hinson Island
Darrell Island
Hamilton Harbour
Ferry
Middle Rd.
Little Sound
Harbour Rd.
Middle Rd.
WARWICK
South Rd.
PAGET
SOUTHAMPTON

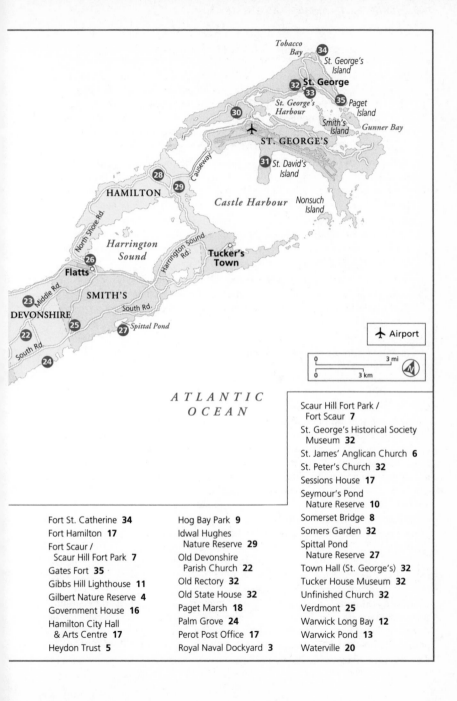

Airport ✈

| 0 | | 3 mi |
| 0 | | 3 km |

ATLANTIC
OCEAN

Insider Tours: "Bermuda Explorers Program"

Visitors to Bermuda have the opportunity to gain an even deeper under-standing of local attractions through the **Bermuda Explorers Program**, a series of tours and programs. The island's cultural leaders, business owners, and other local residents are creating opportunities to present travelers with an in-depth and unique look at Bermuda. The following is a list of tours currently available through **Bermuda Explorers Program**:

Art and Architecture Walk: A pre-opening-hours tour starts at the Bermuda National Gallery with a museum curator, then continues into the town of Hamilton. Guests receive a map of art in public places and local gal-leries and can meet with the gallery owners or artists on their own.

Gumba Trail: A historic journey through time via a cultural nature walk, the trail describes the background of the Caribbean Junkanoo dancers and their connection to the Gombeys of Bermuda, along with commentary on the Island's plant life and its uses.

Verdmont Historic House Museum: A historian from the National Trust accompanies visitors on a private tour of Verdmont. Built in 1710, the house contains Bermuda's most notable collection of antique cedar-wood furni-ture, portraits, and toys.

Arrangements for tours can be made through the Visitors Service Bureaus (p 49). Most tours charge admission fees that range from $20 to $35.

ENVIRONMENTAL TOURS

The not-for-profit **Bermuda Biological Station for Research** has collected the world's most comprehensive data on the oceanographic absorption of human-released carbon dioxide. It has tracked carbon dioxide levels for more than 40 years over a 21km (13-mile) area southeast of Bermuda. The National Science Foundation awarded the station a $500,000 grant to study climate change, the greenhouse effect, and the carbon cycle. The station has also compiled an extensive record on acid rain in the North American atmosphere.

You can learn firsthand what the station's scientists are studying by taking a free 60-minute guided tour of the grounds and laboratory in St. George. Guides explain what scientific studies are being conducted in Bermuda and how they relate to the overall world environment. They also discuss the island's natural areas, including the coral reefs, which are protected by strict conservation laws, and how humans have produced changes in the fragile ecological environment.

Trained volunteers and scientists who are carrying out studies conduct the educational tours, offered at 10am on Wednesday. Visitors should assemble before 10am in the Bio-logical Station's Hanson Hall. For more information, contact the **Bermuda Biological Station for Research,** 17 Biological Lane, Ferry Reach, St. George (© **441/297-1880**). The tour lasts 1 hour.

3 Sandys Parish

Sandys Parish is one of the island's real beauty spots. If you're looking for a place to just wander about and get lost on a summer day, this lovely parish is well worth your time. Fort Scaur and the Royal Naval Dockyard on Ireland Island are the major attractions. If you're pressed for time, skip the Gilbert Nature Reserve and St. James' Anglican Church.

To explore this tip of the fishhook that is Bermuda, it's best to take a ferry (the fare is $4). The trip from the City of Hamilton to Watford Bridge takes 45 minutes, and you can take your bike onboard free (there's a $4 charge for scooters and mopeds). Ferries originating in Hamilton also stop at Cavello Bay, Somerset Bridge, Boaz Island, and the Royal Naval Dockyard. The **Visitors Service Bureau** is at the Royal Naval Dockyard (*C* **441/234-3824**), across from the ferry terminal. From May to October, hours are Monday to Friday and Sunday 9am to 5pm (closed Sat).

Gilbert Nature Reserve (aka National Trust)   In the center of the island lies the Gilbert Nature Reserve, 2 hectares (5 acres) of unspoiled woodland. It bears the name of the family that owned the property from the early 18th century until 1973, when the Bermuda National Trust acquired it (in conjunction with the Bermuda Audubon Society).

Somerset Rd. *C* **441/236-6483**. Free admission. Daily 9am–5pm. Organized tours available. Bus: 7 or 8 from the City of Hamilton.

Scaur Hill Fort Park *ℱ*   On the highest hill in Somerset, Fort Scaur was part of a ring of fortifications constructed in the 19th century, during a period of troubled relations between Britain and the United States. Intended as a last-ditch defense for the Royal Naval Dockyard, the fort was skillfully constructed, taking advantage of the land contours to camouflage its presence from detection at sea. The fort has subterranean passages and a dry moat that stretches across the land from Ely's Harbour to Great Sound.

Open to visitors since 1957, Fort Scaur has become one of Somerset's most popular tourist attractions. The fort has panoramic views of Ely's Harbour and Great Sound; using the free telescope, you'll see such faraway points as St. David's Lighthouse and Fort St. Catherine. The fort sits on 9 hectares (22 acres) of parkland filled with interesting trails, picnic areas, a rocky shoreline for fishing, and a public dock. Picnic tables, benches, and restrooms are available.

Ely's Harbour, Somerset Rd. *C* **441/236-5902**. Free admission. Daily 9am–6pm. Closed Dec 25, Jan 15. Bus: 7 or 8 from the City of Hamilton.

St. James' Anglican Church   This is one of the most beautiful churches on Bermuda. It was constructed on the site of a structure that was destroyed by a hurricane in 1780. The present church was built 9 years later. A unique feature is the altar, which faces west instead of the customary east. The north and south aisles were added

---

Fun Fact **Just Where Is Bermuda?**

Bermuda is definitely not a Caribbean island. Many visitors learn with surprise that it lies closer to Nova Scotia than to any island in the Caribbean.

Especially for Kids

Bermuda is a great destination for the entire family. Most resorts offer children's activities and special family packages. Most of the larger properties also give Mom and Dad an opportunity to spend some time alone by offering babysitting services for minimal fees.

Even more important, Bermuda offers many activities that will keep kids interested all day long. Kid-friendly activities include sailing, water-skiing, snorkeling, and glass-bottom-boat trips from April to October, plus tennis, visits to museums and caves, and a wide array of walking tours. Here are some of Bermuda's top sights and activities for kids:

Bermuda Aquarium, Museum & Zoo (p. 178)   This complex offers kids a wonderful introduction to the undersea world. Hand-held cassette recordings let you listen to a history of marine life as you visit live exhibits of Bermuda's native fish.

Bermuda Bell Diving (p. 147)   Kids can explore the ocean floor on their own—all they need is an underwater helmet and a little guidance. Following a predive educational lecture aboard the ship, the kids can walk along the ocean floor for face-to-face encounters with friendly sea creatures. For children 8 years and older only.

Bermuda Maritime Museum (p. 169)   Everyone in the family takes equal delight in seeing the exhibits of Bermuda's nautical history in this authentic Victorian fortress museum.

Bermuda Railway Trail   This nature walk, with strolls overlooking the seashore and along quiet tree-lined alleyways, is suitable for the entire family. You can pick up the 34km (21-mile) trail at many points and explore as many sections as you like, according to your stamina and interests. See "Rattle & Shake: The Bermuda Railway Trail," in chapter 8, "Island Strolls."

Crystal Caves (p. 178)   Two boys chasing a runaway ball in 1907 discovered an enormous cavern and an underground lake. Easily navigable walkways, and good guides, take parents and kids down into the caverns in Hamilton Parish.

---

in 1836, the entrance gate in 1872, and the spire and chancel in 1880. The church was struck by lightning in 1939 and restored shortly thereafter.

90 Somerset Rd. (£) 441/234-0834. Free admission. Daily 8am–5pm. Bus: 7 or 8 from the City of Hamilton.

IRELAND ISLAND & THE ROYAL NAVAL DOCKYARD

Bermuda Arts Centre   Works by local artists are the focus in this gallery, with exhibits changing about every 6 weeks. An eclectic range of original art and prints is for sale. Local artists in residence include a cedar sculptor and a jewelry maker. On the premises you'll see four artists laboring in their respective mediums: wood-sculpting, jewelry making, oil painting, and weaving. There's a small gift shop on-site, displaying and selling the wares of these and other artists.

Maritime Lane. ℭ 441/234-2809. www.artbermuda.bm. Free admission. Daily 10am–5pm. See transportation information under the Royal Naval Dockyard listing below.

Bermuda Craft Market   This is the prime place to watch local artists at work and to buy their wares, which make ideal souvenirs. Established in 1987, this market offers items made from Bermuda cedar, candles, clothing, dolls, fabrics, hand-painted goods, jewelry, metal and gem sculpture, needlework, quilts, shell art, glass panels, and woven-cane goods, among other things.

In the Cooperage Building, 4 Freeport Rd. ℭ 441/234-3208. Free admission. Nov–Mar daily 10am–4pm; Apr–Oct daily 9:30am–6pm. See transportation information under the Royal Naval Dockyard listing below.

Bermuda Maritime Museum 🐂🐂 *(Kids)*   Housed in a 19th-century fortress built by convict labor, this museum exhibits artifacts, models, and maps pertaining to Bermuda's nautical heritage. The fortress's massive buildings of fitted stone, with their vaulted ceilings of English brick, are worth a visit on their own. So are the 9m (30-ft.) defensive ramparts; the underground tunnels, gun ports, and magazines; and the water gate and pond designed for boats entering from the sea. Exhibits in six large halls illustrate the island's long, intimate connection with the sea—from Spanish exploration to 20th-century ocean liners; from racing dinghies to practical fishing boats; from shipbuilding and privateering to naval exploits.

The museum's most famous exhibit is in the 1837 **Shifting House,** which opened in 1979. You can see such artifacts as gold bars, pottery, jewelry, silver coins, and other items recovered from 16th- and 17th-century shipwrecks. The collection includes some earthenware and pewter that belonged to the English settlers on their way to Jamestown aboard the *Sea Venture,* which was wrecked in 1609. Most visitors come here to gaze at the Tucker Treasure. A well-known local diver, Teddy Tucker, made a significant find in 1955 when he discovered the wreck of the *San Antonio,* a Spanish vessel that had gone down off the coast of Bermuda in a violent storm in 1621. One of the great treasures of this find, the Pectoral Cross, was stolen in 1975 just before Queen Elizabeth II officially opened the museum. The priceless original cross was replaced by a fake. The original cross has not been recovered, and its mysterious disappearance is still the subject of much discussion.

As you enter the Parade Ground at the entrance to the museum, you'll notice a 3m-high (9¾-ft.) figure of King Neptune. This has been duplicated in Indiana limestone from a figure that was recovered from HMS *Irresistible,* when the ship was broken up in 1891. The **Queen's Exhibition Hall** houses general maritime exhibits, including displays on navigation, whaling, and cable and wireless communications. A "Bermuda in Five Hours" exhibit focuses on Pan American's early "flying boats." The building itself was constructed in 1850 for the purpose of storing 4,860 barrels of gunpowder.

The **Forster Cooper Building** (1852) illustrates the history of the Royal Navy in Bermuda, and includes the Bromby Bottle Collection, boasting more than 2,000 rare

---

(Fun Fact **The World's Smallest Drawbridge**

After leaving Fort Scaur, you can continue over the much-photographed 17th-century **Somerset Bridge,** the world's smallest drawbridge. When it's open for marine traffic, the space between the spans is a mere 56 centimeters (22 in.) at road level—just large enough for the mast of a sailboat to pass through.

and antique bottles that have washed up on Bermuda's shores. Princess Margaret opened the exhibit in 1984. The **Boatloft** houses part of the museum's boat collections, including the century-old fitted dinghy *Victory,* the 5m (16-ft.) *Spirit of Bermuda,* and the *Rambler,* the only surviving Bermuda pilot gig (a commanding officer's light boat kept on a large ship). On the upper floor, the original dockyard clock, which is still working, chimes every quarter-hour. In 2000, one of the Dockyard's most impressive colonial-era buildings, the **Commissioner's House,** was restored and opened to the public. The ground floor of its stately looking interior is devoted to exhibits showing the contribution of Bermudians to World War I; the second floor is devoted to exhibitions about the history of marine traffic and sailing in Bermuda; and the third floor contains some of the many watercolors that ladies of distinction used to paint, usually of the Dockyards, during the 19th and early 20th centuries. Admission to the Shifting House, Queen's Exhibition Hall, Forster Cooper Building, Boatloft, and Commissioner's House are included in the entrance price to the Bermuda Maritime Museum.

Royal Naval Dockyard. (C) **441/234-1418.** www.bmm.bm. Admission $10 adults, $8 seniors, $5 children 5–15, free for children 4 and under. Daily 9:30am–4pm. Closed Dec 25. See transportation information under the Royal Naval Dockyard listing below.

The Royal Naval Dockyard *✹✹* The Dockyard, with its Bermuda Maritime Museum, is the number one tourist attraction on Bermuda. Even if you plan to spend all your precious Bermuda time on the pink sandy beaches, try to schedule at least a half-day to check it out.

The Royal Naval Dockyard has been transformed into a park, with Victorian street lighting and a Terrace Pavilion and bandstand for concerts. When the Bermudian government bought this dockyard, which had been on British Admiralty land, in 1953, it marked the end of British naval might in the western Atlantic. A multimillion-dollar cruise-ship dock has been built and a tourist village has emerged; today, vendors push carts filled with food, dry goods, and local crafts. There's a full-service marina with floating docks, a clubhouse, and showers. The area also houses the Bermuda

---

Finds **A Park of Your Own**

Just when you thought that everything in "Paradise" (as locals call Bermuda) had been discovered, you happen upon 15-hectare (37-acre) **Hog Bay Park.** In spite of its unattractive name, this is one of the beauty spots of Bermuda, and one of its least visited attractions. To reach the park from the City of Hamilton, take a ferry across Great Sound, getting off at the Somerset Bridge ferry stop. Cross the Somerset drawbridge and follow the trail of the old Bermuda Railway. Cross Middle Road into the park. Once at the park you'll pass ruins of lime kilns once used for making lime to paint the famous whitewashed roofs of island homes. As you meander, you'll come across old abandoned cottages, finally reaching Sugar Loaf Hill with its Look Out Point. From here, you'll be rewarded with one of the greatest panoramic views on Bermuda. As Barbra Streisand might put it: "On a clear day, you can see forever."

> **Moments   Stepping Back into the Ice Age**
>
> Bermuda has one of the highest concentrations of limestone caves in the world. Most began forming during the Pleistocene Ice Age. As early as 1623, the adventurer Capt. John Smith wrote that he had encountered "vary strange, darke, cumbersome caves."
>
> In Bermuda, nature's patient, relentless underground sculpting has left behind a dream world for even the casual spelunker. Deep in the majestic silence of the earth's interior, you can roam in caverns full of great stalactites and stalagmites of Gothic grandeur, delicacy, and beauty. This awesome underground has been the inspiration for creative achievements as diverse as Shakespeare's *The Tempest* and Henson Associates' *Fraggle Rock*.
>
> You can visit Crystal Caves on guided tours; the cave complex is along Harrington Sound Road in Hamilton Parish (p. 178).

Maritime Museum, the Neptune Theatre (a 118-seat cinema showing feature films two times a night, with matinees Fri–Sun; *©* 441/291-2035), the Crafts Market, and the Bermuda Arts Centre, which are all described above. Closed Good Friday and Christmas Day. Call the Visitors Service Bureau for more information (*©* 441/234-3824).

Ferries from the City of Hamilton stop at Ireland Island, at the western end of Bermuda, once each hour 7am–6pm. Fare $4 each way. Buses (no. 7 or 8) leave the City of Hamilton for the Royal Naval Dockyard Mon–Sat every 15 min. 6:45am–11:45pm. The trip takes 1 hr. and costs $4 for adults, $1 for children 5–15, free for children 4 and under. **Note:** Drivers accept this exact bus fare in coins only.

4 Southampton Parish

Most visitors stop by Southampton for the beaches, if for no other reason. Even if you're not staying here, it's worth a journey to see the view from Gibbs Hill Lighthouse—there's no finer panorama in all of Bermuda.

Gibbs Hill Lighthouse *☞* Southampton's main attraction is this completely restored lighthouse, built in 1846. It's the oldest cast-iron lighthouse in the world. Although there's a 185-step climb to the top, the panoramic view of Bermuda and its shoreline from the balcony make the exertion worthwhile. You can also view the same panorama that Queen Elizabeth II gazed on in 1953; just find the commemoration plaque by the entrance to the lighthouse. The lighthouse keeper will explain the workings of the machinery. If you visit in the spring, you may spot migrating whales beyond the south-shore reefs.

Gibbs Hill, Lighthouse Rd. (between South Rd. and Middle Rd.). *©* 441/238-8069. www.gibbshilllighthouse.com. Admission $2.50, free for children 4 and under. Daily 9am–4pm. Closed Feb. Bus: 7 or 8 from the City of Hamilton.

5 Warwick Parish

This parish has few sightseeing attractions, but it is a place of natural beauty. Visitors come here mostly for the sandy beach, **Warwick Long Bay,** on South Road—it's one of the finest on Bermuda (see "Beaches," in chapter 6, "Fun in the Surf & Sun," for details). Nearby, you can visit **Christ Church,** across from the Belmont Hotel on Middle Road. Built in 1719, it's one of the oldest Scottish Presbyterian churches in the New World.

Warwick is also the site of some of the best golf and horseback riding in Bermuda. See chapter 6, "Fun in the Surf & Sun," for specifics on these activities.

6 Paget Parish

On every visit to Bermuda, we schedule a long stopover at the Botanical Gardens. They are worth the trip, even if you're staying in the East End. Once you're here, Waterville, one of the oldest houses in Bermuda, merits a look. You could cap your visit with a walk through unspoiled Paget Marsh, although you might skip it if you've already seen Spittal Pond (see "Smith's Parish," later in this chapter).

The Birdsey Studio Jo Birdsey Lindberg, daughter of the island's best-known artist, Alfred Birdsey (1912–96), sells original artwork, watercolors, and oils. An experienced painter, she continues a family tradition by producing and showing her work here, in a garden setting. Her impressionistic style appears in compositions ranging from landscapes of Bermuda to architectural and nautical themes. Prices range from $50 to $350 for watercolors, $700 to $1,000 for oils. Also available are notecards reproduced from paintings by Alfred Birdsey. It's always best to call ahead to make sure the studio is open.

5 Stowe Hill. ✆ **441/236-6658** or 441/236-5845 in the evening. Free admission. Mar–July and Sept–Nov Mon–Fri 11am–1pm; other times by appointment only. Bus: 8 from the City of Hamilton.

Botanical Gardens ⚶ This 14-hectare (35-acre) landscaped park, maintained by the Department of Natural Resources, is one of Bermuda's major attractions. Hundreds of clearly identified flowers, shrubs, and trees line the pathways. Attractions include collections of hibiscus and subtropical fruit, an aviary, banyan trees, and even a garden for the blind. It's best to take one of the 90-minute walking tours from the visitor center. The cafe sells sandwiches and salads (soup and chili in winter). **Masterworks Foundation** has built a growing art exhibit in the gardens, displaying various types of oil paintings and watercolor paintings.

Point Finger Rd. (at South Rd.). ✆ **441/236-4201.** Free admission. Daily 9:30am–5:30pm. Tours Tues–Wed and Fri 10:30am. Bus: 1, 2, 7, or 8. By bike or moped, turn left off Middle Rd. onto Tee St.; at Berry Hill Rd., go right; about 1km (⅔ mile) farther on the left is the signposted turnoff to the gardens; take a right fork to the parking lot on the left.

Paget Marsh This nature reserve comprises 10 hectares (25 acres) of unspoiled native woods and marshland, with vegetation and bird life of ecological interest. Because it's a fully protected area with few trails, prospective visitors should call first and make special arrangements, and obtain a map from the Bermuda National Trust. A boardwalk allows you to view the marsh better.

Middle Rd. ✆ **441/236-6483.** Free admission. Mon–Fri 9am–5pm by special arrangement. Bus: 2, 7, or 8.

Waterville Built before 1735, Waterville is one of the oldest houses on Bermuda. It was home to seven generations of the prominent Trimingham family. From the house's cellar storage rooms in 1842, James Harvey Trimingham started the business that was to become Trimingham Brothers—now one of Bermuda's finest Front Street department stores. Major renovations were undertaken in 1811, and the house has been restored in that period's style. The two main rooms hold period furnishings, mainly Trimingham family heirlooms specifically bequeathed for use in the house.

Waterville is the headquarters of the Bermuda National Trust, and houses its offices and reception rooms. It's just west of the Trimingham roundabout, near the City of Hamilton.

29 The Lane (Harbour Rd.), at Pomander Rd. ⓒ **441/236-6483.** Free admission. Mon–Fri 9am–5pm. Closed on holidays. Bus: 7 or 8 from the City of Hamilton.

7 Pembroke Parish & the City of Hamilton

For first-time visitors, the ideal way to see the City of Hamilton and its parish, Pembroke, is to sail in through Hamilton Harbour, past the offshore cays.

In 1852, the cornerstone was laid for the Hamilton Hotel, Bermuda's first hotel, completed in 1863. It survived until a fire destroyed it in 1955. When the Hamilton Princess opened in 1887, it overshadowed the Hamilton Hotel and became the island's hotel of choice. The Hamilton Hotel's colorful history includes being taken over by Allied agents during World War II.

If Queen Victoria's daughter Princess Louise were to visit Bermuda today, she would probably stay at **Government House,** on North Shore Road and Langton Hill. Because this is the residence of the governor of the island, it's not open to the public. This Victorian home has housed many notable guests, including Queen Elizabeth II and Prince Philip, Prince Charles, Sir Winston Churchill, and Pres. John F. Kennedy. In 1973, Gov. Sir Richard Sharples, his aide, Capt. Hugh Sayers, and the governor's dog were assassinated while they were walking on the grounds. The killer, a local named Erskine Burrows, was hanged in 1977 after being found guilty of these murders as well as that of Police Commissioner George Duckett in 1972 and an armed robbery in 1973. The tragedy led to a state of emergency in Bermuda.

While touring Pembroke Parish, visitors often stop at **Black Watch Well,** at the junction of North Shore Road and Black Watch Pass. Excavated by a detachment of the Black Watch Regiment, the well was dug in 1894, when Bermudians were suffering through a long drought.

Another choice spot to visit is **Admiralty House Park,** off North Shore Road at Spanish Point Road. In 1816, a house was erected here to offer accommodations for the commanding British admiralty, who worked at the naval base at the dockyard. Over the years, the house was rebuilt several times. In the 1850s, it gained a series of subterranean tunnels, plus a number of galleries and caves carved into the cliffs above the sea. By 1951, the Royal Navy withdrew, and most of the house was torn down— except for a ballroom, which survives. Today, you can explore the parklike grounds. The sheltered beach at Clarence Cove is good for swimming.

THE CITY OF HAMILTON ✹✹✹

The capital of Bermuda was once known as the "show window of the British Empire." Both Mark Twain and Eugene O'Neill, who lived in lodgings that opened onto Hamilton Harbour, cited its beauty.

Named for former governor Henry Hamilton, the City of Hamilton was incorporated in 1793. Because of its central location and its large, protected harbor, it replaced St. George as the island's capital in 1815. The city encompasses only 73 hectares (180 acres) of land, so most visitors explore it on foot.

Long before it became known as "the showcase of the Atlantic," the City of Hamilton was a modest outlet for the export of Bermuda cedar and fresh vegetables. Today, it's the hub of the island's economy.

⟨Tips⟩ From the Land & from the Sea

The City of Hamilton should be seen not only from land but also from the water. Try to make time for a boat tour of the harbor and its coral reefs. If you're visiting from another parish, the ferry will let you off at the west end of Front Street, which is ideal if you'd like to drop by the Visitors Service Bureau, which is right near the Ferry Terminal, and pick up a map. The staff also provides information and helpful brochures; hours are 9am to 5pm Monday to Saturday.

More popular for its shops and restaurants than for its attractions, The City of Hamilton boasts the largest number of dining spots and bars on Bermuda, especially on and near Front Street. The restaurants have a wide range of prices, and there are many English-style watering holes if you'd like to go for a traditional pub-crawl. And religion isn't neglected—there are 12 churches within the city limits, the most interesting being the Cathedral of the Most Holy Trinity (p. 175).

If you'd like to go sightseeing, take our walking tour (see chapter 8, "Island Strolls") for a comprehensive view of the City of Hamilton. The only sights that are worth in-depth visits are Fort Hamilton (seen on the walking tour), the Bermuda Historical Society Museum, and the Bermuda National Gallery. You can safely skip the rest if you're pressed for time.

A stroll along **Front Street** ✿ will take you by some of the City of Hamilton's most elegant stores, but you'll also want to branch off into the little alleyways to check out the shops and boutiques. If you get tired of walking or shopping (or both), you can go down to the docks and take one of the boats or catamarans waiting to show you the treasures of Little Sound and Great Sound.

Ferries back to Paget, Warwick, and Sandys parishes leave daily between 6:50am and 11:20pm. On Saturday and Sunday, there are fewer departures.

On certain days you may be able to see locals buying fresh fish—the part of the catch that isn't earmarked for restaurants—right from the fishers at the **Front Street docks.** Rockfish is the most abundant, and you'll also see snapper, grouper, and many other species.

Opposite the Visitors Service Bureau stands the much-photographed **"Birdcage,"** where you used to be able to see a Bermuda-shorts-clad police officer directing traffic on a pedestal likened to a birdcage. Such a sight is rare now. Visitors often wondered if the traffic director was for real or placed there for tourist photographs.

Nearby is Albouy's Point, site of the Royal Bermuda Yacht Club, founded in 1844. The point, named after a 17th-century professor of "physick," is a public park overlooking Hamilton Harbour.

To reach the sights listed below, take bus no. 1, 2, 10, or 11.

Bermuda Historical Society Museum After leaving the harbor, proceed up Queen Street to the public library and the Bermuda Historical Society Museum. The museum has a collection of old cedar furniture, antique silver, early Bermuda coins (hog money), and ceramics imported by early sea captains. You'll see the sea chest and navigating lodestone of Sir George Somers, whose flagship, the *Sea Venture,* became stranded on Bermuda's reefs in 1609, resulting in Bermuda's first European settlers. You'll also find portraits of Sir George and Lady Somers, and models of *Patience, Deliverance,* and the ill-fated *Sea Venture.*

The museum is in Par-la-Ville Park on Queen Street. It was designed by William Bennett Perot, the City of Hamilton's first postmaster (1818–62), who was a somewhat eccentric fellow; as he delivered mail around town, he is said to have placed letters in the crown of his top hat in order to preserve his dignity.

13 Queen St., Par-la-Ville Park. (✆ 441/295-2487. Free admission. Mon–Sat 9:30am–3:30pm.

Bermuda National Gallery   Located on the second floor of City Hall in the heart of Hamilton, this national gallery is the home of the island nation's art collection, showing both Bermudian and world art. The museum displays a diverse permanent collection as well as changing exhibitions. Both past and contemporary work from local and international painters not only tells the story of Bermuda's history but reflects its heritage. The gallery opened in 1992 with a core collection of European masters, including Gainsborough, Reynolds, and Murillo. The collection was bequeathed to Bermuda by the Hon. Hereward T. Watlington on the condition that the art be housed in a climate-controlled environment to protect it from humidity and damaging sunlight.

In addition to the Watlington Collection, the museum has an African collection (African figures, masks, and royal regalia), a Bermuda Collection (which ranges from 17th-century decorative arts to contemporary Bermudian work), and a wide range of Bermudian and international photographs, prints, and modern art.

City Hall, 17 Church St. (✆ 441/295-9428. www.bermudanationalgallery.com. Free admission. Mon–Sat 10am–4pm. Tours Thurs at 10:30am.

Cathedral of the Most Holy Trinity (Bermuda Cathedral)   This is the mother church of the Anglican diocese in Bermuda. It became a cathedral in 1894 and was formally consecrated in 1911. The building features a reredos (ornamental partition), stained-glass windows, and ornate carvings. If you have the stamina, climb the 157 steps to the top of the tower for a panoramic view of the City of Hamilton and the harbor.

Church St. (✆ 441/292-4033. www.anglican.bm. Free admission to cathedral; admission to cathedral tower $3 adults, $2 children 6 and under and seniors 65 and over. Cathedral daily 8am–5pm and for Sun services; tower Mon–Fri 10am–3:30pm.

African Diaspora Heritage Trail

The African Diaspora Heritage Trail commemorates the role African slaves played in the formation of Bermuda. Free brochures, available from tourist offices, direct you along this self-guided tour that highlights peak points in the black cultural history of the island. A plaque marks each site.

Thirteen sites have been identified, including the site of the slave ship *Enterprise* incident, which, like the similar, better-known *Amistad* affair, involved the rescuing of slaves seeking refuge and freedom; and the historic Slave Graveyard at St. Peter's Church (ca. 1612), both located in St. George's (UNESCO's newest World Heritage Site); the Crow Lane site of the execution of Sally Bassett, slave revolt leader; sites associated with Mary Prince, the Bermudian slave who wrote the first account of slavery actually authored by a slave, which played a key role in the struggle to abolish slavery; and Cobb's Hill Wesleyan Methodist Church, built by slaves by moonlight.

Hamilton City Hall & Arts Centre   The City Hall, also home of the **Bermuda Society of Arts,** is an imposing white structure with a giant weather vane and wind clock to tell maritime-minded Bermudians which way the wind is blowing. Completed in 1960, the building is the seat of the City of Hamilton's municipal government. The theater on the first floor books stage, music, and dance productions throughout the year, and is the main site of the Bermuda Festival. The Bermuda National Gallery (see above) is also here.

Since 1956, the Bermuda Society of Arts has encouraged, and provided a forum for, contemporary artists, sculptors, and photographers. Its gallery, with ever-changing exhibitions, displays the work of local and visiting artists.

17 Church St. ✆ **441/292-1234** or 441/292-3824. Free admission to City Hall and Bermuda Society of Arts. City Hall Mon–Fri 9am–5pm; Sat 9am–4pm. Bermuda Society of Arts Mon–Sat 10am–4pm.

Perot Post Office   Bermuda's first stamp was printed in this landmark building. Beloved by collectors from all over the world, the stamps—signed by William Bennett Perot, Bermuda's first postmaster—are priceless. It's said that Perot and his friend J. B. Heyl, who ran an apothecary, conceived the first postage stamp to protect the post office from cheaters. People used to stop off at the post office and leave letters, but not enough pennies to send them. The postage stamps were printed in black or carmine.

Philatelists can purchase contemporary Bermuda stamps here. For its 375th anniversary, Bermuda issued a series of stamps honoring its discovery in 1609. One stamp portrays the admiral of the fleet, Sir George Somers, along with Sir Thomas Gates, the captain of the *Sea Venture.* Another depicts the settlement of Jamestown, Virginia, which was on the verge of extinction when Sir George and the survivors of the Bermuda shipwreck finally arrived with supplies late in 1610. A third shows the *Sea Venture* stranded on the coral reefs of Bermuda. Yet another shows the entire fleet, originally bound for Jamestown, leaving Plymouth, England, on June 2, 1609.

Queen St., at the entrance to Par-la-Ville Park. ✆ **441/292-9052** or 441/295-5151. Free admission. Mon–Fri 9am–5pm.

Sessions House   This Italian Renaissance–style structure was originally built in 1819. Its clock tower, added in 1887, commemorates the Golden Jubilee of Queen Victoria. The House of Assembly meets on the second floor from November to May, and visitors are permitted in the gallery. Call ahead to learn when meetings are scheduled. On the lower level, the chief justice presides over the Supreme Court.

21 Parliament St. ✆ **441/292-7408**. Free admission. Daily 9am–12:30pm and 2–3pm.

8 Devonshire Parish

If you're passing through Devonshire, consider a stop at the following attractions.

Old Devonshire Parish Church   The Old Devonshire Parish Church is believed to have been built on this site in 1624, although the present foundation dates from 1716. An explosion virtually destroyed the church on Easter in 1970, but it was reconstructed. Today, the tiny structure looks more like a vicarage than a church. Some of the church's contents survived the blast, including silver dating from 1590, which may be the oldest on the island. The Old Devonshire Parish Church is about a 15-minute walk northwest of the "new" Devonshire Parish Church, which dates from 1846.

Middle Rd. ✆ **441/236-3671**. Free admission. Daily 9am–5:30pm. Bus: 2.

Palm Grove This private estate, 4km (2½ miles) east of the City of Hamilton, is one of the delights of Devonshire Parish. It's famous for its pond, which features a relief map of Bermuda in the middle. On the map, each parish is an immaculately manicured grassy division. The site, which has well-landscaped flower gardens, opens onto a view of the sea.

38 South Rd. No phone. Free admission. Mon–Thurs 8:30am–5pm. Bus: 1.

9 Smith's Parish

Even if you're staying in remote Sandys Parish, the 18th-century mansion of Verdmont is worth checking out. If you're in the area, Spittal Pond Nature Reserve also merits some attention.

Spittal Pond Nature Reserve Follow steep Knapton Hill Road west to South Road, turning at the sign for Spittal Pond, Bermuda's largest wildlife sanctuary. The most important of the National Trust's open spaces, it occupies 24 hectares (59 acres) and attracts about 25 species of waterfowl, from November to May. Visitors are asked to stay on the scenic trails and footpaths provided. Bird-watchers especially like to visit in January, when as many as 500 species can be observed wintering on or near the pond.

South Rd. ℭ 441/236-6483. Free admission. Daily sunrise–sunset. Bus: 1 or 3.

Verdmont ℛ This 18th-century mansion is especially significant to Americans who are interested in colonial and Revolutionary War history. It stands on property that was owned in the 17th century by William Sayle, who left Bermuda to found South Carolina and become its first governor. The house was built before 1710 by John Dickinson, a prosperous ship owner who was also speaker of the House of Assembly in Bermuda from 1707 to 1710. Verdmont passed to Mr. Dickinson's granddaughter, Elizabeth, who married the Hon. Thomas Smith, collector of customs. Their oldest daughter, Mary, married Judge John Green, a Loyalist who came to Bermuda in 1765 from Philadelphia. During and after the American Revolution, Green was judge of the Vice-Admiralty Court and had the final say on prizes brought in by privateers. Many American ship owners lost their vessels because of his decisions. The house, which the National Trust now administers, contains many antiques, china, and portraits, along with the finest cedar stair balustrade on Bermuda.

6 Verdmont Lane, Collectors Hill. ℭ 441/236-7369. Admission $5 adults, $2 ages 6–18, free for ages 5 and under. Tues–Sat 10am–4pm. Bus: 1.

Moments The Sounds of Silence (& Gregorian Chant)

In crowded Bermuda, finding solitude and tranquillity grows increasingly more difficult. But one of our staff stumbled upon the 18-hectare (43-acre) **Heydon Trust**, Heydon Drive (ℭ **441/234-1831**), in Sandys Parish, open daily dawn to dusk. This setting, which is also a sanctuary for migratory birds, is Bermuda the way it used to be. The grounds are filled with flower gardens, citrus orchards, walkways, and even a tiny chapel dating from 1620. Chapel services are held Monday, Tuesday, Thursday, and Friday at 7:30am. There is also a chant service Monday to Saturday at 3pm. Park benches are found throughout the preserve where you can sit and contemplate nature (or your navel).

---

10 Hamilton Parish

Even if you have limited sightseeing time, try to budget at least a half-day for Hamilton Parish. It has some of the most intriguing attractions on the island, notably the Bermuda Aquarium, Museum & Zoo, and Crystal Caves and Leamington Caves. If you have time for only one set of caves, we recommend Crystal Caves. However, if you've seen some of the great caves of America or Europe (or beyond), you may find Bermuda's caves less thrilling.

Bermuda Aquarium, Museum & Zoo 𝄞 *Kids*　This complex is home to a large collection of tropical marine fish, turtles, harbor seals, and other forms of sea life. In the museum, you'll see exhibits ranging from the geological development of Bermuda to deep-sea exploration to humpback whales. The zoo is home to alligators, monkeys, and Galapagos tortoises, along with a collection of birds, including parrots and flamingos.

The North Rock Exhibit, in a 140,000-gallon tank, allows visitors to experience a coral reef washed by ocean surge. The tank houses a living coral reef, as well as reef and pelagic fish species. It's the first living coral exhibit on this scale in the world, made possible by the Bermuda Aquarium, Museum & Zoo's success in the science of coral husbandry.

There's parking for cycles and cars across the street from the aquarium.

40 N. Shore Rd. (in Flatts Village). ℂ **441/293-2727.** Admission $10 adults, $5 seniors and children 5–12, free for children 4 and under. Daily 9am–5pm. Closed Dec 25. Bus: 10 or 11 from the City of Hamilton or St. George. From the City of Hamilton, follow Middle Rd. or N. Shore Rd. east to Flatts Village; from St. George, cross the causeway and follow N. Shore Rd. or Harrington Sound Rd. west to Flatts Village.

Crystal Caves 𝄞 *Kids*　This network of subterranean lakes, caves, and caverns houses translucent formations of stalagmites and stalactites, and includes the crystal-clear Cahow Lake. A sloping path and a few steps lead to Crystal Caves, which was discovered in 1907; at the bottom, about 36m (118 ft.) below the surface, is a floating causeway. It follows the winding cavern, where hidden lights illuminate the interior. In 2002, a second cave was opened to visitors. All tours through Crystal Caves are guided. Using the lighting system, the guides make shadow puppets and are fond of pointing out the similarity to the skyline of Manhattan. If you suffer from claustrophobia, you might find this space too tight. A small cafe and a gift shop are on-site.

8 Crystal Caves Rd., off Wilkinson Ave., Bailey's Bay. ℂ **441/293-0640.** Admission $12 adults, $7 children 5–12, free for children 4 and under. To visit 2 caves $18 adults, $8 children. May–Sept Mon–Fri 9:30am–5:30pm, Sat–Sun 9:30am–4:30pm. Oct–Apr daily 9:30am–4:30pm. Bus: 1, 3, 10, or 11.

11 St. George Parish

A great way to explore this historic town is by following the "Historic St. George Town" walking tour in chapter 8, "Island Strolls."

THE TOWN OF ST. GEORGE 𝄞𝄞𝄞

King's Square, also called Market Square and King's Parade, is the center of life in St. George. It holds the colorful **White Horse Tavern,** where you may want to stop for a drink after your tour of the town.

The street names in St. George evoke its history. Petticoat Lane (sometimes called Silk Alley) reputedly got its name when two newly emancipated slaves paraded up and down the lane rustling their colorful new silk petticoats. Barber's Lane is also named for a former slave. It honors Joseph Hayne Rainey, a freedman from the Carolinas who

---

Fun Fact **That'll Teach You!**

Right on King's Square you'll see a pillory and stock. Honeymooners like to be photographed in them today, but in earlier times they were used in deadly earnest. Victims were placed in the pillory for a certain number of hours— sometimes with one ear nailed to the post! Criminals were burned on the hand or branded, fined in tobacco, nailed to the post, or declared "infamous." Often, they had their ears cut off or were forced to "stand in a sheet on the church porch."

The list of offenses for which Bermudians were punished in the early 1600s offers a glimpse into the life of the time. Along with such "usual" crimes as treason, robbery, arson, murder, and "scandal," punishable offenses included concealing finds of ambergris, exporting cedar wood, railing against the governor's authority, hiding tobacco, being "notorious cursers and swearers," leading an "uncivil life and calling her neighbor an old Bawd and the like," neglecting to receive Holy Communion, acting in a stage play of any kind, and playing at unlawful games such as dice, cards, and ninepins.

---

fled to Bermuda during the Civil War aboard a blockade runner and became a barber. After the war, he returned to the United States and was elected to Congress, becoming the first black member of the House of Representatives during Reconstruction.

The St. George branch of the **Visitors Service Bureau** is on King's Square (© **441/ 297-1642**); it's open Monday to Saturday 9am to 5pm. Here you can get a map, transportation passes for the bus and ferry, and other information before setting out to explore. The bureau is to the right of the Town Hall, on the waterfront.

If you're pressed for time, don't worry that you're missing out if you skip interior visits to the sights listed below. The entire town of St. George, with its quaint streets and old buildings, is the attraction, not just one particular monument. If you have time to visit only one attraction's interior, make it St. Peter's Church. Otherwise, just wander around, do a little shopping, and soak in the atmosphere.

To reach these attractions, take bus no. 1, 3, 8, 10, or 11 from the City of Hamilton.

The Bermuda National Trust Museum   This was once the Globe Hotel, headquarters of Maj. Norman Walker, the Confederate representative in Bermuda. Today, it houses relics from the island's involvement in the American Civil War—from a Bermudian perspective. St. George was the port from which ships carrying arms and munitions ran the Union blockade. A replica of the Great Seal of the Confederacy is fitted to a Victorian press so that visitors can emboss copies as souvenirs. There's also a video presentation, *Bermuda: Centre of the Atlantic,* tracing the island's early history.

At the Globe Hotel, King's Sq. © 441/297-1423. Admission $4 adults, $2 children 6–18, free for children 5 and under; $5 combination ticket good for all three Trust museums (Bermuda National Trust Museum, Tucker House, Verdmont). Mon–Sat 10am–4pm. Closed Dec 25 and Good Friday.

Bridge House Gallery   This long-established gallery displays antiques and collectibles, old Bermudian items, original paintings, and Bermuda-made crafts. It contains a studio belonging to Jill Amos Raine, a well-known Bermuda watercolor artist. The house, constructed in the 1690s, was home to several of the colony's governors. Its most colorful owner was Bridger Goodrich, a Loyalist from Virginia, whose privateers

⟮Moments⟯ Special Places Where You Can Be Alone

Bermuda is both popular and small—but that doesn't mean that you can't escape the crowds and find peace and serenity in a lovely spot, hopefully with someone you love.

Hamilton Parish   The Bermuda National Trust (② **441/236-6483**) administers 25 hectares (62 acres) of land at Walsingham, along Harrington Sound Road in Hamilton Parish. Bus no. 1 or 3 runs to the site, and hours are daily dawn to dusk, with no admission charged. The site of Walsingham that visitors find most appealing, especially bird-watchers, is called the **Idwal Hughes Nature Reserve**, which takes up only .5 hectare (1¼ acres) of the lush Walsingham wilderness area sometimes called "Tom Moore's Jungle" by islanders. Walking is rather challenging here but rewarding because of the scenic landscape and the bird life. Access to the Idwal Hughes Nature Reserve is from the road leading down to Tom Moore's Tavern off Harrington Sound Road. Access is also possible through **Blue Hole Park** (take bus no. 1, 3, 10, or 11 to the Grotto Bay Hotel bus stop), which features its own trails for bird-watching and a wooden deck where you can view a water-filled sunken cave.

Sandys Parish   Visitors don't seem to spend a lot of time here, but for wandering about, getting lost, and finding enchanting little vistas, Sandys is without equal on Bermuda. Where Daniel's Head Road meets Cambridge Road, paths will take you to Somerset Long Bay Park, where you can swim. After that, take one of the unmarked trails to the Bermuda Audubon Society Nature Reserve, a gem of nature. The place is often deserted on weekdays. When the white-eyed vireos and the bluebirds call to you from fiddlewood trees, you'll really feel close to nature.

Southampton Parish   In this windswept, tourist-trodden parish, you'd think there was no place to find solitude. Not so! Signposted from Middle Road, a trail goes 1km (⅔ mile) down to the entrance to Seymour's Pond Nature Reserve. Under the management of the Bermuda Audubon Society, this 1-hectare (2½-acre) site attracts the occasional birder as well as romantic couples looking for a little privacy. Just past the pond, you'll spot pepper trees and old cedars that escaped the blight; you might encounter bluebirds and an egret or two as well. After traversing Cross Church Road, you'll come upon the old Bermuda Railway Trail, where in summer you can see fennel

once blockaded Chesapeake Bay. So devoted was he to the king that he sabotaged Bahamian vessels trading with the American colonies.

1 Bridge St. ② 441/297-8211. Free admission. Wed and Sat 10am–6pm.

Carter House (St. David's Island Historical Site)   Low-slung and historic, and set on a hillside about 1.5km (1 mile) east of Swing Bridge, Carter House is believed to be the oldest dwelling place in St. David's parish, at least 3½ centuries old. Reopened in September 2001, after a 3-year renovation, it's now a museum dedicated to the life and values of the people of St. David's, one of the most rugged and hardy

growing wild. In the distance are panoramic views of shipwreck-clogged Black Bay and Five Star Island.

Warwick Parish   With its beautiful pink-sand beaches, seaside parklands, natural attractions, and winding country lanes, this is one of the most charming parishes for exploring and escaping the crowds. Even many long-time local residents haven't seen some of Warwick's beauty spots. The place to head is Warwick Pond, a sanctuary for several rare species of birds. Administered by the Bermuda National Trust, it's open daily from sunrise to sunset. You can reach it by following the Bermuda Railway Trail until you come to Tribe Road No. 3; climb this road for a few hundred yards before it dips down a hill to the pond. You might spot the occasional birder in search of a kiskadee, blue heron, or cardinal. The pond, fed by a subterranean channel from the sea, reminds us of Thoreau's Walden Pond.

St. David's Island   Part of St. George Parish, St. David's is Bermuda "the way it was." Virtually unknown to the average visitor, it awaits your discovery. This is real down-home Bermuda—it's said that some St. David's Islanders have never even visited "mainland" Bermuda. You can begin your walk at Great Head Park in the eastern part of St. David's, southeast of the cricket fields. At the end of the parking lot, follow the trail into a wooded area filled with cherry trees and palmettos. After about 225m (738 ft.), bear right at the fork. Eventually you'll spot St. David's Lighthouse, an octagonal red-and-white tower in the distance to the southwest. The trail forks left until you come to a ruined garrison with a panoramic sea view. It's one of the remotest, loveliest spots on the island—and, chances are, you'll have it all to yourself.

Devonshire Parish   This parish is off the beaten track but home to some lovely spots—if you're adventurous enough to seek them out. Old Devonshire Church on Middle Road is a landmark; almost directly across the road lies Devonshire Marsh, a natural water basin still in an untamed state. You'll also find two nature reserves, Firefly and Freer Cox Memorial, on some 4 hectares (10 acres) of marshland. The Bermuda Audubon Society has set aside this protected area as a bird sanctuary for many endangered wild species. You can also see some of the most unusual Bermudian plants, including orchids. The marsh is always open to the public.

districts of Bermuda. The museum houses exhibitions on the history of whaling, piloting, fishing, and farming. Various artifacts of Bermudian life are displayed here, including a 4m (13-ft.) Bermuda sailing dinghy, dolls and children's toys crafted from palmetto leaves, and artifacts and paneling crafted from Bermuda cedar.

S. Side Rd. (St. David's). ℂ 441/293-1642. Free admission (donations accepted). Apr–Oct Tues–Thurs and Sat 10am–4pm; Nov–Mar Sat 10am–4pm.

Deliverance   Across from St. George's town square and over a bridge is Ordnance Island, where visitors can see a full-scale replica of *Deliverance*. The shipwrecked survivors

---

Fun Fact **St. George: A World Heritage Site**

Historic St. George and its related fortifications are now a World Heritage Site designated by UNESCO. The architecturally rich, 400-year-old town joins such select sites as the Great Wall of China, Statue of Liberty, Taj Mahal, and historic center of Florence.

As the oldest continuously inhabited town of English origin in the Western Hemisphere, St. George and its surrounding buildings, monuments, and structures illustrate the residents' lifestyles through the 17th, 18th, and 19th centuries. Historic St. George remains in authentic condition, featuring unique and diverse examples of Bermudian architecture spanning the past 4 centuries. The town's various forts are like a textbook illustrating British artillery and the changing styles of fort architecture from 1612 to 1956.

---

of the *Sea Venture* built the pinnace (small sailing ship) in 1610 to carry them on to Virginia. The full-scale replica of *Deliverance* is still anchored full-time to Ordnance Island. It's one of the Disney-style adventure sights associated with the King's Square (St. George's main square). In midsummer, its caretakers are outfitted in 18th-century sailor's garb.

Adventure Enterprises owns *Deliverance* and also runs sightseeing and snorkeling adventures aboard its boat *ARGO*. Bermuda's only high-speed tour boat, *ARGO* (which fits neatly into small harbors) takes passengers along the barrier reef, the south-shore beaches, the historic forts, and the billionaires' mansions at Tucker's Town. Call for details, which change seasonally.

Ordnance Island. © **441/297-1459.** Admission $3 adults, $1 children 11 and under. Apr–Nov daily 9am–5pm; Dec–Mar call for hours.

Old Rectory   Built by a reformed pirate in 1705, this charming old cottage was later home to Parson Richardson, who was nicknamed "the Little Bishop." Now a private home, it's administered by the Bermuda National Trust.

At the head of Broad Alley, behind St. Peter's Church. © **441/297-4261.** Free admission (donations appreciated). Nov–Mar Wed noon–4pm.

Old State House   Behind the Town Hall is Bermuda's oldest stone building, constructed with turtle oil and lime mortar in 1620. Unless there's a special event, the landmark building doesn't offer much to see—you might settle for a look at the exterior, then continue on with your sightseeing. The Old State House, where meetings of the legislative council once took place, was eventually turned over to the Freemasons of St. George's. The government asked the annual rent of one peppercorn and insisted on the right to hold meetings here upon demand. The Masonic Lodge members, in a ceremony filled with pageantry, still turn over one peppercorn in rent to the Bermuda government every April.

The annual **Peppercorn Ceremony,** a 45-minute spectacle, takes place in early to mid-April. The ceremony begins around 11am with the gathering of the Bermuda Regiment on King's Square. Then the premier, mayor, and other dignitaries arrive, amid the bellowing introductions of the town crier. As soon as all the principals have taken their places, a 17-gun salute is fired as the governor and his wife make a grand entrance. His Excellency inspects a military guard of honor while the Bermuda Regiment Band plays. The stage is now set for the presentation of the peppercorn, which sits on a silver plate atop a velvet cushion. Payment is made in a grand and formal manner, after which the Old State House is immediately used for a meeting of Her Majesty's Council.

Princess St. ✆ **441/292-2480;** for information on the Peppercorn Ceremony, call ✆ **800/223-6106.** Free admission. Wed 10am–3pm or by appointment.

Somers Garden   The heart of Sir George Somers was buried here in 1610; a stone column perpetuates the memory of Bermuda's founder. The garden was opened in 1920 by the Prince of Wales (later King Edward VIII, and then the Duke of Windsor). A large beautiful fountain has been built in the middle of the garden to enhance its beauty, where visitors may also take pictures, using the foundation for a background.

Duke of York St. ✆ **441/297-1532.** Free admission. Apr–Nov daily 7:30am–8pm; off season daily 7:30am–5pm.

St. George's Historical Society Museum   Set in a home built around 1700, this museum contains an original 18th-century Bermuda kitchen, complete with utensils from that period. Other exhibits include a 300-year-old Bible, a letter from George Washington, and Native American ax heads. Some early settlers on St. David's Island were Native Americans, mainly Pequot.

Duke of Kent St. ✆ **441/297-0423.** Admission $5 adults, $2 children 11 and under. Mon–Thurs 10am–4pm; Fri 10am–2pm.

St. Peter's Church ⚓   From King's Square, head east to Duke of York Street, where you'll find St. Peter's Church, believed to be the oldest Anglican place of worship in the Western Hemisphere. Colonists built the original church in 1612 almost entirely of cedar, with a palmetto-leaf thatched roof. A hurricane in 1712 destroyed it almost completely. Some of the interior, including the original altar from 1615 (still used daily), was salvaged, and the church was rebuilt in 1713. It has been restored many times since, providing excellent examples of the architectural styles of the 17th to the 20th century. The tower was added in 1814. Before the Old State House was built, the colony held public meetings in the church. The first assize (legislative assembly) convened here in 1616, and the first meeting of Parliament was held in 1620. The church holds Sunday and weekday services.

Some of the tombstones in the Graveyard of St. Peter's (entrance opposite Broad Alley) are more than 3 centuries old; many tombs mark the graves of slaves. Here you'll find the grave of Midshipman Richard Dale, an American who was the last victim of the War of 1812. The churchyard also holds the tombs of Gov. Sir Richard Sharples and his aide, Capt. Hugh Sayers, who were assassinated while strolling on the grounds of Government House in 1973.

Duke of York St. ✆ **441/297-8359.** www.anglican.bm. Free admission (donations appreciated). Daily 10am–4:30pm; Sun services 11am; guide available Mon–Sat.

Town Hall   Officers of the Corporation of St. George's, headed by a mayor, meet in the Town Hall, located near the Visitors Service Bureau. There are three aldermen and five common councilors. The Town Hall holds a collection of Bermuda cedar furnishings, along with photographs of previous mayors.

7 King's Sq. ✆ **441/297-1532.** Free admission. Mon–Sat 10am–4pm.

Tucker House Museum   This was the home of the well-known Tucker family of England, Bermuda, and Virginia. It displays a notable collection of Bermudian furniture, portraits, and silver. Also in the Tucker House is the Joseph Rainey Memorial Room, where the African-American Civil War refugee (mentioned above in the section on "The Town of St. George") practiced barbering. A new exhibit on the ground floor traces the archaeological history of the site. The kitchen, now restored, has become an exhibit for visitors to see.

5 Water St. ✆ 441/297-0545. Admission $5 adults, $2 children 6–18, free for children 5 and under. Mon–Sat 10am–4pm.

Unfinished Church   After leaving Somers Garden, head up the steps to the North Gate, which opens onto Blockade Alley. The structure here is known as the "folly of St. George's." The cathedral, begun in 1874, was intended to replace St. Peter's. But the planners ran into money problems, and a schism within the church developed. As if that weren't enough, a storm swept over the island, causing considerable damage to the structure. Result: the Unfinished Cathedral.

Blockade Alley. No Phone. Free admission. Open year-round.

HISTORIC FORTS THAT NEVER SAW MUCH ACTION

From its earliest days, St. George has been fortified. Although it never saw much military action, reminders of that history are interesting to explore. Take Circular Drive to reach the forts, on the outskirts of town. As forts go, these two are of relatively minor interest (unless, of course, you're a fort buff—in that case, be our guest). If you have time for only one fort on Bermuda, Fort Hamilton on Happy Valley Road is the most intriguing. See "Walking Tour 1: The City of Hamilton," in chapter 8, "Island Strolls," for details.

Along the coast is Building Bay, where the shipwrecked victims of the *Sea Venture* built their vessel, the *Deliverance,* in 1610.

Fort St. Catherine ✯   Towering above the beach where the shipwrecked crew of the *Sea Venture* came ashore in 1609 is Fort St. Catherine, completed in 1614 and named for the patron saint of wheelwrights and carpenters. The fortifications have been upgraded over the years. The last major reconstruction took place from 1865 to 1878, so the fort's appearance today is largely the result of work done in the 19th century.

In the museum, visitors first see a series of dioramas, "Highlights in Bermuda's History." Figures depict various activities that took place in the magazine of the fort, restored and refurnished as it was in the 1880s. In the keep, which served as living quarters, you can see information on local and overseas regiments that served in Bermuda. Also here are a fine small-arms exhibit, a cooking-area display, and an exhibit of replicas of England's crown jewels. There's a short audiovisual show on St. George's defense systems and the forts of St. George.

15 Coot Pond Rd. ✆ 441/297-1920. Admission $5 adults, $2 children 11 and under. Daily 10am–4pm. Closed Dec 25.

Gates Fort   This small-scale, partially ruined two-story watchtower is capped with a cannon that (symbolically) monitors the entrance to St. George's harbor. With an interior of only two square and angular rooms, it was originally built in 1609 by its namesake, Sir Thomas Gates. Gates, who was one of the original band of settlers from the *Sea Venture* who colonized Bermuda, was later the governor-designate for the Colony of Virginia. In midsummer, when cruise ships drop their anchors for short sojourns in St. George, a gatekeeper in 18th-century costume sometimes hails onboard passengers with a "welcome to Bermuda" spate of bell ringing and an occasional cannon blast. There's virtually nothing to see inside—the allure is entirely a byproduct of its isolated charm near the harbor's entrance.

Cut Rd. No phone. Free admission. Daily 10am–4:30pm.

8

Island Strolls

You can cover much of Bermuda, especially the harbor City of Hamilton and the historic town of St. George, on foot. Indeed, if you had the time, you could walk or bike through all of the parishes and visit the major attractions. Some visitors would rather devote their vacation time to less taxing pursuits, such as relaxing on the beach or playing a leisurely game of golf. If you're interested in seeing the island's sights, however, do consider taking at least one walking tour.

WALKING TOUR 1 · THE CITY OF HAMILTON

Start:	The Visitors Service Bureau/Ferry Terminal.
Finish:	Fort Hamilton.
Time:	2½ hours.
Best Time:	Any sunny day.
Worst Time:	When cruise ships are anchored in Hamilton Harbour.

Begin your tour along the harborfront at the:

❶ Visitors Service Bureau/ Ferry Terminal

Pick up some free maps and brochures of the island here.

From the bureau, you'll emerge onto Front Street, the City of Hamilton's main street and principal shopping area. Before 1946, there were no cars here. Today, the busy traffic includes small automobiles (driven only by Bermuda residents), buses, mopeds, and bicycles. You'll also see horse-drawn carriages, which are the most romantic (and, alas, the most expensive) way to see the City of Hamilton.

At the docks behind the Ferry Terminal, you can find the ferries to Warwick and Paget parishes; for details on their attractions, see chapter 7, "Seeing the Sights." You can also take a ferry across Great Sound to the West End and Somerset.

Walk south from the Ferry Terminal toward the water, taking a short side street between the Visitors Service Bureau and the large Bank of Bermuda. You'll come to:

❷ Albouy's Point

This is a small, grassy park with benches and trees, which opens onto a panoramic vista of the boat- and ship-filled harbor. Nearby is the Royal Bermuda Yacht Club, which has been an elite rendezvous for the Bermudian and American yachting set—including the rich and famous—since the 1930s. To use the word *royal* in its name, the club obtained special permission from Prince Albert, Queen Victoria's consort. The club sponsors the widely televised Newport–Bermuda Race.

After taking in the view, walk directly north, toward Front Street. Continue east along Front Street to the intersection with Queen Street. This is the site of the:

Tips Planning Pointer

It's enlightening to take a ferry ride around the inner harbor before or after your City of Hamilton walking tour. You can get an overview of the City of Hamilton before concentrating on specific landmarks or monuments, or gain a new perspective on what you've just seen.

❸ "Birdcage"

This is the most photographed sight in Bermuda. Here you can sometimes find a police officer directing traffic. If the "bobby" is a man, he's likely to be wearing regulation Bermuda shorts. The traffic box was named after its designer, Michael "Dickey" Bird. It stands at Heyl's Corner, which was named for an American southerner, J. B. Heyl, who operated a nearby apothecary in the 1800s.

Continue north along Queen Street until you reach:

❹ Par-la-Ville Park

This was once a private garden attached to the town house of William B. Perot, Bermuda's first postmaster. Perot, who designed the gardens in the 19th century, collected rare and exotic plants from all over the globe, including an Indian rubber tree, which was seeded in 1847. Mark Twain wrote that he found the tree "disappointing" in that it didn't bear rubber overshoes and hot-water bottles.

Also opening onto Queen Street at the entrance to the park is the:

❺ Bermuda Historical Society Museum

This museum, at 13 Queen St., is also the Bermuda Library. It's filled with curiosities, including cedar furniture, collections of antique silver and china, hog money, Confederate money, a 1775 letter from George Washington, and other artifacts. The library has many rare books, including a 1624 edition of John Smith's *General Historie of Virginia, New England and the Somers Isles,* which you can ask to view. If you'd like to rest and catch up on your reading, you'll also find a selection of current local and British newspapers and periodicals here.

Across the street is the:

❻ Perot Post Office

William Perot ran this post office from 1818 to 1862. It's said that he'd collect the mail from the clipper ships, then put it under his top hat in order to maintain his dignity. As he proceeded through town, he'd greet his friends and acquaintances by tipping his hat, thereby delivering their mail at the same time. He started printing stamps in 1848. A Perot stamp is extremely valuable today—only 11 are known to exist, and Queen Elizabeth II owns several. The last time a Perot stamp came on the market, in 1986, it fetched $135,000.

Continue to the top of Queen Street, then turn right onto Church Street to reach:

❼ Hamilton City Hall

Located at 17 Church St., the city hall dates from 1960 and is crowned by a white tower. The bronze weather vane on top is a replica of the *Sea Venture*. Portraits of the queen and paintings of former island leaders adorn the main lobby. The Bermuda Society of Arts holds frequent exhibitions in this hall. The Benbow family's collection of rare stamps is also on display.

TAKE A BREAK
The **Paradiso Cafe** (p. 131), on the ground floor of the Washington Mall, a shopping and office complex on Reid Street, which is parallel to Church Street to the south (℃ **441/295-3263**), serves the most irresistible pastries in town. You can also order ice cream, tartlets, quiches, croissant sandwiches, espresso, and cappuccino.

Walking Tour 1: The City of Hamilton

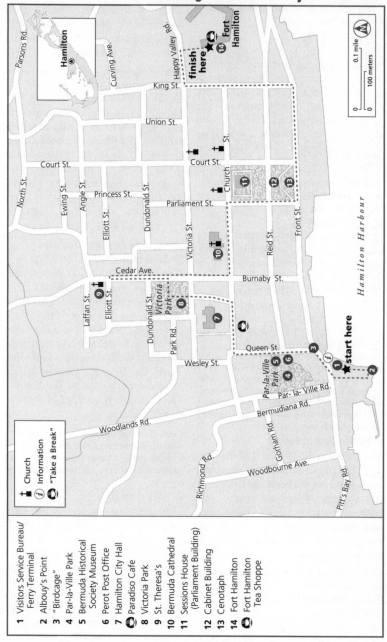

Church ■

Information ⓘ

"Take a Break" ◖

1 Visitors Service Bureau/
  Ferry Terminal
2 Albouy's Point
3 "Birdcage"
4 Par-la-Ville Park
5 Bermuda Historical
  Society Museum
6 Perot Post Office
7 Hamilton City Hall
  ◖ Paradiso Cafe
8 Victoria Park
9 St. Theresa's
10 Bermuda Cathedral
11 Sessions House
   (Parliament Building)
12 Cabinet Building
13 Cenotaph
14 Fort Hamilton
   ◖ Fort Hamilton
     Tea Shoppe

In back of Hamilton City Hall, opening onto Victoria Street, lies:

⑧ Victoria Park

Office workers frequent this cool, refreshing oasis on their lunch breaks. It features a sunken garden, ornamental shrubbery, and a Victorian bandstand. The 1.6 hectare (4-acre) park was laid out in honor of Queen Victoria's Golden Jubilee in 1887. Outdoor concerts are held here in summer. Contact the tourist office for dates.

Cedar Avenue is the eastern boundary of Victoria Park. If you follow it north for 2 blocks, you'll reach:

⑨ St. Theresa's

This Roman Catholic cathedral is open daily from 8am to 7pm and for Sunday services. Its architecture was inspired by the Spanish Mission style. Dating from 1927, it's one of a half-dozen Roman Catholic churches in Bermuda; its treasure is a gold-and-silver chalice—a gift from Pope Paul VI when he visited the island in 1968.

After seeing the cathedral, retrace your steps south along Cedar Avenue until you reach Victoria Street. Cedar Avenue now becomes Burnaby Street; continue south to Church Street and turn left. A short walk along this street (on your left) will bring you to the:

⑩ Bermuda Cathedral

Also known as the Cathedral of the Most Holy Trinity, this is the seat of the Anglican Church of Bermuda, and it towers over the city skyline. Its style is neo-Gothic, characterized by stained-glass windows and soaring arches. The lectern and pulpit duplicate those of St. Giles in Edinburgh, Scotland.

Leave the cathedral and continue east along Church Street to the:

⑪ Sessions House (Parliament Building)

Located on Parliament Street, between Reid and Church streets, the Sessions House is open to the public Friday at 10am. The speaker wears a full wig and a flowing black robe. The Parliament of Bermuda is the third oldest in the world, after Iceland's and England's.

Continue south along Parliament Street to Front Street, and turn left toward the:

⑫ Cabinet Building

The official opening of Parliament takes place here in late October or early November. Wearing a plumed hat and full regalia, the governor makes his "Throne Speech." If you visit on a Wednesday, you can see the Bermuda Senate in action. The building is located between Court and Parliament streets, and is open Monday to Friday from 9am to 5pm.

In front of the Cabinet Building is the:

⑬ Cenotaph

The Cenotaph is a memorial to Bermuda's dead from World War I (1914–18) and World War II (1939–45). In 1920, the Prince of Wales laid the cornerstone. (In 1936, as King Edward VIII, he abdicated to marry an American divorcée, Wallis Simpson, and during World War II, as the Duke of Windsor, he served as governor of The Bahamas.) The landmark is a replica of the Cenotaph in London.

Continue east along Front Street until you reach King Street, then turn left and head north until you come to Happy Valley Road. Go right on this road until you see the entrance (on your right) to:

⑭ Fort Hamilton

This imposing old fortress lies on the eastern outskirts of town. The Duke of Wellington ordered its construction to protect Hamilton Harbour. Filled with underground passageways and complete with a moat and 18-ton guns, the fort was outdated before it was even completed, and it never fired a shot. It does, however, offer panoramic views of the city and the harbor, and it's worth a trip just for the view. In summer, try to be here at noon, when the kilted Bermuda Isles Pipe Band performs a skirling ceremony on the green, accompanied by dancers and drummers.

WINDING DOWN
Enjoy old-fashioned tea at the **Fort Hamilton "Victoria Castle" Tea Shoppe** (no phone), where you can also order light refreshments.

WALKING TOUR 2 HISTORIC ST. GEORGE TOWN

Start:	King's Square.
Finish:	Somers Wharf.
Time:	2 hours, not counting the time you spend inside the buildings.
Best Time:	Any sunny day except Sunday, when many destinations are closed.
Worst Time:	When a cruise ship is anchored in the harbor.

At the eastern end of Bermuda, St. George was the second English town established in the New World (after Jamestown, Virginia). For the history buff, it holds more interest than the City of Hamilton.

We'll begin the tour at:

❶ King's Square

Also known as Market Square and King's Parade, the square is the very center of St. George. Only about 200 years old, it's not as historic as St. George itself. This was formerly a marshy part of the harbor—at least when the shipwrecked passengers and crew of the *Sea Venture* first saw it. At the water's edge stands a branch of the Visitors Service Bureau, where you can pick up additional information on the area. On the square you'll notice a replica of a pillory and stocks. The devices were used to punish criminals—and, in many cases, the innocent. You could be severely punished here for such "crimes" as casting a spell over your neighbor's turkeys.

From the square, head south across the small bridge to:

❷ Ordnance Island

The British army once stored gunpowder and cannons on this island, which extends into St. George's Harbour. Today, the island houses the *Deliverance*, a replica of the vessel that carried the shipwrecked *Sea Venture* passengers on to Virginia. Alongside the vessel is a ducking stool, a contraption used in 17th-century witch trials.

Retrace your steps across the bridge to King's Square. On the waterside stands the:

❸ White Horse Tavern

This restaurant juts out into St. George's Harbour. Consider the tavern as a possible spot for lunch later (for a review, see chapter 5, "Where to Dine"). For now, we'll focus on its history: It was once the home of John Davenport, who came to Bermuda in 1815 to open a dry goods store. Davenport was a bit of a miser; upon his death, some £75,000 ($135,000) in gold and silver was discovered stashed away in his cellar.

Across the square stands the:

❹ Town Hall

Located near the Visitors Service Bureau, this is the meeting place of the corporation governing St. George. It has antique cedar furnishings and a collection of photographs of previous lord mayors. *Bermuda Journey,* a multimedia audiovisual presentation, is shown here several times a day.

From King's Square, head east along King Street, cutting north (left) on Bridge Street. You'll come to the:

⑤ Bridge House

Constructed in the 1690s, this was once the home of several governors of Bermuda. Located at 1 Bridge St., it's furnished with 18th- and 19th-century antiques and houses an art gallery and souvenir shop.

Return to King Street and continue east to the:

⑥ Old State House

The Old State House opens onto Princess Street, at the top of King Street. This is the oldest stone building in Bermuda, dating from 1620, and was once the home of the Bermuda Parliament. It's the site of the Peppercorn Ceremony, in which the Old State House pays the government a "rent" of one peppercorn annually. See chapter 7, "Seeing the Sights," for details on this grand ceremony.

Continue your stroll down Princess Street until you come to Duke of York Street and the entrance to:

⑦ Somers Garden

The heart of Sir George Somers, the admiral of the *Sea Venture,* is buried here. The gardens, opened in 1920 by the Prince of Wales, contain palms and other tropical plants.

Walk through Somers Gardens and up the steps to the North Gate onto Blockade Alley. Climb the hill to the structure known as "the folly of St. George's," the:

⑧ Unfinished Cathedral

This cathedral was intended to replace St. Peter's Church (see stop no. 12 on this tour). Work began on the church in 1874, but ended when the church was beset by financial difficulties and a schism in the Anglican congregation.

After viewing the cathedral, turn left onto Duke of Kent Street, which leads down to the:

⑨ St. George's Historical Society Museum

Located at Featherbed Alley and Duke of Kent Street, the museum building is an

example of the rather plain 18th-century Bermudian architecture. It contains a collection of Bermudian historical artifacts and cedar furniture.

Around the corner on Featherbed Alley is the:

⑩ Featherbed Alley Printery

Here you can see a working replica of the type of printing press invented by Johannes Gutenberg in Germany in the 1450s.

Go up Featherbed Alley and straight onto Church Street. At the junction with Broad Lane, look to your right to see the:

⑪ Old Rectory

The Old Rectory is located at the head of Broad Alley, behind St. Peter's Church. Now a private home administered by the National Trust, it was built in 1705 by a reformed pirate. You can go inside only on Wednesdays from noon to 5pm.

After seeing the Old Rectory, go through the church's backyard, opposite Broad Alley, to reach:

⑫ St. Peter's Church

The church's main entrance is on Duke of York Street. St. Peter's is believed to be the oldest Anglican place of worship in the Western Hemisphere. In the churchyard, you'll see many headstones, some 300 years old. The assassinated governor, Sir Richard Sharples, was buried here. The present church was built in 1713, with a tower added in 1814.

Across the street is the:

⑬ Bermuda National Trust Museum

When it was the Globe Hotel, this was the headquarters of Maj. Norman Walker, the Confederate representative in Bermuda. It was once a hotbed of blockade running (artillery smuggling during the Civil War).

Go west along Duke of York Street to:

⑭ Barber's Alley & Petticoat Lane

Barber's Alley honors Joseph Hayne Rainey. A former slave from South Carolina, Rainey fled to Bermuda with his French wife at the outbreak of the Civil War. He became a barber in St. George

Walking Tour 2: Historic St. George Town

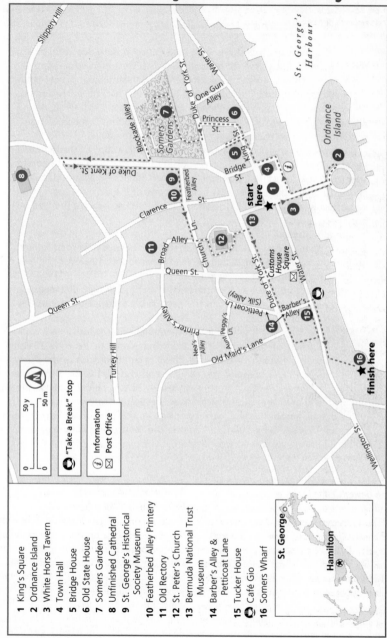

1 King's Square
2 Ordnance Island
3 White Horse Tavern
4 Town Hall
5 Bridge House
6 Old State House
7 Somers Garden
8 Unfinished Cathedral
9 St. George's Historical
    Society Museum
10 Featherbed Alley Printery
11 Old Rectory
12 St. Peter's Church
13 Bermuda National Trust
    Museum
14 Barber's Alley &
    Petticoat Lane
15 Tucker House
⦿ Café Gio
16 Somers Wharf

Rattle & Shake: The Bermuda Railway Trail

One of the most unusual sightseeing adventures in Bermuda is following the Bermuda Railway Trail (or parts thereof), which stretches for 34km (21 miles) along the old railroad way, across three of the interconnected islands that make up Bermuda. Construction of this rail line may have been one of the most costly ever on a per-kilometer basis. Opened in 1931, the Bermuda Railway ceased operations in 1948. Once the island's main mode of transportation, the train eventually gave way to the automobile.

Before setting out on this trek, arm yourself with a copy of the *Bermuda Railway Trail Guide*, which is available at the Bermuda Department of Tourism in the City of Hamilton and the Visitors Service Bureaus in Hamilton and St. George. You're now ready to hit the trail of the old train system that was affectionately called "Rattle and Shake." You can explore the trail on horseback, bicycle, or foot.

Although the line covered 34km (21 miles), from St. George in the east to Somerset in the west, a 5km (3-mile) stretch has been lost to roads in and around the capital city of Hamilton. For the most part, however, the trail winds along an automobile-free route.

In the West End, the trail begins near the Watford Bridge, but there are many convenient access points. In the East End, it's easiest to pick up the trail on North Shore Road.

Along the way, you'll see some rare Bermuda cedar, which nearly vanished as a result of the blight that struck the island in the early 1940s. There's also much greenery and semitropical vegetation, such as the poinsettia, oleander, and hibiscus. You can see and visit Fort Scaur, the 1870s fortress, in Sandys Parish. The tour of Sandys Parish, below, follows the detailed section of the route that includes Fort Scaur. If you only have time to see a small part of the trail, we recommend you take in something of the 2-hectare (5-acre) Gilbert Nature Reserve. The most scenic view begins at Somerset Bridge; head west from there.

and eventually returned to South Carolina, where in 1870 he was elected to the U.S. House of Representatives—the first African American to serve in Congress.

Nearby is Petticoat Lane, also known as Silk Alley. The name dates from the 1834 emancipation, when two former slave women who'd always wanted silk petticoats like their former mistresses finally purchased some—and paraded up and down the lane to show off their new finery.

Continue west until you reach:

⓯ Tucker House

Opening onto Water Street, this was the former home of a prominent Bermudian family, whose members included an island governor, a treasurer of the United States, and a captain in the Confederate Navy. The building houses an excellent collection of antiques, including silver, portraits, and cedar furniture. One room is devoted to memorabilia of Joseph Hayne Rainey.

TAKE A BREAK
Near Tucker House is the family-friendly **Café Gio**, 36 Water St. (☏ **441/297-1307**), with its outdoor terrace overlooking the harbor. It features everything from an ice-cream parlor to a pizza oven, and even full meals, in its tutti-frutti–colored dining room.

End your tour across the street at:

⑯ Somers Wharf

This multimillion-dollar waterfront restoration project contains shops, restaurants, and taverns.

WALKING TOUR 3   SANDYS PARISH

Start: Somerset Bridge.
Finish: Somerset Long Bay Park.
Time: 7 hours.
Best Time: Any sunny day.
Worst Time: When the weather's bad.

Sandys (pronounced *sands*), the far western parish of Bermuda, consists of Somerset Island (the largest and southernmost island), and Watford, Boaz, and Ireland islands. When Bermudians cross into Somerset on Somerset Bridge, they say they are "up the country."

Craggy coastlines, beaches, nature reserves, fisher's coves, old fortifications, winding lanes, and sleepy villages characterize this area. All of Sandys' major attractions lie along the main road from Somerset Bridge to the Royal Naval Dockyard, which is at the end of Ireland Island.

Although we describe this as a walking tour, you may want to rent a bicycle or moped to help you cover the longer stretches.

From the center of the City of Hamilton, you can take a ferry to Somerset. Check the schedule: Some boats take only 30 minutes, others up to an hour. The longer trip affords a more leisurely opportunity to enjoy the waters of Great Sound. You can bring your cycle or moped aboard the ferry. You can also see the West End by bus (see "Getting Around," in chapter 3).

To begin the tour, take the ferry from the City of Hamilton to:

❶ Somerset Bridge

This bridge links Somerset Island with the rest of Bermuda. It was among the first three bridges constructed on Bermuda in the 1600s, and it's said to be the smallest drawbridge in the world—its opening is just wide enough to accommodate a sailboat mast. Near the bridge you can see the old Somerset Post Office and an 18th-century cottage known as Crossways.

Next, walk up Somerset Road about 69m (226 ft.) to the entrance to the:

❷ Railway Trail

Open only to pedestrians and bikers, the trail follows the path of old "Rattle and Shake," the Bermuda Railway line that once ran the length of the island. This section of the trail—between Somerset Bridge and Sound View Road—is one of the most attractive segments (good to know if you don't want to walk the whole trail—although some hearty visitors do just that). Parts of the trail open onto the coast, affording panoramic vistas of the Great Sound. See "Rattle & Shake: The Bermuda Railway Trail," above, for more information.

> **TAKE A BREAK**
> The trail goes across the parkland of Fort Scaur (see below), with its large moat. If you're here around noontime, you might want to consider this as a picnic spot (get your picnic fixings in the City of Hamilton). If you can spend all day in Somerset (which we highly recommend), you might also want to take time out for a swim before returning to your walking or cycling.

Follow the signposts to:

❸ Fort Scaur

In the 1870s, the British feared an attack from the United States, so they built this fort on the highest hill in Somerset to protect Her Majesty's Royal Naval Dockyard. It sits on 9 hectares (22 acres) of land and opens onto Somerset Road; the huge dry moat cuts right across Somerset Island. You can wander around this fort, which proved to be unnecessary because the American invasion never materialized. If you stand on the ramparts, you'll be rewarded with a marvelous view of Great Sound. Through a telescope, you can see such distant sights as St. David's Lighthouse and Fort St. Catherine in the East End of Bermuda. If you follow the eastern moat all the way down to the Great Sound shore, you'll find ideal places for swimming and fishing.

After exploring the surrounding Scaur Hill Fort Park, resume your walk along the railway track and continue north for more than 1.5km (1 mile), then turn right onto:

❹ Sound View Road

Take a stroll along this sleepy residential street, which has some of the finest cottages in Bermuda.

Continue around a wide arc, passing Tranquillity Hill and Gwelly and Saltsea lanes. When you come to Scott's Hill Road, take a right and go about 78m (256 ft.) to East Shore Road. At the first junction, take a little road, Cavello Lane, which branches off to the right; it will take you to:

❺ Cavello Bay

The sheltered cove is a stopping point for the City of Hamilton ferry.

Wait for the next ferry and take it (with your cycle or moped) to Watford Bridge or directly to the:

❻ Royal Naval Dockyard

There's so much to see here, you could spend an entire afternoon exploring the area. The dockyard is a sprawling complex encompassing 2½ hectares (6¼ acres) of Ireland Island. The major attraction is the **Bermuda Maritime Museum** (see chapter 7), opened by Queen Elizabeth II in 1975. There's an exhibit of Bermuda's old boats, documenting the island's rich maritime history. You can cross a moat to explore the keep and the 9m-high (30-ft.) defensive ramparts.

Across the street from the Bermuda Maritime Museum is the Old Cooperage Building, site of the Neptune Cinema. Adjacent to the cinema is the Craft Market, which sells interesting items. Next door is the:

❼ Bermuda Arts Centre

Princess Margaret opened the Centre in 1984. Showcasing the visual arts and crafts of the island, this not-for-profit organization has a volunteer staff.

From the dockyard, it's a long walk to Somerset Village, but many people who have walked or cycled the distance considered it one of the highlights of their Bermuda trip. You'll find some of the best beaches here, so if you get tired along the way, take time out for a refreshing dip in the ocean.

Leave through the dockyard's south entrance and walk down Pender Road about 1km (⅔ mile). Cross Cockburn's Cut Bridge and go straight along Cockrange Road, which will take you to:

1 Somerset Bridge
2 Railway Trail
3 Fort Scaur
4 Sound View Road
5 Cavello Bay
6 Royal Naval Dockyard
7 Bermuda Arts Centre
8 Lagoon Park
9 Somerset Village
Somerset Country Squire
Pub & Restaurant
10 Somerset Long Bay Park

Sandys Parish

Hamilton

⑧ Lagoon Park

Enter the park as you cross over the Cut Bridge onto Ireland Island South. Walking trails crisscross the park, which has a lagoon populated with ducks and other wild fowl. There are places for picnicking in the park, which is free and open to the public.

To continue, cross Grey's Bridge to Boaz Island, and walk or cycle along Malabar Road. On your right you'll see the calm waters of Mangrove Bay. You'll eventually arrive at:

⑨ Somerset Village

Somerset is one of the most charming villages on Bermuda. Only one road goes through the village. Most of the stores are branches of larger stores in the City of Hamilton.

TAKE A BREAK
Somerset Country Squire Pub & Restaurant (© 441/224-0105; p. 110) is an English-style pub that serves sandwiches, burgers, and such pub grub as steak-and-kidney pie and bangers and mash (sausages and mashed potatoes). The kitchen is also noted for its desserts.

Follow Cambridge Road west to:

⑩ Somerset Long Bay Park

Families like this park because of its good beach and shallow waters, which open onto Long Bay. You can picnic here. The Bermuda Audubon Society operates the nature reserve, and the pond attracts migrating birds, including the Louisiana heron, the snowy egret, and the purple gallinule, in both spring and autumn.

9

Shopping

Retailers on less prosperous islands attribute Bermuda's continuing reputation as a shopping mecca not only to the superb climate, but also to many years of skillful marketing. Indeed, no one has ever accused Bermudians of not knowing how to sell their island—or their rich inventories of goods.

Bermuda, once widely hailed as a "showcase of the British Empire," is still that, at least in its variety of goods. The retail scene draws upon its British antecedents: Shopkeepers are generally both polite and discreet, and merchandise is unusual and well made. In addition, most retailers take

full advantage of location. Shops usually occupy charming cottages or historically important buildings, making shopping even more fun. Even visitors who intend to do no more than window-shop are likely to break down and make a purchase or two.

In most cases, shopping on Bermuda is about quality, not bargains. Shops face huge import tariffs, plus employee-related taxes, leading to what some view as outrageously high prices. And it rarely pays to comparison shop—the price of a watch in a branch store in St. George is likely to be exactly the same as it is in the main shop in the City of Hamilton.

BERMUDA'S BEST BUYS

Most of Bermuda's best shops are along Front Street in the City of Hamilton, where shopping is relaxed and casual. Among the choicest items are imports from Great Britain and Ireland, such as Shetland and cashmere sweaters, Harris tweed jackets, Scottish woolen goods and tartan kilts, and even fine china and crystal. Many items cost appreciably less than in their country of origin.

Because of a special "colony-like" arrangement with Great Britain, certain British goods are cheaper in Bermuda than in the United States, thanks to lower import tariffs. Some frequent visitors stock up on porcelain, crystal, silverware, jewelry, timepieces, and perfume, perhaps anticipating a wedding gift several months in advance. The island abounds with merchandisers of fine tableware, including Royal Copenhagen, Wedgwood, and Royal Crown Derby. Crystal is also plentiful, with many of the finest manufacturers in Europe and North America providing wide selections of merchandise. For a fee, most items can be shipped.

Liquor is also a good buy in Bermuda. U.S. citizens are allowed to bring back only 1 liter duty-free, but even adding U.S. tax and duty, you can save 35% to 50% on liquor purchases, depending on the brand. Liqueurs offer the largest savings.

The island's wealth of antiques and collectibles is extraordinary. Antiques lovers appreciate Bermuda's fusion of British aesthetic and mid-Atlantic charm. The island has a wealth of antique engravings and 19th-century furniture. Its modern artwork and handmade pottery and crafts are elegant souvenirs. And anyone interested in carrying home a piece of Bermuda's nautical heritage can choose from oversize ship's propellers, captain's bells, brass nameplates, scale models of sailing ships, or maybe even an old-fashioned ship's steering wheel from a salvaged shipwreck.

Other good buys are "Bermudiana"—products made on Bermuda or manufactured elsewhere exclusively for local stores. They include cedar-wood gifts, carriage bells, coins commemorating the 375th anniversary of the island's settlement, flower plates by Spode, pewter tankards, handcrafted gold jewelry, traditional-line handbags with cedar or mahogany handles, miniature cottages in ceramic or limestone, shark's teeth polished and mounted in 14-karat gold, decorative kitchen items, Bermuda shorts (of course), silk scarves, and watches with a map of Bermuda on their faces.

Although some items might be less expensive than they are stateside, be aware that this isn't always the case. In fact, many, many items are overpriced. You should be familiar with the prices of comparable goods back home before making any big purchases.

1 The Shopping Scene

WHERE TO GO
THE CITY OF HAMILTON
The best and widest range of shopping choices is in the City of Hamilton (see "In the City of Hamilton," below). Most shops are on Front Street, but you should explore the back streets as well, especially if you're an adventurous shopper.

The Emporium on Front Street, a restored building constructed around an atrium, houses a number of shops, including jewelry stores. Windsor Place on Queen Street is another Bermuda-style shopping mall.

HISTORIC ST. GEORGE
The "second city" of St. George also has many shops, stores, and boutiques, including branches of the City of Hamilton's famous Front Street stores. King's Square, the center of St. George, is home to many shops. The other major centers are Somers Wharf and Water Street.

In recent years, this historic port has emerged as a big-time shopping competitor to the City of Hamilton. It's easier to walk around St. George than the City of Hamilton, and St. George is more architecturally interesting than the City of Hamilton; so more and more customers are choosing to do their shopping here. Of course, St. George doesn't have as vast an array of merchandise as the City of Hamilton, so the serious shopper might want to explore both cities.

SANDYS PARISH
Don't overlook the shopping possibilities of the West End. Somerset Village in Sandys Parish has many shops (though quite a few are branches of the City of Hamilton stores). At the Royal Naval Dockyard area on Ireland Island, you can visit the Craft Market, Island Pottery, and the Bermuda Arts Centre at Dockyard, where you'll see local artisans at work.

WHAT YOU SHOULD KNOW
STORE HOURS
Stores in the City of Hamilton, St. George, and Somerset are generally open Monday to Saturday 9am to 5:30pm. When large liners are in port, stores sometimes stay open later, and are sometimes open on Sundays.

(Tips **The Eternal Search for Bargains**

During the off season (autumn and winter), stores often reduce prices to make way for goods for the new season. But sales come and go year-round—there's no particular season. Keep an eye out for SALE signs no matter when you're in Bermuda.

FINDING AN ADDRESS

Some Front Street stores post numbers on their buildings; others don't. Sometimes the number posted or used is the "historic" number of the building, which has nothing to do with the modern number. You can always ask for directions, and most Bermudians are willing to help. Outside the City of Hamilton, don't expect to find numbers on buildings at all—or even street names in some cases.

SALES TAX & DUTY

There's no sales tax in Bermuda, but it's not a duty-free island. Depending on which country you're returning to, you may have to pay duty. See "Entry Requirements & Customs," in chapter 2, for details.

Note: Bermuda is covered by the U.S. law regarding "Generalized System of Preferences" status. That means that if at least 35% of an item has been crafted in Bermuda, you can bring it back duty-free, regardless of how much you spent. If you've gone beyond your $800 allotment, make a separate list of goods made in Bermuda. This will make it easier for the customs officials (and for you).

2 In the City of Hamilton

DEPARTMENT STORES

Since 1842, generations of Bermuda-bound visitors made Trimingham's, along Front Street, their number one place for shopping. In 2005, though, the venerable department store closed its doors.

H. A. & E. Smith, Ltd.   This store has been selling top-quality merchandise since 1889, at substantial savings over U.S. prices. Smith's comprehensive stock includes sweaters for men and women (in cotton, cashmere, lamb's wool, and Shetland), British cosmetics, and a collection of top French perfumes. Smith's is noted for its selection of handbags, gloves, a very limited array of Liberty fabrics by the yard, and children's clothing. It also carries such merchandise as Burberry's rainwear from London and Rosenthal china. A subsidiary, "The Treasure Chest," located across the street from the main store, carries a full line of French perfumes and gifts, plus souvenirs.
35 Front St. (**441/295-2288.**

Marks & Spencer   This branch of the famous British chain (sometimes oddly called "St. Michael") carries the same reliable merchandise as its sibling stores in the British Isles. You'll find men's, women's, and children's fashions in everything from resort wear to sleepwear, including lingerie. There are also well-tailored dresses and suits, dress shirts, blazers, and British-tailored trousers, as well as swimwear, toiletries, and English sweets and biscuits.
18 Reid St. (**441/295-0031.**

GOODS A TO Z
ANTIQUES
Heritage House   This outlet sells nautical prints, English antiques, old maps, modern porcelain, and the largest collection of Bermudian fine art on the island. Heritage House also boasts one of the best collections of costume jewelry in town. Look for the large collection of "Halcyon Days" pillboxes.

26 Church St. W. (♪ **441/295-1902.**

ART
Bermuda Society of Arts   Loosely associated with the Bermudian government, this store is devoted to the exhibition of works by Bermuda-based artists and is one of the focal points of the island's arts scene. The West Wing of Hamilton's City Hall (the island's Fine Arts Museum occupies the East Wing) is the permanent home of the oldest arts society on Bermuda. The site contains two separate exhibition areas, where the artwork changes every 2 to 3 weeks. Themes range from the moderately avant-garde to the conservative, and every show includes dozens of examples of Bermudian landscapes, seascapes, or architectural renderings, any of which would make worthwhile souvenirs of your stay on the island. All merchandise can be packed for airplane transport.

West Wing of City Hall, 17 Church St. (♪ **441/292-3824.**

Burnaby Gallery   In the heart of the City of Hamilton, this new yet prestigious gallery is dedicated to showcasing the best of Bermuda's artists. Deborah Harper runs the gallery with the aid of a panel of local art experts who help select the pieces that are exhibited here. Every 4 to 6 weeks a new exhibition opens.

The LOM Building, corner of Burnaby and Reid sts. (♪ **441/292-8641.**

Masterworks Foundation Gallery   Established in 1987 by a group of international philanthropists, this foundation showcases paintings by renowned European, Bermudian, and North American artists. It serves to some extent as the island's most visible arts center. The foundation sponsors frequent art exhibitions, which have included works by Georgia O'Keeffe (who painted in Bermuda during the early 1930s), seascapes by Winslow Homer, and watercolors by Ogden Pleissner. The foundation also arranges guided art and architectural tours around the island and coordinates other artistic endeavors and exhibitions throughout the year.

Bermuda House Lane, 97 Front St. (♪ **441/295-5580.** www.bermudamasterworks.com.

Michael Swan Studio and Art Gallery   For almost 3 decades, Michael Swan has been one of the best-known artists in Bermuda, using the medium of the airbrush and acrylic paints. Praised by critics for the energy that seemingly bursts out of the shadows he creates, he's noted for his strong, simple designs that appeal to anyone with a sense of architectural form. His depictions of clouds are particularly evocative. He usually paints at night, when shoppers and art lovers are far from his gallery, but in his absence, a staff displays and sells his work.

Butterfield Place, Front St., Hamilton. (♪ **441/296-5650.**

Windjammer Gallery   In a coral cottage, this gallery exhibits paintings and bronze sculptures by local and international artists. It also carries an extensive selection of cards, prints, and limited editions. Adjacent to the gallery is the last private garden in the city, used for the display of sculpture and exhibitions.

Reid and King sts. (♪ **441/292-7861.** Closed Nov to mid-Feb.

Shopping in the City of Hamilton

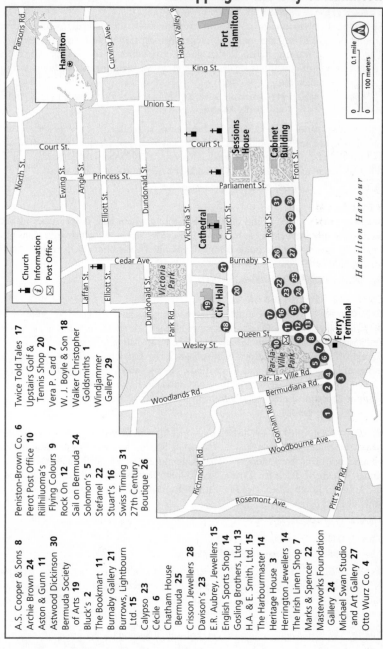

A.S. Cooper & Sons **8**
Archie Brown **24**
Aston & Gunn **11**
Astwood Dickinson **30**
Bermuda Society
 of Arts **19**
Bluck's **2**
The Bookmart **11**
Burnaby Gallery **21**
Burrows, Lightbourn
 Ltd. **15**
Calypso **23**
Cécile **6**
Chatham House
 Bermuda **25**
Crisson Jewellers **28**
Davison's **23**
E.R. Aubrey, Jewellers **15**
English Sports Shop **14**
Gosling Brothers, Ltd. **13**
H.A. & E. Smith, Ltd. **15**
The Harbourmaster **14**
Heritage House **3**
Herrington Jewellers **14**
The Irish Linen Shop **7**
Marks & Spencer **22**
Masterworks Foundation
 Gallery **24**
Michael Swan Studio
 and Art Gallery **27**
Otto Wurz Co. **4**

Peniston-Brown Co. **6**
Perot Post Office **10**
Riilhiluoma's
Flying Colours **9**
Rock On **12**
Sail on Bermuda **24**
Solomon's **5**
Stefanel **22**
Stuart's **16**
Swiss Timing **31**
27th Century
Boutique **26**

Twice Told Tales **17**
Upstairs Golf &
 Tennis Shop **20**
Vera P. Card **7**
W. J. Boyle & Son **18**
Walker Christopher
 Goldsmiths **1**
Windjammer
 Gallery **29**

201

BEACHWEAR & SUNGLASSES

Calypso   Calypso carries casual, fun fashions (including unusual garments from around the world) and the most comprehensive selection of swimwear on Bermuda. The shop also features Italian leather goods, espadrilles, hats, bags, pareus, Italian ceramics, and whimsical gift items. It's the exclusive island retailer of Louis Vuitton luggage and accessories.

23–24 Front St. ✆ **441/295-2112.** Additional branches at the Fairmont Southampton, Elbow Beach Hotel, Wyndham Bermuda Resort, Coral Beach Club, and the dockyard.

Sail on Bermuda   The locals shop at this store, which carries a unique collection of casual wear, bathing suits, and gifts. A recent poll of shoppers named Sail on Bermuda's T-shirts the best on Bermuda. A small addition, called "Shades of Bermuda," has the finest collection of sunglasses on the island. The store also sells sailing suits.

Old Cellar, Front St. ✆ **441/295-0808.** www.sailonbermuda.com.

BOOKS

The Bookmart   This is the biggest bookstore on Bermuda. It specializes in best-sellers—mainly from the U.S. market—and carries works by British authors as well. One section is devoted to books about the island. There's also a well-stocked section for the kiddies.

Phoenix Centre, 3 Reid St. ✆ **441/295-3838,** ext. 412.

CHINA & GLASSWARE

A. S. Cooper & Sons   Bermuda's oldest and largest china and glassware store—family owned since 1897—offers a broad range of fine bone china, earthenware, glassware, and jewelry. Among the famous names represented are Minton, Royal Doulton, Belleek, Aynsley, Wedgwood, and Royal Copenhagen. The Crystal Room displays Orrefors, Waterford, Royal Brierley, and Kosta Boda, among others. The Collector's Gallery is known for its limited editions of Bing & Gröndahl, Royal Doulton, and Lladró. The perfume department offers selections from the world's greatest perfumeries.

59 Front St. ✆ **441/295-3961.**

Bluck's   Established in 1844, Bluck's is well-known for carrying some of the finest names in china, including Royal Worcester, Spode, Aynsley, Royal Doulton, and Herend porcelain from Hungary. The choice in crystal is equally impressive: Kosta Boda, Waterford, Baccarat, Daum, and Lalique (exclusive with Bluck's). Upstairs is the Antiques Room, filled with fine English furniture, antique Bermuda maps, and an array of old English silver.

4 Front St. ✆ **441/295-5367.**

FASHION

Also see "Shoes," "Sportswear," and "Woolens," p. 206 and 207.

Aston & Gunn   This shop sells career-oriented clothing for men (imported from Germany and Holland). In addition to the usual collection of shirts, ties, jackets, and suits, Aston & Gunn is the exclusive island distributor of Hugo Boss.

2 Reid St. ✆ **441/295-4866.**

Cécile   Well-stocked Cécile is the center for high fashion on Bermuda. Management boasts that visiting one of Cécile's shops (the others are in England) is like calling upon the fashion capitals of the world—you'll find everything from German high fashion to Gottex swimwear. Its sweater and accessory boutique is also outstanding. 15 Front St. W. (near the Visitors Service Bureau and the Ferry Terminal). ℂ **441/295-1311**.

Stefanel   This is the island's only outlet for the clothing of Carlo Stefanel, a well-known Italian designer. Stocking merchandise for women, the store sells handmade skirts (some of them knit) with contrasting jackets. There are a stylish array of accessories and a line of clothing for infants and children. 7 Reid St. or 12 Walker Arcade. ℂ **441/295-5698**.

27th Century Boutique   Long known as a stylish, trendsetting shop, this high-fashion boutique carries designer clothing, silver costume jewelry, and accessories. The European clothing is styled for women ages 13 and up—on our recent visit, a 16-year-old and a grandmother bought the same shirt. The clothing is rather conservative and in good taste. 4 Burnaby St. (between Front and Church sts.). ℂ **441/292-2628**.

GIFTS
Riihiluoma's Flying Colours   This is everybody's favorite catchall emporium for inexpensive, impulse-purchase souvenirs and T-shirts with perky slogans. You'll also find paperweights; beach coverups; sarongs like actress Dorothy Lamour used to wear; key chains shaped like Bermuda; and arts and crafts. The establishment's hard-to-spell name comes from the Finnish-born family that established it in 1937 and still manages it today. 5 Queen St. ℂ **441/295-0890**.

Vera P. Card   Vera P. Card is known for its "gifts from around the world," including the island's largest collection of Lladró and Hümmel figurines. Famous-name watches include Nivada, Borel, and Rodania. The dinnerware collection features such brands as Rosenthal, and the crystal department offers a wide assortment of Czech and Bohemian crystal, giftware, and chandeliers. Look for the "Bermuda Collection" of 14-karat gold jewelry. 11 Front St. ℂ **441/295-1729**. Other branches are at 7 Water St. in St. George and at the Sonesta Beach Resort.

HAIR
The Hair Salon   Those pursuing beauty head here. Catering to both men and women, this renewed salon is bold and sassy, the decor reflecting the personality of its owner, Sharon Bartram. Her daughter, Kim Scott, is known locally as a "hair artist." This is a cutting-edge salon—the type of place visiting celebrities might frequent. 92 Reid St. ℂ **441/295-2258**.

JEWELRY
Astwood Dickinson   Here you'll find a treasure-trove of famous-name watches, including Patek Philippe, Cartier, Tiffany, Tag Heuer, Tissot, and Omega, plus designer jewelry, all at prices generally below U.S. retail. From the original Bermuda collection, you can select an 18-karat gold memento of the island (jeweled representations of local flora, fauna, and landmarks). 83–85 Front St. ℂ **441/292-5805**. There is a branch in the Walker Arcade.

Crisson Jewellers   Crisson is the exclusive Bermuda agent for Rolex, Ebel, Seiko, Cyma, and Gucci watches, and for other well-known makers. It also carries an extensive selection of fine jewelry and gems. 55 and 71 Front St. ℂ **441/295-2351**.

Finds **Counterculture Shopping**

If Bermuda is a bit prim for your tastes, we have a couple unusual stores to suggest: Try dropping in at **Twice Told Tales,** 34 Parliament St. (📞 **441/296-1995**), in the City of Hamilton, where kindred spirits gather at one of the few tables for coffee and conversation. We can't think of a better name for this store, which is a secondhand bookshop.

Here's a chance to meet the locals—**Rock On,** 67 Front St. (📞 **441/295-3468**), in the City of Hamilton, provides a full range of herb teas, nutritional supplements, and books and magazines devoted to health issues.

E. R. Aubrey, Jewellers   This shop carries an extensive collection of gold chains, rings with precious and semiprecious stones, and charms, including one of the Bermuda longtail bird.
19 Front St. W. (opposite the Ferry Terminal). 📞 441/295-3826.

Herrington Jewellers   This leading jewelry store offers a good selection of gold and silver items. It is the authorized dealer for Citizen watches, sells Timex watches, and carries a vast selection of 14-karat gold chains and rings set with precious and semiprecious stones.
1 Washington Mall. 📞 441/292-6527.

Solomon's   Some aficionados of the shopping scene consider Solomon's one of Bermuda's most appealing jewelry stores. Don't expect a supermarket-style emporium with vast inventories: Solomon's is small, select, and ever so polite, with a range of valuable stones mostly set in 18-karat gold (and, to a lesser degree, in platinum).
17 Front St. (across from the Bank of Bermuda). 📞 441/292-4742.

Swiss Timing   All the best names in Swiss watchmaking are found here, including Maurice Lacroix, Michel Herbelin, and Versace, along with a selection of semiprecious jewelry, gold chains, and bracelets.
95 Front St. 📞 441/295-1376.

Walker Christopher Goldsmiths   For the past decade or so, the *Bermudian* magazine has cited this goldsmith for selling the finest jewelry on the island. The shop showcases everything from classic diamond bands to strands of South Sea pearls to modern hand-hammered chokers. The store also carries a collection of rare coins—gold doubloons and silver "pieces of eight" salvaged from sunken galleons, as well as Greek and Roman coins which can be mounted and worn as pendants, earrings, and cuff links. Even Egyptian artifacts have been transformed into wearable art. Customers who have their own design in mind can work with a master jeweler to craft a one-of-a-kind piece. The on-site workshop also produces Bermuda-inspired gold jewelry and sterling silver Christmas ornaments.
9 Front St. 📞 441/295-1466.

LEATHER GOODS
The Harbourmaster   This is your best bet for luggage and leather goods. These good-value items are from Colombia and are often sold at prices 30% lower than in

the United States. There are more expensive leather goods from Italy (such as hand-bags), plus an extensive collection of wallets, and nylon and canvas tote bags. The shop also stocks travel accessories, including luggage carts.

Washington Mall. © **441/295-5333.**

LINENS

The Irish Linen Shop   At Heyl's Corner, near the "Birdcage" police officer post, this shop stocks pure linen tablecloths from Ireland and a large variety of other merchandise from Europe—everything from quilted place mats to men's shirts in French cotton from Souleiado of Provence. The shop also carries a large selection of Le Jacquard Français table linens. They are the biggest distributors of luxury bed linens. The owners go to Europe twice a year and bring back exceptional items such as Madeira hand embroidery and Belgian lace. You can often save as much as 50% over American prices.

31 Front St. (at Queen St.). © **441/295-4089.**

LIQUOR & LIQUEURS

You are allowed to take what U.S. Customs calls a "reasonable amount" of liquor from Bermuda to the United States. There is a duty-free allowance, but you merely pay overage to U.S. Customs at the airport. Even with the duty, prices are often lower than those in the States.

Orders must be placed 24 hours before you leave Bermuda, except on Sunday, when a 48-hour advance purchase is required. "In-bond" items cannot be consumed on the island; they can only be exported. The bottle you drink on the island is likely to cost 50% more than the "in-bond" bottle.

Burrows, Lightbourn Ltd.   This is the best and most comprehensive liquor store on island, carrying a wide array of spirits in various price ranges. You can put together your own package of Bermuda liquors at in-bond or duty-free prices. The store will deliver your packages to the airport or to your ship.

57 Front St. © **441/295-0176.** There are additional locations at Main Rd. in Somerset (© 441/234-0963), at Harbour Rd. in Paget Parish (© 441/236-0355), and at Water St. in St. George's (© 441/297-0552).

Gosling Brothers, Ltd.   The leading competitor of Burrows, Lightbourn, Gosling has also been selling liquor on Bermuda since 1806. You can buy Gosling's Black Seal dark rum—perhaps one bottle to sample on the island and another to take home with you. In addition to their own rum, the store stocks a wide selection of liquors, liqueurs, and wines. If you want to buy liquor to take home under your duty-free allowance, you can arrange to have it sent to the airport.

Front and Queen sts. © **441/298-7337.** www.goslings.com. There are 2 other locations, the Black Seal Shop (under the same ownership despite having a different name), at 17 Dundonald St. and at the airport.

(*Tips* **Shoppers Beware**

Many of our readers carry only the Discover Card. But be warned in advance that the popular U.S. card isn't accepted in Bermuda. One reader, John Fisher, wrote us to say that, because Discover is not accepted: "Many of the items we had looked forward to purchasing in Bermuda we had to pass up." MasterCard and Visa are accepted by most stores.

Branching Out

You'll often find branches of City of Hamilton's stores at major resorts. The prices—even when there's a sale—are the same as those charged by the parent stores in the City of Hamilton. Although the selection is more limited, resort boutiques remain open on Sunday, when most stores in the City of Hamilton are shuttered.

PERFUMES

Peniston-Brown Co.   This shop carries almost all of the world's most popular perfumes. Its "fragrance specialists" will be happy to teach you something about the art of choosing and wearing perfume.

23 Front St. W. (opposite the Ferry Terminal). ℭ **441/295-0570.** There is another location On the square in St. George.

PHOTOGRAPHIC EQUIPMENT

Stuart's   This is Bermuda's leading outlet for photographic and electronic equipment. It is the official rep for Minolta, Canon, Sony, Nikon, Pentax, and other big names. The store also carries top-of-the-line picture frames and camera bags. Also sold are tapes, film, tape recorders, and other supplies.

5 Reid St. ℭ **441/295-5496.**

SHOES

W. J. Boyle & Son   In business since 1884, this shop offers footwear for men, women, and children. With the best collection in town, it specializes in brand-name footwear from England, Spain, Brazil, and the United States (including Clarks of England, Cole Haan, and Enzo Angiolini).

Queen St. ℭ **441/295-1887.**

SILVER

Otto Wurz Co.   Otto Wurz is at the western end of Front Street, past the Ferry Terminal and the Bank of Bermuda. It specializes in articles made of silver, including jewelry, charms, and bracelets. One section of the store is devoted to gift items, such as pewter ware, cute wooden signs, and glassware, which the store can engrave for you.

2 Vallis Building, 3–5 Front St. (between Par-la-Ville Rd. and Bermudiana Rd.). ℭ **441/295-1247.**

SPORTSWEAR

Davison's   Sportswear with a Bermudian flair is the specialty at this emporium. Along with virtually anything you'd need to wear for almost any sport on Bermuda— or to the country club at home—it carries accessories and sporting equipment. The store features bags by Vera Bradley. Also available are culinary gift packages including such items as Bermuda fish or clam chowder, fish-based sauces, and island herbs.

27 and 93 Front St. ℭ **441/292-1556.** Other locations are at Water St. in St. George, and at the Fairmont Southampton.

Upstairs Golf & Tennis Shop   Everything you'll need for the tennis courts or the golf links is available in this amply stocked store. For golfers, there's merchandise by Ping, Callaway, Titleist, and Adams. Tennis enthusiasts will recognize products by Dunlop, Slazenger, and many others. There is also men's and women's rainwear from Scotland, which is suitable for Bermuda's wet winters.

26 Church St. ℭ **441/295-5161.**

STAMPS

Perot Post Office   Philatelists from all over the world visit this office to buy postage stamps from Bermuda. Highly prized by collectors, the stamps often feature historic figures and the island's flora and fauna. A stamp showing the *Sea Venture* stranded on coral reefs is one of the most coveted stamps. Open Monday to Friday from 9am to 5pm.

Queen St., at the entrance to Par-la-Ville Park. (C) **441/292-9052** or 441/295-5151, ext. 1192.

TOBACCO

Many Americans come to Bermuda to enjoy Cuban cigars, which can't be brought back into the United States but must be smoked while abroad.

Chatham House Bermuda   This shop seems as if it's been around since Columbus discovered Taino Indians smoking the leaves of a plant called *cohiba* in 1492. Chatham House is a historic retailer of Cuban cigars. Bermuda used to harvest its own tobacco, but Castro blessed those on sale here—well, almost. The store also carries pipes, Swiss Army knives, lighters, and postcards.

65 Front St. (C) **441/292-8422.**

WOOLENS

Archie Brown   In business for more than half a century, this shop features sweaters for men and women in cashmere, cotton, lamb's wool, and Shetland; it also carries matching kilts for ladies and children. Men's kilts can be specially ordered. Colors range from neutral to vibrant.

51 Front St. (C) **441/295-2928.**

English Sports Shop   This shop, established in 1918, is one of the island's leading retailers of quality classic and British woolen goods for men, women, and children. This store features brands like Pringles and Marks and Spencer.

95 Front St. (C) **441/295-2672.**

3 Around the Island

As you leave the City of Hamilton and tour the island, you may want to continue looking for typical Bermudian items at the shops listed below.

For other shopping suggestions, consider the **Bermuda Craft Market** (see "Sandys Parish," in chapter 7) and the **Birdsey Studio** in Paget Parish (see "Paget Parish," in chapter 7).

Finds   Searching for That Little Treasure

In Southampton Parish, **Deja-Vu Flea Market**, 40 Middle Rd. ((C) **441/238-8525;** take bus no. 3), has recently started to attract a lot of attention from shoppers looking for offbeat and secondhand items. You never know what's been resting in those Bermudian attics all these years—on this island of seagoing men, many unusual finds were brought back from around the world. As you rummage around, you could find anything from Tibetan rubbings to a complete dinner set used by the Carringtons on the TV soap *Dynasty.*

SANDYS PARISH

IRELAND ISLAND

Bermuda Arts Centre at Dockyard   In one of the stone-sided warehouses originally built by the British during their military tenure in Bermuda, this art gallery specializes in paintings, sculptures, and crafts, mostly by Bermudian artisans. New artists are featured every 6 weeks. Not to be confused with the nearby Bermuda Crafts Centre, with which it is not associated, it's sponsored by a local foundation and strives for more than a purely commercial approach to art. Canvases range in price from $175 to around $5,000; less expensive craft items are also for sale. Some of the staff members are well versed in the nuances of the art.

Museum Row, 4 Freeport Rd., Royal Naval Dockyard. *C* **441/234-2441**. www.artbermuda.bm. Bus: 7 or 8.

SOUTHAMPTON PARISH

Desmond Fountain Gallery   Bermuda's most prominent sculptor, Desmond Fountain, has created some of the island's most visible public art. In recent years much of his work has been commissioned for upscale private homes and gardens around the world. The gallery also features original works by local artists.

On the ground floor of the Emporium, 69 Front St. *C* **441/296-3518**. www.desmondfountain.com.

Rising Sun Shop   This eclectic outlet, the only real "country store" left on Bermuda, lies 1km (⅔ mile) west of the Waterlot Inn. The owner, Anne Powell, has assembled a little bit of everything. We always like to stop in just in case we see something we can't live without. In addition to one of Bermuda's warmest welcomes, it offers a frequently changing inventory. You'll find everything from weather vanes to old hobbyhorses, saddlery to wine coolers.

159 Middle Rd. *C* **441/238-2154**. Bus: 3.

Sharon Wilson Gallery   At a gallery just minutes by foot from Horseshoe Beach, local artist Sharon Wilson is known for going beyond the picture-postcard view of island life in an attempt to portray Bermuda's spirit in more depth. She explores the scope of Bermudian life and its people through limited and open-edition lithographs and notecards. The gallery is also home to her picture book illustrations, the most well-known being the award-winning *The Day Gogo Went to Vote.*

2 Turtle Place. *C* **441/238-2583**. Bus: 7.

HAMILTON PARISH

Bermuda Glass-Blowing Studio and Showroom   This glass-blowing studio employs both locally trained Bermudians and Europeans. Although some of the studio's glass pieces have been commissioned, most are inspired by cutting-edge developments

---

Tips Comparison Shopping at Somers Wharf

The best place to begin shopping is at the new **Somers Wharf & Branch Stores** along Water Street (take bus no. 7), a coterie of shops that includes all the big names from the City of Hamilton such as A. S. Coopers and the Crown Colony Shop. Of course, the parent stores in the City of Hamilton are better stocked, but Somers Wharf makes shopping a pleasure because all the island's "name" shops are clustered together, making comparison shopping much easier.

Tips **Last-Minute Purchases**

The international airport in Bermuda offers duty-free shops for those last-minute purchases. One shop is in the international departures lounge, and the other lies near the U.S. departures lounge. U.S. citizens clear customs before flying back to the States. For that specialty purchase, you should still shop around the island, but now you can buy routine duty-free purchases such as perfume, cigarettes, and liquor right before getting on the plane. That sure beats buying such goods a day or so in advance and having them delivered to the airport.

---

in the art-glass world. Pieces on display cost $5 to $850. The minimum commission accepted is usually more than $500. The studio offers a workshop where customers can create a dish or paperweight of their own design for $150 per hour. The custom pieces are then taken home by the customer. There are also demonstrations held by experts from Monday to Friday 10am to 5pm.

16 Blue Hole Hill. ℂ **441/293-2234**. Bus: 1, 3, 6, 10, or 11.

PAGET PARISH

Masterworks   In the Botanical Gardens, this new home is for Bermuda artwork that has been collected from around the world. The first phase of the gallery is slated to open in the autumn of 2006. At the Visitors' Centre in the gardens, you can visit the Double Fantasy Café and Gift Shop, not only for morning coffee and afternoon tea, but to purchase original souvenirs and gifts. There is also a wide selection of books on local botany and Bermuda itself.

Point Finger Rd. (at South Rd.). ℂ **441/236-2950** for Masterworks; ℂ **441/236-5291** for Double Fantasy Café and Gift Shop. Bus: 1, 2, 7, or 8.

ST. GEORGE PARISH

The Book Cellar   Built in the 18th century, this small but choice bookshop lies below Tucker House, a National Trust property. It caters to both visitors and locals, including a lot of "yachties" who stop by to pick up reading material for their time at sea. A lot of people come here for the Cellar's line of books on Bermuda. There's also a wide array of fiction and nonfiction by British and American writers. Parents might be interested in picking up one of the children's books published in Britain—many are quite different from similar editions in America.

Water St. ℂ **441/297-0448**. Bus: 7.

Frangipani   This is a world of fun, colorful, "dressy casual" fashion for women. You'll find a large selection of comfortable cottons, bright silks, and soft rayons. The store is known for its unusual merchandise, including exclusive island designs. There's also a fine collection of swimwear and unusual accessories.

16 Water St., Somers Wharf. ℂ **441/297-1357**. Bus: 7.

Taylors   Go here for the finest selection of kilts, skirts, and other tartans from Scotland, even if you can't play the pipes.

30 Water St. ℂ **441/297-1626**. Bus: 7.

10

Bermuda After Dark

As we mentioned already, nightlife is not one of the compelling reasons to go to Bermuda, although there is some after-dark action, mainly in the summer. If you visit during the winter, we trust you'll be content to nurse a drink in a pub.

In the summer, activity seems to float from hotel to hotel, which makes it hard to predict which pub or nightspot will have the best steel-drum or calypso band at any given time. Many pubs feature sing-alongs at the piano, a popular form of entertainment in Bermuda. Most of the big hotels offer shows after dinner, with combos filling in between shows for couples who like to dance.

The island's visitor centers and most hotels distribute free copies of such publications as *Preview Bermuda, Bermuda Weekly,* and *This Week in Bermuda,* which list the latest scheduled activities and events. There's a calendar of events in the *Bermudian,* sold at most newsstands.

You can also tune in to the local TV station, which constantly broadcasts information for visitors, including details on cultural events and nightlife offerings around the island. From 7am to noon daily, radio station 1160 AM (VSB) broadcasts news of Bermuda's cultural and entertainment events.

1 The Club & Music Scene

PAGET PARISH

After Hours   The idea of an after-hours spot in sleepy Bermuda, where many guests turn in at 9pm, seems incongruous—but there is such a place. Local night owls flock here for good burgers and good times, downing food and drink until they're turned away. The cafe is very popular with locals, especially those who don't have to get up at 7am to report to work. The kitchen also turns out well-stuffed sandwiches, Indian curries, roti, and steak, for those late-night munchies. Open Monday to Friday 7pm to 3am; Saturday to Sunday 7pm to 4am.

117 South Rd. (past the intersection with Middle Rd.). ✆ 441/236-8563. Bus: 7 or 8.

The Deep   Bermuda's hottest nightclub is found on the sea terrace of the Elbow Beach Hotel. The club attracts a young crowd, but not that young: you must be 25 or over to enter. You'll find the hottest DJs playing the latest U.S. and European music. There is multilevel seating. The mezzanine offers a bird's-eye view of all the action, and the dance floor is spacious. Deep also features a custom-built stage for entertainment. Free entrance is granted to patrons of the Cafe Lido. The club is open Monday to Saturday from 10am to 3am (very late for early-to-bed Bermuda).

60 South Rd. ✆ 441/236-9884. Cover $20. Bus: 1, 2, or 7.

PEMBROKE PARISH (CITY OF HAMILTON)

Coconut Rock   With a name more evocative of the Caribbean than of Bermuda, this restaurant has two of the most active bars in town. It draws locals and visitors (in equal numbers) with background music and videos of the hottest acts in the U.K. and America. The Yashi Bar is a sushi bar. Happy hour is Monday to Friday from 5 to 7pm. Open daily 11:30am to 1am.

Williams House, 20 Reid St. ℂ **441/292-1043**. Bus: 7 or 8.

The Ozone Nightclub & the Lucky Strike Casino   One of Bermuda's leading clubs, the Ozone is on the third floor of a stylish commercial building in the center of the City of Hamilton. It has been renovated into a modern, trendy club, and there's lots of special-effects lighting. The extensive music repertoire includes the top hits climbing the charts. After the Ozone, visit the small Lucky Strike Casino to try your luck at the slots. Drink prices range from $5 to $8. Open Tuesday to Saturday noon to 3am.

In the Emporium Building, 69 Front St. ℂ **441/292-3379**. Cover: free Tues, otherwise $10, rising to $20 after midnight Fri–Sat. Bus: 3, 7, or 11.

The Spinning Wheel   If you'd like to escape from the tourist hordes and enjoy a pint with the locals, head to this longtime favorite, a virtual institution since opening in 1970. Named for the Fifth Dimension (remember them?) song, it's a relaxing place that has an outdoor pool area with a bar. There's live music downstairs. An upstairs section for disco dancing draws a young crowd. Happy hour is noon to 8pm Monday through Friday. Open daily noon to 3am.

33 Court St. ℂ **441/292-7799**. Cover upstairs $15–$20 Fri–Sun. Bus: 7 or 8.

Splash ℛ   Located next to the restaurant Portofino (see chapter 5, "Where to Dine," for a review), this split-level club—with two full-service bars and a cozy lounge atmosphere—evokes nightlife in New York City. Both visitors and islanders alike enjoy the best DJs on island, and they dance until 3am. The martini-and-wine bar is a chic rendezvous, and you can also enjoy the outdoor patio, ideal for meeting friends or for making new ones. Happy hour is from 5 to 9pm, and the club is open nightly from 5pm to 3am.

Bermudiana Rd. ℂ **441/296-3848** or -3849. Cover $20 after 9pm Fri–Sat. Free admission with dinner at Portofino. Bus: 1, 2, 10, or 11.

SOUTHAMPTON PARISH

Henry VIII   This restaurant (see chapter 5, "Where to Dine," for a review) is also a good bet for music and comedy. Piano tunes and singing are often featured, as are comedians. Performances begin at 9:45pm and last until the restaurant closes at 1am. The stage is visible from the pub and from one of the restaurant's three dining areas.

56 South Shore Rd. ℂ **441/238-1977**. Bus: 7 or 8.

2 The Bar Scene

HAMILTON PARISH

Swizzle Inn   The home of the Bermuda rum swizzle, this bar and restaurant lies west of the airport, near the Crystal Caves and the Bermuda Perfumery. You can order a Swizzleburger and fish and chips throughout the day (see chapter 5, "Where to

Dine," for a review). There is live entertainment every night except Mondays and Wednesdays. In the old days, you might've run into Ted Kennedy here; now his wife steers him to more sedate places. The tradition is to tack your business card to anyplace you can find a spot, even the ceiling. The jukebox plays both soft and hard rock. Happy hour is Monday to Friday 5 to 7pm. Open daily 11am to 1am.

3 Blue Hole Hill, Bailey's Bay. ✆ **441/293-1854**. Bus: 3 or 11.

PEMBROKE PARISH (CITY OF HAMILTON)

Casey's   There's nothing flashy about this long, narrow room, which seems to be a favorite with locals. Look for yellowed photographs of old Bermuda and a carefully preserved, wall-mounted marlin caught by the owner in 1982. Friday nights here are the most popular on the island, and the joint overflows. Go here if you like to wander far off-the-beaten tourist trail and want to hang out with local Bermudians. Open Monday to Saturday 10am to 10pm.

25 Queen St. (between Reid and Church sts.). ✆ **441/292-9994**. Bus: 1, 2, 10, or 11.

Docksider   This sports bar on the City of Hamilton's main drag is lively into the early-morning hours. At a long cedar bar you'll find some of the most avid sports fans on Bermuda. There are 15 TVs (including three large plasma screens). One section is a wine bar, which is more intimate; another section is a pool bar. You can order pub grub, such as fish and chips or shepherd's pie. On some Fridays, there is a live DJ. Happy hour is daily from 5 to 7pm. Open daily 11am to 1am (until 2am Fri and Sat).

121 Front St. ✆ **441/296-3333**. Bus: 1, 2, 10, or 11.

Flanagan's   On the second floor of a landmark building, this restaurant-pub is the domain of Irishman Thomas Gallagher, who extends a *cead mile failte,* or "100,000 welcomes." This club has some of the town's best music—reggae, Top 40, rock, soca, and what is often called "party music." There are two bars that feature exotic drinks. Happy hour is daily from 5 to 7pm. In the sports bar, you can watch European soccer matches or other sports; there are eight 27-inch screens. Open daily 11am to 1am.

Emporium Building, 69 Front St. ✆ **441/295-8299**. Bus: 7 or 8.

The Pickled Onion   For years, Ye Old Cock & Feather was one of Bermuda's landmark pubs. In 1997, it glaringly changed its image (as well as its name), and the once fairly staid pub became a stop on the after-dark circuit. Funky fabrics cover the booths and tables where patrons listen to music that ranges from Top 40 to blues to oldies and hits of the past 50 years. Live music starts at 10pm during the summer season. Happy hour is Monday to Friday from 5 to 7pm. Open daily 11:30am to around 1am (until 2am Fri–Sat).

53 Front St. ✆ **441/295-2263**. Bus: 7 or 8.

Robin Hood Pub & Restaurant   The merry women and men of Bermuda flock here for a variety of entertainment options. Robin Hood serves fine pub fare, including some of Bermuda's best pizzas. It's also the island's number one sports bar, with video coverage of various U.S. and British league competitions. The pub has recently been renovated. On some nights you can enjoy everything from casual trivia quizzes with other patrons to jukebox nights devoted to reggae or rock. Sometimes prizes are awarded to the patron who can drink a pint of ale the fastest. Open Monday to Saturday 11am to 1am, Sunday noon to 1am.

25 Richmond Rd. ✆ **441/295-3314**. Bus: 1 or 2.

Square One   This convivial indoor/outdoor nightspot opened in 2000, when Guido Esposito, one of the owners of the also-recommended Tuscany restaurant (see chapter 5, "Where to Dine," for a review), headed from his restaurant upstairs to what at the time had functioned as a laundry room opening onto an outdoor courtyard. After a few drinks, he got the idea for a nightspot like the ones in his native island of Capri, off the coast of Naples. The result is the most European-style nightclub in Bermuda, with an indoor bar and an outdoor courtyard with aluminum tables and chairs soaking up the moonlight. Both areas are steeped in techno music that you'd hear in a nightclub in Rome, without too much of an emphasis on the loud and throbbing house and garage music you might expect at a late-night spot in, say, New York or L.A. (This is, after all, downtown Hamilton, and noise restrictions are somewhat strict.) Attracting a hip and permissive crowd of good-looking people of all genres and sexual persuasions, it's the local bar for many Hamilton residents. Open Monday to Saturday noon to 3am.

95 Front St., off Bermuda House Lane. © **441/292-1959.** Bus: 1 or 2.

SANDYS PARISH

The Frog & Onion Pub   Converted from an 18th-century cooperage, or barrel-making factory, this British-style pub is in the Royal Naval Dockyard (see chapter 5, "Where to Dine," for a restaurant review). It serves bar snacks throughout the afternoon and evening. Operated by a "frog" (a Frenchman) and an "onion" (a Bermudian), the pub is open daily 11:30am to 1am.

The Cooperage, Royal Naval Dockyard, Ireland Island. © **441/234-2900.** Bus: 7 or 8.

SMITH'S PARISH

North Rock Brewing Company   If you want to find us in Bermuda, chances are we'll be at this watering hole, Bermuda's first brewpub. The draft beer is brewed on the premises right before your eyes. Pub seating envelops the glass-enclosed brewery where Old Colony Bitters and Somers Ale are brewed. You may be surprised to find that some of the mugs are 22 ounces. These brews are only for local consumption and not sold elsewhere. You'll find a selection of fresh ales on any given day, including "Whale of a Wheat" and "North Rock Porter." The outdoor roadside patio adds a British flavor. See the restaurant recommendation in chapter 5, "Where to Dine," for more details. The pub is open daily from 11am to 11pm.

10 South Rd. © **441/236-6633.** Bus: 1.

SOUTHAMPTON PARISH

Jasmine   In the restored Fairmont Southampton, this club has become the ideal spot for meeting and enjoying the quintessential martini. Along with your favorite drink, a selection of light dishes, snacks, sandwiches, and even pizza are served. The bar skips a beat when live entertainment is featured. Drinks begin at $8, and there is no cover. Open daily 11am to midnight.

In the Fairmont Southampton, 101 South Rd. © **441/238-8000.** Private ferry to Fairmont Hamilton.

ST. GEORGE PARISH

The little port of St. George and adjoining St. David's Island are a pubber's haven. Our favorite is **Black Horse Tavern** (p. 136), a perfect spot for a congenial evening in good company. It lies on St. David's Island immediately adjoining St. George, and is worth the trek over. If you get hungry, you can always order a plate of shark hash to go with your beer. Back in St. George itself, **Freddie's Pub on the Square** (p. 137) is always a lot of fun. Its selection of draft beers is among the best on the island. The oldest pub in St. George, **White Horse Tavern** (p. 138), remains an enduring favorite. It's jammed most evenings with a mixture of locals and visitors. We especially like the location of this one, as it stands at the water's edge overlooking the harbor. Don't expect speedy service in any of these joints.

3 The Performing Arts

You can order tickets for Bermuda's major cultural events through the box office at the **Visitors Service Bureau** in the City of Hamilton (© 441/292-8572) with your MasterCard, Visa, or American Express card. Students and senior citizens are sometimes eligible for discounts to various entertainment events.

BALLET

The Bermuda Civic Ballet presents classical ballets at various venues. On occasion, a major European or American guest artist appears with the troupe. The National Dance Theater of Bermuda also stages performances, both classical and modern, around the island. Ask at the tourist office or call the box office at the Visitors Service Bureau (see above) to check the troupe's schedules during your visit; prices vary with the performance.

CLASSICAL MUSIC

The **Bermuda Philharmonic Society,** conducted by Graham Garton, presents four regular concerts during the season. Special outdoor **"Classical Pops" concerts** are presented on the first weekend in June in St. George and at the Royal Naval Dockyard. Concerts usually feature the Bermuda Philharmonic orchestra, the choir, and guest soloists. You can get tickets and concert schedules by calling © **441/295-5333.** Tickets generally cost $18 to $21; seniors and students are often granted discounts, depending on the performance.

GOMBEY DANCING

Ask at the tourist office or call the box office at the Visitors Service Bureau (see above) to see whether the gombey dancers will be performing during your stay. Gombey

---

Tips **The Big Event: The Bermuda Festival**

Bermuda's major cultural event is the Bermuda Festival, staged every January and February. Outstanding international classical, jazz, and pop artists perform, and major theatrical and dance companies from around the globe stage productions. During the festival, performances take place on varying nights. Ticket prices start at $40. Some festival tickets are reserved until 48 hours before curtain time for visitors. Visitors who'd like tickets can contact **Axiom** (© **441/236-4034**; www. resqwest.com), which holds back a number of tickets that locals cannot access. Most performances are at **City Hall Theatre**, City Hall, Church Street, the City of Hamilton. For more information and reservations, contact the **Bermuda Festival,** P.O. Box HM 297, Hamilton HM AX, Bermuda (© **441/295-1291**; fax 441/295-7403).

(commonly pronounced *goom*-bee or *gom*-bay) is the island's single most important cultural expression of African heritage. Once part of slave culture, the tradition dates from the mid-1700s. The local dance troupe of talented men and women often performs at one of the big hotels in winter (and, on occasion, aboard cruise ships for passengers). On holidays, you'll see the gombeys dancing through the streets of the City of Hamilton in their colorful costumes.

MUSICAL THEATER

An all-volunteer organization based in the City of Hamilton, the **Gilbert & Sullivan Society of Bermuda,** P.O. Box HM 3098, Hamilton HM NX (© **441/295-3218**), is known for producing at least one large-scale musical per year. These days, only about 20% of the repertoire is based on the works of Gilbert and Sullivan; it now includes such musicals as *Cabaret, Les Misérables, Chicago, Fiddler on the Roof, Into the Woods,* and *Carmen,* among others. The society performs at the City of Hamilton's City Hall, on Church Street. Be warned that this is a volunteer organization; the sole production runs for 2 weeks at most, usually in October. Tickets cost $35. Society members sometimes contribute their talents to the Bermuda Festival (see the box above).

Bermuda is the only place outside of Cambridge where Harvard University's **Hasty Pudding Theatricals** are staged. Performances have been presented in Bermuda during College Weeks (in Mar and Apr) since the 1960s. They're staged at the City Hall Theatre on Church Street in the City of Hamilton; call the box office at the Visitors Service Bureau (see above) for tickets, which cost about $25 each.

Appendix:
Bermuda in Depth

Welcome to an island of no pollution, no billboards, no graffiti, no litter, no rental cars, no unemployment (well, almost), no tolerance for drugs, no illiteracy (well, almost), and no nude or topless beaches. In a changing world, Bermuda remains . . . well, Bermuda.

If there's a sore point among Bermudians today, it's their extreme desire to separate themselves from the islands of the Caribbean, particularly from The Bahamas, in the eyes of the world. They often send angry letters to publishers of maps, reference sources, and travel guides, insisting that Bermuda is not in the Caribbean. As one irate Bermudian put it, "You don't claim that Washington, D.C., is part of Dallas, Texas. They're the same distance apart that Bermuda is from the Caribbean."

Bermuda prides itself on its lack of economic, socioeconomic, and racial problems, many of which plague the Caribbean islands. Bermuda does not tolerate unsavory businesses. What the island would really like to be known for is its stellar performance in banking and multinational business.

During this first decade of the millennium, international business is positioning itself to overtake tourism as Bermuda's primary source of revenue. Before China's takeover of Hong Kong, Bermuda persuaded some of the biggest names in world business to create official domiciles on the island. The trend began in the 1970s, when some Hong Kong businesspeople formed low-profile shipping, trading, and investment companies in Bermuda—companies that became, in essence, corporate cash cows. That trend continues to positively affect Bermuda's economy.

When Britain surrendered Hong Kong to China in 1997, Bermuda became the largest British colony. A local businessman watched the televised ceremonies in which Britain handed over control, and gleefully remarked, "All we can say is: Thank you very much, Hong Kong, because here come the insurance companies and pension funds." By the end of the 20th century, nearly half of the companies listed on the Hong Kong Stock Exchange—and even some of the Chinese government's own holding companies—had established a legal presence in Bermuda, because Bermuda provides such hefty tax breaks. Amazingly, tiny Bermuda has emerged as the biggest and most prosperous of all of Britain's colonies, the bulk of which are now in the Caribbean.

In the early years of the 21st century, Bermuda continues to attract a growing number of American companies that are incorporating in Bermuda to lower their taxes without giving up the benefits of doing business in the United States. Insurance companies have led the way, but now manufacturers and other kinds of companies are following. It's been heralded in the press as "profits over patriotism." Becoming a Bermuda company is a paper transaction that can save millions annually.

And as aggressively as Bermuda is pursuing business, it's also more aware than ever of its fragile environment. Bermuda's population density is the third highest in the world, after Hong Kong's and Monaco's. Because the number of annual visitors is 10 times higher than the population, Bermuda has had to take strong initiatives to protect its environment and natural resources. Environmental protection takes the form of stiff anti-litter laws, annual garbage cleanup campaigns, automobile restrictions, cedar replanting (a blight in the '40s and '50s wiped out the native trees), lead-free gasoline, a strict fishing policy, and other measures.

Along the shaky road to self-government, Bermuda had some ugly racial conflicts. Riots in 1968 built up to the assassination of the British governor in 1973. But that was a long time ago; today, Bermuda has the most harmonious race relations in this part of the world, far better than those in the United States, the Caribbean, or The Bahamas. There's still a long way to go, but Bermudians of African descent have assumed important political, administrative, and managerial posts in every aspect of the local economy. Bermuda hasn't quite reached the point where the color of your skin is unimportant, but it has made more significant advancement toward that goal than its neighbors to the south.

In the early 21st century, Bermuda's average household income rose to a healthy $68,500—contrast that with some of the less fortunate islands in the south, many of which don't even have the budgets to compile such statistics. Compared with residents of Puerto Rico, Jamaica, and certainly Haiti, no one is really poor in Bermuda. On the downside, home prices in Bermuda are at least three times the median cost of a house in the United States or Canada.

As a tourist destination, Bermuda has impeccable credentials. It was a resort long before Florida, Hawaii, Mexico, and many other places. Over the years, it has successfully exploited its position in the northwest Atlantic between North America and Europe. It is even working to throw off its image as a staid resort, hoping to project a lively, more with-it atmosphere (although it has a long way to go in that department). The United States remains its largest market—about 86% of visitors are Americans—but in recent years more and more visitors from Europe, the Far East, and the Near East have been seen dining, drinking, and shopping in the City of Hamilton.

1 The Natural World: An Environmental Guide to Bermuda

Lying 918km (570 miles) east-southeast of Cape Hatteras, North Carolina, Bermuda is actually a group of some 300 islands, islets, and coral rocks clustered in a fishhook-shaped chain about 35km (22 miles) long and 3km (2 miles) wide at its broadest point. The archipelago, formally known as "The Bermudas," forms a landmass of about 54 sq. km (21 sq. miles).

Only 20 or so of the islands are inhabited. The largest one, called the "mainland," is Great Bermuda; about 23km (14 miles) long, it's linked to nearby major islands by a series of bridges and causeways. Bermuda's capital, the City of Hamilton, is on Great Bermuda.

The other main inhabited islands include Somerset, Watford, Boaz, and Ireland in the west, and St. George's and St. David's in the east. This chain of major islands encloses the archipelago's major bodies of water, which include Castle Harbour, St. George's Harbour, Harrington Sound, and Great Sound. Most of the other smaller islands, or islets, lie within these bodies of water.

Bermuda is far north of the Tropic of Cancer, which cuts through the Bahamian archipelago. Bermuda's archipelago is based on the upper parts of an extinct volcano, which may date from 100 million years ago. Through the millennia, wind and water brought limestone deposits and formed these islands far from any continental landmass. Today, the closest continental landmass is the coast of the Carolinas. Bermuda is about 1,250km (775 miles) southeast of New York City, some 1,660km (1,030 miles) northeast of Miami, and nearly

5,555km (3,445 miles) from London. It has a balmy climate year-round, with sunshine prevailing almost every day. The chief source of Bermuda's mild weather is the Gulf Stream, a broad belt of warm water formed by equatorial currents. The stream's northern reaches separate the Bermuda islands from North America and, with the prevailing northeast winds, temper the wintry blasts that sweep across the Atlantic from west and north. The islands of Bermuda are divided, for administrative purposes, into parishes. (See "Orienting Yourself: The Lay of the Land," in chapter 3, "Getting to Know Bermuda.")

MORE THAN ONIONS: THE ISLAND'S FLORA

Bermuda's temperate climate, abundant sunshine, fertile soil, and adequate moisture account for the exceptionally verdant gardens that you'll find on the archipelago. Some of the best gardens, such as the Botanical Gardens in Paget Parish, are open to the public. Bermudian gardeners pride themselves on their mixtures of temperate-zone and subtropical plants, both of which thrive on the island, despite the salty air.

Bermuda is blessed with copious and varied flora. Examples include the indigenous sea grape, which flourishes along the island's sandy coasts (it prefers sand and saltwater to more arable soil), and the cassava plant, whose roots resemble the tubers of sweet potatoes. When ground into flour and soaked to remove a mild poison, the cassava root is the main ingredient for Bermuda's traditional Christmas pies. Also growing wild and abundant are prickly pears, aromatic fennel, yucca, and the Spanish bayonet, a spiked-leaf plant that bears a single white flower in season.

Bermuda's only native palm, the palmetto, proved particularly useful to the early settlers. Its leaves were used to thatch roofs, and when crushed and fermented, the palm fronds produced a strong alcoholic drink called bibby, whose effects the early Puritans condemned. Palmetto leaves were also fashioned into women's hats during a brief period in the 1600s, when they represented the height of fashion in London.

The banana, one of Bermuda's most dependable sources of fresh fruit, was introduced to the island in the early 1600s. It is believed that Bermudian bananas were the first to be brought back to London from the New World. They created an immediate sensation, leading to the cultivation of bananas in many other British colonies.

The plant that contributed most to Bermuda's renown was the Bermuda onion *(Allium cepa)*. Imported from England in 1616, it was grown from seeds brought from the Spanish and Portuguese islands of Tenerife and Madeira. The Bermuda onion became so famous along the East Coast of the United States that Bermudians themselves became known as "Onions." During the 1930s, Bermuda's flourishing export trade in onions declined due to high tariffs, increased competition from similar species grown in Texas and elsewhere, and the limited arable land on the island.

Today, you'll see oleander, hibiscus, royal poinciana, poinsettia, bougainvillea, and dozens of other flowering shrubs and vines decorating Bermuda's gently rolling land. Of the island's dozen or so species of morning glory, three are indigenous; they tend to grow rampant and overwhelm everything else in a garden.

CLOSE ENCOUNTERS WITH THE LOCAL FAUNA
AMPHIBIANS

Because of the almost total lack of natural freshwater ponds and lakes, Bermuda's amphibians have adapted to seawater or slightly brackish water. Amphibians include tree frogs *(Eleutherodactylus johnstonei* and *Eleutherodactylus gossei),* whose nighttime chirping newcomers sometimes mistake for the song of birds. Small and camouflaged by the leafy matter of the forest floor, the frogs appear between April and November.

More visible are Bermuda's giant toads, or road toads *(Bufo marinus)*, which sometimes reach the size of an adult human's palm. Imported from Guyana in the 1870s in hopes of controlling the island's cockroach population, giant toads search out the nighttime warmth of the asphalt roads—and are often crushed by cars in the process. They are especially prevalent after a soaking rain. The road toads are not venomous and, contrary to legend, do not cause warts.

Island reptiles include colonies of harmless lizards, often seen sunning themselves on rocks until approaching humans or predators scare them away. The best-known species is the Bermuda rock lizard *(Eumeces longirostris)*, also known as a skink. It's said to have been the only nonmarine, nonflying vertebrate on Bermuda before the arrival of European colonists. Imported reptiles include the Somerset lizard *(Anolis roquet)*, whose black eye patches give it the look of a bashful bandit, and the Jamaican anole *(Anolis grahami)*, a kind of chameleon.

BIRD LIFE

Partly because of its ample food sources, Bermuda has a large bird population; many species nest on the island during their annual migrations. Most of the birds arrive during the cooler winter months, usually between Christmas and Easter. Birders have recorded almost 40 different species of eastern warblers, which peacefully coexist with martins, doves, egrets, South American terns, herons, fork-tailed flycatchers, and even some species from as far away as the Arctic Circle.

Two of the most visible imported species are the cardinal, introduced during the 1700s, and the kiskadee. Imported from Trinidad in 1957 to control lizards and flies, the kiskadee has instead wreaked havoc on the island's commercial fruit crops.

The once-prevalent eastern bluebird has been greatly reduced in number since its preferred habitat, cedar trees, was depleted by blight. Another bird native to Bermuda is the gray-and-white petrel, known locally as a cahow, which burrows for most of the year in the sands of the isolated eastern islands. During the rest of the year, the cahow feeds at sea, floating for hours in the warm waters of the Gulf Stream. One of the most elusive birds in the world—it was once thought to have been extinct—the petrel is now protected by the Bermudian government.

Also native to Bermuda is the cliff-dwelling tropic bird, which you can identify by the elongated plumage of its white tail. The bird resembles a swallow and is the island's harbinger of spring, appearing annually in March.

Although the gardens and golf courses of many of the island's hotels attract dozens of birds, some of the finest bird-watching sites are maintained by the Bermuda Audubon Society (www.audubon.bm) or the National Trust. Isolated sites known for sheltering thousands of native and migrating birds include Paget Marsh, just south of the City of Hamilton; the Idwal Hughes Nature Reserve in Hamilton Parish; and Spittal Pond in Smith's Parish.

SEA LIFE

In the deep waters off the shores of Bermuda are some of the finest game fish in the world: blackfin tuna, marlin, swordfish, wahoo, dolphin, sailfish, and barracuda. Also prevalent are bonefish and pompano, both of which prefer sun-flooded shallow waters closer to shore. Any beachcomber is likely to come across hundreds of oval-shaped chitons *(Chiton tuberculatus)*, a mollusk that adheres tenaciously to rocks in tidal flats; locally, it is known as "suck-rock."

Beware of the Portuguese man-of-war *(Physalia physalis)*, a floating colony of jellyfish whose stinging tentacles sometimes reach 15m (49 ft.) in length. Give this dangerous and venomous marine creature a wide berth: Severe stings may require hospitalization. Avoid the creature when it washes up on Bermuda beaches, usually between March and July—the man-of-war can sting even when it appears to be dead.

The most prevalent marine animal in Bermuda is responsible for the formation of the island's greatest tourist attraction—its kilometers of pale pink sand. Much of the sand consists of broken shells, pieces of coral, and the calcium carbonate remains of other marine invertebrates. The pinkest pieces are shards of crushed shell from a single-celled animal called foraminifer. Its vivid pink skeleton is pierced with holes, through which the animal extends its rootlike feet *(pseudopodia)*, which cling to the underside of the island's reefs during the animal's brief life, before its skeleton is washed ashore.

2 Life in the Onion Patch

GETTING TO KNOW THE "ONIONS"

Even though Bermuda isn't in the onion business the way it used to be, a born and bred islander is still called an "Onion." The term dates from the early 20th century, when the export of Bermuda onions and Easter lilies to the U.S. mainland were the island's major sources of income.

The "Onions"—a term that still carries a badge of pride—have their own lifestyle and even their own vocabulary. For example, "Aunt Haggie's children" are frustrating, stupid people; "married by 10 parsons" is a reference to a woman with huge breasts; "backin' up" means gay. You don't vomit in Bermuda, you "Go Europe." "Cockroach killers" (a term you may also hear in the American Southwest) are pointy-toed shoes. Although you'll rarely see it on local menus, the bream fish is called a "shit-bubbler."

Residents of more troubled islands to the south often look with envy upon the "Onions," who have a much higher standard of living than Caribbean islanders do; they also pay no personal income tax and suffer from only a 7% unemployment rate. The literacy rate is high: An estimated 99% of females age 15 and older can read and write, as can 98% of all Bermudian males.

Today's 61,000 residents are mostly of African, British, and Portuguese descent. Bermuda's population density, one of the highest in the world, is about 3,210 per 2.5 sq. km (1 sq. mile). The population is about 61% black, 39% white. Many ethnic minority groups are represented, the largest and most established being the Portuguese; the majority of inhabitants, however, are islanders from the Caribbean or The Bahamas. Some Bermudians can even trace their ancestry back to the island's first settlers, and some to successful privateers and freed slaves.

Britain's influence in Bermuda is obvious in the predominantly English accents, police who wear helmets like those of London bobbies, and cars that drive on the left. Schools are run along the lines of the British system and provide a high standard of preparatory education. Children 5 to 16 years of age must attend school. The Bermuda College, which offers academic and technical studies, boasts a renowned hotel and catering program.

WHO'S MINDING THE STORE?

In essence, Bermuda is a self-governing dependency of Britain, which protects its security and stability. The governor, appointed by the Queen, represents Her Majesty in the areas of external affairs, defense, and internal security.

> **Fun Fact** **Bermuda Shorts: Not Too Far Above the Knee**
>
> Most Bermudians consider the winter months too cold for Bermuda shorts; but by May, just about every businessman along Front Street has traded in his trousers for a pair. Bermuda shorts weren't initially Bermudian; they originated when the British army was sent to India. Later, when British troops were stationed in Bermuda, they were issued the shorts as part of the military's tropical kit gear.
>
> By the 1920s and 1930s, the shorts had become quite fashionable, although they were not considered acceptable at dinner parties or at church. Now suitable attire for businessmen, the shorts are worn with a blazer, collared shirt, tie, and knee socks. They shouldn't be more than 3 inches above the knee, and they must have a 3-inch hem.

By choosing to remain a British dependency, Bermuda rejected the trail that many former colonies in the Caribbean (including Antigua) blazed by declaring their independence. Although they remain under the protection of the British, Bermudians manage their own day-to-day affairs. And ever since the people of Bermuda were granted the right to govern themselves in 1968, they have done so admirably well.

Bermuda has a 12-member cabinet headed by a premier. The elected legislature, referred to as the Legislative Council, consists of a 40-member House of Assembly and an 11-member Senate. Bermuda's oldest political party is the Progressive Labour Party, formed in 1963. In 1964, the United Bermuda Party was established; it stayed in power until it was toppled by the Progressive Labour Party in 1998.

Bermuda's legal system is founded on common law. Judicial responsibility falls to the Supreme Court, headed by a chief justice in a powdered wig and a robe. English law is the fundamental guide, and in court, English customs prevail.

The island consists of nine parishes, each managed by an advisory council. The capital, the City of Hamilton, is in Pembroke Parish. (For details on the individual parishes, see "Orienting Yourself: The Lay of the Land," in chapter 3.)

TOURIST DOLLARS & NO INCOME TAX

Bermuda's political stability has proved beneficial to the economy, which relies heavily on tourism and foreign investment.

For much of the island's early history, the major industry was shipbuilding, made possible by the abundant cedar forests. In the second half of the 19th century, when wooden ships gave way to steel ones, the island turned to tourism. Today, tourism is the country's leading industry, with annual revenues estimated at $450 million. Approximately 550,000 visitors come to Bermuda each year; an estimated 86% arrive from the United States, 4% from Britain, and 7% from Canada. Bermuda enjoys a 42% repeat-visitor rate.

Because Bermuda has enacted favorable economic measures, more than 6,000 international companies are registered there. The companies engage mostly in investment holding, insurance, commercial trading, consulting services, and shipping—but fewer than 275 companies are actually on the island. The reason for this curious situation? Bermuda has no corporate or income tax, so companies register on Bermuda but conduct business in their home countries, thereby avoiding taxes that their home countries would otherwise deduct.

The island's leading exports are pharmaceuticals, concentrates (primarily black rum and sherry peppers), essences, and beverages. Leading imports include foodstuffs, alcoholic beverages, clothing, furniture, fuel, electrical appliances, and motor vehicles. Bermuda's major trading partners are the United States, Great Britain, Canada, the Netherlands, and the Caribbean states.

3 History 101

THE EARLY YEARS

The discovery of the Bermudas is attributed to the Spanish—probably the navigator Juan Bermúdez—sometime before 1511, because in that year a map published in the *Legatio Babylonica* included "La Bermuda" among the Atlantic islands. A little over a century later, the English staked a claim to Bermuda and began colonization.

In 1609, the flagship of Admiral Sir George Somers, the *Sea Venture,* was wrecked on Bermuda's reefs while en route to the colony at Jamestown, Virginia. The dauntless crew built two pinnaces (small sailing ships) and headed on to the American colony, but three sailors hid out and remained on the island. They were Bermuda's first European settlers. Just 3 years later, the Bermuda islands were included in the charter of the Virginia Company, and 60 colonists were sent there from England. St. George Town was founded soon after.

Bermuda's status as a colony dates from 1620, when the first parliament convened.

Bermuda's is the oldest parliament in continuous existence in the British Commonwealth. In 1684, Bermuda became a British Crown Colony under King Charles II, and Sir Robert Robinson was appointed the colony's first governor.

Slavery became a part of life in Bermuda shortly after the official settlement. Although the majority of slaves came from Africa, a few were Native Americans. Later, Scots imprisoned for fighting against Cromwell were sent to the islands, followed in 1651 by Irish slaves. This servitude, however, was not as lengthy as that of plantation slaves in America and the West Indies. The British Emancipation Act of 1834 freed all slaves.

RELATIONS WITH AMERICA

Early on, Bermuda established close links with the American colonies. The islanders set up a thriving mercantile trade on the Eastern Seaboard, especially with southern ports. The major commodity sold by Bermuda's merchant ships was salt from Turks Island.

Dateline

- **ca. 1503** Juan Bermúdez discovers Bermuda while sailing aboard the Spanish ship *La Garza.*
- **1609** The British ship *Sea Venture* is wrecked on the reefs of Bermuda; all onboard make it to shore safely and the settlement of Bermuda begins.
- **1612** The Virginia Company dispatches the *Plough* to

Bermuda with 60 colonists onboard. Richard Moore is appointed governor of Bermuda.
- **1620** The first Bermuda parliament session is held in St. Peter's Church, St. George.
- **1684** The British Crown takes over the Bermuda Company's charter. Sir Robert Robinson is appointed the Crown's first governor of Bermuda.

- **1775** Gunpowder is stolen in St. George and shipped to the American colonies for use against the British.
- **1861** Bermuda becomes involved in the American Civil War when it runs supplies to the South to undermine the Union's blockade.
- **1919–33** Bermudians profit from Prohibition in the United States by engaging in rumrunning.

During the American Revolution, the rebellious colonies cut off trade with Loyalist Bermuda, despite the network of family connections and close friendships that bound them. The cutoff in trade proved a great hardship for the islanders, who, having chosen seafaring over farming, depended heavily on America for their food. Many of them, now deprived of profitable trade routes, turned to privateering, piracy, and "wrecking" (salvaging goods from wrecked or foundered ships).

Britain's loss of its important American colonial ports led to a naval buildup in Bermuda. Ships and troops sailed from Bermuda in 1814 to burn Washington, D.C., and the White House during the War of 1812.

Bermuda got a new lease on economic life during the American Civil War. The island was sympathetic to the Confederacy. With the approval of the British government, Bermuda ran the blockade that the Union had placed on exports, especially of cotton, by the Southern states. St. George's Harbour was a principal Atlantic base for the lucrative business of smuggling manufactured goods into Confederate ports and bringing out cargoes of cotton and turpentine.

When the Confederacy fell, so did Bermuda's economy. Seeing no immediate source of income from trading with the Eastern states, the islanders turned their attention to agriculture and found that the colony's fertile soil and salubrious climate produced excellent vegetables. Portuguese immigrants arrived to farm the land, and soon celery, potatoes, tomatoes, and especially onions were being shipped to the New York market. So brisk was the onion trade that the City of Hamilton became known as "Onion Town."

During Prohibition, Bermudians again profited from the situation in the United States—they engaged in the lucrative business of rumrunning (smuggling alcohol to the U.S.). The distance from the island to the East Coast was too great for quick crossings in small booze-laden boats, which worked well from The Bahamas and Cuba. Nevertheless, Bermuda accounted for a good part of the alcoholic beverages transported illegally to the United States before the repeal of Prohibition in 1933.

A HOTBED OF ESPIONAGE

Bermuda played a key role in World War II counterespionage for the Allies. The story of the "secret war" with Nazi Germany is told dramatically in William Stevenson's *A Man Called Intrepid.*

Beneath the Hamilton Princess Hotel, a carefully trained staff worked to decode radio signals to and from German

- **1940–45** Bermuda plays an important role in World War II counterespionage for the Allies.
- **1946** The automobile is introduced on Bermuda.
- **1957** Great Britain withdraws military from Bermuda after 2 centuries of rule.
- **1963** Voter registration is open to all citizens.
- **1968** Bermudians are granted a new constitution that, while protecting them

under the umbrella of the British Commonwealth, allows them to govern themselves.
- **1973** The governor, Sir Richard Sharples, and an aide are assassinated.
- **1979** Bermudians celebrate as their own Gina Swainson wins the Miss World contest.
- **1987** Hurricane Emily causes millions of dollars' worth of damage; some 70 people are injured.

- **1990** Prime Minister Margaret Thatcher confers with President George H. W. Bush in Bermuda.
- **1991** Prime Minister John Major meets with President George H. W. Bush in Bermuda.
- **1995** Bermudians vote to maintain traditional ties with Britain.

continues

submarines and other vessels operating in the Atlantic, close to the United States and the islands offshore. Unknown to the Germans, the British, early in the war, had broken the Nazi code using a captured German coding machine called "Enigma." The British also intercepted and examined mail between Europe and the United States.

Bermuda served as a refueling stop for airplanes flying between the two continents. While pilots were being entertained at the Yacht Club, the mail would be taken off the carriers and examined by experts. An innocent-looking series of letters from Lisbon, for example, contained messages written in invisible ink. The letters were part of a vast German spy network. The British became skilled at opening sealed envelopes, examining their written contents, and carefully resealing them.

The surreptitious letter-readers were called "trappers." Many of them were young women without any previous experience in counterespionage work, yet a number of them performed very well. As Stevenson wrote, it was soon discovered that "by some quirk in the law of averages, the girls who shone in this work had well-turned ankles." A medical officer involved with the project reported it as "fairly certain that a girl with unshapely legs would make a bad trapper." So, amazingly, the word went out that women seeking recruitment as trappers would have to display their gams.

During the course of their work, the trappers discovered one of the methods by which the Germans were transmitting secret messages: They would shrink a whole page of regularly typed text to the size of a tiny dot, then conceal the dot under an innocuous-looking punctuation mark! The staff likened these messages, with their secret-bearing dots, to the English dessert plum duff, for these "punctuation dots [were] scattered through a letter like raisins in the suet puddings." The term "duff method" came to be applied to the technique that the Germans used to send military and other messages through the mail.

When the United States entered the war, FBI agents joined the British in their intelligence operations in Bermuda.

BERMUDA COMES INTO ITS OWN

In 1953, British Prime Minister Winston Churchill chose Bermuda, which he had visited during the war, as the site for a conference with U.S. President Dwight D. Eisenhower and the French premier. Several such high-level gatherings have followed in the decades since; the most recent one, between former British Prime

- **1997** Pamela Gordon, 41, becomes the island's first female prime minister.
- **1998** The Labour Party sweeps into power with another female prime minister.
- **2000** It's announced that 75% of U.S. Fortune 500 companies make Bermuda their home port.
- **2003** Bermuda launches its quincentennial celebrations; Hurricane Fabian devastates the island.
- **2004** Bermuda hoteliers launch massive restorations in the wake of Fabian.
- **2005** U.S. passes law stipulating that Americans will need passports to reenter the United States after a visit to Bermuda.

Minister John Major and former U.S. President George H. W. Bush, took place in 1991.

Bermuda's increasing prominence led to changes in its relations with Great Britain and the United States, as well as significant developments on the island itself. In 1957, after nearly 2 centuries of occupation, Britain withdrew its military forces, and decided to grant self-government to its oldest colony. Under the Lend-Lease Agreement signed in 1941, the United States continues to maintain a naval air station at Kindley Field, in St. George Parish. The agreement is due to expire in 2040.

As Bermudians assumed greater control over their own affairs, they began to adopt significant social changes, but at a pace that did not satisfy some critics. Although racial segregation in hotels and restaurants ceased in 1959, schools were not integrated until 1971. Women received the right to vote in 1944, but the law still restricted suffrage to property holders. That restriction was rescinded in 1963, when voter registration was opened to all citizens.

On the rocky road to self-government, Bermuda was not without its share of problems. Serious rioting broke out in 1968, and British troops were called back to restore order. Then, in 1973, Sir Richard Sharples, the governor, was assassinated; in 1977, those believed to have been the assassins were executed.

These events, which occurred at a time when several of the islands in the region and in the Caribbean were experiencing domestic difficulties, proved to be the exception rather than the rule. In the years since, the social and political climate in Bermuda has been markedly calm—all the better for the island's economic well-being, because it encourages the industries on which Bermuda depends, including tourism.

In 1972, the Bermuda dollar gained its independence from the pound sterling;

it's now pegged through gold to the U.S. dollar on an equal dollar-for-dollar basis.

During the 1990s, the political status of the island again became a hot topic among Bermudians. Some people felt it would be advantageous to achieve complete independence from Britain, whereas others believed it was in Bermuda's best interest to maintain its ties to the Crown. In 1995, the majority of voters in an independent referendum rejected a proposal to sever ties with Great Britain, preferring to maintain their status with Great Britain.

In 1997, the governing party of Bermuda, the United Bermuda Party, chose the daughter of a well-known civil rights leader as its prime minister. Pamela Gordon, former environment minister, was named to the post at the age of 41, the youngest leader in the island nation's 400-year history and the first woman to be prime minister. David Saul, the reigning prime minister, resigned in favor of this younger and more popular leader. In her first months in office, Ms. Gordon, a relative political newcomer, pledged to bridge differences between Bermuda's majority black population and its white business elite.

In that stated goal, at least based on subsequent election returns, she did not succeed. In November 1998, the Progressive Labour Party, supported by many of Bermuda's blacks, ended 30 years of conservative rule by sweeping its first victory in general elections. Although Ms. Gordon is black, as was most of her cabinet, many locals saw her party as "part of the white establishment."

The Labour Party's leader, Jennifer Smith, became the new prime minister, claiming Bermuda's residents had met their "date with destiny." The Labour Party has moved more from the left to the center in recent years, and Ms. Smith has sought to reassure the island's white-led business community that it will be "business as usual" with her in power. The Labour Party made the economy an issue in the campaign, promising higher wages and better benefits to workers, even though Bermuda residents enjoy one of the highest standards of living in the world. In 2003, W. Alexander Scott replaced Ms. Smith as the prime minister and head of the party.

In the 21st century, Bermuda faces many problems, including what many see as a declining quality of life. There are environmental concerns—notably overfishing and damage to precious reefs. Traffic jams are now common despite the ban against visitors' renting automobiles. Affordable housing becomes scarcer year by year. Nonetheless, the more unfortunate islands to the south still envy Bermuda's standard of living.

As more cruise lines launch megaliners, Bermuda is also concerned that its tight harbors will not be able to accommodate the traffic.

Although Bermuda and tourism seemed linked like a horse and carriage, the Bermuda-shorts-wearers' businesses dominated the focus at the turn of the

new century when it was announced that 75% of U.S. Fortune 500 companies had made Bermuda their home base.

In 2003, Bermuda honored its past as the island nation commemorated the 500th anniversary of Bermuda's first sighting by Spanish explorer Juan Bermúdez in 1503.

Also in 2003, tragedy struck the island in the roaring fury called Hurricane Fabian, Bermuda's worst hurricane in 40 years. For some 12 hours, Fabian pummeled the island with 193 to 225kmph (120–140-mph) winds. This caused small tornadoes to spawn and unleashed a towering surge of ocean that drenched almost all of Bermuda in saltwater, uprooting trees.

In Washington in April 2005, it was announced that Americans will need passports to reenter the United States after a visit to Bermuda. The change won't be phased in until 2008. Until the new rules become law, American citizens returning from Bermuda need only a government-issued photo identification card plus proof of U.S. citizenship such as an original birth or naturalization certificate.

4 Bermuda Style at Its Best: Island Architecture

Today, Bermuda's unique style is best represented by its architecture: primarily, those darling little pink cottages that grace postcards. The architecture of the island—a mélange of idiosyncratic building techniques dictated by climate and the types of building materials available—is the archipelago's only truly indigenous art form.

Bermuda's early settlers quickly recognized the virtues of the island's most visible building material, coral stone. A conglomerate of primeval sand packed with crushed bits of coral and shells, this stone has been quarried for generations on Bermuda. Cut into oblong building blocks, it is strong yet porous. However, it would be unusable in any area where the climate has cycles of freezing and thawing,

because it would crack. Mortared together with imported cement, the blocks provide solid and durable foundations and walls.

Bermuda's colonial architects ingeniously found a way to deal with a serious problem on the island: the lack of an abundant supply of fresh water. During the construction of a house or any other sort of building, workers excavated a water tank, or cistern, first. The cistern was created either as a separate underground cavity away from the house or as a foundation for the building. These cisterns served to collect rainwater funneled from rooftops via specially designed channels and gutters. The design of these roof-to-cellar water conduits led to the development of what is Bermuda's most distinct architectural feature, the gleaming rooftops of its houses. Gently sloping, and invariably painted a dazzling white, they are constructed of quarried limestone slabs sawed into "slates" about an inch thick and between 77 and 116 sq. cm (12 and 18 sq. in.). Roofs are installed over a framework of cedar-wood beams (or, more recently, pitch pine or pressure-treated wood beams), which are interconnected with a series of cedar laths. The slates are joined together with cement-based mortar in overlapping rows, then covered with a cement wash and one or several coats of whitewash or synthetic paint. This process corrects the porosity of the coral limestone slates, rendering them watertight. The result is a layered effect, since each panel of limestone appears in high relief atop its neighbor. The angular, step-shaped geometry of Bermudian roofs has inspired watercolorists and painters to emphasize the rhythmically graceful shadows that trace the path of the sun across the rooflines.

Unlike those in the Caribbean, Bermudian houses are designed without amply proportioned hanging eaves. Large eaves may be desirable because of the shade they afford, but smaller ones have proved to be structurally more sound during tropical storms. The interiors of Bermudian houses are usually graced with large windows and doors, and, in the older buildings, floors and moldings crafted from copper-colored planks of the almost extinct Bermuda cedar. Also common is a feature found in colonial buildings in the Caribbean and other western Atlantic islands as well: tray ceilings, so named because of their resemblance to an inverted serving tray. This shape allows ceilings to follow the lines of the inside roof construction to create what would otherwise be unused space. The effect of these ceilings, whether sheathed in plaster or planking, gives Bermudian interiors unusual height and airiness.

Despite the distinctively individualistic nature of Bermuda's architecture, decor remains faithfully—some say rigidly—British, and somewhat more formal than you might expect. Interior designs seem to be a felicitous cross between what you'd find in a New England seaside cottage, and how a nautically minded society hostess would accent her drawing room in London. Bermuda homes usually have lots of Chippendale or Queen Anne furniture (sometimes authentic, sometimes reproduction). Decorators love to include, whenever possible, any piece of antique furniture crafted from almost-extinct copper-colored Bermuda cedar. Combine these features with the open windows, gentle climate, and carefully tended gardens of the fertile, mid-Atlantic setting, and the result is some very charming and soothing interiors.

No discussion of Bermudian architecture should neglect to mention a garden feature that many visitors consider unique to Bermuda: the moon gate. A rounded span of coral blocks arranged in a circular arch above a wooden gate, the moon gate was introduced to Bermuda around 1920 by the Duke of Westminster's landscape architect, who got his inspiration from such gates in China and Japan.

5 The Rhythms of Bermuda

Modern Bermudian music, which you hear today mainly in hotel lounges, is a blend of traditional Bermudian music with sounds from Jamaica, Trinidad, and Puerto Rico, as well as the United States and Britain. However, these aren't the sounds you'll predominantly hear: As elsewhere, American and British rock, modified by local rhythms, has proved the strongest and most lasting influence.

Visitors are often pleased to discover that the island's best-known singers and musicians, some of whom are discussed below, can be heard at many of the hotels and nightclubs. Inquire about which local artist is performing during the cocktail hour at your hotel; chances are it may be one of the most popular.

GOMBEY DANCING

Despite new pop forms, Bermuda is proud of its original musical idioms. Gombey dancing is the island's premier folk art. Gombey (commonly pronounced *goom*-bee or *gom*-bay) combines West Africa's tribal heritage with the Native American and British colonial influences of the New World. Gombey dancers are almost always male; in accordance with tradition, men pass on the rhythms and dance techniques from generation to generation in their family. Dancers outfit themselves in masquerade costumes, whose outlandish lines and glittering colors evoke the brilliant plumage of tropical birds.

Gombey (spelled goombay in some other places, such as The Bahamas) signifies a specific type of African drum, as well as the Bantu word for "rhythm." These rhythms escalate into an ever faster and more hypnotic beat as the movements of the dancers become increasingly uninhibited, and the response of the spectators grows ever more fervent. The most strenuous dances are usually performed during the Christmas season.

Although gombey dancing, with its local rituals and ceremonies, can be seen as one of Bermuda's major cultural contributions, it's not unique to the island. Variations are found elsewhere in the western Atlantic, as well as in the Caribbean. Indeed, during its development, Bermuda's gombey dancing was significantly influenced by some of these other versions. In colonial times, for example, when African Caribbeans were brought to Bermuda as slaves or convicts to help build the British military installations on the island, they carried with them their own gombey traditions, which eventually combined with those that had already taken root in Bermuda. What's unique about the Bermudian version of gombey, however, is its use of the British snare drum, played with wooden sticks, as an accompaniment to the dancing.

A handful of gombey recordings are available, enabling you to hear the sounds of this African-based music, with its rhythmic chanting and rapid drumbeat. Among the recordings, the album *Strictly Gombey Music* (Edmar 1165), performed by four members of the Pickles Spencer Gombey Group, offers a good selection of gombey dances.

Aficionados of this art form, however, will argue that gombey's allure lies not so much in the music as in the feverish—almost trancelike—dancing that accompanies it, as well as in the colorful costumes of the dancers. For that reason, they say, audio recordings can't convey the full mesmerizing power of a gombey dance the way a visual recording can. So, while you're in Bermuda—and if you have a camcorder—consider filming a gombey dance to show when you get back home,.

Regrettably, there's no one place in Bermuda where you can always see gombey. Your best bet is to inquire at your hotel to see what events and performances might be staged during your visit. Sometimes hotels present gombey shows, but they don't follow a fixed schedule.

THE BALLADEER TRADITION

Bermuda also has a strong balladeer tradition. Although its exponents are fewer than they used to be, local balladeers continue to enjoy considerable popularity among islanders and visitors alike. A wry, self-deprecating humor has always distinguished their compositions, and balladeers can strum a song for any occasion on their guitars. Today, many of their songs have to do with Bermuda's changing way of life.

By virtually everyone's estimate, the musical patriarch of Bermuda was Hubert Smith, who was the island's official greeter in song. A balladeer of formidable talent and originality, Smith composed and performed songs for the visits of nearly all the foreign heads of state who graced Bermuda's shores in recent memory. His performances for members of the British royal family included one of the most famous songs ever written about the island, "Bermuda Is Another World." The song is now the island's unofficial national anthem; it's included in the best-selling album *Bermuda Is Another World* (Edmar 1025).

6 Island of the Sunday Painter

Art in Bermuda has never reached the status enjoyed by such islands as Haiti and Jamaica. A critic once wrote that "Bermuda is the perfect place for the Sunday painter." Some serious art, however, is displayed at such places as the Masterworks Foundation Gallery at Bermuda House in the City of Hamilton (see chapter 9, "Shopping"). Still, a great deal of Bermuda art is of the watercolor variety, with idyllic landscapes and seascapes sold at various shops around the island.

Bermuda's earliest works of art were portraits painted by itinerant artists for the local gentry. Most of these were by the English-born Joseph Blackburn, whose brief visit to Bermuda in the mid-1700s led to requests by local landowners to have their portraits painted. Many of these portraits can be found today in the Tucker House Museum in St. George's. A handful of portraits from the same period were done by the American-born artist John Green. Also prized are a series of paintings from the mid–19th century depicting sailing ships; they're signed "Edward James," but the artist's real identity remains unknown.

During the 19th century, the traditions of the English landscape painters, particularly the Romantics, came into vogue in Bermuda. Constable, with his lush and evocative landscapes, became the model for many. Other than a few amateur artists, however, whose works showed great vitality but little sense of perspective, most of Bermuda's landscape paintings were executed by British military officers and their wives. Their body of work includes a blend of true-to-life landscapes with an occasional stylized rendering of the picturesque or Romantic tradition then in vogue in England. Among the most famous of the uniformed artists was Lt. E. G. Hallewell, a member of the Royal Engineers, whose illustrations of the island's topography were used for planning certain naval installations.

Another celebrated landscapist was Thomas Driver, who arrived as a member of the Royal Engineers in 1814 and remained on the island until 1836. Trained to reproduce detailed landscape observations as a means of assisting military and naval strategists, he later modified his style to become more elegant and evocative. He soon abandoned the military and became a full-time painter of Bermuda scenes. Because of Driver's attention to detail, his works are frequently reproduced by scholars and art historians who hope to recapture the aesthetic and architectural elements of the island's earliest buildings.

Later in the 19th century, other artists depicted the flora of Bermuda. Lady Lefroy, whose husband was governor of the island between 1871 and 1877, painted the trees, shrubs, fish, flowers, and animals of the island in much detail. Later, at scattered intervals during their careers, such internationally known artists as Winslow Homer, Andrew Wyeth, George Ault, and French-born Impressionist and cubist Albert Gleizes all painted Bermudian scenes.

Today, Bermuda has more artists painting and creating than at any point in its history. Among prominent Bermuda-born artists was Alfred Birdsey, who died in 1996. His watercolors represented some of the most elegiac visual odes to Bermuda ever produced. Birdsey's paintings, as well as those of other artists mentioned above, are on display in galleries around the island. Other local favorites include Eric Amos; his illustrations of Bermuda's wild birds are sought by collectors all over the world. Captain Stephen J. Card has developed an international reputation by specializing in marine art. Vivienne Gardner is known not just for her paintings but for her sculpture, stained glass, and mosaics as well. Christine Phillips-Watlington has achieved an international reputation for her botanical paintings.

Protecting artworks from climate damage is a constant problem on the island. As the administrator of one major art gallery explained, "Bermuda's climate is unquestionably the worst in the world for the toll it takes on works of art, with three elements—humidity, salt, and ultraviolet light—all playing their part." Some very valuable Bermudian paintings have been totally destroyed. As a result, more and more galleries and exhibition rooms on the island have installed air-conditioning.

In addition to its painters, Bermuda also boasts several noted sculptors, including Chelsey Trott, who produces cedar-wood carvings, and Desmond Hale Fountain, who creates works in bronze. Fountain's life-size statues often show children in the act of reading or snoozing in the shade.

7 Prospero, a Lovesick Poet & Other Bermudian Literary Legacies

Bermuda has long been a haven for writers. It has figured in many works of literature, beginning with Shakespeare's *The Tempest.* Shakespeare never visited the island himself but was inspired to set his play here by accounts he had read or heard of the island.

The Irish poet Thomas Moore (1779–1852), who visited Bermuda for several months in 1804, was moved by its beauty to write:

> *Oh! could you view the scenery dear*
> *That now beneath my window lies.*

Moore left more memories—literary and romantic—than any other writer who came to Bermuda. He once stayed at Hill Crest Guest House (now Aunt Nea's Inn at Hillcrest) in St. George's (see chapter 4, "Where to Stay") and soon became enamored of Nea Tucker, the adolescent bride of one of the most prominent men in town. "Sweet Nea! Let us roam no more," he once wrote of his beloved.

It's said that the lovesick poet would gaze for hours upon Nea's veranda, hoping that she'd appear. One day a jealous Mr. Tucker could tolerate this no more and banished the poet from his property. Moore was chased down a street that now bears the name Nea's Alley—to commemorate his unrequited romance.

Today, one of the most popular restaurants in Bermuda is Tom Moore's Tavern (see chapter 5, "Where to Dine"). The building was once the home of Samuel Trott, who constructed it in the 17th century. Unlike Mr. Tucker, the descendants of Samuel Trott befriended Moore, who often visited the house. Moore immortalized the calabash tree on the Trott estate in his writing; he liked to sit under it and write his verse there.

Following in Moore's footsteps, many famous writers visited Bermuda in later years. None, however, have left their mark on the island like Tom Moore.

For Americans, it was Mark Twain who helped make Bermuda a popular tourist destination. He published his impressions in the *Atlantic Monthly* in 1877 through

Fun Fact Royalty Comes to "Shangri-La"

The Irish poet Tom Moore and the American humorist Mark Twain publicized the glories of Bermuda, but—for the British, at least—the woman who put Bermuda on the tourist map was Princess Louise. The daughter of Queen Victoria, she spent several months in Bermuda in 1883. Her husband was the governor-general of Canada, so she traveled to Bermuda to escape the fierce northern cold. Although Bermuda hosted many royal visitors in the 20th century, including Queen Elizabeth II, Princess Louise was the first royal personage to set foot in the colony. When she returned to Canada, she told reporters that she'd found the Shangri-La of tourist destinations.

1878, and in his first book, *The Innocents Abroad.* He became so enchanted by the island that, as he wrote many years later to a correspondent, he would fain choose it over heaven.

After Twain, Eugene O'Neill came to Bermuda in 1924, and returned several more times, at least through 1927. While here, he worked on *The Great God Brown, Lazarus Laughed,* and *Strange Interlude.* O'Neill was convinced that cold weather adversely affected his ability to write. He thought that Bermuda would "cure" him of alcoholism. At first, O'Neill and his family rented cottages on what is now Coral Beach Club property. Later, O'Neill bought the house "Spithead," in Warwick. In 1927, however, his marriage ended, and O'Neill left his family—and Bermuda.

During the 1930s, several eminent writers made their way to Bermuda, in hopes of finding idyllic surroundings and perhaps a little inspiration: Sinclair Lewis, who spent all his time cycling around "this gorgeous island"; Hervey Allen, who wrote *Anthony Adverse,* his best-selling novel, at Felicity Hall in Somerset; and

James Ramsey Ullman, who wrote *The White Tower* on the island. James Thurber also made several visits to Bermuda during this time.

In 1956, Noël Coward came with his longtime companion, Graham Payn, to escape "the monstrously unjust tax situation in England." He was not, he said, "really mad about the place," yet he purchased "Spithead" in Warwick (O'Neill's former home) and stayed some 2 years, working on *London Mornings,* his only ballet, and the musical *Sail Away.* "Spithead" is now privately owned.

Other well-known authors who visited Bermuda over the years include Rudyard Kipling, C. S. Forester, Hugh Walpole, Edna Ferber, Anita Loos, John O'Hara, E. B. White, and Philip Wylie.

Bermuda's own writers include William S. Zuill—a former director of the Bermuda National Trust who wrote *The Story of Bermuda and Her People,* an excellent historical account—and Nellie Musson, Frank Manning, Eva Hodgson, and Dale Butler, who have written about the lives of African Bermudians.

Index

See also Accommodations and Restaurant indexes, below.

FROMMER'S® COMPLETE TRAVEL GUIDES

Alaska
Amalfi Coast
American Southwest
Amsterdam
Argentina & Chile
Arizona
Atlanta
Australia
Austria
Bahamas
Barcelona
Beijing
Belgium, Holland & Luxembourg
Belize
Bermuda
Boston
Brazil
British Columbia & the Canadian
   Rockies
Brussels & Bruges
Budapest & the Best of Hungary
Buenos Aires
Calgary
California
Canada
Cancún, Cozumel & the Yucatán
Cape Cod, Nantucket & Martha's
   Vineyard
Caribbean
Caribbean Ports of Call
Carolinas & Georgia
Chicago
China
Colorado
Costa Rica
Croatia
Cuba
Denmark
Denver, Boulder & Colorado Springs
Edinburgh & Glasgow
England
Europe
Europe by Rail
Florence, Tuscany & Umbria

Florida
France
Germany
Greece
Greek Islands
Hawaii
Hong Kong
Honolulu, Waikiki & Oahu
India
Ireland
Israel
Italy
Jamaica
Japan
Kauai
Las Vegas
London
Los Angeles
Los Cabos & Baja
Madrid
Maine Coast
Maryland & Delaware
Maui
Mexico
Montana & Wyoming
Montréal & Québec City
Moscow & St. Petersburg
Munich & the Bavarian Alps
Nashville & Memphis
New England
Newfoundland & Labrador
New Mexico
New Orleans
New York City
New York State
New Zealand
Northern Italy
Norway
Nova Scotia, New Brunswick &
   Prince Edward Island
Oregon
Paris
Peru
Philadelphia & the Amish Country

Portugal
Prague & the Best of the Czech
   Republic
Provence & the Riviera
Puerto Rico
Rome
San Antonio & Austin
San Diego
San Francisco
Santa Fe, Taos & Albuquerque
Scandinavia
Scotland
Seattle
Seville, Granada & the Best of
   Andalusia
Shanghai
Sicily
Singapore & Malaysia
South Africa
South America
South Florida
South Pacific
Southeast Asia
Spain
Sweden
Switzerland
Tahiti & French Polynesia
Texas
Thailand
Tokyo
Toronto
Turkey
USA
Utah
Vancouver & Victoria
Vermont, New Hampshire & Maine
Vienna & the Danube Valley
Vietnam
Virgin Islands
Virginia
Walt Disney World® & Orlando
Washington, D.C.
Washington State

FROMMER'S® DAY BY DAY GUIDES

Amsterdam
Chicago
Florence & Tuscany

London
New York City
Paris

Rome
San Francisco
Venice

PAULINE FROMMER'S GUIDES! SEE MORE. SPEND LESS.

Hawaii

Italy

New York City

FROMMER'S® PORTABLE GUIDES

Acapulco, Ixtapa & Zihuatanejo
Amsterdam
Aruba
Australia's Great Barrier Reef
Bahamas
Big Island of Hawaii
Boston
California Wine Country
Cancún
Cayman Islands
Charleston
Chicago
Dominican Republic

Dublin
Florence
Las Vegas
Las Vegas for Non-Gamblers
London
Maui
Nantucket & Martha's Vineyard
New Orleans
New York City
Paris
Portland
Puerto Rico
Puerto Vallarta, Manzanillo &
   Guadalajara

Rio de Janeiro
San Diego
San Francisco
Savannah
St. Martin, Sint Maarten, Anguilla &
   St. Bart's
Turks & Caicos
Vancouver
Venice
Virgin Islands
Washington, D.C.
Whistler

FROMMER'S® CRUISE GUIDES

Alaska Cruises & Ports of Call
Cruises & Ports of Call
European Cruises & Ports of Call

FROMMER'S® NATIONAL PARK GUIDES

Algonquin Provincial Park
Banff & Jasper
Grand Canyon

National Parks of the American West
Rocky Mountain
Yellowstone & Grand Teton

Yosemite and Sequoia & Kings
Canyon
Zion & Bryce Canyon

FROMMER'S® MEMORABLE WALKS

London
New York

Paris
Rome

San Francisco

FROMMER'S® WITH KIDS GUIDES

Chicago
Hawaii
Las Vegas
London

National Parks
New York City
San Francisco

Toronto
Walt Disney World® & Orlando
Washington, D.C.

SUZY GERSHMAN'S BORN TO SHOP GUIDES

France
Hong Kong, Shanghai & Beijing
Italy

London
New York

Paris
San Francisco

FROMMER'S® IRREVERENT GUIDES

Amsterdam
Boston
Chicago
Las Vegas

London
Los Angeles
Manhattan
Paris

Rome
San Francisco
Walt Disney World®
Washington, D.C.

FROMMER'S® BEST-LOVED DRIVING TOURS

Austria
Britain
California
France

Germany
Ireland
Italy
New England

Northern Italy
Scotland
Spain
Tuscany & Umbria

THE UNOFFICIAL GUIDES®

Adventure Travel in Alaska
Beyond Disney
California with Kids
Central Italy
Chicago
Cruises
Disneyland®
England
Florida
Florida with Kids

Hawaii
Ireland
Las Vegas
London
Maui
Mexico's Best Beach Resorts
Mini Mickey
New Orleans
New York City

Paris
San Francisco
South Florida including Miami &
the Keys
Walt Disney World®
Walt Disney World® for
Grown-ups
Walt Disney World® with Kids
Washington, D.C.

SPECIAL-INTEREST TITLES

Athens Past & Present
Best Places to Raise Your Family
Cities Ranked & Rated
500 Places to Take Your Kids Before They Grow Up
Frommer's Best Day Trips from London
Frommer's Best RV & Tent Campgrounds
in the U.S.A.

Frommer's Exploring America by RV
Frommer's NYC Free & Dirt Cheap
Frommer's Road Atlas Europe
Frommer's Road Atlas Ireland
Great Escapes From NYC Without Wheels
Retirement Places Rated

FROMMER'S® PHRASEFINDER DICTIONARY GUIDES

French
Italian
Spanish

THE NEW TRAVELOCITY GUARANTEE

EVERYTHING YOU BOOK WILL BE RIGHT, OR WE'LL WORK WITH OUR TRAVEL PARTNERS TO MAKE IT RIGHT, RIGHT AWAY.

*To drive home the point,
we're going to use the word "right" in every single sentence.*

Let's get right to it. Right to the meat! Only Travelocity guarantees everything about your booking will be right, or we'll work with our travel partners to make it right, right away. Right on!

Here's a picture taken smack dab right in the middle of Antigua, where the guarantee also covers you.

The guarantee covers all but one of the items pictured to the right.

For example, what if the ocean view you booked actually looks out at a downright ugly parking lot? You'd be right to call – we're there for you. And no one in their right mind would be pleased to learn the rental car place has closed and left them stranded. Call Travelocity and we'll help get you back on the right track.

Now, you may be thinking, "Yeah, right, I'm so sure." That's OK; you have the right to remain skeptical. That is until we mention help is always right around the corner. Call us right off the bat, knowing that our customer service reps are there for you 24/7. Righting wrongs. Left and right.

Now if you're guessing there are some things we can't control, like the weather, well you're right. But we can help you with most things – to get all the details in righting,* visit **travelocity.com/guarantee**.

*Sorry, spelling things right is one of the few things not covered under the guarantee.

I'd give my right arm for a guarantee like this, although I'm glad I don't have to.

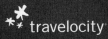

travelocity
You'll never roam alone.